Web Component Development with Zope 3

Philipp von Weitershausen

Web Component Development with Zope 3

With a Foreword by Phillip J. Eby

Second Revised and Enlarged Edition

With 48 Figures and 10 Tables

 Springer

Philipp von Weitershausen
Bernhardstr. 66
01187 Dresden
Germany
philipp@weitershausen.de

Library of Congress Control Number: 2006935572

ISBN-10 3-540-33807-1 Springer Berlin Heidelberg New York
ISBN-13 978-3-540-33807-9 Springer Berlin Heidelberg New York
ISBN-10 3-540-22359-2 1. Edition Springer Berlin Heidelberg New York

Springer is a part of Springer Science+Business Media

springer.com

Typesetting: PTP, Berlin
Production: LE-TeX Jelonek, Schmidt & Vöckler GbR, Leipzig
Cover: KünkelLopka, Heidelberg

Printed on acid-free paper   33/3100/YL - 5 4 3 2 1 0

Für Mami und Papi.

A common gateway linked code to the net,
Its limitations plain for some to see.
While on a plane an engineer set
This common gateway object-orientedly.

Created through a clown's principia,
All built upon acquisitive ideals:
Dark reservoirs of content will see a
Great framework that an acqueduct reveals.

Alas, ideals of acquisition fall
Beneath the weight of complex modes of use.
Who listens to the new religion's call?
How many will the purer creed seduce?

Foundations that we took such pains to mold
Support a new world better than the old.

> Steve Alexander, inspired by Aroldo Souza-Leite's
> *Sonnets from Pythia*

Subclassing made Zope and TR
much harder to work with by far.
   So before you inherit,
   be sure to declare it
Adapter, not PyObject*

> Glyph Lefkowitz in the docstring of
> `twisted.python.components.Adapter`

Foreword

Where Zope leads, Python follows.

So it has been for a decade, and the trend doesn't show any signs of stopping. Whatever the latest buzzword—be it RESTful web programming, standardized interfaces, pluggable components, or practical restricted-execution environments, Zope has quietly led the way, delivering the goods years ahead of anyone else. Not just as technology concepts, but shipped and working in *paying* clients' offices.

And yet, strangely, Zope's role in the ongoing development of Python is little-known and little-appreciated among Python developers. It is frequently the case that some new and much-touted development in the Python community—especially in the web application and object security arenas—is something that Zope has already been doing for many years.

I'm somewhat baffled by this peculiar blind spot in the Python community. Even when I tell people that Zope's already done something that they're working on, the response is usually a blank look, or no response at all. It's almost as if the innovations of Zope don't really exist until somebody else reinvents them. In fact, the pattern has led me coin this little saying:

Those who do not study Zope, are condemned to reinvent it.

It doesn't matter if you don't plan to actually use Zope. Frankly, I haven't used Zope in years. But the lessons I learned from Zope, I use constantly. Studying Zope—Zope 3 in particular—will make you a better programmer, without question.

Of course, "better programmer" begs the question: better how? Better at achieving what? Zope was created so that Zope Corporation (originally Digital Creations) could do contracting business more efficiently. It allows them to keep an ever-growing toolkit of reusable solutions for their clients, reducing the costs of development and maintenance of these applications. Its purpose is to let you "write once, use many": a multiplier of *economic* effectiveness.

If this is the path your career is taking, you can only benefit from studying how this has been achieved in Zope, whether you actually use Zope for this purpose or not.

If you are developing any new or cutting-edge technology for Python, you can only benefit by asking, "Does Zope already have this, or something like it? And if not, how would Zope use this?" These are the questions I asked when developing Python Eggs, setuptools, and even the WSGI (Python Web Server Gateway Interface) specification. The success of these projects is a *direct* reflection of me asking WWZD: What Would Zope Do (with this idea)?

That's because what's good for Zope, is usually good for Python. Not in the language sense—Python's "Benevolent Dictator" and the "Zope Pope" often disagree quite strenuously on how the language should change. What I mean is, tools that make Zope a better platform, make Python a better platform. If you study Zope diligently, you may begin to understand why.

And maybe, just maybe, you'll find yourself a little bit ahead of other programmers, especially when it comes to new ideas... but hopefully, not *so* far ahead, that they begin to act as though *you* don't exist, either!

Good luck!

Phillip J. Eby

Foreword to the First Edition

Zope 3 is here! Congratulations to Jim Fulton, the Zope Pope, and the global team that made it happen. Now the rest of us can start putting its power to use. Truly, with the arrival of the component architecture, Zope can now change its tagline from "Brilliant but clunky" to just "Brilliant".

The world of Zope and its offspring such as Plone have now matured to the point of mainstream legitimacy. In fact, one major European telecom recently told me, "If you bid on a government CMS project, and you don't use Zope, you have to explain why." Incredible!

The world of Zope is big. There are hundreds of add-on packages that integrate into the system in ways that other architectures simply don't anticipate. However, the full potential of Zope's broad basis for business has been held back by limitations that we didn't expect when Zope 2 was designed.

Enter the component architecture! With these lessons from Zope 2, and particularly from the trail blazed by the CMF, software packages can be plugged in and replaced on a more robust and industrial-strength basis. This will help raise the level of basic capabilities common to all Zope-based software, thus accelerating a trend towards enterprise-class services such as versioning.

Most exciting, though, is the business integration. Small companies are specializing in certain platform services and working together for full solutions. The component architecture is crucial for making this work to level of quality demanded by consulting deployments. Also, the often-overlooked upside of Zope 3's test-oriented culture gives us all a boost into better ways of working.

Just like Zope 3 will prove indispensible to the business of Zope, so too will this book. Zope 3 is a commercial-class platform for application services. This book is an in-depth guide to Zope 3, written by one of the most important developers of Zope 3 itself. The overview of core concepts in Chapter 2 is, alone, worth the price of the book. And because the writing style is thoroughly instructive, while also entertaining, the book makes getting started with Zope 3 a pleasure.

This book appears only shortly after a first version of Zope X3 has been released. This is a monumental accomplishment, serving as a testimony to several factors: the discipline of the author, the dedication of the team of developers that managed the last phase of the project in a professional way, and the now-provable wisdom of Jim Fulton's design decisions. Compared to the early days of Zope 1 and 2, the upside of having this book to accompany Zope 3's launch cannot be overstated. It's a big deal.

I've been lucky to know Philipp for a few years, even working with him on some consulting projects. Not only is he great fun to be around, he is also a real leader in the world of Zope. He has the credibility, the reliability, and the right touch for working with the far-flung army of volunteers that are producing Zope. And atop all that, he has written for us the guide to developing killer apps for Zope 3.

I hope you enjoy this book as much as I have, and good luck in your start on Zope 3.

Paul Everitt, co-founder of Zope Corporation

Contents

Part III Expert

Part IV Appendices

Part I

Beginner

1

Introduction

1.1 About this book

Is this book for me?

This book is for web developers. If you are migrating from Zope 2 or have experience in competing technologies, such as J2EE or Vignette StoryServer, or Python-based frameworks like Django and TurboGears—this book is for you! It is probably not for you if you are looking for an introduction to web application development.

This book introduces the web developer step-by-step to the world of Zope 3 and its Component Architecture. It describes how to build web applications with Zope 3 step by step using detailed examples. It is not a "cookbook" with recipes for specific tasks or solutions to problems.

Examples in this book

To demonstrate Zope's wide range of features, we will use a consistent example application throughout the whole book. Whenever a new feature of Zope 3 is covered, this example application will be extended accordingly. It is supposed to drive the fictitious *World Cookery* website which allows hobby cooks from around the globe to share their recipes online. This particular application was chosen because it incorporates the most important characteristics of the majority of Zope-based web applications:

- A limited set of content object types. In the World Cookery example application, the primary type of content object is a *recipe*.
- Content is added in a management interface accessible through-the-web using a web browser.
- The layout of the application follows a common theme, for example a *corporate identity*.
- The application has to cope with multiple or even numerous users with different roles and responsibilities.

- The target audience is international, thus internationalization is required.
- Existing features must easily be extensible and new functionality easily be addable.

Apart from source code examples, there are hands-on sessions with the Python interpreter. In these sessions we quickly try out things or test components from the example listings.

This book also features...

- *Summaries* at the end of each section allow you to review a chapter and also serve as good reminders in case you need to go back and restudy a certain section.
- *Flashback* boxes explain how a Zope 3 feature compares to its Zope 2 or CMF equivalent.
- Explanations entitled *Using Zope 2* indicate that a Zope 3 feature is available in Zope 2 (see *Zope 2 and backwards-compatibility* below).
- Rocky Burt, a J2EE developer as well as Zope and Plone expert, compares some of Zope's features with those of the J2EE world in *Rocky says...* sections.

1.2 What is Zope?

The rest of this chapter and the next chapter introduce Zope. They give an overview of how Zope works and what Zope can do. If you are eager to get started, you can skip them and go on to install Zope in Chapter 3 or dive directly into the code with Chapter 4.

Zope is

- *a collection of free software*
- *jointly developed by Zope Corporation and a large community of software developers*
- *that you can use in whole or in part*
- *to manage complexity in gluing software components together,*
- *securely publish objects on the web and other systems,*
- *and make it easy to do Quality Assurance.*

Steve Alexander at EuroPython 2004

a collection of free software: Zope is not just a web application server product, it is also a large collection of mostly web-related Python software. It is also freely distributable under the *Zope Public License* [29] and maybe modified and improved by anyone. This increasingly successful concept is called *Open Source* [10].

jointly developed by Zope Corporation and a large community of software developers: When Zope Corporation opened Zope 2's source code to the public, the development process was also opened to encourage contributions from other developers. Zope 3 is a pure community effort from the beginning, with the majority of the contributions coming from a community of software developers around the globe. The benefits for the single developer, the whole community as well as the quality of the software have proven to be enormous.

that you can use in whole or in part: Zope the web application server product is modular and its parts can be used independently from Zope. That is why we need to differentiate between *Zope-the-product* which is the web application server and *Zope-the-project* which produces a collection of reusable software components written in Python.

to manage complexity in gluing software components together: There is a demand for web-based applications to be more and more complex. This can be a time consuming challenge to many applications. Zope solves this problem elegantly by separating activities into many different components. The way these components are then "glued together" determines the behaviour of the overall application.
Secondly, complex applications require a lot of planning and resources. Zope 3's Component Architecture allows the responsibilities for components to be divided across a team. Zope is an excellent platform for collaborative development.
Thirdly, refactoring is easy because only the components needing refactoring are worked on. One example is the customization of presentation and layout components, work can be carried out on HTML pages and CSS style sheets, while the underlying software components are not touched.

securely publish objects on the web and other systems: Zope's main focus is to allow people to manage objects that are published on the web as part of a larger application, not just a static website.
Zope values security very highly. Compliance to international IT security norms is a major part of the Zope 3 philosophy. Zope 3 is undergoing a development-concurrent examination process run by an official IT security agency in Germany. As a result, the Common Criteria Certificate (ISO-15854), a security certificate accepted in Europe, North America and many other countries, will be issued to Zope. An invaluable byproduct of this will also be that Zope's security model in its full extent is being documented in an ISO-compliant manner.

and make it easy to do Quality Assurance: The developers of Zope 3 have enforced a high level of quality during development. Zope is tested by several thousand automated tests; any modifications need to assure that the tests still pass, any new feature needs to be covered by new tests. This ensures the quality of Zope and makes it a great platform to do quality assurance with.

Zope runs on all major Unix platforms, including Mac OS X, as well as Microsoft Windows operating systems. It comes with its own webserver but can interoperate with an existing webserver such as Apache.

Content Management

As an object-oriented web application server with features such as object persistency, Zope provides an excellent platform for building content management systems (CMS). Additional open source party libraries jointly developed by content management vendors allow a custom CMS to be built on Zope. Zope itself is *not* a content management system. However its whole machinery is geared towards managing content. This is why the main focus of this book is the construction of applications that manage content.

"Take Five:" Zope 2 and backwards-compatibility

Zope 3 started out as a complete rewrite of the Zope code base and is not backwards compatible with its predecessor, Zope 2. While many of the concepts had been borrowed from Zope 2 and the Content Management Framework (CMF), Zope 2 and Zope 3 initially shared only very little actual code. That started to change with the formation of the Five project[1] which aims to bring Zope 3 technology into existing Zope 2 applications. Five was integrated into the Zope 2 source code with version 2.8. This has started an evolution process that has led and will continue to lead to an increasingly larger shared code base. This is not an instant process, of course. Vendors of existing Zope 2-based technologies have to be given adequate time to adjust their software.

This book's focus is on Zope 3. There is no explicit chapter covering Zope 2 and Five, although the *Flashbacks* throughout the book give helpful comparisons for Zope 2 developers. Because more and more Zope 3 technology can be used in Zope 2, many solutions presented in this book also apply to Zope 2 and Five. Whenever this is the case, a *Using Zope 2* box will mention it. Apart from that, the concepts and lessons taught in this book can also be applied (even if a bit differently) in the Zope 2 world. It is good to develop Zope 2-based software with Zope 3's way of doing things in mind to be fit for the future.

---

[1] Five project website <http://codespeak.net/z3/five>

1.3 Zope's features

It is Zope's goal to make the web application developer's life easier. Therefore Zope provides as much of the "application" as possible. The developer only has to link the components together and customize and extend Zope's features as needed. The following is an overview of Zope's major features:

Component Architecture. Zope 3 is a collection of software components. Components are objects with a clear understanding of their functionality and responsibility. Describing this in a formal way is the role of interfaces, a concept introduced by the Component Architecture. With the Component Architecture it is then possible to group components together to form a greater piece of software—the application. All of this is not very web-specific, the Component Architecture (`zope.component`) and the interface implementation (`zope.interface`) may be used outside of Zope. Chapter 2 gives a thorough introduction to the Component Architecture and Chapter 4 introduces Zope interfaces.

Object database. One of the strengths of Zope is the Zope Object Database (ZODB) which stores data as objects. Since Zope is all about object publishing, it makes a sense to store the data as objects, too. Developers can persist Python objects nearly transparently into a transactional database that can have load-balancing capabilities. The ZODB is not bound to Zope and can also be used in other Python applications. Chapter 6 covers the ZODB in detail.

HTML/XML templating. For decent web development, it is important to have an easy and productive way of producing HTML and other XML markup. Zope uses Zope Page Templates (ZPT), an XML templating system. This system retains the template as a well-formed XML document and, apart from a few namespaced tags and elements, also as a valid document as far as the original XML schema is concerned. The implementation (mainly in `zope.pagetemplate`) can also be used in other Python projects. Chapter 7 gives a full introduction to ZPT.

Form generation and validation. Many web applications need to process data that is entered through browser forms. Since the construction of a form in HTML and the validation of the user's input data is not only tedious but quite repetitive, Zope's form library (`zope.formlib`) can do both for you according to your content's data schema (`zope.schema`). This is covered in Chapter 8.

Internationalization. Zope software is used all over the world and needs to support different languages and locale-specific date and number formatting. Zope's internationalization (i18n) and localization (l10n) machinery in `zope.i18n` greatly aids the developer to create multilingual and locale-dependent applications. These aids are not tied to Zope. Internationalization is the covered in chapter, Chapter 9.

Security Zope allows for very fine-grained security checks. The publishing and storage mechanism is object-centric and so is the security system. Both the security policy and the authentication system are pluggable and allow the modelling of a flexible security system. Chapter 21 and Chapter 22 tell you how to do that.

Cataloguing. Storing content is one thing, finding and retrieving content is another. Zope has a cataloguing and indexing machinery that can make data stored in Zope easily searchable. This is demonstrated in Chapter 19.

Testing. Zope 3 puts a strong emphasis on testing and software maturity. Its own source code contains over 5000 automated tests that ensure its stability even when big changes to the code base are introduced. These include low-level unit tests as well as integration tests and functional, HTTP-based tests. Zope has also taken taken part in the propagation and improvement of innovative ways of testing such as doctests. Doctests provide developer documentation in forms of automated tests. Most of the testing machinery is available through the very generic `zope.testing` package which also employs a very capable test runner. All of Chapter 12 is devoted to automated tests in Zope.

Playing well with others. Zope has inspired Python technologies such as new-style classes, the WSGI specification, doctests and the `datetime` module. It also reuses code from other Python projects such as Twisted, pytz, docutils and wwwsearch. Zope has in return contributed code and concepts back to these projects. Because of its modularity, many of the above mentioned features can be and are used outside of Zope.

Superseded and emerging features

Zope is under constant development by a world-wide community of developers. This means that features in use now may be superseded in later versions. Why are they documented here? Because Zope 3.3, the Zope 3 version that this book is based on, can be used *now*. Unlike the development code, Zope 3.3 is being used in production successfully. Constant improvement is a good thing. It shows that Zope development is not standing still. Having stable versions to work with is important. The Zope 3 development cycle guarantees both.

Here are some emerging features that have not yet gained the maturity needed to be fully covered in this book:

Workflow Content management systems often need a workflow where people or the system have to do certain actions in a certain order. With the zope.wfmc package Zope already features a workflow engine that follows the standard of the Worfklow Management Coalition (WfMC). Apart from that engine, however, there is not a lot of machinery yet for making custom applications easily workflow-aware.

Relational database access. Zope 3 has rudimentary support for relational databases through Python's database connectors. In Zope these are enhanced with a bit of glue code that makes them play well within Zope. There they are called *database adapters*. This only provides a connection to a relational database, though. It cannot be considered an adequate approach for Zope which is about publishing objects, not rows from a relational database. Projects like SQLObject[2] and sqlos[3] are aiming to solve this.

XML. Zope 3 uses XML in quite a few places (Page Templates, ZCML, etc.), however it does not yet have a framework dedicated to XML processing. There have been initial prototypes that were developed in external projects and there are plans to ship an XML library like lxml[4] with Zope, thus allowing Zope to depend on XML features on a broader basis. These plans are not yet definite enough to make them part of this book.

If you think that a vital feature is missing from Zope, do not hesitate to participate in development. Everyone can contribute and the community welcomes even the smallest contribution.

1.4 The history of Zope

Although the Zope community was small when I joined, it already had its myths. "Jim wrote the first version of Zope on a plane" the Zope birthing myth said. Fact is that Jim Fulton was not happy with web development in Python when he returned from the International Python Conference in 1998. He had just given a tutorial on CGI programming at the conference, certainly not the nicest way of doing web development. Back at Digital Creations, he started writing Bobo, an object database and object request broker capable of publishing Python objects over the web. Later, the commercial Principia,

---

[2] SQLObject project website <http://sqlobject.org/>
[3] sqlos project website <http://codespeak.net/z3/sqlos>
[4] lxml project website <http://codespeak.net/lxml>

Zope's predecessor, joined its little brother Bobo. Their heritage in Zope 2 even lives on today in method and attribute names of the Zope 2 API such as bobobase_modification_time and isPrincipiaFolderish.

Open Source success story

In 1998, Hadar Pedhazur from the venture capital firm Verticality Investment Group invested into Digital Creations and convinced them to make their successful web applications open source. Paul Everitt, CEO of Digital Creations at the time, announced the opening of the source code at the Python Conference 1998. That same year, Bobo and Principia became Zope, the *Z Object Publishing Environment*, and was released under the Zope Public License. Zope 2.0 followed the next year and has been the basis for all stable Zope 2 releases.

Digital Creations—later renamed to Zope Corporation—now sells its services as a software consultant implementing solutions using Zope open source software. Many other companies around the world now also base their services on Zope and have developed successful solutions such as Plone, Silva, and CPS. Due to the wide-spread network of solution providers, professional Zope support and consultancy is available around the world. Zope itself is now maintained and further developed by developers from these solution providers. In March of 2006, the Zope Foundation was founded to govern the Zope source code and to provide a platform for the Zope community to drive the Zope project.

Zope 2's success from a technical point of view is based on two revolutionary concepts. Firstly, it publishes data on the web via objects that are able to presents themselves to a web browser. Secondly, its web application development process enables people to configure pre-coded software components through a web browser or, as the Zope world calls it, *through-the-web* (TTW). These processes are carried out through a web interface, the *Zope Management Interface* (ZMI) and are stored in Zope's own object database, the ZODB. While this was a great way for developers to quickly get started with Zope, it also meant that the transition from a quickly sketched web application to a larger, filesystem-based software project that needed version control and the like was not easy to do. Hence the phrase Zope's "Z-shaped learning curve" was coined, which meant that Zope made things very easy in the beginning, then required a lot of work to understand the filesystem-based development model at which point it could be considered easy again.

How Zope 3 was born

The Zope 3 project started in 2001 when Zope Corporation experimented with the *Component Architecture*. The goal was to split up the responsibilities and functionality of current Zope 2 objects because they had grown to be incredibly large with respect to their functionality and code in their classes.

The new approach coupled several smaller objects together rather than having one big bloated one. It also included a move away from through-the-web development. One of the goals of this was to smooth Zope's learning curve. A number of these concepts were prototyped in the Content Management Framework (CMF), a library on top of Zope 2 that is the basis for many Zope-based content management systems, such as Plone and CPS.

Zope 2 had grown to be too complex to incorporate Component Architecture. It was decided to do a complete rewrite, Zope 3, which used Component Architecture as its foundation and at the same time borrowed and learned from the strengths and weaknesses of Zope 2. It was first called Zope 3X (X for *experimental*), then Zope X3, its first stable version was Zope X3 3.0. No longer being experimental, Zope 3 dropped the X for Zope 3.1 and all subsequent releases.

Having two very different versions of Zope was still a problem. Martijn Faassen, an active Zope 2 and Zope 3 developer, and others wanted to use Zope 3 technology in existing Zope 2 software. To solve this the Five project was started. Its goal is to make Zope 3 technology available in Zope 2. Five gained momentum from all over the Zope 2 community and was adopted as the official migration strategy. Zope 2.8 had Five integrated into its source code. Zope 2 development was spurred on and subsequent Zope 2 versions started using more and more Zope 3 technology. Probably the most exciting things we will see in Zope's future will come from this integration project since it allows the tremendous amount of excellent Zope 2 software to work with Zope 3 technology in the future, thus enriching both.

1.5 The Python Programming Language

> *Zope magic is Python magic.*
> Jim Fulton at the EuroZope Conference Berlin 2002

Zope profits from Python's supremacy. Even more, Zope would be impossible without Python. Python is a quick, easy-to-learn, Swiss Army knife-like scripting language—but so is Perl. Python also is an industrial strength, highly dynamic, object-oriented, interpreted programming language—but so is Java. What makes Python special then?

Python is easy to learn. It took me one afternoon to go through the Python tutorial [13]. Sure, I bought a few books on Python afterwards, but not for learning the language. I merely wanted to know what it was capable of.

Python is easy to read. Go and open an arbitrary python source code file in Zope 3. Chances are good you will understand most of what is going on without actually having seen Python before. Using indentation for marking blocks certainly is the most aesthetic aspect of the language, but also one many people have to get used to first. Obviously, it is still possible to write cryptic code in Python, but less likely.

Python is easy to write. I rarely need the library reference when programming. When developing Java, I constantly find myself looking up standard library interfaces, abstract classes, etc. Python is not as wordy as Java, but it is not as cryptic as Perl, either.

Python is easy to develop with. Not having complicated package names and long class names in the standard library, Python can easily be written without an IDE that would ease the development process. In fact, the Zope contributor community is more or less equally split into those who use emacs and those who use vi. Moreover, Python does not require a compiler, obsoleting long compilation sessions.

Python comes with batteries included. The regular Python distribution comes with a rich library of useful modules, ranging from parsers for text formats to email messaging and processing. That means you can get started with Python very quickly without having to collect the basic modules yourself. In case you are looking for third party packages you can use the *Python Cheese Shop* website[5] to find the software package of your desire. There are numerous third party packages available as open source which can easily be used in Zope applications, too.[6]

"Python—it fits your brain" a popular Python t-shirt reads; it sums up my programming experience with Python in one sentence. If you are new to it, you are sure to be converted to Python by the end of this book. In case you are looking for a Python book to accompany your Zope 3 development, the author can strongly recommend the excellent *Dive Into Python* by Mark Pilgrim [4].

1.6 Changes since Zope X3 3.0

Since December 2005, Zope 2 and Zope 3 releases have been synchronized and put on a time-based schedule. This ensures that new features will appear in a stable release at a definite point in time while potentially unstable features will not be able to postpone a major release.

The first edition of this book covered Zope X3 3.0. Three major versions of Zope 3 have been released since then. This book uses Zope 3.3. For those of you who developed Zope applications with the first edition, here is a short overview of the most important changes in Zope 3.1, 3.2 and 3.3:

---

[5] Python Cheese Shop website <http://cheeseshop.python.org/>

[6] In Chapter 13, for example, we will use *ReportLab*, a third party library for PDF generation, to generate PDF documents from Zope content objects.

Restructuring

- Zope's publisher API was rebuilt to the *Python Web Server Gateway Interface* (WSGI) specification [12] and has been given a frontend that acts as a *WSGI application*. Similarly, Zope's own HTTP server (`zope.server`) has been made to act as a *WSGI gateway*. Zope also ships with the Twisted network framework. Its WSGI-capable web server, `twisted.web2`, is the default backend now.
- The Component Architecture has been greatly simplified. The concept of services has been dropped, only two types of components remain: utilities and adapters. While the adapter registry has taken over the responsibility of some services like the presentation service and browser menu service, most former services are now simply available utilities. The utility and adapter registries are now part of the *component registry* (formerly known as site manager), which is the successor to the service registry. Chapter 2 explains this in depth.
- With the abolition of all services including the presentation service, views are now named multi-adapters for the object they represent and request. Resources are named adapters for request. Browser layers and skins simply are interfaces extending `IBrowserRequest`, thus request marker interfaces.
- Menus, formerly registered through the browser menu service, are named utilities providing `IBrowserMenu`. Menu items are named multi-adapters for the context object and the request. Submenu items are also possible now.
- The authentication service has been replaced with the authentication utility. The pluggableauth service has also been replaced by a port of the *Pluggable Auth Service* (PAS) which is now called *Pluggable Auth Utility* (PAU) due to its being a utility. It is located at `zope.app.authentication`. Chapter 22 covers this new system.
- Several packages or modules were moved out of `zope.app` to make them easier to reuse, for example in Zope 2. These are:
  - `zope.app.size`
  - `zope.app.location`
  - `zope.app.annotation`
  - `zope.app.dublincore`
  - `zope.app.copypastemove`
  - `zope.app.mail` (to `zope.sendmail`)
  - `zope.app.rdb`
  - `zope.app.filerepresentation`
  - `zope.app.traversing`
  - `zope.app.event` (to `zope.component.event` and `zope.lifecycleevent`)

- The mutable implementation of i18n message IDs has been replaced with an immutable one, now simply called *i18n messages*. Chapter 9 covers this as well as the new semantics regarding immutability.
- The vocabulary feature is being replaced by *sources*, a simpler and less constraining framework.
- A number of redundant or superfluous ZCML directives have been removed:
  - `factory`
  - `vocabulary`
  - `content` (as an alias of `class`)
  - `modulealias`
  - `browser:addview`
  - `renderer:renderer`

New features

- A new library for form generation and validation, `zope.formlib`, has been added to Zope. Instead of defining forms through ZCML, they are now implemented in Python and thus give the developer much more flexibility over forms while automating the recurring parts of generating and validating forms. Chapter 8 covers the new form system.
- A new machinery for dynamically constructing user interfaces via *content providers* has been added with the `zope.contentprovider` package, along with a content provider implementation called *viewlets* located in `zope.viewlet`. Chapter 10 covers both in detail.
- A reinterpretation of Zope 2's *ZCatalog* for the Component Architecture is now available for Zope 3 at `zope.app.catalog`, along with some indices (`zope.index`) and a unique ID facility (`zope.app.intid`). This makes it possible to efficiently index and search objects in the ZODB. ZCatalog is covered in Chapter 19.
- Zope 3 now has support for browser sessions located in `zope.app.session`. Chapter 20 covers this.
- An engine for the Worfklow Management Coalition (WfMC) workflow standard has been added to Zope with the `zope.wfmc` package.

2

Zope and the Component Architecture

This chapter gives a bird's eye view of Zope as an object publishing environment. It explains how Zope works as well as the principles of its Component Architecture. Make sure you understand the basic concepts explained here before moving on.

2.1 How Zope works—an overview

Zope is a collection of software suitable for building web applications. Zope is typically used as a web application server in which case it consists of three major parts:

Server. The server is the component that lets users connect to Zope by allowing network requests from clients. Typically this means HTTP connections, such as from a web browser, XML-RPC client, or WebDAV client.

The *Python Web Server Gateway Interface* (WSGI) specification [12] calls this the *gateway*. WSGI-capable HTTP gateways that can currently be used with Zope are Zope's own `zope.server` and Twisted's `twisted.web2`.[1]

Publisher. Requests coming in through the server are handled by the publisher. WSGI calls this part the *application*, but in Zope, the application does not deal with such low-level things as parsing the HTTP input stream. This is the publisher's task instead, making it a distinct component between server and application.
The WSGI gateway invokes Zope's publisher via the `zope.app.wsgi.WSGIPublisherApplication` class. This class, among others, con-

---

[1] `twisted.web2` project website <http://twistedmatrix.com/projects/web2>

structs a *request* object from the input stream and hands it off to the actual Zope publishing machinery in `zope.publisher`. This is the machinery which makes Zope unique: object publishing. Zope's object publisher first finds the object addressed by the request and then invokes that object. The former is called *traversing*, the latter *publishing*. In object publishing, the request object and its corresponding *publication* object cooperate. The latter takes care of actions that are related to a particular request, for example starting and committing database transactions.

Application. Basically, the application is everything that the server and the publisher are not. For example, determining *how* the publisher traverses through objects to the one it finally invokes is part of the application, just like other parts such as security.

When we say that we develop Zope applications, we are specifically referring to the application part of Zope. Of course we do not have to write our own security system nor do we have to rethink every detail about object traversal. Zope already has this functionality. It can be used directly, customized, enhanced, or completely replaced for your own application.

Rocky says...

WSGI is about enabling different Python web frameworks to work along side each other. Java developers should see this akin to Java Servlet technology. JSP is an example of a framework built on top of servlets. Even filters as defined by the Servlet specification behave closely to WSGI's middlewares.

2.2 Introducing components

When using large frameworks like Zope, the goal is to avoid starting from scratch. That means Zope application development involves the skilled reuse, customization and extension of the existing functionality. The question is how do this as easily and as flexibly as possible.

Subclassing

Object-orientation provides two approaches to such customization. The first one is subclassing. A subclass derived from one or more superclasses inherits all of their functionality, unless explicitly overridden. That certainly is a very powerful concept, allowing you as the developer to mix as many functions together in one class as you like[2]. That is a very common scheme in Zope

---

[2] As long as the language supports multiple inheritance, which Python does.

2. Many Zope 2 classes only exist because they are to be "mixed in" into application classes. Some of them even carry a `Mixin` suffix in their name.

Subclassing has a weakness in practice: you have to create a new class for every change in functionality. Often, you find your mix-in classes rely on functionality intended to be implemented by subclasses, which is an error-prone scheme. Moreover, changing even presentation behaviour would mean writing Python code (a new subclass) even if only an HTML template has to be customized.

Delegation

Delegation is the other concept. Instead of inheriting functionality from superclasses, work is delegated among several separate objects called *components*. Each component takes a responsibility in a complex action. For instance, a content component is only responsible for storing data while a presentation component is responsible for presenting it. When a component is no longer satisfactory, whether in general or for your particular application, it can be replaced by a better implementation. For example, a presentation component that determines the way a content component is presented to the web browser could be exchanged without any modifications to the underlying content component. The Component Architecture is the tool by which Zope can provide this flexibility and power.

In order to be exchangeable for another implementation, components need to clearly define what kind of functionality they expect from other components and what kind of functionality they provide in return. In the real world, this is often called a *contract*. Objects must have a clear contract in order to be components. Like other systems, the Component Architecture uses interfaces to express such contracts (see below). We can therefore define components as *objects with interfaces*.

We commonly divide components into three categories: Model, View, and Controller (MVC). The model holds the data. It knows about the data's structure, as well as where and how to store it. The model is analogous to what we often call a *content component*. The view presents the data to the user (e.g. as a GUI element or a web page) and the controller processes data in order to change the model or the view. In the Zope Component Architecture, *adapters* can be used to implement controllers and views. They are a generic way of extending existing components with data processing or presentation capabilities. Apart from adapters, the Component Architecture also knows *utilities*. These are components fulfilling a certain task without the context of another component, for example database look-ups or indexing and searching.

The following sections of this chapter will uncover more details on each of those component types.

Benefits of reuse and pluggability

The use of the Component Architecture has two large benefits: increased exchangeability and easier reuse. In Zope, you can exchange nearly any component with a custom one. That applies to "small" components like a simple browser view producing HTML just as well as to "large" parts of the Zope framework like the authentication system.

The other aforementioned benefit is a better ability to reuse existing components. Python has many packages for data handling, processing and presenting functionality. Why should Zope prevent you from using them? Consider a web application for handling email messages. Python already has excellent support for handling emails in the `email` and `smtplib` packages. To use this Python package in Zope you simply add functionality, such as HTML presentation or support for another network protocol like FTP, by adding components.

The Component Architecture is provided by the `zope.component` package.

Summary

- Zope 3 is based on a component architecture in which different responsibilities are covered by different components.
- Components are objects with a clear contract of their functionality, expressed through interfaces.
- The component architecture gives developers the ability to replace implementations with better or different ones later in the development process.
- It is easy to both use non-Zope components from Python inside Zope, as well as use Zope-specific components outside Zope.
- Two explicit types of components are known to the component architecture: adapters and utilities.

Flashback

Zope 3 is the first Zope version completely based on a component architecture, but a prototype was introduced with the Content Management Framework (CMF) in Zope 2. The CMF separates content objects from application logic and presentation. It is still based on Zope 2, though, and therefore inherits limitations. For example, content objects, software components ("tools") and presentation layers still persist in the same folders and namespaces, making the developer rely on naming conventions everywhere in order to avoid name clashes.

On the other hand, the CMF allows the developer to completely customize the default application. In fact, it was designed to be customized, which many developers are happy to do when facing the raw looks of the default presentation skin. A now famous third party product was born out of a customized CMF skin: Plone. It uses the CMF's architecture and many CMF default components, customizing them to the extent of hiding the CMF beneath from the user completely (the developer unfortunately still has to deal with the CMF). Ironically, the Plone documentation nowadays tells developers to customize Plone, just like CMF does.

Rocky says...

J2EE's component model is based on JavaBeans and EJB (Enterprise JavaBeans) but works quite differently from the Zope component model. Plus J2EE itself does not describe any sort of fine-grained web components. However, anyone experienced with the Struts MVC (Model 2) framework for J2EE should have an easy time learning to use view components. Struts action classes to Zope 3's view classes and Struts XML configuration to ZCML are just a few examples of their similarities in implementation.

2.3 Interfaces

When a company delegates work to another company, a legal contract is made. In that contract they agree to deliverables, conditions, and price:

- The vendor has fulfil its promises, per the contract.
- The customer uses the contract as a guarantee of these vendor promises.
- Both know, from the contract, what is expected from the transaction.

Components are no different in this respect. Components need to know what other components promise. For example, a presentation component needs to know what kind of data a content component provides.

Many programming languages have come up with a formalization of the contract concept: *interfaces*. Interfaces describe the methods and attributes an object provides, in other words: the API. They describe the *what* of a component (as in "what can I do with it?"), but not the *how* (as in "how does it do it").

Python does not have built-in support for interfaces. This means Python products needing formalization in terms of responsibility must come up with their own solutions. Zope interface support resides in the `zope.interface` package.

Summary

- Interfaces are the contracts by which components work together.
- Interfaces are not a Python language construct.
- Interfaces can serve as API documentation.

Chapter 4 has a full description of interfaces and covers how to define, declare and use them.

2.4 Content components

Content components are objects containing data. All they should provide is functionality to store and update that data. Data presentation (such as in HTML, XML, etc.) and processing (sorting, interpreting, transforming, etc.) should not be part of their responsibilities. Just like all other components, content components should be exchangeable. As long as the new component implements the same interface, the other parts of the application should not be affected.

Most applications built with Zope are content management systems. Of course, these applications revolve around content components, but even other applications need to deal with content once in a while. Fortunately, it is very easy to reuse existing content components in Zope, so the application developer can focus on the presentation and application logic. As discussed above, one of the benefits of the Component Architecture is the reusability of already existing components. That includes third party components, but also those you write yourself. Writing a content component therefore is usually not much more work than writing a simple Python class for any other application.

Many of today's web content management systems use a relational database for data storage. You can use them with Zope quite well, too. Zope is about publishing *objects*, though. One possibility is to use an object-relational mapper (ORM) to turn relational data into objects. Another possibility is to use a database that stores data in objects rather than in tables. Zope has such a database, the Zope Object Database (ZODB). With the ZODB you can create persistent Python objects with little additional code or knowledge about object persistency. The ZODB is fully compliant with the ACID database properties which means it ensures atomicity, consistency, isolation and durability (more information in Chapter 6). Furthermore, the ZODB supports versioning and has a pluggable backend storage architecture. All of these features are nearly transparent to the developer of content objects and can be used outside of Zope as well. We will dive into the features of the ZODB, as well as the implementation of persistent objects, in Chapter 6.

Summary

- Content components are simple Python classes usable outside Zope applications.
- Their responsibility is only to store data, not to present or process it.
- Typically, content components are persistent, using the transparent object storage of the ZODB.
- Content components are the *model* of the Component Architecture, though they are not as formalized as adapters and utilities.

Rocky says...

In J2EE, entity beans are the equivalent of content components, with CMP style entity beans being the closest to transparent persistence. While using the ZODB is radically different from using entity beans (particularly since entity beans generally work against a RDBMS), most will find that working with the ZODB is much cleaner and more elegant in comparison both from an API perspective and in requirements to make data persistable. Those familiar with the Hibernate ORM project can understand how persisting objects can be much more satisfying than persisting raw data in a relational database.

2.5 Adapters

Zope makes no special requirements on content components They do not have to implement a special interface, nor are certain methods or attributes required for a component to be used in Zope. On one hand, this lets us use nearly any third-party component in Zope. On the other hand, it makes it hard for components to expect certain functionality from each other.

For example, a directory listing may display the size of objects listed. How would the component responsible for generating the directory listing (typically a view) know how to retrieve an object's size (if the object had a size at all)? The answer lies in adapters, a very powerful feature of the component architecture.

Plugging components together

Adapters work like adapters for a stereo. Imagine you have an old European tape deck, and you want to hook it up to your modern amplifier. The amplifier expects RCA plugs, but all the tape deck provides is the old European five prong DIN plug. To connect the two, you would go to an electronics shop and buy an adapter from DIN to RCA or, if you had the parts and the tools, you could solder one yourself. As expected, you will hear the ancient sounds from the tape deck when you plug it all together. To the amplifier, it does not matter what device the music is coming from, nor what kind of plug it has. All it cares about is that it comes in over RCA plugs in the end. We could say that *the amplifier accepts any source device that either provides RCA plugs itself, or for which an adapter to RCA is available.*

Zope adapters work in much the same way. Even if an object does not provide a certain API directly, an adapter may be available to provide it for the object. In the directory listing example, we would not require the object to be able to tell us about its size, but we would assume that an adapter could do it for us. We would therefore adapt the object to an interface that specifies a size API. Then, if we introduced some new type of component and wanted the directory listing to show its size, we would simply supply an adapter to that interface.

In this way, adapters let us extend existing components without having to change the original code. Adapters rarely depend on a certain implementation, only on the interfaces they adapt and provide.

Views

A *view* is a special type of adapter that extends components with presentation capabilities. Views make the bridge between application components and the user, as a user obviously does not know how to talk to a component using its Python API. With Zope being a web application platform, views are of course one of the most important use cases of adapters.

Being adapters, views are subject to the same basic rule as the content components they present: it should be possible to replace their implementation with a different one providing the same interface. Similarly, views cannot rely on a certain implementation. Hence, they are *registered for interfaces.*

As we will see later, this registration is not done in Python, but in special configuration files, allowing the site administrator to enable and disable view registrations without having to dive into code. The same rule applies to "normal" adapters and other types of components.

Summary

- Adapters extend the functionality of existing components without modifying the original code.
- They are registered for the interface they adapt and the one they provide. Similarly, they are looked up for the object they are supposed to adapt (the context) and the target interface.

- Views are adapters that provide a user-oriented presentation of an object according to a certain request.
- Views should be the only parts in an application that deal with request and response objects.
- A view's characteristics are

  - the type of object it presents
  - the type of request it is for
  - its name

Similarly, they are looked up for the object they are supposed to present (the context), the request they are for and their name.

Flashback

Initially, Zope's view concept was roughly derived from the CMF. Since then it has been consolidated with the adapter concept. Zope 3 now only knows adapters, whether they involve the request or not.

Adapters will be covered in depth in Chapter 11. Views will be the topic of Chapter 7 and will then be revisited in Chapter 13.

2.6 Utilities

The second type of components the Component Architecture knows are *utilities*. Like adapters, they provide a well-defined set of functionality to other components. The difference is that utilities do not operate on another component. They just provide a specific service.

In general, we can distinguish between those components that rely on a context and those that do not. Context-dependent components are written as adapters, whereas context-independent ones are utilities. Hence, utilities do not take a context argument.

Singletons vs. named utilities

There are two typical use cases for utilities. In the first one, a certain type of functionality is needed in an application for which one utility is registered as a singleton (meaning there is only one instance per site or application). They are registered and looked up solely by interface, again for exchangeability of implementations. Examples for this type of utilities are:

- database connectivity, indexing, searching

- encoding/decoding, encryption/decryption
- mail delivery, browser sessions, translation negotiation
- sorting, randomizing, etc.

In the second use case, small components that occur more than once and are looked up by name within their group of components are often written as utilities. The components are registered and looked up by *name and interface*. That is why they are called *named utilities*. Typical use-cases include:

- permissions and roles
- factories
- content types
- translation domains
- browser skins

Summary

- A utility is a small software component that provides a certain, limited type of functionality.
- Utilities do not rely on a context.
- A singleton is a utility that occurs only once; it is simply registered and looked up by its interface.
- Several named components of the same kind can be registered as *named* utilities; they are looked up by name and interface.

Rocky says...

While not an exact match, the closest equivalent to a utility in Java would be EJB session beans. Both EJB session beans and utilities are considered components by their respective platforms, and both are used to implement business logic. However, session beans must run within a J2EE server or set of containers, whereas Zope 3 utilities can be accessed via the standard Zope API. This makes it much easier to unit test utilities than EJB session beans. Of course, using the Spring framework to separate testable code into Spring components can alleviate this, but Spring is not core to J2EE.

2.7 Configuring components

If we want to be able to look up components, they must obviously be registered somewhere first. The place where this is done is the *component registry* (formerly known as site manager). Sometimes in addition to a simple registration, other aspects of the application policy needs to be defined, such as security settings. Zope 3 simply calls the definition of such application policy (which includes the registration of components) *configuration*.[3]

How should this configuration take place? It certainly is not the responsibility of the component itself. How would a component know where and how it was going to be registered, or if it was going to be registered at all? In addition, configuration often is not only the responsibility of the site developer, but also of the site administrator. This rules out using Python for the configuration wiring, because site administrators should not have to get involved with Python code.

Zope Configuration Markup Language (ZCML)

Zope 3 uses an XML-based configuration language for global component registration: the Zope Configuration Markup Language, ZCML. Since a form of text and not code is used for configuration, developers cannot mix configuration and implementation. Furthermore, XML is a web standard, and many of today's text editors have facilities to ease markup editing. Using XML also makes it easier for the site administrator to enable, disable or exchange components, all without touching Python code.

Summary

- Component registration and other aspects of application policy are a matter of configuration.
- Zope 3 uses the XML-based ZCML language for configuration.

We will see examples of configuration entries and whole file listings in all of the following chapters.

2.8 Security

Storing, presenting, and processing data is one part of an application. Granting or denying certain functionality based on authentication is another aspect. Security plays an extremely important role for web applications, which are usually accessible over the Internet. This section briefly introduces the key concepts of the Zope security system. More detailed coverage is provided by Chapter 21.

---

[3] Here, configuration is meant in terms of configuring the components of the software. It is not meant in the traditional sense of a configuration file that is read by the application.

Permissions

The smallest "unit" of security assertions Zope knows is a *permission*. Most components require a specific permission to be used while different actions require different permissions. For example, accessing a content object's data requires one permission, while changing the data requires another. Fortunately, the component doesn't worry about who or what has those permissions. Instead, the developer or site developer sets that policy.

Principals

Principals in Zope are entities with certain access privileges. Typically, when we speak of principals we mean users with accounts. Other applications might want to stick additional metadata on principals, for example when the data is retrieved from a directory service such as LDAP that contains not only full names but also addresses, phone numbers and the location within an organization. Then again, a principal does not necessarily have to have a login account. The *unauthenticated principal*, a principal that is always available in Zope and represents users that have not authenticated with the system, does not have a login account. You do not have to login to be unauthenticated. You simply are.

Principals are provided by authenticator plug-ins, a component that is queried by the authentication utility. Thus, with a custom authenticator plug-in, principals can be defined almost anywhere, whether in a file on the file system or in tables of a relational database system. Their login credentials are extracted from the request by login credential utilities. Principals can be joined into groups.

Security policy

In Zope, the security policy is a piece of machinery that decides when to allow and when to deny certain privileges. When doing so, it has to check whether the active principal has permission to perform an action or not. Security policies are pluggable like most other components. That means you can implement your own security policy which authorizes principals in whatever way that fits your application.

Summary

- Components are secured using permissions. Different actions may require different permissions.
- The abstraction of a user in Zope is called a principal.
- Custom credential and authenticator plug-ins allow a custom way of looking up and authenticating principals from a user database.

- A security policy determines whether a principal has permission to perform an action. The default security policy denies everything unless it is explicitly allowed.

Rocky says...

J2EE doesn't specify anything beyond basic security concerns in the specifications themselves. As a result, there are a plethora of security frameworks available from the various J2EE vendors in the form of commercial and open source frameworks. J2EE developers will be delighted when dealing with the more mature Zope security model. Both the fine-grained control of permission checking and the extensibility of PAU (Pluggable Authentication Utility) alleviate problems when dealing with security concerns in Zope applications.

3

Installing Zope

To start, you need to set up Zope on your computer. Firstly, we install Zope and its dependencies. Then we will set up one Zope instance which is a directory with Zope's configuration, database files and extension modules. From this directory we will then start a Zope server.

3.1 Requirements

Zope 3 runs on all major platforms: Microsoft Windows, Linux, Apple Mac OS X, and other Unix flavours. It uses about 100 megabytes of hard disc space. For production systems and development environments, a machine with a reasonable processor and a fair amount of RAM is recommended. You might increase both depending on the complexity of the applications that are to be developed and run.

Python

Zope usually requires a specific version of Python which may change from release to release. Make sure you have the Python version installed that is mentioned in the release notes or README.txt file of your Zope 3 distribution.

Unix and Unix-like systems
Many software distributions, such as Linux, BSD distributions and Mac OS X provide a default installation of Python. You can find out its version number by issuing the following command line:

```
$ python -V
Python x.y.z
```

If you do not have Python installed, or have an older version than required by Zope, consult the packaging system of your Linux or BSD distribution to retrieve the correct version. On Mac OS X, there are third party packaging systems available, such as Fink[1] and DarwinPorts.[2]

Alternatively, you can easily install the correct Python version from source. The source packages are provided on the Python website.[3] First, download the source archive and extract it in a temporary directory, such as /tmp:

```
/tmp$ tar xzf Python-x.y.z.tgz
/tmp$ cd Python-x.y.z
```

On most systems, you can then simply enter the following three typical commands to compile Python:

```
/tmp/Python-x.y.z$ ./configure
/tmp/Python-x.y.z$ make
/tmp/Python-x.y.z$ make install
```

If you would like to install Python into a different location than the standard one in /usr, you can specify extra parameters to the configure script. Enter ./configure --help for a detailed help on the script parameters. No matter where you install Python, though, you should ensure that the Python interpreter is on the command line search path (PATH environment variable) so that you can easily invoke it by simply typing python.

Windows

If you are on Windows, you can simply download and run the installer executable from the Python website. The installer will first ask you where to install Python and its libraries. We will assume that this is the default location at C:\Python24 (depending on the Python version) here, though you are free to choose any other location. Before the actual installation begins, you can choose which components you wish to install apart from the interpreter and libraries. None of these extra items are required but some of them might be useful during development.

As we will be invoking the Python interpreter from the command line a lot, it is recommended to put the directory where you installed Python (e.g. C:\Python24) on the command line search path. This search path is controlled by the PATH environment variable. Environment variables can be set in the *System Properties* dialog which is opened by right-clicking on *My Computer* and choosing *Properties*. Then go to the *Advanced* tab and click on the *Environment Variables* button. In the appearing dialog window you can add new user environment variables, as shown in Figure 3.1.

---

[1] Fink website <http://fink.sourceforge.net>

[2] DarwinPorts website <http://darwinports.opendarwin.org/>

[3] Python website <http://www.python.org>

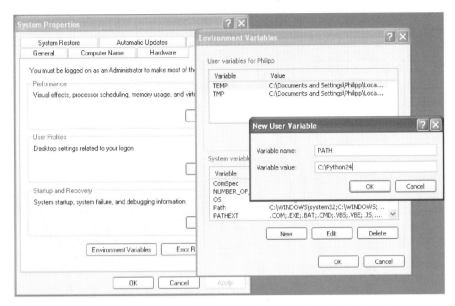

Fig. 3.1. Setting the PATH environment variable so that the Python interpreter will be found on the command line.

C compiler for source downloads

A few parts of Zope 3 are written in C, mostly for optimization. Therefore, unless you are planning to use a binary distribution of Zope, you will also need an ANSI C compiler, such as gcc. Linux and Unix systems should be equipped with the GNU compiler. On Mac OS X, you will have to install the Xcode utilities. On Windows, you may use the cygwin[4] collection of Unix tools which provides a Windows version of gcc, or, alternatively use Microsoft Visual C++ to compile Zope. It is, however, recommended to use the binary package on Windows.

3.2 Download, compilation and installation

Zope packages in Linux/Unix distributions

Apart from being available as a source code archive, Zope might also be available as an installable package in your Linux or Unix distribution. Note that this might not always be the most current version of Zope in which case it is recommended to install Zope from source, at least for development purposes.

---

[4] Cygwin website <http://cygwin.com>

On Debian, Zope 3 is available via the `zope3` package. It installs the Python libraries of Zope directly into the Python site-packages directory (e.g. `/usr/lib/python2.4/sites-packages`) and Zope-related scripts into `/usr/lib/zope3/bin`. In the Gentoo Portage system, Zope 3 is available through the `zope` package. There the whole Zope 3 setup will be installed into `/usr/lib/zope-3.x.y`.

Source installation (Unix)

Unless you are on a Windows system or your packaging system provides a binary install package, you will need to download the source archive from the Zope community website.[5] The compilation and installation follows the standard Unix procedure using a configuration script and the `make` program.

Download the archive and extract it in a temporary directory, such as `/tmp`. Then invoke the `configure` script to generate a `Makefile`:

```
/tmp$ tar xzf Zope-3.x.y.tgz
/tmp$ cd Zope-3.x.y
/tmp/Zope-3.x.y$ ./configure
Configuring Zope installation

Testing for an acceptable Python interpreter...

Python version x.y.z found at /usr/bin/python

The optimum Python version (x.y.z) was found at
/usr/bin/python.
```

If the `configure` script is given no parameters, it will try to detect any installed Python versions and use the optimum one. You can force it to use a specific Python version using the `--with-python` parameter, for example:

```
./configure --with-python=/usr/local/bin/python2.4
```

The Python libraries and executable scripts of Zope will be installed into the *software home*, by default `/usr/local/Zope-3.x.y/`. This can be changed using the `--prefix` parameter, for example:

```
./configure --prefix=/opt/Zope
```

Now that the `Makefile` is generated, the next task is to call the `make` program, once to compile the Zope libraries and once more to install it into the various locations:

```
/tmp/Zope-3.x.y$ make
/usr/bin/python install.py -q build
/tmp/Zope-3.x.y$ make install
/usr/bin/python install.py -q build
/usr/bin/python install.py -q install --home "/usr/local/Zope-3.x.y"
```

---

[5] Zope 3 downloads <http://www.zope.org/Products/Zope3>

Windows

On a Windows system, download the binary archive. This is recommended because it comes in the form of a handy installer program. When you execute the installer, it will search the Windows registry for any installed Python versions. If you have more than one installed, select the appropriate version and advance by clicking the *Next* button. To begin the installation, click on *Next* once more. The installer program will then install the Zope libraries into Python's library directory, usually C:\Python24\Lib\site-packages, and the executable scripts to the scripts directory, usually C:\Python24\Scripts.

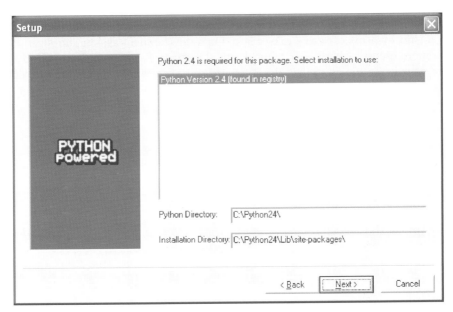

Fig. 3.2. The Windows installer detects installed Python versions automatically.

Zope can be uninstalled like any other Windows program. To remove Zope from your system, go to the *Add or Remove Programs* section in the *Control Panel*, select the entry concerning Zope and invoke the *Change/Remove* button.

3.3 Setting up a Zope instance

Installing Zope is only half of the setup. To run Zope and develop with it you will need to set up at least one *instance* which is a server instance and a database instance running together with a specific configuration and in a specific location. You can create as many parallel instances from one Zope installation as you wish and, provided the servers listen to different TCP/IP ports, run as many as you wish in parallel. We will only be needing one here, but when developing several applications simultaneously, it is often useful to create separate instances for each project. Similarly, in a server environment, different instances can be used to give different users control over their Zope applications.

Creating an instance

On a production system, Zope instances are typically installed where other large data files occur, since instances contain the database files. A good place on Unix systems is /var/lib/zope. On a development system, however, it is more useful to work out of your home directory. To create a Zope instance in your home directory, use the mkzopeinstance script that was installed into the executables directory. Its interactive mode is fortunately quite self-explanatory:

```
~$ /usr/local/Zope-3.x.y/bin/mkzopeinstance
Please choose a directory in which you'd like to install Zope
'instance home' files such as database files, configuration
files, etc.

Directory: Zope3Instance

Please choose a username for the initial administrator
account. This is required to allow Zope's management interface
to be used.

Username: manager

Please select a password manager which will be used for encode
the password of the initial administrator account.

  1. Plain Text
  2. MD5
  3. SHA1

Password Manager Number [1]: 1
'Plain Text' password manager selected

Please provide a password for the initial administrator
account.

Password: *****
Verify password: *****
```

On Windows, use the *Command Prompt* (available in the Start Menu under *Accessories*) to type in the commands. Note that the location of the script is different and that you have to explicitly call it with the Python interpreter:

```
C:\> python \Python24\Scripts\mkzopeinstance
...
```

Instance configuration

We have now created an instance in the Zope3Instance directory, relative to the current working directory. The mkzopeinstance script has also created an initial administrator account in the instance's etc/principals. zcml file. For development purposes, we chose to store the password in plain text. On production sites you might consider choosing the SHA1 encryption option, or simply disable the account altogether.

The server aspects of a Zope instance are largely configured through the etc/zope.conf configuration file. Its syntax is quite similar to the configuration files used by the Apache HTTP server. The default version of zope. conf has the following features enabled:

- an HTTP server listening on port 8080,
- a FileStorage database stored in var/Data.fs,
- an access log written to log/access.log as well as *standard output*,
- and an event log written to log/z3.log as well as *standard output*.

You can easily enable the following features by uncommenting and adjusting the corresponding examples in a stock zope.conf:

- an HTTPS server, typically listening on port 8443. Note that the instance must be a Twisted-based one for this to work. You must have also have the Python bindings to the OpenSSL library[6] installed. Also note that the usual way to serve a Zope site via HTTPS is to put an HTTPS-capable webserver such as Apache in front of Zope (see Chapter 24).
- an FTP server, typically listening on port 8021.
- an SFTP server, typically listening on port 8115. Note that the instance must be a Twisted-based one for this to work. You must have also have the Python Cryptography Toolkit pyCrypto[7] installed.

Starting, stopping and controlling an instance

We can now start up the instance by running the bin/runzope script from the instance directory:

---

[6] pyOpenSSL website <http://pyopenssl.sourceforge.net>
[7] pyCrypto website <http://www.amk.ca/python/code/crypto>

~$ **cd Zope3Instance**
~/Zope3Instance$ **bin/runzope**

This works similar in the Windows *Command Prompt*:

C:\> **cd Zope3Instance**
C:\Zope3Instance> **bin\runzope**

Once Zope has reported the server instances during startup and displayed a message about the startup time, the instance is ready for request. To test whether Zope is operational, open http://localhost:8080/manage in a web browser and log in with the administrator user account we configured when creating the instance. You should now see the *Zope Management Interface* (ZMI) which will be explained in more detailed later. To stop the Zope instance, hit **Ctrl–C** in your terminal or command prompt window.

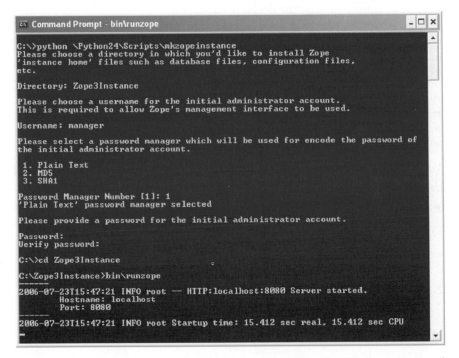

Fig. 3.3. Setting up an instance and starting Zope from the Windows command prompt.

For development purposes, the runzope script is perfectly sufficient to start and terminate an instance. In a server environment, however, one often needs to start a server instance that detaches from the terminal so it will keep on running even after the terminal has been closed. This is especially useful when the server is administrated from a remote location. This functionality and more is provided for each instance in a small script, `bin/zopectl`. It works similarly to Apache's `apachectl` program or even System V init scripts. It accepts the following parameters:

`start` starts the detached server daemon or does nothing in case it is already running.

`stop` stops the detached server daemon or does nothing in case it is not running.

`status` shows the status of the server process, for example if it is running or not.

`reload` reloads the server configuration.

`restart` first stops and then starts the daemon again.

`foreground`, `fg` starts the server process without detaching. This is equal to calling `bin/runzope`.

`run <script> [args]` runs a specified Python script with the whole Zope environment except the servers set up. The script has the root database object exposed as the global `root` variable.

`debug` sets up the whole Zope environment except the servers and then drops into an interactive Python prompt. The root database object is exposed as the `root` variable. This is equal to calling `bin/debugzope`.

`logtail [logfile]` follow the specified log file on the terminal, equivalent to `tail -f`. Use **Ctrl–C** to exit.

`logreopen` sends a `SIGUSR2` signal to the daemon process to tell it to reopen log files, e.g. after the log files have been rotated.

`kill [signal]` sends a signal, by default `SIGTERM` to the daemon process.

`wait` wait for daemon process to finish when shutting down.

`show {options|python|all}` prints options about the controller script itself, the Python environment or both.

`help [command]` prints a list of available commands or displays information about a specific command if given.

Note that because of its nature, bin/zopectl only works on Unix-style operating systems. For more information about controlling instances on Windows, see Chapter 24.

Zope Management Interface (ZMI)

Zope has an online, web-based administrative user interface called the *Zope Management Interface* (ZMI). It can be used not only to manage the content stored in Zope but also to administer run-time settings of the Zope instance. To log into the ZMI, open the following URL in your web browser: http://localhost:8080/manage, provided your Zope instance is in fact listening to port 8080 on the same machine. Zope will then ask you for authentication; use the initial user account for the administrator which you provided when setting up the instance here. You will then be presented a screen similar to what Figure 3.4 shows.

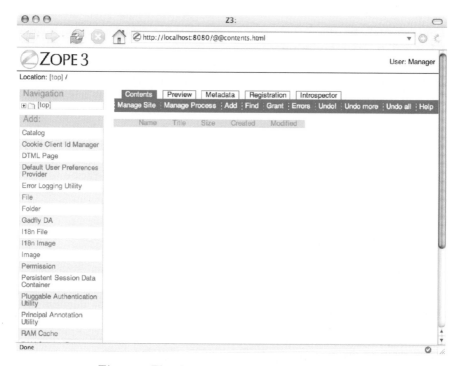

Fig. 3.4. The *Zope Management Interface* (ZMI).

For server administration, the management screens of the process controller are of particular interest. Click on *Manage Process* or enter the URL http://localhost:8080/++etc++process/ in your web browser to

view them. You can review runtime information, shutdown or restart the
Zope server, and do other administrative tasks in separate screens. Note that
restarting Zope only works when started using `bin/zopectl`.

We will use the ZMI in the future mostly to manage our content which can
be added, edited, and deleted in ZMI screens. It is a good idea to familiarize
yourself with the ZMI before starting with the example application.

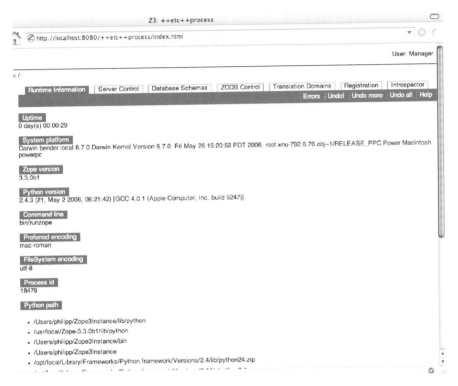

Fig. 3.5. The process administration screens of the ZMI.

Installing additional packages

A Zope instance not only has its own server and security configuration, but
also its own software configuration. Apart from a small set of core packages,
Zope mainly consists of more or less independent packages which, though
they are installed together with Zope, are configured independently. Furthermore, applications running on Zope come as add-on packages that need to
be installed and configured together with the instance.

Add-on packages that are to be used in more than once instance can
be installed into Python's add-on package directory (usually `/usr/lib/`

python/site-packages or C:\Python24\Lib\site-packages). If
the package comes with a setup.py installation script, it will install it there
by default. Instance-specific software, on the other hand, is best installed into
the instance's lib/python directory. You can tell the setup.py script to
use a different directory with the --home parameter, for example:

```
python setup.py --home=~/Zope3Instance
```

This would install the package in our instance's lib/python directory where
it would automatically be importable for Python code running in that instance. If you would like to install packages in Python's new packaging format, *eggs*, into your instance, please refer to Chapter 24.

Most Zope-related packages, whether part of the Zope core, the instance installation or the global Python environment, need to register components with Zope. As we know, component registration and software configuration happens through ZCML, a Zope-specific XML dialect. When
started, the Zope instance processes the site.zcml file or whichever file
the site-definition directive in zope.conf points to. You can enable
and disable individual packages by adding include statements in this file, e.g.:

```
<include package="worldcookery" />
```

You can avoid having to edit site.zcml and instead put the include
statement in a separate ZCML file ending in -configure.zcml, e.g.
worldcookery-configure.zcml. This file is then put into the etc/
package-includes directory. An include statement in site.zcml usually ensures that all files from the package-includes directory ending
in -configure.zcml will be loaded. There are also other types of ZCML
snippets ending in

-meta.zcml for packages that need to register their own ZCML directives,

-overrides.zcml for packages that override configuration of other pack-
    ages (see Chapter 10),

-ftesting.zcml for packages with functional testing configuration (see
    Chapter 12).

Therefore, to enable a package in the instance configuration, you simply need
to drop those small ZCML files into the package-includes directory. To
disable a package, simply move or remove the corresponding include files.

Summary

- Zope instances are created using the `mkzopeinstance` script.
- An instance's server and database configuration can be found and adjusted in `etc/zope.conf`.
- A Zope server instance is either started using the `runzope` script (Windows or development environment) or the `zopectl` program (Unix only).
- Additional packages, if instance-specific, are installed into the instance's `lib/python` directory. Most add-on packages need to be configured in `etc/site.zcml` or using ZCML one-liners in `etc/package-includes`.

Flashback

Focus of the ZMI

Zope 2 developers will be familiar with the *ZMI*, however in Zope 3 its purpose has broadened. The ZMI in Zope 2 is the name of a user interface that allows software developers to persistently add and manage mostly software objects, such as Python scripts, DTML methods and Page Templates. In a few but rare cases, Zope 2's ZMI was even used to manage content, though usually a additional user interface was built for this. The CMF and Silva are prominent examples of that.

The focus of the ZMI has changed in Zope 3. It is now an interface for all purposes, but with a strong focus on content management. Only some sections like the *Site Management* screens go beyond this scope. The ZMI is not used for development anymore. In the early days of Zope 2, through-the-web development using the ZMI was very popular, but this had little to do with developing in Python. This has changed with Zope 3 which gives pure Python development on the file system a much higher priority.

Products vs. packages

The treatment of additional packages in Zope 3 is fundamentally different than it used to be in Zope 2. Zope 2 add-on software is traditionally located in a special directory called `Products` which led to the Zope 2 add-ons being called *products*. Zope 3 add-ons are regular Python packages (hence also referred to simply as packages) and can be located anywhere in the Python interpreter search path. It is still preferable to install software for just a particular instance, which is what an instance's `lib/`

python directory is used for. Again, as the name suggests, the contents are regular Python packages.

It is important to realize the difference in semantics between Zope 2 *products* and Zope 3 *packages*. Zope 2 picks up whatever is dropped into that Products directory. While that makes it easy to install add-ons, it makes it difficult to disable an add-on temporarily. In Zope 3, package configuration is explicit, meaning that you have to explicitly tell Zope 3 to load a package. That is done using small ZCML one-liners in an instance's etc/package-includes directory, as discussed in this chapter.

Using Zope 2

Instances are a concept developed in Zope 2, so much of this section also applies to Zope 2. In particular, Zope 2 instances are also created using a similar mkzopeinstance script and they are started and stopped with bin/runzope or bin/zopectl. Instances of recent Zope 2 versions also deploy etc/site.zcml, an etc/package-includes directory, and a lib/python directory for instance-specific Python packages, as in Zope 3. Regular packages are thus configured as in Zope 3. However, ZCML configuration of Zope 2 add-on packages ("products") is automatically loaded.

3.4 The example application

We will use the example application throughout this book. You will not have to type in all the examples. A download of an archive containing the example application is provided on the book's website.[8]

The example application is modified and extended in each chapter, so there is a version of the worldcookery package available for every chapter. To work with the examples of a particular chapter, copy the corresponding directory from the examples archive (e.g. 04interfaces for Chapter 4) to your instance's lib/python directory and rename it to worldcookery. In later chapters, you will also have to make sure its ZCML configuration is loaded by installing ZCML snippets into etc/package-includes. This was discussed in Section 3.3.

When moving on to a new chapter, simply delete the worldcookery directory from the instance, copy over the directory from the examples archive that corresponds to the new chapter, and rename it to worldcookery again.

---

[8] Book website <http://worldcookery.com>

Conventions

When you encounter a particular example listing, the caption of the listing states the name of the file whose contents is shown in parentheses. E.g. if an example is titled *Configuring a content type (configure.zcml)*, then look for the code in the `configure.zcml` file within that chapter's examples directory. If you installed the chapter's examples directory as the `worldcookery` package in the Zope instance, the path relative to the instance directory will be `lib/python/worldcookery/configure.zcml`.

In a few cases, the same file may be modified several times throughout the course of a chapter. In this case, the package contains the *latest* version of this file under the given filename. Earlier versions are still available, but their filenames are suffixed with numbers, e.g. `configure.zcml.1`.

The coding style and naming conventions of the Python code follow the Zope 3 coding style and naming conventions [2], Guido van Rossum's recommendations [11], and the author's personal taste (in that order).

Interactive interpreter examples

As an interpreted language, Python provides us with an interactive interpreter, which is invoked by running the `python` program without arguments. This interpreter shell allows us to test code or conduct quick experiments. In addition to the code listings of the example application there will also be plenty of sessions with the interactive Python interpreter. You will recognize them by the usual Python prompt ($>>>$). You do not have to type in the code listings of the example application, but consider taking the time to at least type in the interpreter examples. They will give you a better understanding of what is going on.

Most interpreter sessions will be started by simply invoking the Python Interpreter. These examples begin with the following line:

```
$ python
```

That means on most systems you only have to type `python` at the command line, depending on whether the Python interpreter is on your command line search path.

You also need to make sure that both the Zope libraries and the packages you installed in the Zope instance are in the interpreter's search path. This is controlled by the `PYTHONPATH` environment variable. On Unix systems you will most likely have to put both the Zope installation path and the Zope instance path in the variable. Both paths are separated by a colon, e.g.:

```
~$ export PYTHONPATH=/usr/local/Zope-3.x.y/lib/python:\
            ~/Zope3Instance/lib/python
```

Windows users should already have the Zope libraries in their search path, they only need to set the `PYTHONPATH` environment variable to the instance's lib/python directory. This is done exactly like setting the PATH environment variable as described in Section 3.1. To test whether the interpreter can find the Zope libraries, invoke the interpreter and try to import the zope. app package:

```
philipp@bender:~$ python
Python 2.4.3 (#1, May  2 2006, 08:21:42)
[GCC 4.0.1 (Apple Computer, Inc. build 5247)] on darwin
Type "help", "copyright", "credits" or "license" for more information.
>>> import zope.app
Traceback (most recent call last):
  ...
ImportError: No module named zope.app
```

If you see an error like this, the interpreter can obviously not find the Zope libraries. To test whether it can import packages from the Zope instance, install the example application from an arbitrary chapter and repeat the above test with the worldcookery package.

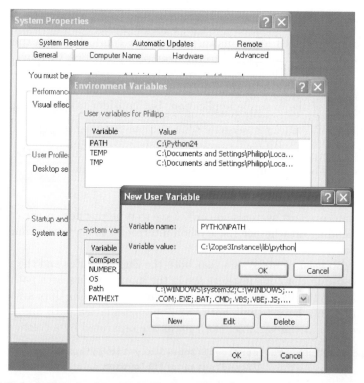

Fig. 3.6. Including the instance's library path in the PYTHONPATH environment variable.

A few interpreter sessions require the whole Zope 3 instance to be set up, especially its ZCML configuration and its database. For this we will use Zope's debug shell, `bin/debugzope`, which is assumed to be invoked from the instance directory. Therefore these interpreter sessions begin with the following line:

```
$ bin/debugzope
```

Note that the PYTHONPATH environment variable does not need to be set up in this case because the `debugzope` script sets all the necessary paths for us.

Sometimes we will keep using the same interpreter shell throughout a whole section of a chapter, sometimes we will have to restart the interpreter in order to re-import modules or reread configuration. The end of a session will be marked by a ■ while a ▼ indicates that the interpreter should not be closed because more examples in that session will follow.

Summary

- The whole book is accompanied by one example application that is extended in each chapter.
- The example application lives inside the `worldcookery` package. There is a version for each chapter.
- The example application comes with interactive interpreter sessions. In contrast to the actual application source code, it is recommended to type these sessions.
- The interpreter sessions will both facilitate the plain interpreter (with the correct package search paths) and the Zope debug shell allowing you to work with configured components or the database.

4

Interfaces

We can now start with our example application. The *World Cookery* website will store information about recipes from around the world. Thus the first thing we need is a component to store recipe information in. As we have discussed in Chapter 2, components that store data are content components. Before we are going to write such a component, we need to define what kind of data it shall store and provide: we need to write an interface!

Interfaces are contracts that define how components work together. They describe the methods and attributes provided by an object. Interfaces describe the *what* of a component, they do not describe the *how*. The modelling of interfaces can be tackled many different ways. As we look at these possibilities we will improve the example implementation with each iteration. This process of *refactoring* occurs a number of times in this book to constantly improve and adjust the code.

Using Zope 2

This chapter applies to Zope 2 as well. Zope 3 interfaces may be declared and used the same way as in Zope 3 itself. The older Zope 2 flavour of interfaces has been deprecated and should no longer be used.

4.1 Interface semantics

It is important to understand the way interfaces are used in Zope. The semantics are different to other languages (such as Java). Thus the name *interface* might be misleading, especially for people coming from languages with different interface semantics.

While in other languages, interfaces are sometimes used to cope with the lack of multiple inheritance, they often only have a symbolic value in Zope. Proper collaboration demands that components comply with promises made in their interfaces, but that is not enforced at language level. Interfaces cannot and do not change the semantics of the Python language.

Interfaces identify components by what functionality they promise to provide. In this they are nothing more than labels or markers. Some interfaces, for example, do not express an API at all but rather an abstract contract. We call those *marker interfaces*. Other uses of interfaces are data schemas where interfaces are used to describe a data format rather than functionality. In case interfaces do describe an API, they can also serve as documentation on that API. If one needed to replace a component with another one, it often suffices to look at the interface, which usually looks clearer and cleaner than the implementation.

Jargon

Being familiar with the jargon that is typically used with interfaces helps the understanding of interface semantics. The jargon also plays a role in Zope's interface API. The main difference between Zope's interface model and others is that it is more object-centric than class-centric. In general, one does not care as much about the implementation of an object but only about the functionality a certain object provides.

In interface jargon, we say that an object *provides* an interface, just like a machine providing functionality or somebody providing a service. Objects in this case is meant in a general sense: class instances, Python modules or even interfaces themselves (since interfaces provide functionality, too!). Yet, it would be tiresome having to declare what interface each object we encounter provides. It is often easier to declare what a class's instances provides. We then say, a class *implements* an interface, which is equivalent to saying that all of the class's instances provide that interface.

Summary

- Interface semantics differ to many other languages because interface compliance in Zope is not enforced but implied.
- Interfaces often serve as markers/identifiers and API documentation.
- Interface jargon reflects the semantics of interfaces in Zope.
- The functionality an object provides is usually more of interest than its particular implementation.
- Classes *implement* interfaces so that their instances *provide* them.

4.2 Defining interfaces

An interface is defined by using the `class` statement and inheriting from `Interface`, which is imported from the `zope.interface` package. By convention, interface names are written in CamelCase[1] like classes, but with a proceeding I to indicate the difference between classes and interfaces. Standard Python syntax is used, for example when defining a class with methods. Interfaces and their methods are documented using standard Python docstrings. A simple docstring as a class or method body satisfies the Python syntax, meaning you do not have to use the pass keyword. When declaring methods for the interface, the self parameter is not declared either, because the interface describes how the method is used, not its implementational details.

It is another convention to put all interfaces of a package in a module called interfaces.py, or in case of a larger software product, in modules which reside in a package called interfaces. A first example interface to put in worldcookery/interfaces.py is shown in Example 4.2.1.

The IRecipeInfo interface from Example 4.2.1 only defines methods for retrieving information about the recipe. If one needed a recipe object whose values can be set, one would either have to extend IRecipeInfo to provide those methods or derive a new interface from it. Deriving an interface from another works like subclassing, as demonstrated in Example 4.2.2.

In these first two interfaces, one interface describes how to get the information contained in a recipe, the other interface also describes how to set the data. Dividing getters and setters up into two separate interfaces has some advantages. There might be components that provide recipe information but do not allow setting it. Also, as we will see later on, it is useful to separate read and write functionality when declaring permissions. For example reading data requires different permissions to the permissions needed for writing data. However, unless you have one of these reasons to write separate interfaces, you might as well put getters and setters in one interface.

Attribute definitions

Using getters and setters like getName() and setName() is not very "pythonic". In Python you can set attributes (e.g. name) on an object from the outside. Why not declare the data as gettable and settable attributes? Consider Example 4.2.3.

As you can see in the rewritten IRecipe interface example, attributes are declared using instances of Attribute which is provided by the zope. interface package as well. Of course, attribute and method definitions can be mixed in an interface.

---

[1] Two or more words are concatenated to one and their first letter is capitalized. Upper and lower case letters in the resulting word suggest the image of a camel, thus CamelCase.

Example 4.2.1 An example interface (`interfaces.py`)

```
1   from zope.interface import Interface
2
3   class IRecipeInfo(Interface):
4       """Give information about a recipe.
5       """
6
7       def getName():
8           """Return the name of the dish described.
9           """
10
11      def getIngredients():
12          """Return a list of ingredients.
13          """
14
15      def getTools():
16          """Return a list of necessary kitchen tools.
17          """
18
19      def getTimeToCook():
20          """Return the time necessary for preparing the meal in
21          minutes.
22          """
23
24      def getDescription():
25          """Return the description of the recipe.
26          """
```

1. The "base" interface must be imported from the `zope.interface` package.

3. Although the `class` statement is used here, there is no class being defined. That is because `Interface` is not a base class, but an object, an interface object to be exact. You could say that the `class` statement really is abused here.[2]

7. As with the `class` statement, the `def` statements suggest a method being defined. The contrary is the case. Since `IRecipeInfo` is not a class but an interface object, the method definitions end up as special definition objects on the interface. Since these method definition objects solely *describe* real callable methods, you should omit the otherwise obligatory `self` parameter, too.

8. A Python docstring fulfils the function body syntax. It is not required to use `pass` or to even raise `NotImplemented` or similar. Any code put in the method definitions will not be executable because there are no methods defined here (if you want to see for yourself, try to call an interface method at the interactive interpreter shell; you will see it fails).

Example 4.2.2 Deriving from an interface (`interfaces.py`)

```
1  ...
2
3  class IRecipe(IRecipeInfo):
4      """Give and store information about a recipe.
5      """
6
7      def setName(name):
8          """Set the name of the dish provided in the 'name' parameter.
9          """
10
11      def setIngredients(ingredients):
12          """Set the ingredients necessary for this recipe provided in
13          the 'ingredients' parameter."""
14
15      def setTools(tools):
16          """Set the list of necessary kitchen tools.
17          """
18
19      def setTimeToCook(time_to_cook):
20          """Set the time necessary for preparing the meal in minutes.
21          """
22
23      def setDescription(description):
24          """Set the description of the recipe.
25          """
```

3. The `class` statement allows us to let interfaces derive from interfaces the same way classes can derive from other classes. Method and attribute definitions are inherited and can be overridden in the derived interface.

Summary

- Interfaces are defined by using the `class` statement, although no class is created.
- Extending an interface works like extending a class (subclassing syntax).
- Docstrings are used to satisfy the Python block syntax and to document the API that is being defined.
- Attributes are defined using `Attribute` objects.

Example 4.2.3 An interface with attribute declarations (`interfaces.py`)

```
1  from zope.interface import Interface, Attribute
2
3  class IRecipe(Interface):
4      """Store information about a recipe.
5      """
6
7      name = Attribute("Name of the dish.")
8
9      ingredients = Attribute(
10         "List of ingredients necessary for this recipe.")
11
12     tools = Attribute("List of necessary kitchen tools.")
13
14     time_to_cook = Attribute(
15         "Necessary time for preparing the meal described.")
16
17     description = Attribute("Description of the recipe.")
```

Rocky says...

Java developers should notice some similarities between Zope interfaces and Java interfaces. While they serve similar purposes, there are a few differences in the implementation details. Being able to define required class attributes is something specific to Zope as is having to use the `class` statement to define an interface. Also getters and setters in a traditional Java sense are heavily frowned upon.

4.3 Declaring that an object provides an interface

When a component wants to promise to provide a certain interface, it needs to do so explicitly, otherwise the component machinery in Zope will not know about it. The most common case is declaring that a class implements an interface so that its instances provide it. That is usually done using the `implements()` function in the class declaration. Consider the simple implementation of `IRecipeInfo` in Example 4.3.1.

Note that, unlike in other programming languages with interfaces, no actual checking is enforced. `RecipeInfo` may choose to implement less than it promises through the interface. That per se will not let the application fail. However, if other components rely on `RecipeInfo` implementing the whole interface, the application will sooner or later break at the point where components are trying to use the part of the interface the class does not im-

Example 4.3.1 A simple implementation of the `IRecipeInfo` interface
(`recipe.py`)

```
1   from zope.interface import implements
2   from worldcookery.interfaces import IRecipeInfo
3
4   class RecipeInfo(object):
5       """Give information about a recipe.
6       """
7       implements(IRecipeInfo)
8
9       def __init__(self, name, ingredients, tools, time_to_cook,
10                     description):
11          self.name = name
12          self.ingredients = ingredients
13          self.tools = tools
14          self.time_to_took = time_to_cook
15          self.description = description
16
17      def getName(self):
18          return self.name
19
20      def getIngredients(self):
21          return self.ingredients
22
23      def getTools(self):
24          return self.tools
25
26      def getTimeToCook(self):
27          return self.time_to_cook
28
29      def getDescription(self):
30          return self.description
```

7. The `RecipeInfo` class promises to implement the `IRecipeInfo` interface by
    using the `implements()` function in the class body. `implements()` takes an
    arbitrary number of arguments, thus you can use it to declare several interfaces
    at one time.

17–30. Below the constructor method (`__init__`), you find the implementations of
    the five methods promised by the interface.

---

plement. In conclusion, interface compliance is *assumed*, not enforced, though
the interface machinery provides utilities for verification (see below).

There also are other ways of declaring that a component implements an
interface. The `classImplements()` function declares an interface on an
already existing class. This is useful when third party components are being
used in Zope 3 and source code modification is not possible or unwanted.

The directlyProvides() function declares an interface on an object that
has already been instantiated. A second call to directlyProvides() will
override anything that has been set during the first call, though. That means
it would remove interfaces from the object unless they were stated explicitly
again. It is therefore safer to use the alsoProvides function which only
adds interfaces to the object and does not remove existing ones. Note that
interfaces that are declared at a class level are not affected by this.

Making a particular object provide an additional interface is mostly used
for marker interfaces. These are interfaces that do not promise any methods
or attributes to be implemented but mark the object that implements them
in a certain way. Zope 3 makes use of a few marker interfaces as we will see
later on. Consider the following example code for classImplements() and
alsoProvides(), typed in at the Python interpreter prompt:

```
$ python
>>> class RecipeInfo:
...      pass
...
>>> from worldcookery.interfaces import IRecipeInfo
>>> IRecipeInfo.implementedBy(RecipeInfo)
False
>>> chilaquiles = RecipeInfo()
>>> IRecipeInfo.providedBy(chilaquiles)
False                                                          ▼
```

Here we actually have a hint that interfaces are not classes but special objects, because they have implementedBy() and providedBy() methods
which return True when the argument implements or provides the interface, respectively, and False otherwise. Interfaces have many more methods
which are all documented in (surprise!) an interface, IInterface.

In the example, the chilaquiles object is an instance of the RecipeInfo
class and does not provide the IRecipeInfo interface. However, we can
change that by using alsoProvides:

```
>>> from zope.interface import alsoProvides
>>> alsoProvides(chilaquiles, IRecipeInfo)
>>> IRecipeInfo.providedBy(chilaquiles)
True                                                           ▼
```

Now the chilaquiles object, and only this object, provides the interface.
We can verify this by checking another RecipeInfo instance:

```
>>> posole = RecipeInfo()
>>> IRecipeInfo.providedBy(posole)
False                                                          ▼
```

If we now let the RecipeInfo class implement the interface, all its instances
will automatically provide it as well, including the posole object:

```
>>> from zope.interface import classImplements
>>> classImplements(RecipeInfo, IRecipeInfo)
>>> IRecipeInfo.implementedBy(RecipeInfo)
True
>>> IRecipeInfo.providedBy(posole)
True                                                          ▼
```

Functions and modules

We have so far only talked about classes implementing interfaces. In general, implementers do not have to be classes, though. Any callable object that creates an object providing an interface can implement this interface. Classes just happen to work this way, but we could also think of *functions* that do this. For example, imagine we have a function that creates RecipeInfo objects, basically a simple factory. Since the created objects provide IRecipeInfo (we made RecipeInfo implement IRecipeInfo, remember?), this factory function can be declared an implementer of IRecipeInfo by using the implementer decorator:

```
>>> from zope.interface import implementer
>>> @implementer(IRecipeInfo)
... def makeRecipeInfo():
...     return RecipeInfo()
...
>>> IRecipeInfo.implementedBy(makeRecipeInfo)
True
>>> IRecipeInfo.providedBy(makeRecipeInfo())
True                                                          ▼
```

The similar semantics between a class factory and a function factory become apparent if we repeat the two last statements with the class instead of the function:

```
>>> IRecipeInfo.implementedBy(RecipeInfo)
True
>>> IRecipeInfo.providedBy(RecipeInfo())
True                                                          ■
```

Another unusual use of interface is to indicate the API of a Python module. Since Python modules are regular objects, they can also provide interfaces. This can be expressed using the moduleProvides() function. For example, the zope.component module provides many standard Component Architecture API functions from one single module (see Appendix A). This API is documented in the IComponentArchitecture interface. Therefore the zope.component module somewhere contains these lines:

```
from zope.interface import moduleProvides
moduleProvides(IComponentArchitecture)
```

That is equivalent to assigning the interface from the outside:

```
$ python
>>> import zope.component
>>> directlyProvides(
...      zope.component,
...      zope.component.interfaces.IComponentArchitecture
... )                                                        ■
```

As we have seen so far, the zope.interface module has a rich API with a lot of functions for declaring interfaces. implements, directlyProvides, etc. are all part of it. This API is also formally defined in an interface called IInterfaceDeclaration. It will of course not surprise you now that the zope.interface module provides this interface.

Summary

- Factories *implement* interfaces so that the objects they create *provide* them; normally these factories are classes, but can be any callable object (such as functions).
- Interfaces are typically declared on classes using the implements() function in the class body.
- It is also possible to declare that a single object or even a Python module provides an interface.
- An interface's providedBy() method informs whether an object provides that interface.

4.4 Verifying implementations

As mentioned before, interfaces are a Zope-specific addition and not part of Python, thus declarations in interfaces are not enforced. The interface package provides a way to verify if an object conforms to an interface it provides. For example, let us create a simple class that obviously does not comply with IRecipeInfo but claims to implement it:

```
$ python
>>> from zope.interface import implements
>>> from worldcookery.interfaces import IRecipeInfo
>>> class NotARecipeInfo:
...      implements(IRecipeInfo)
...
>>> not_a_recipe_info = NotARecipeInfo()                     ▼
```

We can then use `verifyObject` to perform the interface compliance check:

```
>>> from zope.interface.verify import verifyObject
>>> verifyObject(IRecipeInfo, not_a_recipe_info)
Traceback (most recent call last):
  ...
zope.interface.exceptions.BrokenImplementation:
  An object has failed to implement interface
  <InterfaceClass interfaces.IRecipeInfo>

       The getName attribute was not provided.
```
▼

As expected, `verifyObject` finds that the `NotARecipe` instance does not comply with the `IRecipeInfo` interface. The contrary is the case with instances of the `RecipeInfo` class we defined in Example 4.3.1; they fulfil the interface:

```
>>> from worldcookery.recipe import RecipeInfo
>>> recipe_info = RecipeInfo()
>>> verifyObject(IRecipeInfo, recipe_info)
True
```
■

If you want to directly check whether a class complies with an interface without creating an object first, you may use the `verifyClass` function from the `zope.interface.verify` module. Its usage is like `verifyObject`. However, be aware that not all classes that implement an interface comply with it directly. For example, certain required attributes might only be set by the constructor method (`__init__`) when an object is created. `verifyClass` would miss those and falsely report an error.

Summary

- Interface compliance is implied and not enforced at runtime.
- The `zope.interface.verify` module provides tools for the developer to verify that implementations concur with what the interface defines.

4.5 Schemas

As we have discussed before, simple content objects usually do not need methods because all they are responsible for is storing data. That can easily be done in instance attributes; defining setters and getters, while not complicated, is still quite verbose and frankly very unpythonic.

We have also seen that we can describe required attributes in interfaces using `Attribute` objects. However, even in the simple `IRecipeInfo` example above, it is quite obvious that we could supply much more information about each field than just a docstring. For example, we see that name should be a one line text string while time_to_cook should store an integer. Even though Python is dynamically-typed, we are absolutely certain that these attributes should only contain values of a certain type.

If we continue that thought and define the type of each attribute in the interface, we end up with what is called a *schema*. Much like in a table schema known from relational databases, each property is called a *field*. Different fields imply different type constraints.

Defining schemas

Schemas are defined exactly like interfaces. There is no special schema object to derive from. However, instead of using Attribute, we now use fields provided by the zope.schema package to describe attributes. Table 4.1 lists the standard field types provided by Zope 3 and the type they describe. Since schemas and interfaces are semantically and syntactically the same thing, an interface with method definitions can just as well contain schema fields and vice versa. It is all interfaces to Zope. Example 4.5.1 demonstrates what a schema definition looks like.

In Example 4.5.1, we see that all fields are passed nearly the same arguments, such as title and description. Table 4.2 gives an overview over possible field arguments. All arguments to the field constructor listed below are also attributes of the field instance. We see that field parameters/attributes are defined through a schema as well, since they have to comply with certain field constraints (e.g. title has to be a TextLine, that is why we have to pass a Unicode string)[3].

All arguments to the field constructor are optional. However, providing at least the title and a longer descriptive text helps documentation. More usefully, they also support application purposes, such as automatically generated forms (see Chapter 8).

Custom constraints

We said earlier that different fields imply different type constraints. In addition to this implied type constraint, it is also possible to add a custom constraint by using the *constraint* parameter in the field constructor. The field expects any callable that takes one argument for this parameter.

Imagine, for example, an interface that had an email field. There is no special field type for emails, but we can use TextLine with a custom constraint. Verifying email addresses is best done with a regular expression:

---

[3] Like interfaces, schemas also "eat their own dog food" by using a schema to define what fields must look like while schemas are composed of fields.

Example 4.5.1 Defining a schema (`interfaces.py`)

```
1  from zope.interface import Interface
2  from zope.schema import List, Text, TextLine, Int
3
4  class IRecipe(Interface):
5      """Store information about a recipe.
6      """
7
8      name = TextLine(
9          title=u"Name",
10         description=u"Name of the dish",
11         required = True
12         )
13
14     ingredients = List(
15         title=u"Ingredients",
16         description=u"List of ingredients necessary for this recipe.",
17         required=True,
18         value_type=TextLine(title=u"Ingredient")
19         )
20
21     tools = List(
22         title=u"Tools",
23         description=u"List of necessary kitchen tools",
24         required=False,
25         value_type=TextLine(title=u"Tool")
26         )
27
28     time_to_cook = Int(
29         title=u"Time to cook",
30         description=u"Necessary time for preparing the meal described, "
31         "in minutes.",
32         required=True
33         )
34
35     description = Text(
36         title=u"Description",
37         description=u"Description of the recipe",
38         required=True
39         )
```

2. The zope.schema package provides field types for the most common types of objects, such as Python lists, integers, and Unicode strings.

4. As mentioned before, Zope does not distinguish between interfaces and schemas, the difference is pure nomenclature.

8–39. Fields on the schema are specified like `Attribute` definitions on a regular interface, however with a rich set of parameters that document the field and describe the constraints.

Table 4.1. Schema fields from `zope.schema`[4]

Field type	Type constraint
Abstract fields (mostly used for subclassing)	
Field	Simple field without any type constraint (unless a custom one is provided), base class for all other fields.
Container	Object supporting the in operator, meaning it has to provide either __contains__ or __getitem__.
Iterable	Object supporting iteration, meaning it has to provide either __iter__ or __getitem__.
Fields for standard python types	
Bool	Boolean value (`bool`).
Int	Integer (`int`).
Float	Float (`float`).
Text	Unicode text (`unicode`).
TextLine	Like `Text`, but without newline characters.
Bytes	Byte string (`str`), useful for binary data.
BytesLine	Like `Bytes`, but without newline characters.
Tuple	Tuple (`tuple`).
List	List (`list`).
Dict	Dictionary (`dict`).
Set	Set (`sets.Set`).
Date	Date value (`datetime.date`).
Datetime	Date and time value (`datetime.datetime`).
Choice	An object from a source or vocabulary.
Object	Arbitrary object providing a schema.
Fields with special constraints	
Password	A `TextLine` used for storing passwords.
SourceText	A `Text` field that holds the source of some computed output.
ASCII	A string containing only ASCII characters.
InterfaceField	Interface (`zope.interface.Interface`).
URI	A `BytesLine` that holds a Uniform Resource Identifier (URI).
DottedName	A `BytesLine` that contains a dotted name.
Id	A `BytesLine` that contains either a URI or a dotted name.

---

[4] This list does not aim at being complete. It only tries to give an overview over the most important fields.

Table 4.2. Schema field parameters/attributes

Name	Type	Description
`title`	`TextLine`	Label for the field.
`description`	`Text`	Longer description.
`required`	`Bool`	Require the existence of the value (mutually exclusive with `default`). Defaults to `True`.
`readonly`	`Bool`	Determine whether the field's value can be changed.
`default`	`Field`	The default value if none was provided (mutually exclusive with `required`).
`missing_value`	`Field`	In the case of missing input value, the value provided here is used.
`order`	`Int`	Gives information about the order in which fields in a schema are defined. This is a read-only attribute and may not be passed as an argument to the field constructor.
`constraint`	one-parameter callable	A callable (e.g. function) that validates its parameter (the potential field value) in addition to the constraint implied by the field. It may either return a Boolean or raise an exception derived from `ValidationError`.
`min, max`	`Int or Float`	Limit the numeric range of `Int` and `Float` fields.
`min_length,` `max_length`	`Int`	Require a minimum and/or maximum length. Applicable to all bytes, text and sequence fields.
`value_type`	`Field`	The type of values in a collection. Applicable to all collection fields (including sequence fields).
`unique`	`Bool`	Specifies whether the values in a collection must be unique or not. Applicable to all collection fields (including sequence fields).

```
$ python
>>> import re
>>> regex = r"[a-zA-Z0-9._%-]+@([a-zA-Z0-9-]+\.)*[a-zA-Z]{2,4}"
>>> check_email = re.compile(regex).match
>>> bool(check_email("philipp@weitershausen.de"))
True
>>> bool(check_email("this-is-not-an-email-address"))
False                                                          ▼
```

Above we aliased the `match` method of a regular expression object to the `check_email` variable. This is now a one-argument callable which we can use when constructing the `email` field:

```
>>> from zope.schema import TextLine
>>> email = TextLine(
...     title=u"Email",
...     description=u"An email address",
...     constraint=check_email
... )                                                            ▼
```

When we validate a value for the email field now, the field will use the extra constraint expressed through the regular expression:

```
>>> email.validate(u"philipp@weitershausen.de")
>>> email.validate(u"this-is-not-an-email-address")
Traceback (most recent call last):
  ...
zope.schema._bootstrapinterfaces.ConstraintNotSatisfied:
this-is-not-an-email-address                                     ▼
```

Note that for custom constraints that report an invalid value, the very general ConstraintNotSatisfied exception is raised. This may not always be satisfactory, for example when the schema field is used to render forms and a detailed error message should be displayed to the user as to why the input value is not valid. In this case it is possible to create a custom exception deriving from ValidationError and raise this in the custom validator. For automated forms as they are discussed in Chapter 8, the exception's docstring will be presented to the user as the detailed error message:

```
>>> from zope.schema import ValidationError
>>> class NotAnEmailAddress(ValidationError):
...     """This is not a valid email address"""
...
>>> def validate_email(value):
...     if not check_email(value):
...         raise NotAnEmailAddress(value)
...     return True
...
>>> email.constraint = validate_email
>>> email.validate(u'this-is-not-an-email-address')
Traceback (most recent call last):
  ...
__main__.NotAnEmailAddress: this-is-not-an-email-address         ■
```

Invariants

We have seen that the *constraint* parameter lets us add a custom constraint to any field. Such a constraint is bound to that particular field, though. It is not possible to express a constraint between several fields with it.

For example, consider a schema that describes a round-trip flight ticket. Most tickets are not valid for longer than a year. Thus, the date of the departing flight and the date of the returning flight should not be longer than 12 months apart. Of course, the departing flight should also occur before the returning flight. With these constraints it is not possible to validate one or the other separately. Only when knowing *both* values it is possible to say whether they are valid.

A constraint that involves more than one field is called an *invariant*. The flight ticket example can easily be rendered with an invariant. For reasons of brevity, we continue on the interpreter prompt:

```
$ python
>>> from zope.interface import Interface, Invalid, invariant
>>> from zope.schema import Datetime
>>> class IRoundTripTicket(Interface):
...     departing = Datetime(title=u"Departure date")
...     returning = Datetime(title=u"Return date")
...     @invariant
...     def departingBeforeReturning(ticket):
...         if ticket.departing > ticket.returning:
...             raise Invalid("Departing date must be before "
...                           "returning date")
...     @invariant
...     def oneYearValid(ticket):
...         delta = ticket.returning - ticket.departing
...         if delta.days > 365:
...             raise Invalid("Ticket is only valid for one year!")
...
```
▼

As you can see, invariants are one-parameter callables like custom constraints. However, they take a whole object as their argument, not just the value of a particular field. This gives invariants access to all the attributes of an object, allowing checks on one, two or more of them.

Invariants are added to an interface by using the `invariant` function from the `zope.interface` package. When the callable is a mere function, we can write it directly into the interface and use Python's decorator syntax (`@invariant`). Again, looks are deceiving when writing interfaces: the functions created and decorated this way are not callable methods on the interface. In fact, they are not accessible at all from the outside, they are absorbed into the internal interface definition.

Let now create a dummy ticket object and stick some (invalid) dates on it. Note that the interface specifies a `Datetime` field for both dates, so we should use the `datetime` class from the Python standard library:

```
>>> class Ticket:
...     pass
>>> ticket = Ticket()
>>> from datetime import datetime
>>> ticket.departing = datetime(2006, 1, 1, 8, 0, 0)
>>> ticket.returning = datetime(2006, 1, 1, 7, 0, 0)
```
▼

We can now validate the `ticket` object regarding its compliance with the invariants. This is done by using the `validateInvariants` method of interfaces:

```
>>> IRoundTripTicket.validateInvariants(ticket)
Traceback (most recent call last):
  ...
zope.interface.exceptions.Invalid:
Departing date must be before returning date                        ∎
```

As expected we are presented with the right exception. I leave it up to you now to test the other invariant. You will also see that the `validateInvariants` method simply returns if the invariant tests pass.

Introspecting schemas

Sometimes it is useful to introspect schemas, for example when you want to retrieve a list of the fields a schema carries. Schemas are just plain interfaces and can contain standard method or attribute declarations apart from schema fields. Therefore, an interface's `names()` or `namesAndDescriptions()` method would not only return fields, but these other declarations as well. That would not be too useful. If you only need to know about a schema's fields, the `zope.schema` package provides a few functions for introspecting schemas as listed in Table 4.3.

Table 4.3. Schema introspecting functions provided by `zope.schema`

Function	Parameters	Description
getFieldNames	*schema*	Returns a list of the fields' names defined in *schema*.
getFields	*schema*	Returns a dictionary containing a mapping of field names to fields defined in *schema*.
getFieldsInOrder	*schema*	Returns a list of (name, field) tuples in the order the fields are defined in *schema*.
getFieldNamesInOrder	*schema*	Returns a list of the fields' names in the order they are defined in *schema*.

Summary

- Interfaces can be used to describe data schemas.
- Instead of attribute declarations, fields expressing type and other constraints are used to describe the schema.

- The `zope.schema` package provides many basic field types.
- Constraints involving more than one field may be implemented using an invariant.

Writing content objects that provide a schema and the automatic validation of schema compliance will be covered in Chapter 5. Sources and vocabularies, an advanced schema-related topic, are the subject of Chapter 17.

Flashback

Those of you with experience in Plone development are probably already familiar with schemas from the Archetypes product. Archetypes are, among other things, a framework for rapid development of content objects for Plone. Like Zope 3, Archetypes schemas describe the data layout of fields in a content type. Those schemas are just like any object, though, while in Zope 3, a schema is an interface. Since Zope 3 uses interfaces as formal contracts between components, or even for practical things like security assertions, the developer benefits from schemas being an interface everywhere. There are also large differences in the implementation of schema-based content types as we will see in the next chapter.

5

Content Components

5.1 Schema-based content

The previous chapter demonstrated what interfaces for content components can look like. Schemas have proven to be most suitable for this kind of component, since we often think in terms of data schemas. Implementing a schema in a content component is therefore quite easy. All you have to do is provide sane default values for the fields described in the schema, as Example 5.1.1 demonstrates.

Example 5.1.1 Implementing a schema (`recipe.py`)

```
1  from zope.interface import implements
2  from worldcookery.interfaces import IRecipe
3
4  class Recipe:
5      implements(IRecipe)
6
7      name = u''
8      ingredients = []
9      tools = []
10     time_to_cook = 0
11     description = u''
```

That class could not be simpler. Except for the import of the `zope.interface` package, this class could be perfectly usable outside Zope. Maybe you might want to give it a constructor that sets some initial values, but that is not necessary. The fact that it implements a schema does not mean its attributes are constrained to conform with the schema. Remember, interfaces are not enforced! Consider the following example of a schema violation on this class:

```
$ python
>>> from worldcookery.recipe import Recipe
>>> strudel = Recipe()
>>> strudel.time_to_cook
0
>>> strudel.time_to_cook = "Well, about an hour"
>>> strudel.time_to_cook
'Well, about an hour'
```
 ■

The class defines default attributes with the correct types as specified in the schema. But then some "bad application code", like the above, sets the time_to_cook attribute, which is supposed to be an integer, with a string. Since Python is a dynamically typed language and Zope 3 interfaces definitions are not enforced on implementations, no error is raised. However, your application depending on time_to_cook being an integer could fail horribly. Imagine that in one part of the application you would have to sum up the necessary time for preparing several recipes, for example the aperitif, main dish and dessert of a large meal. Then your application would break and the problem would not even be in the aggregation code.

Luckily, Zope has a solution for this. First of all, the form widget framework allows changes to schema-based content object's data through the web. The widget framework validates all input against the schema and if it is validated, converts it to the right data type. Thus, most of the time you do not have to worry about this problem. You can rely on these very simple implementations of a schema. However, if you do need explicit validation, for whatever reason, here are your options:

Validate parameters passed to a method

Let's take Recipe and extend it with a method that validates incoming values according to the schema (Example 5.1.2).

We can now use the update method to update instances of Recipe. When we pass a string for the time_to_cook attribute as before, we expect an error to be raised, while it should let us set an integer:

```
$ python
>>> from worldcookery.recipe import Recipe
>>> strudel = Recipe()
>>> strudel.time_to_cook
0
>>> strudel.update(time_to_cook="Well, about an hour")
Traceback (most recent call last):
  ...
zope.schema._bootstrapinterfaces.WrongType:
('Well, about an hour', (<type 'int'>, <type 'long'>))
```

Example 5.1.2 Using a schema's fields for validation (`recipe.py`)

```
1   from zope.interface import implements
2   from zope.schema import getFieldNames
3   from worldcookery.interfaces import IRecipe
4
5   class Recipe:
6       implements(IRecipe)
7
8       name = u''
9       ingredients = []
10      tools = []
11      time_to_cook = 0
12      description = u''
13
14      def update(self, **kw):
15          # retrieve a list of the names of the schema's fields
16          field_names = getFieldNames(IRecipe)
17          for key, value in kw.items():
18              if key not in field_names:
19                  raise TypeError, "Invalid field to set: %s" % key
20              field = IRecipe[key]
21              field = field.bind(self)
22              field.validate(value)
23              setattr(self, key, value)
```

20. Declarations in interfaces, such as schema fields, can be accessed using the index notation, also known as the ⌐getitem⌐ protocol. For example, `IRecipe['time⌐to⌐cook']` refers to the integer field describing the `time⌐to⌐cook` attribute (see Example 4.5.1, line 28.)

21. Before fields can be used to validate values of an object, they should be bound to that object. While this is not strictly necessary for the simple field types we are using in `IRecipe`, more complex fields might require this.

22. Every field has a `validate` method that validates an object against the field constraint. If the value does not validate, an exception derived from the `ValidationError` exception is raised which indicates why validation failed.

```
>>> strudel.update(time_to_cook=45)
>>> strudel.time_to_cook
45
```
■

As we see, keyword parameters passed to `update()` are validated through every field's `validate` method. When validation fails, this method raises appropriate exceptions, all derived from `ValidationError`. Table 5.1 gives an overview over possible validation exceptions, all of which can be imported from the `zope.schema` package (including `ValidationError`).

Table 5.1. Validation exceptions from zope.schema

Exception name	Description
RequiredMissing	Indicates that input for a required field is missing.
WrongType	The value has a wrong type (raised, for example, when assigning a string object to an integer field).
TooBig	The provided value is too big (typically raised for numeric fields with range limitations).
TooSmall	The provided value is too small (typically raised for numeric fields with range limitations).
TooLong	The provided text is too long.
TooShort	The provided text is too short.
InvalidValue	Simply indicates that the provided value is invalid.
ConstraintNotSatisfied	A field constraint was not satisfied.
NotAContainer	The object in question is not a container (raised by the Container field).
NotAnIterator	The object in question is not an iterator (raised by the Iteratable field.
WrongContainedType	Object within a collection (for example a list or a tuple) is of the wrong type.
NotUnique	One or more objects in a collection that is required to have unique entries are not unique.
SchemaNotFullyImplemented	Raised by the Object field to indicate that the object in question does not fully implement the promised schema.
SchemaNotProvided	Raised by the Object field to indicate that the object in question does not provide the promised schema.
InvalidURI	Raised by the URI field when passed value is not a valid URI.
InvalidId	Raised by the Id field when passed value is neither a dotted name nor a valid URI.
InvalidDottedName	Raised by the DottedName field when passed value is not a valid dotted name.

Validation upon attribute setting

We can now validate values according to schema fields, but we have to do so manually, by calling a special `update` method. It would really be much nicer if we could simply set the attributes on instances and still have the values validated, in case bad application code would ignore the `update` method. Python allows such validation upon attribute setting through `property` objects. They allow us to execute any business logic when an attribute is read from or written to an instance, such as validation.

Fortunately, the Zope schema machinery already provides us with a validating property implementation. `FieldProperty`, provided by the `zope.schema.fieldproperty` module, also returns the default value if an attribute has not yet been set on the instance. With it we can now rewrite our `Recipe` implementation, as shown in Example 5.1.3.

Example 5.1.3 Using the schema machinery to auto-validate instance attributes (`recipe.py`)

```
1  from zope.interface import implements
2  from zope.schema.fieldproperty import FieldProperty
3  from worldcookery.interfaces import IRecipe
4
5  class Recipe(object):
6      implements(IRecipe)
7
8      name = FieldProperty(IRecipe['name'])
9      ingredients = FieldProperty(IRecipe['ingredients'])
10     tools = FieldProperty(IRecipe['tools'])
11     time_to_cook = FieldProperty(IRecipe['time_to_cook'])
12     description = FieldProperty(IRecipe['description'])
```

That implementation is quite compact. There are two things to note about it. First, Python's property feature only works with *new-style classes*[1]. That is why we have to subclass from `object` now. Otherwise, `FieldProperty` cannot assume control over the attribute. Second, `FieldProperty` needs to know which field to validate against. Thus, we have to pass it the corresponding field each time, which we can get from `IRecipe` using the index notation, as already discussed above.

---

[1] New-style classes were introduced in Python 2.2. They are a new implementation of classes in Python supporting a number of new features, such as slots, properties and a new class inheritance resolution. Please refer to A. M. Kuchling's *What's New in Python 2.2* [27] for more information.

Let us now try out the new implementation:

```
$ python
>>> from worldcookery.recipe import Recipe
>>> strudel = Recipe()
>>> strudel.time_to_cook = "Well, about an hour"
Traceback (most recent call last):
  ...
zope.schema._bootstrapinterfaces.WrongType:
('Well, about an hour', (<type 'int'>, <type 'long'>))

>>> strudel.time_to_cook = 45
>>> strudel.time_to_cook
45                                                              ∎
```

As expected, setting a string to the integer attribute time_to_cook fails as
a WrongType exception is raised. Setting an integer works as expected and
the last two lines prove that the instance is storing the value correctly.

Summary

- A simple implementation of a schema is straightforward since it is
  only about storing a certain set of attributes.
- For some applications, it is necessary to validate the values to be
  stored. Fields provide a validate method for that.
- A schema's fields can be accessed through the index notation, a.k.a.
  __getitem__ protocol.
- FieldProperty allows one to transparently validate the attributes
  that are set on a class.

5.2 Configuration via ZCML

We have now reached a common milestone in the development process. We
finished implementing a component and need to tell Zope about it. In most
cases, this means a simple registration with the component registry. In other
cases it also involves other matters of application policy, such as security
settings. The process of defining application policy is casually called *configuration* in Zope. As we saw in Chapter 2, Zope uses ZCML for this.

ZCML files can be placed anywhere, usually they are placed inside their
corresponding Python package. By convention, the main configuration file
inside a Python package is named configure.zcml. If a large ZCML
needs to be split up, additional ZCML files can be placed inside a package.
They can be included via the include directive (see Appendix B for more
info.)

Inside ZCML files, global objects, like classes in modules or packages, are referred to using dotted names describing the objects' full package path, for example `email.Message` or `worldcookery.recipe.Recipe`[2]. When an object in the same package as the configuration file is referred to, the short syntax `.recipe.Recipe` (when used in a configuration file in the `worldcookery` package) can be used. Apart from that, dotted names are often used to indicate namespaces in identifiers of named utilities, for example `zope.View` (a permission) or `worldcookery.RecipeWithInitialValues` (a factory, see below).

Configuring a content component

Let us come back to our example application. We now have several implementations for recipes, each of them useful for different purposes. For future examples however, we will only rely on the implementation shown in Example 5.1.1. If you would like, you can also use the implementation shown in Example 5.1.3. The only difference between them is that the former does not validate attributes being set to its instances, an aspect which shall not be of importance in future examples.

Content components do not need to be registered anywhere, they are retrieved from their storage (e.g. a database). The only aspect of a content component that can be registered is a content *factory* which shall be the topic of Section 5.4. Content components themselves only need security definitions for the read and write access of their data. Example 5.2.1 shows us how to do that.

As we see in the example, the `class` directive is used to configure classes like our content component. It is a *complex directive*, meaning it expects subdirectives. The only subdirective used in this example is the `require` directive. It is used to configure a class's security. The first `require` directive tells the security proxy for recipes to require the `zope.View` permission when accessing the given set of attributes. These happen to be the attributes we defined in the `IRecipe` schema. A method, by the way, is just another attribute from a security perspective and protected the same way as other (read-only) attributes. Attributes can typically be read and written. We therefore also need the second `require` directive to protect write access on the given attributes of `Recipe` instances. That is done using a different permission, `zope.ManageContent`.[3]

If we decide to extend the `IRecipe` schema with another field, we would have to update both `require` directives to list that additional attribute. In

---

[2] think: `from email import Message` or `from worldcookery.recipe import Recipe`, respectively.

[3] What these permissions mean in detail will be covered much later in Chapter 21. For now it is enough to understand that one of them is about viewing things and one is about changing things.

Example 5.2.1 Configuring a content component's security
(`configure.zcml`)

```
 1  <configure xmlns="http://namespaces.zope.org/zope">
 2
 3    <class class=".recipe.Recipe">
 4      <require
 5          permission="zope.View"
 6          attributes="name ingredients tools time_to_cook description"
 7          />
 8      <require
 9          permission="zope.ManageContent"
10          set_attributes="name ingredients tools time_to_cook description"
11          />
12    </class>
13
14  </configure>
```

5 and 9.   Notice the usage of dotted names. The ones used here refer to *permissions* which have been registered with that identifier.

3.   Here we also use a dotted name, but this time it refers to a global python object located in a module or package. The leading dot stands for the package the configuration file is located in, in this case the worldcookery package. This way, we can write .recipe.Recipe instead of worldcookery.recipe.Recipe. This is a real space saver when you have deep package structures, since absolute package paths can get pretty long.

addition, some schemas can be quite large, which would make configuration inconvenient. The ZCML machinery luckily provides a shortcut. In Example 5.2.2, we configure the class's security using the schema. The ZCML machinery knows how to inspect the schema and thus knows which attributes we mean.

Summary

- The ZCML file inside a Python package is typically called `configure.zcml`.
- Global objects are referred to using a dotted path. Both absolute and relative module paths are supported.
- Content components are configured using the complex content ZCML directive.
- A class's attributes, including its methods, are protected using the require subdirective.

Example 5.2.2 Using interfaces/schemas for security declarations
(`configure.zcml`)

```
1  <configure xmlns="http://namespaces.zope.org/zope">
2
3    <class class=".recipe.Recipe">
4      <require
5          permission="zope.View"
6          interface=".interfaces.IRecipe"
7          />
8      <require
9          permission="zope.ManageContent"
10         set_schema=".interfaces.IRecipe"
11         />
12   </class>
13
14 </configure>
```

Flashback

Zope 2 supports several ways of protecting a class's methods and attributes with security declarations. The newest, *declarative security*
which uses the `ClassSecurityInfo` class, is perceived to be the most
elegant. All solutions, however, mix security declarations into the code
that is to be protected. This makes it impossible to use and easily protect
third party classes in Zope 2 and to use classes written for Zope 2 outside
Zope applications. Also, security checking is only activated if the special function `InitializeClass`, formerly `default_class_init_`,
is called on the class. It is a common mistake to forget to call this function, thus leaving class instances openly accessible.

Using Zope 2

The `class` directive including its subdirectives are available in Five.
The security relevant subdirectives map to the Zope 2 security system
and can therefore be used in the normal manner in Zope 2. All default
Zope 2 permissions have corresponding dotted names by which they can
be referenced in ZCML for Five-based software.

Rocky says...

Security declarations in J2EE's `ejb-jar.xml` file work similarly to security declarations in ZCML. The most noticeable difference would be

> that J2EE declares security based on roles while Zope uses the more granular permissions. But ZCML even has the ability to define permissions much like J2EE's method of defining roles.

5.3 Content types

Content management systems usually deal with different types of content, e.g. documents, articles, news items, photos, etc. In our example application, we are dealing with recipes. Of course, it would be convenient for the system to differentiate an article from a photo or a recipe by using a certain marker. In Zope we use interfaces as markers. For example, the `IRecipe` interface is a marker for recipes, meaning that when an object provides `IRecipe`, it is definitely a recipe object.

The only problem with this is that a recipe object could easily provide more than one interface. How can we distinguish the interface that says something about its type of content from the extra interfaces? The solution is to make the interface that tells us about the type of content a special interface, a *content type*. In our example, recipes would be of the content type `IRecipe`. Note the name "IRecipe" is not the identifier but the interface itself is the identifier!

Content types are interfaces with the added notion that they are meant to be for content components. A component might provide several interfaces, but it only provides one content type. We also say "the object is of the type *content type*" or "the object's type is *content type*". The `interface` ZCML directive declares an interface type, as Example 5.3.1 demonstrates.

Example 5.3.1 Configuring a content type (`configure.zcml`)

```
1    ...
2    <interface
3        interface=".interfaces.IRecipe"
4        type="zope.app.content.interfaces.IContentType"
5        />
6    ...
```

The ZCML code in Example 5.3.1 is equal to providing `IContentType` directly on `IRecipe`:

```
$ python
>>> from zope.interface import alsoProvides
>>> from worldcookery.interfaces import IRecipe
>>> from zope.app.content.interfaces import IContentType
>>> alsoProvides(IRecipe, IContentType)
```

It is perfectly okay to stumble at this point. An interface that provides
an interface? Sounds complicated. But if we think about it for a minute,
it makes perfect sense. Interfaces provide `IInterface`, which promises
methods we have already used, like `providedBy` and `implementedBy`.
`IContentType` merely extends `IInterface`, it does not declare additional
methods or attributes. Interfaces providing `IContentType` only promise to
be content types. Since `IContentType` only implies that promise and cannot
express it in terms of methods and attributes, we call it a *marker interface*.
That way, checking whether an interface is a content type or not is simply a
matter of checking whether it provides `IContentType`.

Querying an object's content type

When you deal with content components, you often might want to know its
content type. For example, when you have a tabular folder listing containing
a number of different content objects, you might want to display each object's
name and type. You could use the `providedBy` from the `zope.interface`
package to retrieve a list of interfaces each object provides. The only problem
is that objects can provide many interfaces at a time. It would be quite
complicated having to figure out every time which one of them is a content
type.

Zope has a shortcut for this problem. The `zope.app.interface` package provides the `queryType` function. It takes an object and a type interface
as arguments and returns the first interface it can find on the object that provides the type interface. In case the object does not provide an interface of
that type at all, it returns `None`.

The following interpreter session demonstrates the usage of `queryType`.
First we construct a recipe object that will have an additional interface:

```
$ bin/debugzope
>>> from worldcookery.recipe import Recipe
>>> meatballs = Recipe()
>>> from zope.interface import alsoProvides
>>> from zope.annotation.interfaces import IAttributeAnnotatable
>>> alsoProvides(meatballs, IAttributeAnnotatable)            ▼
```

Now we can see the difference between the output of a mere call to
`providedBy` and `queryType`:

```
>>> from zope.interface import providedBy
>>> from zope.app.interface import queryType
>>> from zope.app.content.interfaces import IContentType
>>>
>>> list(providedBy(meatballs))
[<InterfaceClass interfaces.IRecipe>,
 <InterfaceClass zope.annotation.interfaces.IAttributeAnnotatable>]
>>> queryType(meatballs, IContentType)
<InterfaceClass interfaces.IRecipe>                            ■
```

Our recipe objects do not only provide `IRecipe`, but also the marker interface `IAttributeAnnotatable`. We will cover later what that means, for now it is just important that it provides more than one interface. Only one of them is a content type, as the different outputs of `providedBy` and `queryType` demonstrate.

Summary

- When interfaces describe pure content objects we call them content types.
- Content type interfaces provide `IContentType`, which is derived from `IInterface`.
- Interfaces are made content types through ZCML configuration using the `interface` directive.
- `queryType` returns an object's interface of a certain type, if it has one.

Flashback

Zope 2 distinguishes objects by their *meta type*, a simple string attribute of the objects. In order to make objects work with Zope 2, they need to carry that attribute. Since Zope 2 by itself does not distinguish between application objects such as a session manager and content objects, the Content Management Framework (CMF), gives content objects yet another mandatory attribute, the *portal type*.

Zope 3 has neither meta type nor portal type. It uses a more subtle and at the same time meaningful way: interfaces. Plain interfaces can be seen as the Zope 3 equivalent of the meta type, while content types (which are interfaces, too) replace the portal type attribute.

5.4 Factories

Earlier in this chapter we implemented a simple content component. Like all components, this particular implementation of a recipe storage class is exchangeable. The only problem is that code expecting to create recipes will have to directly import the recipe class, making it impossible to easily exchange it for another implementation. *Factories* are components that take away the responsibility of creating objects from their classes. By doing so they allow us to exchange a content component implementation for another one as long as we also provide a replacement factory along with it.

Factories are utilities that provide the IFactory interface. A simple factory that just creates and returns a recipe object is shown in Example 5.4.1. As a utility, it needs to be registered first before we can look it up through the Component Architecture. The ZCML directive that is needed for this is shown in Example 5.4.2. Note that this configuration does not make any security assertions about the factory. It may be used by anyone, though the object created by the factory might not due to its own security declarations.

Example 5.4.1 Simple factory implementation (recipe.py)

```
 1   ...
 2
 3   from zope.component.interfaces import IFactory
 4   from zope.interface import implementedBy
 5
 6   class RecipeFactory:
 7       implements(IFactory)
 8
 9       title = u"Create a new recipe"
10       description = u"This factory instantiates new recipes."
11
12       def __call__(self):
13           return Recipe()
14
15       def getInterfaces(self):
16           return implementedBy(Recipe)
```

9–10. Factories can carry a title and description. These might be used when a list of factories is presented to the user, for example in an object add menu.

12–16. The __call__ and getInterfaces methods are described by the IFactory interface and need to be implemented here. __call__ is expected to return the created object whereas getInterfaces is expected to return an iterable of interfaces that are provided by the created objects.

Factories from class

The factory we just implemented is not too complicated, it only invokes the Recipe class. Other typical factories are just as simple. They often only create new objects from a class. For this case, Zope has a shortcut for us so that we need not implement the IFactory interface every time. The shortcut is shown in Example 5.4.3. Example 5.4.4 shows the slight change in the ZCML configuration that is now necessary.

Example 5.4.2 Configuring a custom factory (`configure.zcml`)

```
1    ...
2    <utility
3        factory=".recipe.RecipeFactory"
4        name="worldcookery.Recipe"
5        permission="zope.Public"
6        />
7    ...
```

3. The `utility` directive lets us specify the component that is to be registered in two ways. If you already have an instance and want to register that, you can use the `component` parameter. If you have a class (or something else that must be called to create the utility) and want ZCML to instantiate the component, you may use the `factory` parameter. Since `RecipeFactory` is indeed a class, we choose the latter.

4. Factories are named utilities. The ZCML directive lets us specify under which name we register this particular factory. It is a common convention to use *dotted names* for this and using a sensible prefix, for example the name of the Python package.

5. Utilities may optionally be protected with a permission so that their usage is only open to users with the right privileges. Factories are typically protected by the public permission because they only create object, which typically is not a security risk in and of itself. Note that protecting with the public permission is different than stating no permission at all: to security-sensitive components (such as views), unprotected components are inaccessible whereas components protected with e.g. `zope.Public` are available.

Example 5.4.3 Factory from class (`recipe.py`)

```
1    ...
2
3    from zope.component.factory import Factory
4
5    recipeFactory = Factory(
6        Recipe,
7        title=u"Create a new recipe",
8        description = u"This factory instantiates new recipes."
9        )
```

Using factories

We said initially that factories provide a good way to create objects without having to rely on a specific implementation—in other words, a specific

---

Example 5.4.4 Configuring a factory from class (`configure.zcml`)

```
1    ...
2    <utility
3        component=".recipe.recipeFactory"
4        name="worldcookery.Recipe"
5        />
6    ...
```

---

class. Let us therefore now create some recipe objects without importing the
`Recipe` class at all.

As mentioned earlier, factories are utilities. We will therefore use the
`getUtility` function from the Component Architecture to look them up:

```
$ bin/debugzope
>>> from zope.component import getUtility
>>> from zope.component.interfaces import IFactory
>>> recipe_factory = getUtility(IFactory, u"worldcookery.Recipe")
>>> weisswurst = recipe_factory()
>>> weisswurst
<worldcookery.recipe.Recipe object at 0x30469c30>                    ▼
```

We can also instantiate recipes in a shorter way by using the `createObject`
function. It will find and invoke the factory for us:

```
>>> from zope.component import createObject
>>> weisswurst = createObject(u"worldcookery.Recipe")
>>> weisswurst
<worldcookery.recipe.Recipe object at 0x308d8210>                    ■
```

This is much shorter since neither `IFactory` has to be imported nor a factory
be instantiated.

Custom factories

Note that in the above examples, the recipe class or module is not imported,
yet we end up with a `Recipe` object. This code solely relies on a factory
with the id `worldcookery.Recipe`, not on the implementation itself.

Summary

- Factories are responsible for making new instances of a class, typically, but not limited to content objects.
- Factories are named utilities providing `IFactory`; they are registered using the `utility` ZCML directive.

- Factories are *code components*, thus they are not protected by a permission but publicly usable; the objects they create are security-aware and protected.
- For simple factories based on classes or other callables, `Factory` from the `zope.component.factory` module provides a shortcut.

Rocky says...

Factories are a common design pattern used throughout various languages and Python and Java are no exception. Although not part of core Java, Java has the Spring framework which enables Java to generate various components including (but not limited to) persistent components.

6

Persistency

In the previous chapters, we have seen what content objects can look like. You can store and provide data with getters and setters, or you can use the pythonic attribute approach. In either case, the values were stored inside the object instance. That means when the instance is gone, the data the instance is holding is gone, too. This is obviously not a practical approach. When we make a content component that is designed to store data over a period of time, we would like to be able to restart our application without losing that data. This chapter will show you how to do that.

Using Zope 2

Zope 2 and Zope 3 share the same persistency mechanism. This chapter therefore also applies to Zope 2. Similarly, if you are already familiar with Zope's persistency mechanism (the ZODB), you can skip this chapter and continue with Chapter 7. Just note that recent ZODB versions introduce several improvements and new features that are also available in Zope 2:

- Classes inheriting from `Persistent` are new-style classes, which allows you to use all new-style class features on them, such as `property` and `super`.
- In order to reduce read conflicts on concurring transactions, the ZODB now implements multi-version concurrency control (MVCC). More details are given below.
- Transactions that change a lot of data in the database can use *save-points* to save intermediate work to disk and thus free memory.

6.1 The problem of object storage

Many web applications that are driven by scripting languages such as Perl, PHP, ASP, and Ruby use relational databases to store and query data, for good reasons. Relational databases provide a reliable, efficient, scalable, and often cost-effective way to store large amounts of complex data. By making use of Python database connectors, Zope also supports relational database connectivity very well. However, being object-centric, Zope does not want to lose the simplicity of content objects. It would only feel natural if there were a way to store objects transparently.

While there are popular object-relational mapper (ORM) solutions for Python (*SQLObject*[1] and *SQLAlchemy*[2]), they lack the transparency of a native object storage. Moreover, complex data structures, when modelled in a relational database, often require a complicated set of tables and corresponding join logic. With a pure object-oriented approach, this is not necessary.

Zope has always had its own storage solution called the *Zope Object Database* (ZODB). Python already provides mechanisms to represent objects as byte streams so they can be saved to files or sent over a network connection in the `pickle` module. The ZODB uses this mechanism to provide a sophisticated database that implements the ACID properties. This means it ensures the following:

Atomicity. Modifications to the database happen in transactions that are either carried out as a whole or aborted. That means changes are atomic. Partial changes that could leave inconsistencies do not occur. A new transaction is automatically started when the first change to a persistent object is made. Zope will commit the transaction after every request or, in case an error occurs, abort it. This is completely transparent to the developer.

Consistency. After a transaction has been committed or aborted, the database is always left in a consistent state. This does not only refer to referential integrity. It just means that inconsistent transactions are not be allowed to be committed and reading transactions will always see the database in a consistent state.

Isolation. Multiple transactions executed at the same time have no impact on each other. A reading transaction cannot see the modifications of a concurrent writing transaction. If the writing transaction has been committed while the reading transaction is still running, the database's concurrency control mechanism needs to make sure that the reading transaction still deals with consistent data. The ZODB uses a *multi-version concurrency control* (MVCC) mechanism. For example, take a transaction reading data from objects. While this transaction is still running, another one is committed that modifies some of those objects. MVCC will make sure that the reading transaction will still use an appropri-

---

[1] SQLObject website <http://sqlobject.org>

[2] SQLAlchemy website <http://www.sqlalchemy.org>

ate version of the objects that correspond to a point in time when the
database was definitely consistent.

Durability. Once a transaction has been committed successfully, its changes
are written to the database and persist there. That means the data would
survive a system failure, for example, because the data no longer is in
memory but safely stored on disk.

In addition to that, the ZODB provides the following features:

Transparency. The fact that an object is persistent is nearly completely
transparent to it and other components working with it. No special methods have to be called to store or retrieve data nor does one have to implement a special interface for persistency compliance. That makes it possible to persist any picklable object[3]. The only requirement is that the
majority of the objects involved subclass `persistent.Persistent`.
In practice, we simply subclass it for all objects that need to be stored
in the ZODB, as we will see below.

Undo. Even when a transaction has long been committed and written to
the database, one might still want to undo a change. The ZODB not
only supports a simple undo function for this, it can actually keep every
revision of every stored object, thus allowing simple revision control of
stored data. This feature has its limits, though, especially when an object
has been changed over the course of several transactions and an undo
would lead to inconsistencies.

Pluggable Storages. The ZODB can store persistent data in many ways.
By using a different storage backend, you can choose where and how
you would like to store persistent objects. The most common storage is
FileStorage which stores data in one large file usually called `Data.fs`.
Another popular storage is *DirectoryStorage*[4] which stores each object's
revision in a separate file. It also has replication and hot backup features.
The ZODB also features a network storage system called *Zope Enterprise
Objects* (ZEO) with which one or many Zope instances (the ZEO clients)
delegate storage to a central storage server (the ZEO server) over the
network. Such a setup is typically used in high-availability, scaling or
distributed environments.

---

[3] Picklable objects include all class instances except file objects, network connection objects, and the like.
[4] DirectoryStorage homepage <http://dirstorage.sourceforge.net>

Summary

- Since Zope deals with objects (e.g. content components), it is desirable to store data as objects as well.
- Zope's object database ZODB is based on Python's support to serialize objects as pickles.
- The ZODB implements the ACID properties for databases and provides features generally expected from an industrial strength database.

Rocky says...

Java developers will probably realize at this point that most of the persistence options available to Zope developers are also available to Java developers (in concept, at least). Direct SQL access as provided by JDBC functions very closely to Python's DBAPI. And the Hibernate ORM is very similar (functional-wise) to Python's SQLObject. The largest difference is that the most common J2EE approach to persistence is usually via EJB's whereas Zope developers tend to use the ZODB.

6.2 Making persistent objects

It is not possible to make a single instance persistent. The persistence machinery needs to take advantage of certain Python hooks which why persistence happens at the class level. Classes of persistent objects need to derive from a special base class, `Persistent` from the `persistent` package. This package is part of the ZODB and can be used outside Zope.

Let us look back at our recipe class as we defined it in Example 5.1.1. To make its instances support persistency, we simply have to derive from `Persistent` now (Example 6.2.1).

Since we have not changed anything except a base class, the configuration of this class is identical to the one in the previous chapter. This is a good demonstration of the transparency of the persistence machinery.

Creating persistent objects on the debug prompt

Before we dive into creating components for the web browser interface that will eventually let us create and edit recipes through the web, we will look at a useful feature of the debug shell: access to the ZODB database.

First we create a recipe object (now of the persistent kind). The data we put in it is not of importance now but will be useful later in the next chapter:

Example 6.2.1 Simple persistent class (`recipe.py`)

```
1  from persistent import Persistent
2  from zope.interface import implements
3  from worldcookery.interfaces import IRecipe
4
5  class Recipe(Persistent):
6      implements(IRecipe)
7
8      name = u''
9      ingredients = []
10     tools = []
11     time_to_cook = 0
12     description = u''
```

1 and 5.   By deriving from the `Persistent` base class, we automatically make all
recipe instances persistent. Because of its simplicity the rest of the class does
not have to be changed.

```
$ bin/debugzope
>>> from worldcookery.recipe import Recipe
>>> minestrone = Recipe()
>>> minestrone.name = u'Minestrone'
>>> minestrone.ingredients = [u'onions', u'celery', u'garlic']
>>> minestrone.time_to_cook = 15
>>> minestrone.description = u'Cook at a gentle boil.'            ▼
```

Now we can store the recipe object in the database. The root folder is available
as the `root` variable in the debug shell. As we will discover later in Chapter
15, folders behave like dictionaries, which allows us to store objects inside a
folder quite easily:

```
>>> root[u'minestrone'] = minestrone                             ▼
```

We could now be tempted to close the interpreter session, but our changes
would not not be saved. The ZODB is a transactional database, remember?
To make any changes effective, we first need to commit the transaction:

```
>>> import transaction
>>> transaction.commit()                                         ■
```

When we now take a web browser to navigate to the root folder listing at `http://localhost:8080/@@contents.html` we see that the
`minestrone` object has been successfully stored (see Figure 6.1). There is
not much else to do with it at this point. More will follow in the next chapter.

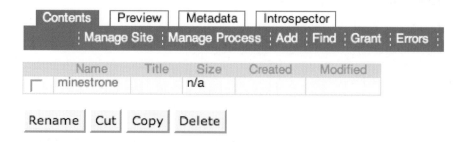

Fig. 6.1. Root folder listing showing the recipe added with the debug shell.

Summary

- Persistent classes need to inherit from `Persistent` provided by the `persistent` package.
- Configuration of a persistent class is identical to its non-persistent equivalent.
- Zope's debug shell can be used to access an instance's database and make changes to it, provided the transaction is properly committed.

6.3 Working with persistent objects

Even though basic persistence is quite transparent, understanding the characteristics of the persistence machinery is important for storing data efficiently. In this section we will discuss some design questions that arise when dealing with persistent objects.

In a relational database, tables are used to model different data. Each row in a table represents a particular set of the data to be modelled. We can say that rows and tables are the *boundaries* by which we divide and structure the data in the model. In the ZODB, persistent classes can be compared to tables and instances of persistent classes can be compared to rows in those tables. Here, the classes and objects make up the boundaries.

Much like a row can make key references to a row in another table, persistent objects can also reference other objects. For example, a recipe object references several other objects, such as Unicode strings that hold a name and description. Referencing simple objects like this is usually trivial, it becomes more complicated when the referenced objects become more complicated.

Referenced objects

Firstly we are confronted with the question of which objects are to be made persistent and which are not. We shall illustrate this with an example.

Imagine we have *dinner* objects. These are objects that hold a bunch of individual recipes. For example, there could be a Christmas dinner object that references three recipe objects (appetizer, main course, dessert). If these recipe objects do not inherit from `Persistent` themselves, the persistence machinery will still make sure they are stored in the database. However, since they are referenced by the Christmas dinner object, they will be stored as part of this object. That has two consequences:

- If some other dinner object references the same recipe object as the Christmas dinner object, then that recipe object will be stored twice: once as part of the Christmas dinner and once as part of the other dinner. That means it will eventually become two separate objects and the object's identity is lost.
- If the recipe object changes (and the persistence machinery will get notice of that), the whole dinner object will have be stored again in the database. That is because the recipe object is not stored by itself but as part of the dinner object. Having to store the whole dinner object when just a recipe changes would obviously be highly inefficient because all other recipes would also be stored again. In other words, data that might not have changed at all would have to be serialized and written to the database for no direct reason.

The solution to this is to make recipes persistent themselves. Then, the recipes will be stored separately from the dinner objects and will neither affect other objects when they change nor lose their identity. In a relational database, we would say that recipes are now stored in their own table and that the dinner table simply holds a foreign key reference to the recipe table.

Divide and conquer

As discussed, making referenced objects individually persistent has several advantages. One that has not been mentioned is separating and dividing large data.

Imagine we wanted to add the ability to associate a picture with recipes. One solution would be to add another field to `IRecipe` that specified a bytes string holding the binary data of the picture. Because strings are not persistent by themselves, the binary data would be stored as part of the recipe. That could make recipe objects very large which means that large changes to the database occur even when only the title or description of a recipe is changed (because the whole recipe object has to be serialized again).

A better solution would therefore be to put the large bytes string on its own persistent object and make recipes simply reference this object. That way, changes of recipe objects will not include the potentially large binary data. When binary data gets very large, it would be recommended to divide it into several persistent objects so that when the data is read, not the all of it is pulled into memory at once but only a portion at a time as each individual persistent object is deserialized.

Volatile data

The ZODB facilitates Python's *pickling* mechanism to serialize objects. That means all attributes on an object need to be picklable themselves. In case you absolutely need to reference an unpicklable object in a persistent object, you need to mark it as *volatile*, in other words non-persistent. Volatile attributes are prefixed with _v_ and always need to be used for file handle objects, network connections or cached values whose change shall not invoke a persistence transaction. Consider the following short example:

```
$ python
>>> from persistent import Persistent
>>> class File(Persistent):
...     def __init__(self, filename):
...         self.filename = filename        # persistent
...         self._v_file = file(filename)    # volatile
...     def read(self):
...         self._v_file.read()
```

The objects this class instantiates are persistent, since it derives from `Persistent`. The `filename` attribute is also persistent, since it would normally be a simple string or Unicode object. However, the file handle object needs to be stored as a volatile attribute and is thus prepended with a _v_.

> **Warning**
>
> Note that volatile attributes are not guaranteed to last through a transaction. When a subtransaction is triggered or the persistent object is serialized again because there is no reference to it anymore, volatile attributes may be lost.

Object changes

To ensure the great deal of transparency, the persistence machinery notices whenever an attribute is set or reset on an object, no matter whether that happens inside an object's method using `self`, for example `self.name = u"Risotto"` or outside to the object, `risotto.name = u"Risotto"`. Yet, it is not able to keep track of any changes to the attributes that will not result in a re-setting of them. Consider the following example:

```
$ python
>>> from worldcookery.recipe import Recipe
>>> risotto = Recipe()
>>> risotto.ingredients
[]
>>> risotto.ingredients.append(u"Rice")
>>> risotto.ingredients
[u"Rice"]
```
▼

Here, we have successfully added an ingredient to our recipe object. However, the problem is that the recipe object itself was not modified at all; all we did was append something to the `ingredients` list. The persistence machinery would not notice anything.

There are two solutions for this common problem. The less transparent one is to set a special attribute called _p_changed on the object[5]. This will let the persistence machinery know that the object has changed for sure:

```
>>> risotto._p_changed = True
```
■

The problem with this solution is that one loses a great deal of transparency. One has to make sure to always set the _p_changed attribute. While that is not so much of a problem when encountering such cases inside object methods, it is from the outside of an object. When would some code know that it is dealing with a persistent component or not?

One way to get around this is changing the `IRecipe` interface so that the `ingredients` and `tools` fields are not lists but tuples. Tuples are immutable and cannot be changed, they must therefore be reassigned as attributes. That way the persistence machinery would always notice a change.

Another option is to make the list objects persistent themselves. That way, the persistent machinery gets notified when they change automatically and transparently to outside code. For two of the built-in data structures in Python, lists and dictionaries, the `persistent` package provides persistent flavours: `PersistentList`, provided by the `persistent.list` module, and `PersistentDict`, provided by the `persistent.dict` module. Using those, we can update our recipe class to use `PersistentList` instead of Python's built-in list (see Example 6.3.1).

You should note that `PersistentList` and `PersistentList` are very inefficient for storing large data structures. If you want to persistently store several hundred items or more in a list or mapping, consider using one of the BTree structures that are introduced in the next section instead.

---

[5] Attributes starting with _p_ are special to the ZODB machinery. Persistent classes may not have custom attributes with that prefix.

Example 6.3.1 Persistent attributes (`recipe.py`)

```
1  from persistent import Persistent
2  from persistent.list import PersistentList
3  from zope.interface import implements
4  from worldcookery.interfaces import IRecipe
5
6  class Recipe(Persistent):
7      implements(IRecipe)
8
9      name = u''
10     ingredients = PersistentList()
11     tools = PersistentList()
12     time_to_cook = 0
13     description = u''
```

Summary

- The persistence machinery only takes notice of direct changes to persistent objects; in cases of indirect change, setting the _p_changed attribute on the persistent object invokes the machinery manually.
- It is usually preferable to make sub-objects persistent as well, using PersistentList and PersistentDict as a replacement for Python's mutable data structures.
- Attributes that should not be persisted need to be prefixed with _v_ to mark them as volatile.

6.4 BTrees

An advanced feature of the ZODB are balanced binary trees called *BTrees*. A BTree object is a persistent mapping object that stores its items in a tree form. Using this special form of storage and an appropriate search algorithm, BTrees perform much better than regular dictionaries when looking up items. While the mean time needed to look up an item from a dictionary increases linearly with the number of items stored in the dictionary, BTrees perform the search proportionally to the logarithm of the number items stored.

In computer science literature, the BTree implementation that comes with the ZODB is sometimes referred to as B^+ trees. The individual nodes of a BTree are persistent objects. That means that large trees which are stored persistently can be searched for items efficiently because only the nodes that are needed for the search algorithm are deserialized from the database and pulled into memory, not the whole tree. This in combination with the fast search algorithm makes BTrees the perfect data storage structure when managing thousands of items in a dictionary-like object, especially in a persistent environment.

There are four different flavours of BTrees that you can use depending on your needs. All of the following can be imported from their subpackage below the `BTrees` package:

IIBTree A BTree whose keys and values are integers.

IOBTree A BTree whose keys are integers and whose values are arbitrary objects. This kind of BTree can be used to mimic a sequence of objects that is persistent and has the fast look up capabilities of BTrees.

OIBTree A BTree whose keys are arbitrary objects and whose values are integers. This kind of BTree is useful for keeping count of object occurrences or similar use-cases.

OOBTree A BTree whose keys and values are arbitrary objects. This is the most general kind of BTree and commonly used for object containers.

In addition to the mapping objects, each BTree flavour also supports a set object. `IITreeSet` and `IOTreeSet` manage sets of integers while `OITreeSet` and `OOTreeSet` manage sets of arbitrary objects. Their advantages over the set implementation built into Python are their fast look-up mechanism (thanks to the underlying BTree) and their persistence support.

Set operations

Apart from the regular mapping API, BTree mappings and sets also support operations known from mathematical sets, such as unions, intersections and differences. Consider the following small example using `IOBTree`:

```
$ python
>>> from BTrees.IOBTree import IOBTree, union, intersection
>>> odd = IOBTree({1: 'one', 3: 'three'})
>>> even = IOBTree({2: 'two', 4: 'four'})                          ▼
```

The union of these two BTrees obviously contains all four numbers, while the intersection is empty:

```
>>> union(odd, even)
IOSet([1, 2, 3, 4])
>>> intersection(odd, even)
IOSet([])                                                          ■
```

It is not only convenient that these operations are already implemented so that one can use an existing implementation when it is needed; because of the underlying BTree storage, these operations are also relatively fast.

Summary

- BTrees are an implementation of persistent mappings and sets that can efficiently store and look up large amounts of items.
- There are four different flavours of BTree for different key/value type combinations.
- BTrees efficiently supports the union and intersection set operations.

7

Simple Views and Browser Pages

How much functionality do the recipes have now? We can describe their API using interfaces and their data structure using schemas. We have a minimal implementation as a Python class which we have made persistent. Its instances can be stored in the ZODB. We can also add recipes to a Zope folder via the debug shell. That is all.

What we cannot do is display the data stored inside a recipe to a web browser. Our content component is only useful for interaction on a Python API level. What we need are components that allow recipes to do user interaction. Such components are adapters, more specifically views.

Using Zope 2

Most of this chapter applies to Zope 2 as well, at least so far as browser pages and Page Templates are concerned. Due to Zope 2's security machinery, all browser views need to support the Zope 2 acquisition machinery, either by subclassing `Acquisition.Explicit` or the convenience base class `Products.Five.BrowserView`. Also, Five's variant of `ViewPageTemplateFile` which is available from `Products.Five.browser.pagetemplatefile` should be used to bind Page Templates to browser page classes.

7.1 Introduction to views

In Zope, the user or the user application is represented by two related objects: the request invoked by the application on behalf of the user, for example the HTTP request of a web browser, and the response that will be sent back to it. A view presents components in an understandable way for the *user application*. For example, if the user application is a web browser, a view may provide HTML. To ensure proper separation, views should be the only part of an application dealing with request and response objects.

Different views for different user interfaces

Views are *named multi-adapters*. Multi-adapting means that instead of adapting a single object, views adapt both the object and the request. Hence, different views of the same object are invoked for different types of requests. Zope knows the following request types:[1]

- HTTP/WebDAV
  (`zope.publisher.interfaces.http.IHTTPRequest`)

- Browser
  (`zope.publisher.interfaces.browser.IBrowserRequest`)

- XML-RPC
  (`zope.publisher.interfaces.xmlrpc.IXMLRPCRequest`)

- FTP
  (request interface `zope.publisher.interfaces.ftp.IFTPRequest`)

Views are *named* multi-adapters. They have a name because different operations on an object require different views. Displaying an object is obviously different from editing it. Hence two separate views might exist for those two different operations, perhaps one named `index.html` for the display and one named `edit.html` for editing. Once registered, these views can be looked up by name, for example in a URL:

`http://worldcookery.com/recipes/lasagne/@@edit.html`

The path to the content object to be displayed is `recipes/lasagne`. The `@@` is a shortcut for `++view++` and indicates that a view name follows and not another element in an object traversal graph.[2] What follows is the name of the view, in this case `edit.html`.

Simple browser pages

The most common views in Zope 3 are browser views. They typically produce HTML. For now, though, let us implement a simple browser page for recipes that outputs the recipe's name in plain text. Generating HTML is covered in the next section.

Example 7.1.1 shows the implementation of a simple browser page generating some plain text. As you maybe have noticed from the filename, we

---

[1] Of course, it is possible to extend Zope's publishing machinery to deal with other request types.

[2] Think of the `@@` as two eyes, as Jim Fulton suggested once.

are now working inside a subpackage of the `worldcookery` package called
`worldcookery.browser`. We will use it for all browser-specific components. It is a Zope convention to separate components that are specific to
a certain type of representation into different modules or, when the amount
of code is substantial, into different packages. Since we will be adding many
more browser-specific components and files in this and subsequent chapters,
it makes sense to start this subpackage now.

Example 7.1.1 Simple browser page (`browser/recipe.py`)

```
1  from zope.publisher.browser import BrowserPage
2
3  class ViewRecipe(BrowserPage):
4
5      def __call__(self):
6          response = self.request.response
7          response.setHeader('Content-Type', 'text/plain')
8          return self.context.name
```

1 and 3. The `BrowserPage` base class provides all the necessary functionality to
make this class publishable as a view.

6. The request object is made available by the base class as `self.request`. The
response associated with this request is available as the `response` attribute of
the request object.

As with any component, we need to register the browser page first before
we can use it. Example 7.1.2 shows the necessary ZCML directive for this.
Since we have put this ZCML file in the `worldcookery.browser` subpackage, we need to make sure that it is properly loaded together with the rest
of the *World Cookery* configuration. Therefore, we add the following line to
the bottom of `configure.zcml`:

```
<include package=".browser" />
```

Now we are nearly ready to look up the browser page using the debug
shell. We will once again use the shell to ensure that the configuration of the
page is loaded. First we need to create test objects. Views are multi-adapters
for the object and the request, so we need to create a recipe object and a test
request:

```
$ bin/debugzope
>>> from worldcookery.recipe import Recipe
>>> lasagne = Recipe()
>>> lasagne.name = u"Lasagne"
>>> from zope.publisher.browser import TestRequest
>>> request = TestRequest()                                    ▼
```

Example 7.1.2 Configuring a browser page (`browser/configure.zcml`)

```
1   <configure
2       xmlns="http://namespaces.zope.org/zope"
3       xmlns:browser="http://namespaces.zope.org/browser"
4       >
5
6     <browser:page
7         for="worldcookery.interfaces.IRecipe"
8         name="index.html"
9         class=".recipe.ViewRecipe"
10        permission="zope.View"
11        />
12
13  </configure>
```

3. All browser-related ZCML directives are part of this namespace. It is a convention to bind it to the `browser` prefix. Thus we will refer to it as the `browser` namespace from now on.

7. As with any type of adapter, we prefer to register it for an *interface*, not a particular implementation. That way we can replace the implementation and still have the view.

8. The name argument specifies the page's name (or the multi-adapter's name, respectively). The page will be accessible in a URL under this name. By convention, the name for the default view of an object is `index.html`; in other words, when Zope is given the URL of an object without any view suffix, it will try to use the `index.html` view.[3]

10. Views are components that deal with user interaction. We therefore have to protect views with a permission that will be required for using them. Since this browser page does not expose an editing form or any other management functionality, we can protect it with a less restraining permission. Typically, all anonymous users (unauthenticated users) have the permission `zope.View` which allows them to view most content.

Now do the lookup using the API provided by `zope.component`. Note how we are adapting the tuple (`lasagne, request`):

```
>>> from zope.component import getMultiAdapter
>>> view = getMultiAdapter((lasagne, request), name=u'index.html')
>>> view()
u'Lasagne'                                                        ■
```

So much for the interpreter shell. Now that we have written a browser view, the much more interesting test is to open a web browser and display the recipe object we created in the last chapter. The result is shown in Figure 7.1.

Fig. 7.1. Simple browser page displaying a recipe's name in plain text.

Summary

- Views present other components to the user. Different kinds of views deal with different user agents (Browser, WebDAV, XML-RPC, FTP).
- Views communicate with the user agent through the request and response objects.
- Views are named multi-adapters, adapting the object they present and the request.
- Browser-related components such as browser pages are commonly placed in a `browser` module or subpackage.

Rocky says...

The quick J2EE study will notice that view components are similar in style to Java Servlets. Both Java Servlets and Zope view components are mapped to URLs via configuration in XML. The biggest difference here is that servlets are mapped to direct URL paths whereas Zope takes a more object-oriented approach where a view component would be mapped to any object providing a specific interface.

7.2 Page Templates

We now know how to write browser pages in Python. With this knowledge, we could create pages to generate HTML instead of plain text. Doing this in Python is tedious, though. Most of the HTML markup of generated pages is static, only the content coming from the component presented in the page changes. Using Python for this would almost be overkill, which is the reason why templating technologies exist.

As you can see from the previous section, the expectations of a browser page are very basic. It only needs to provide a __call__ method that returns the desired output. This means that many Python templating choices are available to you. Zope already ships with the powerful and flexible Page Templates system, also referred to as ZPT (Zope Page Templates). This section introduces Page Templates, the next section uses Page Templates in our *World Cookery* application.

7.2.1 TAL

Page Templates contain the basic markup structure of the output page and special commands executed when the page is invoked, thus making the output dynamic. For the dynamic commands, the *Template Attribute Language* (TAL) is used. The commands are element attributes that are placed on the element they are supposed to modify. By putting these commands into a special namespace,[4] Page Templates remain valid XHTML documents and can still be edited using a WYSIWYG editor or directly viewed in a browser.

XML does not know an order of attributes. Even though one attribute can be defined before another one in an XML text, this order is arbitrary. For the same reason it does not matter to the TAL interpreter which attribute is defined first; it will execute TAL commands in a predefined order. The following list gives an overview over TAL commands in the order they are executed by the TAL interpreter. Note that some commands cannot occur on the same element at the same time, for example content and replace.

define defines new variable(s) with the return value(s) of the corresponding expression(s) in the current scope. If a definition is preceded by global, the variable is available throughout the whole template. Also see Section 7.2.3.

condition removes the element from the output if the expression evaluates to false; the element will only appear if the expression evaluates to true. Values are evaluated according to Python Boolean rules.

repeat Repeat the current element for every item in the sequence returned by an expression. The current item in the sequence is bound to a local variable within the repeated element's variable scope.

content Fills the contents of the element with the return value of an expression. The element and its attributes are preserved, only its contents including all child elements is replaced.

---

[4] http://xml.zope.org/namespaces/tal

`replace` replaces the element with the return value of an expression. The element will not be appear in the result. This command is mutually exclusive with the `content` command on the same element.

`attributes` defines or replaces attribute(s) on the current element with the value(s) of the corresponding expression(s).

`omit-tag` removes the element itself from the output but leaves its contents and child elements in if the given expression evaluates to true. True is assumed for the expression value if no expression is provided.

`on-error` inserts the return value of an expression if an error occurs in subelement processing.

For more information, please refer to the TAL specification [24].

7.2.2 TALES

You might have noticed, most TAL commands deal with expressions. The values of expressions determine the outcome of a condition or what is inserted into the template, either as a text node or an element attribute. Expressions follow the *TAL Expression Syntax* (TALES), which allows multiple types of expressions. The following list gives an overview of them:

Path expressions allow the access of attributes, items and methods through a file system or URL path-like notation. If the resulting object is callable (meaning a method, function or class), it will be called with no arguments. Examples:

```
<!-- Call the values() method of the my_recipes folder -->
<p tal:repeat="recipe context/my_recipes/values">
  Name of the dish: <span tal:replace="recipe/name" />.
</p>
```

String expressions allow the direct insertion of text. They also allow the result of path expressions to be inserted within an expression. Example:

```
<div tal:define="global message string:
    The ${recipe/name} recipe was modified" />
```

Python expressions make it possible to evaluate a piece of Python code in a TALES expression. This is especially useful for Boolean expressions in a condition or for calling functions explicitly or functions that require parameters. Examples:

```
<p tal:condition="python: recipe.time_to_cook &lt; 60">
  Cooking <span tal:replace="recipe/name/title" />
  will take less than an hour.
</p>
```

Expressions can also be preceded by a modifier that changes its behaviour or result:

not : negates the Boolean value of an expression. In Python, everything except the number 0, an empty string, list, tuple, or dictionary and None are treated as True in a Boolean expression. Example:

```
<div tal:define="takes_little_time python: recipe.time_to_cook < 60">
  <p tal:condition="takes_little_time">
    Cooking will take less than an hour.
  </p>
  <p tal:condition="not:takes_little_time">
    This dish takes more than an hour to prepare!
  </p>
</div>
```

nocall : prevents the following path expression from potentially calling a function, method or class. Examples:

```
<div tal:define="pop nocall:recipe/ingredients/pop;
                 lastitem pop"
     tal:content="lastitem">last ingredient goes here</div>
```

structure lets the result of an expression be inserted unquoted. Normally, all characters sensible to XML are quoted using entities. Sometimes you need to prevent this (for example when directly inserting HTML markup). Notice that structure is separated from the expression by a *space*, not a colon. Example:

```
<p tal:define="html string:<b>bold</b>"
   tal:content="structure html">insert html here</p>
```

| (pipe) allows the specification of a fallback if a path expression fails. It is not an *or* operator in a Boolean sense since the result of the expression to its left is still returned, even if it evaluates to False. The operator only becomes active when the path expression to its left cannot be resolved. It therefore works more like a try/except clause.

```
<div tal:define="name_of_dish recipe/name | string:Unknown dish"
     tal:content="name_of_dish">name of the dish goes here</div>
```

For more information, please refer to the TALES specification [25].

7.2.3 Scopes

From the world of programming languages such as Python, you will be familiar with global and local scopes for variables. Page Templates make use of the
same concept. A new variable scope in ZPT begins with each new XML child
element. Child element scopes inherit everything defined in a higher scope.
Using the TAL command `define`, you can set new variables inside a scope.
Unless these definitions are preceded by a `global` statement, they are only
effective in the current scope and the ones of child elements. Consider the
following example:

```
<div tal:define="recipe_name string:Kebab"></div>
<p tal:condition="python: recipe_name=='Kebab'">
  Yummy, Kebab!
</p>
```

This will fail because the variable `recipe_name` is defined in the `div` element, thus not accessible in the paragraph element. This could easily be fixed
by making the `div` element the parent element so that the p will inherit its
variables:

```
<div tal:define="recipe_name string:Kebab">
  <p tal:condition="python: recipe_name=='Kebab'">
    Yummy, Kebab!
  </p>
</div>
```

or even simpler:

```
<p tal:define="recipe_name string:Kebab"
   tal:condition="python: recipe_name=='Kebab'">
  Yummy, Kebab!
</p>
```

Alternatively, we could have made `recipe_name` a global variable:

```
<div tal:define="global recipe_name string:Kebab" />
<p tal:condition="python: recipe_name=='Kebab'">
  Yummy, Kebab!
</p>
```

Of course, with just being able to define our own variables we will not
get far. Luckily, a Page Template provides some useful variables in the root
scope, thus accessible everywhere in the template:

`request` is an object representing the request from the browser, usually a
HTTP request. It can be used to access CGI variables passed in from the
browser or even the authenticated principal, for example:

```
<p>You are
<span tal:replace="request/principal/title" />
using
<span tal:replace="request/HTTP_USER_AGENT" />
</p>
```

nothing represents a false and empty value. It is useful in conditions whenever a false value is needed and in string insertions whenever "nothing" should be inserted, for example:

```
<p tal:condition="nothing">This paragraph will not be printed</p>
<p tal:replace="nothing">Neither will this one</p>
```

default is a marker that indicated that the provided default value should be used. This is usually used in a fallback when a path expression fails to look up an object or attribute, for example:

```
<p>
  You are using
  <span tal:content="request/HTTP_USER_AGENT | default">
    a browser
  </span>
</p>
```

This is a variation of an example used above. The difference is that this will not fail if the browser did not send the CGI variable HTTP_USER_AGENT with the request. In that case, the standard text ("a browser") will be printed to the user as a fall-back.

repeat provides auxiliary functionality in loops invoked by the repeat TAL command, such as the current number of repetition both in Arabic and Roman numbers:

```
<p>You will need the following tools to prepare this dish:</p>

<div>
  <p tal:repeat="tool recipe/tools">
    <span tal:replace="repeat/tool/number" />.
    <span tal:replace="tool" />
  </p>
</div>
```

Of course, in a real Page Template, we could simply use the HTML element ol which automatically makes an ordered list.

modules makes it possible to import Python modules in a Page Template. Since Page Templates are not intended to execute heavy application logic, this should generally be avoided. Example:

```
<p tal:define="IRecipe
    modules/worldcookery.interfaces/IRecipe"
   tal:condition="python:
                    IRecipe.providedBy(context)">
  The object is indeed a recipe.
</p>
```

context is the object that the Page Template is supposed to display. Page Templates are generally used to present a particular type of object's data to the browser, thus acting as mediators between the browser and the object. In Component Architecture terms, we say that the Page Template is a *view* for the object. The object that a view is displaying is always called its context. Example:

```
<h2 tal:content="context/name/title">recipe name goes here</h2>

<p>Cooking <span tal:replace="context/name" />
will take
<span tal:replace="context/time_to_cook" />
minutes.</p>
```

view represents the view component that the Page Template is part of in case the Page Template is used as a view. Page Templates are usually used without an extra view component. Then such a component is created for them automatically. However, if you specify such an extra component in the configuration, you can have access it to through this variable. Enhanced view components will be covered in Chapter 13.

Summary

- Zope is equipped with an extensive HTML/XML templating system called *Page Templates* or *ZPT*.
- Page Templates interoperate with any HTML/XML capable application, such as WYSIWYG editors, as they remain well-formed XML documents.
- ZPT's templating language, TAL, uses attributes in a special namespace to specify commands.
- Page Templates interact with other components by means of various expressions, most importantly *path expressions*.

Flashback

Page Templates are a part of Zope since version 2.5 and probably one of the greatest innovations of Zope 2. The implementation shipping with Zope 3 is very similar to its Zope 2 predecessor. Therefore, if you are already familiar with Page Templates, you can apply all of that knowledge in Zope 3, too. The few and minimal differences include

- partially different set of global variables, for example `here` is now called `context`,
- traversal namespaces like in URLs, for example `@@` for traversing to views,
- TALES namespace adapters as described in Chapter 14.

Note that DTML is not used for rendering HTML markup at all anymore.

Rocky says...

The endless debate of which templating or scripting display page technology is best reaches beyond that of just J2EE. Zope itself has several options, although Page Templates tend to be the prevalent of these much like JSP is for J2EE. Anyone familiar with JSP or any other Java based templating language should have no problem handling the differences in page templates. The big difference between JSP and ZPT being that ZPT makes it much harder (but not impossible) to implement business logic right in the display logic.

7.3 A simple view Page Template

Having seen how to generate HTML using Page Templates, let us put this knowledge to use and write a Page Template to present the information we have saved in a recipe. See Example 7.3.1 for the code listing.

Page Templates remain valid XHTML documents, so nothing prevents us from viewing them in a regular browser off the file system. Figure 7.2 shows `recipeview.pt` being displayed in a browser. Since the browser does not interpret TAL, we see the default text we put in instead of actual values of a recipe. It would not have been necessary to fill elements with a default text, but it makes it easier to view the template without a TAL interpreter, for example directly from the file system (see Figure 7.2).

The template in its current form is not very pretty. We can therefore send it to a designer who could edit it using regular HTML design software. The

Example 7.3.1 View Page Template for displaying recipes
(`browser/recipeview.pt`)

```
1   <html xmlns="http://www.w3.org/1999/xhtml"
2          xmlns:tal="http://xml.zope.org/namespaces/tal">
3   <head>
4     <title tal:content="context/name/title">recipe name goes here</title>
5   </head>
6   <body>
7
8     <h2 tal:content="context/name/title">recipe name goes here</h2>
9
10    <table>
11      <tbody>
12        <tr>
13          <td>Time needed for preparation:</td>
14          <td><tal:var replace="context/time_to_cook">xyz</tal:var> mins</
               td>
15        </tr>
16
17        <tr>
18          <td>Ingredients:</td>
19          <td>
20            <ul>
21              <li tal:repeat="ingredient context/ingredients"
22                  tal:content="ingredient">ingredients go here</li>
23            </ul>
24          </td>
25        </tr>
26
27        <tr>
28          <td>Needed kitchen tools:</td>
29          <td>
30            <ul>
31              <li tal:repeat="tool context/tools"
32                  tal:content="tool">tools go here</li>
33            </ul>
34          </td>
35        </tr>
36
37      </tbody>
38    </table>
39
40    <p tal:content="context/description">Longer description goes here.</p>
41
42  </body>
43  </html>
```

2. In order to let the Page Template remain a valid XHTML document, we define
   an XML namespace for TAL commands. By convention, the namespace prefix
   is `tal`.

Example 7.3.1 (continued)

4 and 8. We use the global context variable to access the current recipe's values. Thanks to path expressions, it is quite obvious even to non-programmers what is inserted into the markup.

21 and 31. Recipes store two lists: a list of ingredients and a list of tools. Here in the Page Template, we want to display these lists as *unordered lists* (ul), each entry being a list item (li). Therefore, we generate an li element for each item in the list and display the item value inside.

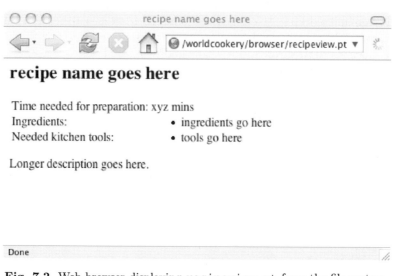

Fig. 7.2. Web browser displaying recipeview.pt from the file system.

default values will give the designer an idea where the real text will appear in the dynamic version. As long as the TAL commands we put into the template remain there, a designer is free to work with any HTML-capable tools, which is another benefit of Page Templates being valid XHTML documents.

Using and registering view Page Templates

We now have the Page Template sitting in a file in the worldcookery. browser package. How do we tell Zope that we want to use it as the index.html view for recipes?

The browser:page ZCML directive which we have used in Section 7.1 already to register the simple, Python-based browser page provides a shortcut for Page Templates. Instead of specifying a class parameter, we can use the template parameter and pass the filename of the Page Template. The result would look like this:

```
...
<browser:page
    for="worldcookery.interfaces.IRecipe"
    name="index.html"
    template="recipeview.pt"
    permission="zope.View"
    />
...
```

This would register the Page Template as a browser page. The effect is the same of the original configuration we provided in Example 7.1.2.

We shall not use the shortcut here. Firstly, we already have a class that's configured and working. We only have to adjust it to refer to the Page Template. Secondly, we will need the class in the next section again. It would not make much sense to throw it away now and recreate it later.

When views, especially browser pages are published, they are called. In other words, their __call__ method is invoked. That is why we did the plain text "rendering" in the __call__ method before. It is also why we now have to replace the __call__ method with something that refers to the Page Template. Example 7.3.2 shows how that is done.

Example 7.3.2 Referring to a Page Template from a browser page class (`browser/recipe.py`)

```
1  from zope.publisher.browser import BrowserPage
2  from zope.app.pagetemplate import ViewPageTemplateFile
3
4  class ViewRecipe(BrowserPage):
5
6      __call__ = ViewPageTemplateFile('recipeview.pt')
```

Since the browser page class itself has stayed where it is, its initial configuration does not change. We could now once again fire up the debug shell and test the view lookup. The bare HTML is not exactly easy on the eyes, though. Let us therefore go directly to the browser and once again display the recipe. Figure 7.3 shows us the result of the Page Template rendering.

Previewing content

As a bonus, we can also add a management interface tab that lets one preview recipes. Zope already provides a template called preview.pt for this in the zope.app.preview package. We will only have to register it for recipes (using a browser:page directive) and add an entry to the zmi_views browser menu. This menu contains common ZMI views. These are browser pages that make up the *Zope Management Interface* (ZMI) and typically

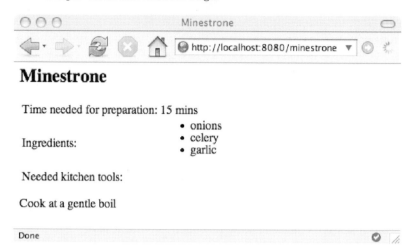

Fig. 7.3. Displaying a recipe using the simple view Page Template.

include pages for editing an object's data or metadata, adding contents to a container, etc. The zmi_views menu provides a visible list of such ZMI pages for an object.

Example 7.3.3 shows how to configure the *Preview* page, including the menu entry. The result will look something like Figure 7.4. Note that the user warnings resulting from this configuration can be safely ignored for now. We will discuss them in Chapter 9.

Summary

- Simple Page Templates can be viewed off of the file system for preview or demonstration purposes.
- View Page Templates are either be registered directly using the browser:page ZCML directive or attached to an existing view class using ViewPageTemplateFile.
- Files in ZCML directives are found relative to the current package.

7.4 Enhanced browser pages

We can now easily display recipes as HTML using Page Templates. ZPTs are a great way to make XML markup dynamic. Their functionality is limited otherwise, though. This is intended because their only role is to cover presentation. If Page Templates had the same functionality as the Python environment, you could be tempted to mix application logic and presentation. Separating the two is essential for Component Architecture.

Example 7.3.3 Configuring a *Preview* page
(`browser/configure.zcml`)

```
1   <configure
2       xmlns="http://namespaces.zope.org/zope"
3       xmlns:browser="http://namespaces.zope.org/browser"
4       >
5
6     <browser:page
7         for="worldcookery.interfaces.IRecipe"
8         name="index.html"
9         class=".recipe.ViewRecipe"
10        permission="zope.View"
11        />
12
13    <configure package="zope.app.preview">
14      <browser:page
15          for="worldcookery.interfaces.IRecipe"
16          name="preview.html"
17          template="preview.pt"
18          permission="zope.ManageContent"
19          menu="zmi_views" title="Preview"
20          />
21    </configure>
22
23  </configure>
```

13 and 21. The `preview.pt` file lies in the `zope.app.preview` package. Since files are found relative to the current package, we wrap the following `browser:page` directive in another `configure` directive and set the current package explicitly. This way, `browser:page` will look in `zope.app.preview` and not in `worldcookery.present` where the configuration file actually is located.

19. We would like the *Preview* page to appear in the manage interface tabs. `browser:page` allows you to automatically define a menu entry for the registered page, which we here do for the `zmi_views` menu, the menu that contains management tabs. The `title` parameter refers to the text displayed for the menu item.

Sometimes you might need presentation logic that is outside the scope of ZPTs. For example when additional components are needed to perform extra computation on the data to be presented. The solution is to provide additional methods on the browser page class used earlier this chapter.

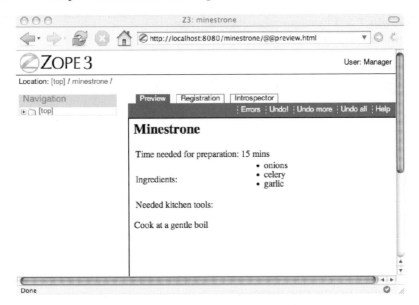

Fig. 7.4. A *Preview* page in the management interface.

Rendering plain text

The `description` field of recipes is usually plain text. Any HTML that a
user would enter would already be escaped by the Page Template. However,
any plain text formatting, such as empty lines for starting paragraphs, is
ignored when inserted into the HTML. Browsers do not interpret this formatting.

Zope has support for rendering different types of plain text to HTML.
Among fancier renderers for StructuredText [22] and reStructuredText [30],
it can also render simple plain text to HTML. This support for text rendering
can be found in the `zope.app.renderer` package.

To render a portion of text to HTML, we have to tell the renderer machinery what type of text we are dealing with. For this, three factories that
create marked Unicode objects are provided:

- `zope.source.plaintext`[5] for regular plain text,
- `zope.source.stx` for StructuredText,
- and `zope.source.rest` for reStructuredText.

When text is fed to one of these factories, a rendering view can render it to
HTML. Example 7.4.1 demonstrates this by treating the `description` field
of recipes as a plain text source.

---

[5] These dotted names do not describe Python import paths but factory names
(utility names). It is common practice to prepend such names with package
names to avoid ambiguities.

Example 7.4.1 Browser page class with additional view logic
(`browser/recipe.py`)

```
1   from zope.component import createObject, getMultiAdapter
2   from zope.publisher.browser import BrowserPage
3   from zope.app.pagetemplate import ViewPageTemplateFile
4
5   class ViewRecipe(BrowserPage):
6
7       __call__ = ViewPageTemplateFile('recipeview.pt')
8
9       def renderDescription(self):
10          plaintext = createObject('zope.source.plaintext',
11                                   self.context.description)
12          view = getMultiAdapter((plaintext, self.request), name=u'')
13          return view.render()
```

9–13. This method will be called later from the Page Template. As introduced
in Chapter 5, the `createObject` function creates new objects by invoking
factories. Here, we use the plain text factory to convert the recipe's description
attribute into a marked source text for which we can one line later get a view
that will render us the HTML.

Although rendering plain text to HTML is a simple operation requiring
just a few lines of Python code, it is preferable to *not* put this code in the
Page Template. Page Templates should only contain basic rules for generating
dynamic markup. They should not be bloated with Python expressions which
make them hard to read and hard to maintain and exchange. The solution is
to add the code as a method of the view class, and to call this method from
the Page Template. This is described in Example 7.4.2.

To test the effects of this change, create a recipe with a description containing formatted text, for example text containing several new-line characters, and see what happens when you display it.

Summary

- Application logic in Page Templates should be limited.
- Methods of the browser page class can aid the Page Template when
  more complex logic is needed than Page Templates can or should
  handle.
- Zope provides rendering functionality for a few different types of
  plain text in the `zope.app.renderer` package.

Example 7.4.2 Recipe view template using the view class's rendering functionality (`browser/recipeview.pt`)

```
1   <html xmlns="http://www.w3.org/1999/xhtml"
2         xmlns:tal="http://xml.zope.org/namespaces/tal"
3         xmlns:metal="http://xml.zope.org/namespaces/metal"
4         xmlns:i18n="http://xml.zope.org/namespaces/i18n"
5         metal:use-macro="context/@@standard_macros/page"
6         i18n:domain="worldcookery">
7   <head>
8     <title metal:fill-slot="title"
9            tal:content="context/name/title">recipe name goes here</title>
10  </head>
11  <body>
12  <div metal:fill-slot="body">
13
14    <h2 tal:content="context/name/title">recipe name goes here</h2>
15
16    <table>
17      <tbody>
18
19        ...
20
21      </tbody>
22    </table>
23
24    <p tal:content="structure view/renderDescription">
25      Longer description goes here.
26    </p>
27
28  </div>
29  </body>
30  </html>
```

24–46. To access the browser page class's method, we use the top-level `view` variable. The TALES expression will automatically call the method and we end up with the rendered HTML. Thus, it is important not to forget to use the `structure` modifier in the TALES expression, otherwise the resulting HTML would be escaped by ZPT.

8

Browser Forms

We are nearing the end of Part I. So far we have learned to describe a recipe's data model, to make a persistent implementation and to display this data to a web browser. To bring the first part to its grand finale, we will *modify* a recipe's data. The most common way to do that in a web environment is through browser forms.

Using Zope 2

Most of what is presented in this chapter can also be done with Zope 2. In particular, `zope.formlib` can be used just as well as Zope 3's widget library. Just note that instead of importing the page form base classes from `zope.formlib.form` you should use the ones from `Products.Five.formlib.formbase` as they provide the necessary compatibility for Zope 2. Other than that, the rule regarding `ViewPageTemplateFile` as discussed in the last chapter still applies.

8.1 Schema-based forms

As you know, to write HTML forms you need a `form` element with several `input` or `select` elements inside. This is not hard but it is tedious if it is done manually every time. The hard part is actually writing form handlers. Values submitted from forms need to be processed, validated and applied. Fortunately, Zope provides a lot of automation here.

Having used a schema to describe each property in the recipe API now pays off. Zope has several mechanisms to provide automatic views for such components. Using this information, Zope can ask the user for input regarding each field. This means little code is necessary for basic schema-based forms.

Furthermore, Zope can do automatic validation of the user input. In Chapter 4, we have validated an object according to a schema using the Python interpreter. Here, the form machinery uses the same mechanism to validate the user's input. The object in question is not modified if the input does not validate according to the schema. That way, we can be sure that the time_to_cook variable only contains an integer, and so on. If the user enters something that does not validate, the form machinery will present an error message next to the input field.

A simple edit form

The simplest form is a form that lets the user edit the data of an object according to a certain schema. We call this type of form an *edit form*. Zope's form machinery, zope.formlib provides a convenient base class for implementing edit forms. Example 8.1.1 demonstrates a simple edit form.

Example 8.1.1 Simple edit form (browser/recipe.py)

```
1   ...
2
3   from zope.formlib.form import EditForm, Fields
4   from worldcookery.interfaces import IRecipe
5
6   class RecipeEditForm(EditForm):
7       form_fields = Fields(IRecipe)
8       label = u"Edit recipe"
```

1 and 6. The EditForm class provides all the necessary form generation and validation functionality. It is very convenient to subclass it and override certain attributes or methods to customize the behaviour (more on that later). The customizable API is documented in zope.formlib's IFormBaseCustomization interface.

1 and 7. To tell the form generator which fields should occur in our form, we need to provide the form_fields attribute. It contains a collection of *form fields* (not to be confused with schema fields). The easiest way to create form fields is to generate them from their corresponding schema fields. Here we obviously use the IRecipe schema since the form is for editing recipe objects.

From a technical point of view, forms are just browser pages. Their registration happens the same way as the browser pages registration in the last chapter. Example 8.1.2 shows the ZCML directive.

Customizing the template

We can now walk up to a recipe object in the Zope Management Interface and edit it by choosing the *Edit* tab. The form we see looks like the one shown in Figure 8.1. However, errors that might occur due to invalid input data are not displayed in a user-friendly manner.

Example 8.1.2 Registering a simple edit form
(`browser/configure.zcml`)

```
1    ...
2    <browser:page
3        for="worldcookery.interfaces.IRecipe"
4        name="edit.html"
5        class=".recipe.RecipeEditForm"
6        permission="zope.ManageContent"
7        menu="zmi_views" title="Edit"
8        />
9    ...
```

6. Last chapter we protected the index.html view with the zope.View permission. This edit form lets us change the data of recipes. We therefore pick
   a permission for this view that is not available to everyone but to authorized
   content editors only.

7. Like the *Preview* page, we would like this edit form to appear in the ZMI tabs,
   thus register it for the zmi_views menu.

Fig. 8.1. A simple edit form for recipes

In order to take more control over a form, zope.formlib allows us to supply a custom template to render the form. This gives us as much freedom as we want when designing a form. We would still want to use the framework's ability to display the input widgets, action buttons, etc. Custom templates usually just change the arrangement of the form elements. Example 8.1.3 shows an example of a customized edit form template displaying validation errors next to the respective widget. Binding this custom template to the form again happens via a ViewPageTemplateFile instance, as shown in Example 8.1.4.

Example 8.1.3 Customized template for an edit form (browser/form.pt)

```
1   <html xmlns="http://www.w3.org/1999/xhtml"
2         xmlns:tal="http://xml.zope.org/namespaces/tal"
3         xmlns:metal="http://xml.zope.org/namespaces/metal"
4         metal:use-macro="context/@@standard_macros/view">
5   <body>
6   <div metal:fill-slot="body">
7   <form class="edit-form" enctype="multipart/form-data" method="post"
8         action="." tal:attributes="action request/URL">
9
10    <h1 tal:content="view/label">Edit something</h1>
11
12    <div class="summary" tal:condition="view/status"
13         tal:content="view/status">Status</div>
14
15    <div class="row" tal:repeat="widget view/widgets">
16      <div class="label">
17        <label for="field.name" title="The widget's hint"
18               tal:attributes="for widget/name; title widget/hint"
19               tal:content="widget/label">Label</label>
20      </div>
21
22      <div tal:condition="widget/error"
23           tal:content="structure widget/error">Error</div>
24
25      <div class="field">
26        <input tal:replace="structure widget" />
27      </div>
28    </div>
29
30    <span class="actionButtons" tal:condition="view/availableActions">
31      <input tal:repeat="action view/actions"
32             tal:replace="structure action/render"
33             />
34    </span>
35
36  </form>
37  </div>
38  </body>
39  </html>
```

Example 8.1.3 (continued)

3–4. This command from the `metal` namespace will let the page adopt the common layout of all other Zope Management Interface pages. This feature is described in detail in the next chapter.

8. A form always submits to itself because the form view not only provides the rendering capabilities but also the data handling and validation facilities.

10, 12–13, 15, and 30–34. We know from the previous chapter that Page Templates that are bound to a page can access this page object via the `view` variable. In this case, it is an instance of the `RecipeEditForm` class. Forms provide a specific API that allows templates to get the necessary information to render the form properly, such as the label, a status message, a list of widgets and action buttons. For more information, consult the `IFormBaseCustomization` interface from the `zope.formlib` package.

17–19, 22–23, and 16. Here we see a demonstration of how to deal with individual widgets. They also have labels and hints (which are typically derived from the schema fields' titles and descriptions) and they might have errors associated with them. Simply calling them will render their HTML code. The widget API for input widgets is documented in the `IInputWidget` interface from the `zope.app.form` package.

Example 8.1.4 Binding a custom template to a form
(`browser/recipe.py`)

```
1   ...
2
3   from zope.formlib.form import EditForm, Fields
4   from worldcookery.interfaces import IRecipe
5
6   class RecipeEditForm(EditForm):
7       form_fields = Fields(IRecipe)
8       label = u"Edit recipe"
9
10      template = ViewPageTemplateFile('form.pt')
```

Named templates

Up until now, we have used `ViewPageTemplateFile` to bind a Page Template to an existing browser page class. For the `ViewRecipe` browser page that merely displays recipes, this has been perfectly fine because both the template and class are meant to work together as a single component. With the edit form we just implemented, however, the class itself is already a functional component and the template just expresses a certain customization of that form. Furthermore, it might be desirable to once more customize the template, without having to reimplement the whole form class, just so that it refers to the new template.

Example 8.1.5 Edit form referring to a template by name (named template) (`browser/recipe.py`)

```
1   ...
2
3   from zope.formlib.form import EditForm, Fields
4   from zope.formlib.namedtemplate import NamedTemplate
5   from zope.formlib.namedtemplate import NamedTemplateImplementation
6   from worldcookery.interfaces import IRecipe
7
8   class RecipeEditForm(EditForm):
9       form_fields = Fields(IRecipe)
10      label = u"Edit recipe"
11
12      template = NamedTemplate('worldcookery.form')
13
14  form_template = NamedTemplateImplementation(
15      ViewPageTemplateFile('form.pt'))
```

4 and 12.   The form class now refers to the template via a `NamedTemplate` instance which is passed a name (an ID) of the template, not a specific file name. The template will be looked up as an adapter for the class, named according to the name.

5 and 14–15.   Here we declare the template that shall be the result of the named template lookup. This is the implementation of the named template, the opposite end to the statement described above, so to speak. The implementation of a named template is done by passing the actual template object (which we still create using `ViewPageTemplateFile`) to `NamedTemplateImplementation`. The second argument is the page class (or an interface) for which the template will be registered as an adapter.

Zope's `zope.formlib` package offers a solution for this: *named templates*. Unlike templates bound to classes via `ViewPageTemplateFile`, named templates are bound to a page class by a simple identifier, a name. This name, in turn, is used to look up the template as an adapter. By customizing this adapter you can customize the template. The original class that refers to the template just by its name does not have to altered. Example 8.1.5 depicts the changes to the edit form class. Since the form class will now look up the template as a named adapter, we will also have to register the

Example 8.1.6 Registering a named template
(`browser/configure.zcml`)

```
1   ...
2   <adapter
3       factory=".recipe.form_template"
4       for=".recipe.RecipeEditForm"
5       name="worldcookery.editform"
6       />
7   ...
```

template as such. The template itself is already defined in Example 8.1.5, it
only needs to be registered as an adapter. The short piece of ZCML that is
necessary to do this is listed in Example 8.1.6.

Fig. 8.2. A customized edit form template with improved error display

It is now possible for third party code to supply a different edit form template for recipes without having to supply a completely new form class. All they have to do is provide a different named template implementation and register it as an adapter under the correct name. Note that named templates are not limited to forms; they can be used on any browser page class, but the extra indirection usually only pays off for complicated browser pages such as forms.

Summary

- Zope can render HTML forms and validate form input based on the type specifications in a schema.
- Zope's form machinery is available from the `zope.formlib` and `zope.app.form` packages.
- Forms are browser pages inheriting from a base class such as `EditForm`. They may use a custom template to render the form.
- Instead of referencing a hard-coded template object, browser page classes can refer to templates by name (*named templates*) to allow customization of just the template.

8.2 Adding objects and add forms

Until now we have been creating recipes through the interactive debugger prompt. We can edit and display recipes, but we cannot add them through the web interface. We will now look at ways to create and add objects.

The *Add* menu

The most convenient way to create and add objects to folders is through an entry in the *Add* browser menu. We have discussed the zmi_views menu which lists all the Zope Management Interfaces views of an object. The *Add* menu lists all the types of objects that are addable to a container. It is displayed on the right hand side in the default Zope Management Interface. Example 8.2.1 shows how to configure an entry for this menu.

Menus are browser specific features. A menu would not make much sense in an FTP or WebDAV context. That is why we usually speak of *browser menus* and use the `browser` XML namespace in ZCML, as we do for all browser-related configuration. Browser menus will be covered in detail in Chapter 13.

If you now start Zope and go to a folder's *Contents* view (e.g. in the root folder), you will see there is a new content type to add: Recipe. When you click to add one, Zope will ask you for a name of the new object in that

Example 8.2.1 Configuring an *Add* menu item
(`browser/configure.zcml`)

```
1    ...
2    <browser:addMenuItem
3        title="Recipe"
4        factory="worldcookery.Recipe"
5        permission="zope.ManageContent"
6        />
7    ...
```

4. The `factory` parameter refers to a content factory as we know it from Chapter 5 (the `IFactory` utility). We refer to the factory we registered in that chapter by name. Alternatively, we could use the `class` parameter and refer to the `Recipe` class directly.

folder, much like a filename. Once a valid name is provided and **Enter** has been pressed, Zope will create a new recipe object and add it to the folder. The recipe object is created by calling the factory we specified in the ZCML directive.

(a) The *Add* menu now containing an entry for recipes

(b) Providing a name for the recipe in the container

Add forms

We can now create recipes and later edit their data. We should be happy. However, it would be nicer if we could supply the recipe data *before* the object was created and added to the folder. To do this we need a form that does not operate on an existing object, but creates one for us, based on the initial data we have entered. Such forms are called *add forms* (as opposed to the *edit forms* we discussed in the last section). We have discussed the basics of form generation in Zope, we will now discuss the difference between an edit from and an add form.

The biggest difference is that edit forms can work on an existing object while add forms cannot. Add forms have to take care of creating the object in question, filling it with the data from the form input and then adding it to the folder. Fortunately, most of this is automated using an *adding view*. This view component takes care of all the processes involved when adding objects through-the-web, such as presenting add forms, checking object names and actually adding the object. The adding view is usually registered under the simple name of +. You can easily verify this by looking at some of the URLs of entries in the *Add* menu.

While edit forms operate on the object they modify, add forms operate on the adding view. That is, their context is the adding view (since there is no other object to deal with at the moment). Adding views provide the IAdding interface from the zope.app.container package. The add form uses the API from this interface to operate on the adding view. In Example 8.2.2, this is not apparent because the AddForm base class saves us this work. We only have to take care of creating the object and settings its data. It does become apparent, however, when registering the add form, as shown in Example 8.2.3.

Summary

- A convenient way to add objects to a folder is using the *Add* browser menu.
- Add forms create and add objects with some initial data from a form.
- Add forms are views for the adding view which is described by the IAdding interface and whose name simply is +.

8.3 Custom widgets

We have seen that generated add and edit forms can be enormously convenient. Not only is the rendering of the form automated but validation is also handled automatically. We have also seen how to customize the arrangement of form elements (widgets) by supplying a custom template. In this section, we will learn how to customize a form element. We will implement a custom widget.

Example 8.2.2 An add form implementation (`browser/recipe.py`)

```
1   ...
2
3   from zope.formlib.form import AddForm, applyChanges
4
5   class RecipeAddForm(AddForm):
6       form_fields = Fields(IRecipe)
7       label = u"Add recipe"
8
9       template = NamedTemplate('worldcookery.form')
10
11      def create(self, data):
12          recipe = createObject(u'worldcookery.Recipe')
13          applyChanges(recipe, self.form_fields, data)
14          return recipe
```

3 and 5. We now use the `AddForm` base class, not `EditForm`.

9. We refer to the same named template as the edit form. Note that this would still allow us to use different templates for add and edit forms because the form object itself is adapted. Different adapters for add and edit forms would therefore yield different named templates. In our case, they will not.

11–14. Implementing this method is the least an add form implementation must do. Its responsibility is to create a new object (we use the factory from Chapter 5) and apply the form input data (`data` parameter) to it, which is best done using the `applyChanges` function. Other methods take care of providing a correct name for the object and adding it to the folder. All of these are customizable and documented in the `IAddFormCustomization` interface.

Widgets

An automatically generated form is composed of components called *widgets* which are representations of schema fields. Widgets are *views* for schema fields, because they are a request-specific representation of them and are mediators between the field and the user. Being adapters, they can easily be customized.

Different types of widgets provide different functionality. Widgets that display field data to the user agent, be it a browser or something else, provide `IDisplayWidget` from the `zope.app.form.interfaces` module. Widgets that provide editing functionality and retrieve input from the user, provide `IInputWidget`. Therefore, widgets are not looked up by name (like other views) but by the interface they provide.

Browser widgets typically present themselves as HTML form fields. Simple browser widgets facilitate the text input field, more complex ones use radio buttons, check boxes and/or other input fields. In the forms we have seen so

---

Example 8.2.3 Registering an add form and its named template
(browser/configure.zcml)

```
1     ...
2     <browser:addMenuItem
3         title="Recipe"
4         factory="worldcookery.Recipe"
5         view="worldcookery.Recipe"
6         permission="zope.ManageContent"
7         />
8
9     <browser:page
10        for="zope.app.container.interfaces.IAdding"
11        name="worldcookery.Recipe"
12        class=".recipe.RecipeAddForm"
13        permission="zope.ManageContent"
14        />
15
16    <adapter
17        factory=".recipe.form_template"
18        for=".recipe.RecipeAddForm"
19        name="worldcookery.form"
20        />
21    ...
```

10. Add forms are registered for the adding view, therefore we specify the `IAdding` interface here.

11 and 5. Because add forms are views of the adding view, the name of an add form should be unique among all other possible add forms. Thus it is a good idea to use a dotted name here. Note that we also create a reference to the add form in the `addMenuItem` directive (via its view name). That way, the adding view will know about the add form and redirect to it from the menu item.

---

far, the browser widget for `TextLine` and `Int` fields use a simple text input box. The `List` field, however, which is used to describe a recipe's ingredients and tools, requires a much more complex browser widget.

A better sequence widget

Since the default list widget provided by Zope tries to be as general as possible, it is complex and not user-friendly. The form has to be reloaded every time one adds or removes an item of the sequence. It would really be much more convenient if one could add, remove, and sort entries right away. The typical way to do this is making the page dynamic in the browser using *ECMAScript*.

Before we can dive into client-side programming, we shall implement the widget component. Our widget needs to be an adapter *for* the list field

Table 8.1. Alternate input widgets for selected fields

Field[a]	Widget[b]	Description
Bool	CheckBoxWidget	Represents a Boolean field with a checkbox. This is the default widget.
Bool	BooleanRadioWidget	Displays two radio buttons labelled *on* and *off* to indicate Boolean true or false.
Bool	BooleanSelectWidget	Displays a list with two options, *on* and *off*, that indicate Boolean true or false.
Bool	BooleanDropdownWidget	Presents a drop-down list with two options, *on* and *off*.
Choice (with vocabulary)	SelectWidget	Displays items from the vocabulary in a list.
Choice (with vocabulary)	DropdownWidget	Presents a drop-down list with items from the vocabulary. This is the default widget.
Choice (with vocabulary)	RadioWidget	Displays a radio box for every item from the vocabulary.
Choice (with source)	source.SourceSelectWidget	same as SelectWidget
Choice (with source)	source.SourceDropdownWidget	same as DropdownWidget
Choice (with source)	source.SourceRadioWidget	same as RadioWidget

[a] Listed fields can be imported from zope.schema.

[b] Listed widgets can be imported from zope.app.form.browser.

Fig. 8.3. An automatically generated add form.

(zope.schema.List) and the browser request (IBrowserRequest). It will *provide* input functionality (IInputWidget). Luckily, the zope.app. form package provides us with a base class, SimpleInputWidget, that implements most of the functionality required by an input widget, making our custom component shown in Example 8.3.1 quite short. SimpleInputWidget offers the following methods for custom implementations to override:

_getFormInput extracts the input value from the submitted form. This typically just accesses the right form field from the request.

_toFieldValue converts an input value to a value suitable for the field. Usually the widget will already have ensured this, the default implementation makes sure that the field's default value is returned when input is missing.

_toFormValue converts a field value to a string that can be inserted into the form.

_getFormValue returns a field value to a string that can be inserted into the form. The difference to _toFormValue is that it also takes into account when a form has already been submitted but needs to be re-rendered (e.g. due to an input error).

Since Page Templates do a much better job of assembling HTML than Python, we delegate all the actual widget markup off to a template whose source code is shown in Example 8.3.2. The Page Template in turn tells the browser to load a file (sequence.js) which contains the necessary EC-MAScript functions to make the widget dynamic in the browser.

Even though the widget's Page Template is technically not a full HTML document (it is lacking the required document and body elements), most browsers will be able to display it. Since we again provided sensible default values where TAL commands make the widget dynamically work in a form, we can view it in a browser without a problem. Even better, the dynamic features provided by the ECMAScript functions work, too, so we can actually test the widget in a browser before embedding it into a form, as shown in Figure 8.4.

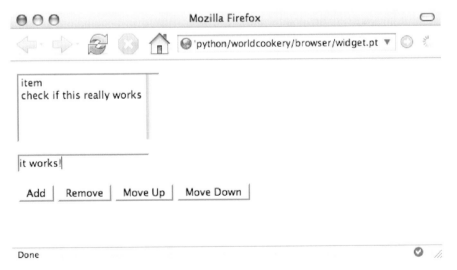

Fig. 8.4. Testing the widget's functionality from the file system.

Example 8.3.1 Custom sequence widget class (`browser/widget.py`)

```
1   from zope.component import getMultiAdapter
2   from zope.app.form.interfaces import IInputWidget
3   from zope.app.form.browser.widget import SimpleInputWidget
4   from zope.app.pagetemplate.viewpagetemplatefile import
        ViewPageTemplateFile
5
6   class DynamicSequenceWidget(SimpleInputWidget):
7
8       __call__ = ViewPageTemplateFile('widget.pt')
9
10      def _getFormInput(self):
11          value = super(DynamicSequenceWidget, self)._getFormInput()
12          # Make sure that we always retrieve a list object from the
13          # request, even if only a single item or nothing has been
14          # entered
15          if value is None:
16              value = []
17          if not isinstance(value, list):
18              value = [value]
19          return value
20
21      def hasInput(self):
22          return (self.name + '.marker') in self.request.form
23
24      def hidden(self):
25          s = ''
26          for value in self._getFormValue():
27              widget = getMultiAdapter(
28                  (self.context.value_type, self.request), IInputWidget)
29              widget.name = self.name
30              widget.setRenderedValue(value)
31              s += widget.hidden()
32          return s
```

3 and 6. We import and subclass `SimpleInputWidget` which already provides most of the basic functionality for a browser input widget specified in `IInputWidget`.

8. When widgets are rendered, they are called as if they were functions; the returned HTML is pasted into the form. To support callability, we provide a `__call__` attribute. However, instead of assembling the HTML ourselves in a method, we use a Page Template file called `widget.pt` to render the markup (see Example 8.3.2).

10–19. Here we extend a method of the `SimpleInputWidget` base class which retrieves the input value from the form. Normally, it does the right thing, except when the list widget only contains one item. That is why need to make sure that the returned input value is always a list.

Example 8.3.1 (continued)

21–22. Widgets need to be able to determine whether the request contains an input value for them. In case of sequence widgets, an empty sequence could also be a valid input value. We therefore do not check for occurrence of input data but for the occurrence of a special marker that is inserted by the Page Template.

24–32. Sometimes browser widgets need to be rendered as hidden fields, for example when only a part of the overall form should be editable, for example in a wizard. The `hidden` method takes care of this by getting a widget for all elements in the sequence and having their hidden field rendered.

To enable the new widget in the forms we need to adjust the add and edit form classes once more. This change is explained in Example 8.3.3. We also must not forget to register the ECMAScript file as a browser resource, as mentioned in Example 8.3.2. Like all registrations, this is done in ZCML, with the following simple directive:

```
<browser:resource name="sequence.js" file="sequence.js" />
```

After restarting Zope, you should see a recipe edit form as shown in Figure 8.5.

Summary

- Automatically generated forms are composed of widget components which can be customized.
- Widgets represent schema fields; they are unnamed *views* providing functionality.
- `SimpleInputWidget` from the `zope.app.form.browser.widget` module provides most of the functionality needed for a browser input widget.
- Custom widgets are assigned to the `custom_widget` attribute of the corresponding form field.

Rocky says...

Java developers who are accustomed to using JavaServer Faces already know how to construct reusable UI components. With Zope's `formlib` package they can now combine UI components to build larger components cutting down on code duplication further.

Example 8.3.2 Custom sequence widget template (`browser/widget.pt`)

```
1   <div xmlns:tal="http://xml.zope.org/namespaces/tal">
2
3   <script type="text/javascript" src="sequence.js"
4           tal:attributes="src context/++resource++sequence.js">
5   </script>
6
7   <p tal:define="form_value view/_getFormValue">
8     <input type="hidden" name="foo.marker" id="foo.marker"
9            tal:define="marker string:${view/name}.marker"
10           tal:attributes="name marker; id marker" />
11     <tal:loop tal:repeat="item form_value">
12       <input type="hidden" name="foo" id="value.0.foo" value="item"
13              tal:condition="item"
14              tal:attributes="name string:${view/name};
15                              id string:value.${repeat/item/index}.${view/
                                  name};
16                              value item" />
17     </tal:loop>
18     <input type="hidden" id="foo" tal:attributes="id view/name" />
19     <select id="select.foo" size="5"
20             tal:attributes="id string:select.${view/name};
21                             size python:min(max(len(form_value), 5), 12)">
22       <tal:loop tal:repeat="item form_value">
23         <option tal:condition="item" tal:content="item"
24                 tal:attributes="value item">item</option>
25       </tal:loop>
26     </select>
27   </p>
28
29   <p>
30     <input type="text" id="input.foo"
31            tal:attributes="id string:input.${view/name}"
32            value="Click here to add an item" onfocus="this.value=''" />
33   </p>
34   <p>
35     <button
36         type="button" onclick="sequenceAddItem('foo')"
37         tal:attributes="onclick string:sequenceAddItem('${view/name}')">
38       Add
39     </button>
40     <button
41         type="button" onclick="sequenceRemoveItem('foo')"
42         tal:attributes="onclick string:sequenceRemoveItem('${view/name}')">
43       Remove
44     </button>
45     <button
46         type="button" onclick="sequenceMoveItem('foo', -1)"
47         tal:attributes="onclick string:sequenceMoveItem('${view/name}', -1)
                  ">
48       Move Up
49     </button>
```

Example 8.3.2 (continued)

```
50    <button
51       type="button" onclick="sequenceMoveItem('foo', 1)"
52       tal:attributes="onclick string:sequenceMoveItem('${view/name}', 1)
                ">
53       Move Down
54    </button>
55  </p>
56  </div>
```

3–5. As mentioned before, we want to make our widget dynamic in the browser; we therefore need to use a set of ECMAScript functions that we load from a separate file, a browser resource. For more information on browser resources, please refer to Chapter 10.

8–10. Here we insert a marker field that will let the widget know whether it was part of a form or not, even when the widget has no input data.

12–16. These hidden input elements will store the entered items. The ECMAScript code will create more of them when new items are entered. When the form is eventually submitted, Zope will decode these values to a sequence.

19–26. We use a select box to show all entered values. The box will be pre-filled with the sequence data if there is any available.

30–32. One can enter a new item into this input field. When the *Add* button is pressed, it will be added to the above select box.

35–54. Four buttons allow one to edit the sequence items in the select box dynamically. When a button is clicked, a corresponding ECMAScript function is called to operate on the items, such as adding or deleting one, or moving them around.

Example 8.3.3 Using a custom widget in forms (`browser/recipe.py`)

```
1   ...
2
3   from zope.formlib.form import EditForm, AddForm, Fields, applyChanges
4   from zope.formlib.namedtemplate import NamedTemplate
5   from zope.formlib.namedtemplate import NamedTemplateImplementation
6   from worldcookery.interfaces import IRecipe
7   from worldcookery.browser.widget import DynamicSequenceWidget
8
9   class RecipeEditForm(EditForm):
10      form_fields = Fields(IRecipe)
11      form_fields['ingredients'].custom_widget = DynamicSequenceWidget
12      form_fields['tools'].custom_widget = DynamicSequenceWidget
13      label = u"Edit recipe"
14
15      template = NamedTemplate('worldcookery.form')
16
17  class RecipeAddForm(AddForm):
18      form_fields = Fields(IRecipe)
19      form_fields['ingredients'].custom_widget = DynamicSequenceWidget
20      form_fields['tools'].custom_widget = DynamicSequenceWidget
21      label = u"Add recipe"
22
23      template = NamedTemplate('worldcookery.form')
24
25      def create(self, data):
26          recipe = createObject(u'worldcookery.Recipe')
27          applyChanges(recipe, self.form_fields, data)
28          return recipe
29
30  form_template = NamedTemplateImplementation(
31      ViewPageTemplateFile('form.pt'))
```

11–12 and 19–20.   Here we specify which form fields the custom widget shall apply to. In our case, these are the `ingredients` and `tools` fields. We tell the form machinery to use our `DynamicSequenceWidget` by setting the custom_widget property of the corresponding form fields. *Form fields* are not to be confused with *schema fields* that occur in interfaces and know nothing about presentation concerns such as forms.

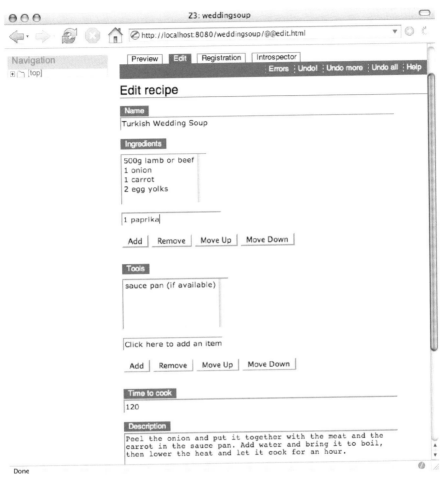

Fig. 8.5. The custom widget being used in an edit form.

Part II

Intermediate

9

Internationalization

The web is a multilingual and multicultural medium. Many websites and services offered over the web need to cope with users that have diverse language backgrounds. It is common for European websites to deal with four languages or more at a time. Even in countries like the United States, an increasing number of websites with nationwide audiences provide their content in Spanish as well as English.

Internationalization covers more than just adding another content language to a website. Time and dates are formatted differently in different countries, as well as numbers. Web applications need to be aware of the differences. Fortunately, Zope provides an excellent framework for internationalization (*i18n*) and localization (*l10n*)[1] which is the subject of this chapter.

Using Zope 2

Everything discussed in this chapter also applies to recent Zope 2 versions. Special attention is required when using the localization features (see last section of this chapter) and custom language extraction (see Section 11.3).

Rocky says...

Python has one major drawback compared to Java, strings are not naturally Unicode aware. Fortunately Python has a Unicode object (denoted by u' ') and Java developers are encouraged to use this in place of regular strings for all human-readable text.

---

[1] The numbers 18 and 10 in i18n and l10n, respectively, refer to the number of letters omitted in the abbreviations.

9.1 Overview

When internationalizing an application, it is usually the application itself that needs to be translated, not the data the application works with. In Zope terms, that means content objects are often not i18n-aware; views, on the other hand, are. In the context of our *World Cookery* application, it would make little sense to request a translation to many different languages for every recipe that is added to the site. However, the user interface for the application that lets us add recipes should be available in the language the user prefers.

Most of the text that would be subject to translation is part of a browser view, such as a Page Template. Sometimes, though, text comes from different components that are not view-specific per se. In case of auto-generated forms, for example, the schema carries descriptive strings that are used to construct the form. Even configuration carries text that is visible in a user interface and thus subject to translation. In all cases, it is necessary to tag the strings that are to be translated so that the Zope machinery can pick them up.

Messages

In i18n jargon, strings that need to be translated are referred to as *messages*. They are identified by a *message id* which can be the string itself or an abstract but unique value. The message id is used to look up the translation of the message, the *message string*. If the look-up fails, the translation machinery falls back to a *default value*. Additionally, message strings are looked up by a certain context, the *domain*. Different domains hold messages for different groups of messages. In Zope, it is the convention that each add-on package or application uses its own domain. Zope itself uses the `zope` domain. For our example application, we will use the `worldcookery` domain.

To demonstrate the concept of messages, consider the translation of the English word *view*. This word has several different meanings in Zope; people can usually find out the proper meaning from the context, but a translation machinery cannot. In Zope, *view* is used as

- the name of components that take care of presentation, *view components*,
- the title of a permission that represents the action of viewing, the *view permission*,
- the actual action of viewing, as displayed on buttons or management tabs.

The dilemma here is two-fold. Not only are slightly different meanings involved; the English language also often does not distinguish between nouns and verbs, as in this case. To allow the proper translation of terms like these, the application developer needs to clarify using unique message ids. For example, one could use

- `view-component` to identify the message for the component type,

- `view-permission` for the permission title,
- `view-button`, `view-tab`, etc. whenever the action of viewing is described.

Of course, all these messages would default to *view*.

Fortunately, this example is an edge case. The longer the message that needs to be translated is, the more likely it is that it is unique in its meaning. Whole sentences are usually unique and can be used as their own message ids. In any case, it is preferable to include as much context in the message as possible. It is often tempting to use shortcuts when assembling user strings, especially when they are similar and can easily be computed. Such behaviour is not constructive for translators and can hinder proper translation.

Most of the translation in Zope happens in an automated manner because browser presentation usually works through Page Templates. Once a portion of text is marked as a message, Page Templates automatically do the translation. To know which language they need to translate to, they ask the request for a set of preferred languages by adapting it to `IUserPreferredLanguages`. Most of today's browsers send a special HTTP header, `Accept-Language` in which they tell the server which languages they prefer. The default adapter in Zope uses the value from this HTTP header to build a list of preferred languages. Then a negotiator utility compares the list of preferred languages with the list of available languages and chooses the best match. Both the languages adapter and the negotiator utility can, of course, be overridden with custom ones to change the language look-up or negotiation policy.

Summary

- Zope's translation machinery can be used to automatically translate messages that are part of an application's presentation.
- Messages are identified by their message id, which is usually the string itself.
- Explicitly unique message ids can be used to distinguish ambiguous messages.
- For browser views, the `IUserPreferredLanguages` adapter extracts the user preferences regarding languages from the request and a negotiator finds the optimum language to be translated to.

9.2 Messages and translation domains

To give you an overview of the Zope components handling translation, it is probably best to "play" with them on the interactive interpreter shell. It is not that you frequently need to get in touch with them, but knowing how they work helps to understand the concepts behind them.

In order to be able to work with messages, we need to setup some basic machinery. In Zope, the components that are responsible for the actual translation are *translation domains*. They carry the mappings between message ids and message strings of a certain domain and provide a translation API which is documented in the `zope.i18n.interfaces.ITranslationDomain` interface. Translation domains are *named utilities* registered for this interface and the name of the domain that they represent. The way translation domains acquire the translated message strings does not matter to the translation machinery. Zope 3 has support for translation domains from *gettext*[2] catalogs or from data stored in the ZODB.

For our experiments on the interactive interpreter shell, we can use a demo implementation of translation domains called `SimpleTranslationDomain`. Instead of reading data from a file, we can simply pass in a mapping of message ids to message strings:

```
$ python
>>> messages = {
...      ('es', u'Time to cook'): u'Tiempo para cocinar',
...      ('de', u'Time to cook'): u'Zeit zum Kochen',
...      ('es', u'Necessary kitchen tools'):
...       u'Herramientas necesarias',
...      ('de', u'Necessary kitchen tools'):
...       u'Benoetigte Kuechengeraete'
... }
>>> from zope.i18n.simpletranslationdomain import \
...      SimpleTranslationDomain
>>> worldcookery = SimpleTranslationDomain('worldcookery', messages) ▼
```

We now have a domain object, but in order for the translation machinery to find it, we need to register it as a named utility:

```
>>> from zope.component import provideUtility
>>> provideUtility(worldcookery, name=u'worldcookery')          ▼
```

Now we can start our interactive session with messages. In order to make a string or a Unicode object aware of translation, it needs to be converted into a `Message` object. These objects represent the message within Zope; apart from the message id, they also carry the domain they belong to and an optional default value. Since the domain of messages in one Python module is generally the same and making an instance of `Message` for every string in the module is tiresome, it is common practice to use a message factory as a shortcut. The factory creates messages of the same domain and is simply named _ (underscore) by convention:

---

[2] *gettext* is a Unix library for internationalization and localization. Python has built-in *gettext* support.

```
>>> from zope.i18nmessageid import MessageFactory
>>> _ = MessageFactory('worldcookery')                          ▼
```

It is fairly easy now to convert regular Unicode to message ids, and even though they still appear to be Unicode objects, they now carry the translation domain they are part of:

```
>>> time_to_cook = _(u"Time to cook")
>>> time_to_cook
u'Time to cook'
>>> time_to_cook.domain
'worldcookery'                                                  ▼
```

We have successfully tagged a user string as a message and can now have it automatically translated. The zope.i18n package provides the necessary function for this:

```
>>> from zope.i18n import translate
>>> translate(time_to_cook, target_language='es')
u'Tiempo para cocinar'
>>> translate(time_to_cook, target_language='de')
u'Zeit zum Kochen'                                              ▼
```

Since we did not provide a message string for French, the translate function will simply return the default value for the message when we request a French translation:

```
>>> translate(time_to_cook, target_language='fr')
u'Time to cook'                                                 ■
```

Variable interpolation

Sometimes, messages are not static but have to include some dynamic values. Imagine the sentence "It takes x minutes to cook" where x is a number to be dynamically inserted. This trivial task turns into a real problem when you need to translate the string. What do you translate? Just "It takes" and "minutes to cook"? That is unlikely to work because the order of a sentence is different in other languages. There is no guarantee that it will always be at the same place of the sentence.

Fortunately, the translation machinery provides a solution since it is a common problem. You can define placeholders in your message strings that will later then be interpolated automatically. The message id object carries the values to be interpolated. The placeholder syntax follows the one of embedded path expressions in Page Templates' string expressions.

So, let us take the above sentence and turn it into a message id:

```
$ python
>>> from zope.i18nmessageid import MessageFactory
>>> _ = MessageFactory('worldcookery')                          ▼
```

```
>>> time_report = _(u'time-report',
...     u"It takes ${time_to_cook} minutes to cook")
>>> time_report
u'time-report'
>>> time_report.default
u'It takes ${time_to_cook} minutes to cook'                    ▼
```

Because it is a rather long sentence, we now use an abstract message id, time-report and provide an English default value which carries a placeholder for x called time_to_cook. Now, let us provide some translations for this message, making sure that we include the placeholder there, too:

```
>>> messages = {
...     ('es', u'time-report'):
...     u'Necesita ${time_to_cook} minutos para cocinar',
...     ('de', u'time-report'):
...     u'Es werden ${time_to_cook} Minuten zum Kochen benoetigt'
... }
>>> from zope.i18n.simpletranslationdomain import \
...     SimpleTranslationDomain
>>> worldcookery = SimpleTranslationDomain('worldcookery', messages)
>>> from zope.component import provideUtility
>>> provideUtility(worldcookery, name=u'worldcookery')          ▼
```

Before requesting a translation, we need to fill the placeholder with a value. Message objects are immutable which means we cannot change the existing one to add the placeholder value. We have to create a new message object based on the existing one by calling the Message constructor. The values for the variable interpolation are passed in as a dictionary via the mapping argument. We fill the dictionary with a value for the time_to_cook placeholder; then we can ask for a translation:

```
>>> from zope.i18nmessageid import Message
>>> time_report = Message(time_report, mapping={'time_to_cook': 45})
>>> from zope.i18n import translate
>>> translate(time_report, target_language='de')
u'Es werden 45 Minuten zum Kochen benoetigt'
>>> translate(time_report, target_language='es')
u'Necesita 45 minutos para cocinar'                            ▼
```

As you can see, the translation machinery replaced the placeholder with the actual value we provided in the message id's mapping. Of course, it will do the interpolation even when a translation is not found and the fallback value has to be used:

```
>>> translate(time_report, target_language='fr')
u'It takes 45 minutes to cook'                                 ■
```

If all the values for the variable interpolation are known when the message object is constructed, the mapping parameter may also be passed to the message factory:

```
>>> time_report = _(u'time-report',
...          u"It takes ${time_to_cook} minutes to cook",
...          mapping={'time_to_cook': 45})
```

Summary

- The translation functionality is provided by translation domain components which are registered as *named utilities*.
- Unicode strings are turned into message objects using *message factories*, which create messages of the same domain.
- Apart from the message id itself, message objects carry the domain they belong to, an optional default value and an optional mapping for variable interpolation.
- Dynamic messages are made by putting placeholders in message strings which are then interpolated using the message object's mapping.

Rocky says...

Java developers will quickly find using Zope's `MessageFactories` very similar to Java's `ResourceBundles`. The only real code-level difference is in convention of use where the message factory will typically be referred to as a variable named _.

9.3 Internationalizing an application

After our tour through the translation components we can now make our Python code "i18n-aware". A typical task is identifying all the places where a (Unicode) string needs to be turned into an i18n message or where the appropriate TAL commands need to be applied. Zope has a very simple tool which will help you identify untranslatable strings in the user interface: the `test` language.

The test language "translates" i18n messages to a string of the format `[[domain][message id (default text)]]`. That way, when displaying a page in the test language, it is very easy to spot strings that have not yet been marked as translatable as they will not appear in this format. Moreover, the test language can also be used for debugging purposes, for example to check which translation domain a particular message is coming from.

How do you invoke the test language? Obviously web browsers usually do not know how to request a language with such a special name. The `++lang++` traversal namespace is the solution here. With it you can directly control the language of the page displayed in Zope. The following URL will switch the standard contents listing of the root folder to the test language:

```
http://localhost:8080/++lang++test/@@contents.html
```

Of course, if you substitute test for something else (e.g. de for German), you can display pages in other languages.

9.3.1 Python code

Python code is probably the most difficult of all three (Python, ZPT, ZCML) to internationalize because it can be difficult to find out which strings are shown to the user. A rule of thumb is that whenever a string does not hold some identifier but real words or even a whole sentence, it should be made translatable. Examples include

- titles, labels, and description, for example in schema fields or browser widgets,
- report and status messages, such as "Your changes have been saved",
- error messages, even when raising exceptions (exceptions, too, are displayed to the user through views such as Page Templates).

Python code is internationalized the same way as the example we have just completed in the interactive interpreter session. We create a message factory for our translation domain and then convert all strings with it. It is important to call the message factory _ (underscore) because Zope provides us with automatic extraction utilities that search our source code for occurrences of i18n messages and compile a message catalog for us (more on that later). Consider the following technically correct but useless piece of code:

```
if successful:
    msg = u"The recipe has successfully been saved"
else:
    msg = u"An error has occurred while saving"
return _(msg)
```

Here, the programmer was aware of the fact that all messages that are to be displayed to the user need to be turned into message strings. However, the automatic extract utility will not be able to collect the message ids because they were defined above and do not appear when the message id is created. The following code fixes the problem:

```
if successful:
    return _(u"The recipe has successfully been saved")
else:
    return _(u"An error has occurred while saving")
```

Here, the strings are directly turned into messages, allowing the extract utility to pick them up. Even though this code might seem less elegant because the same action—turning a string into a message—is spelled out twice, it is the more functional one.

After this bit of theory, we can finally internationalize the Python code we have written in the previous chapters. Fortunately, there are currently only a few places where user strings appear in Python: the `IRecipe` schema from which the add and edit forms are rendered and the add and edit form classes themselves. Though by now you can probably predict what it has to look like, Example 9.3.1 shows you what the internationalized version of `IRecipe` should look like. Turning the labels in the add and edit form classes we wrote earlier into translatable messages is left to you as an exercise.

With a translation provided for the messages in the schema, the automatically generated add and edit forms for recipes are now translated as Figure 9.1 shows.

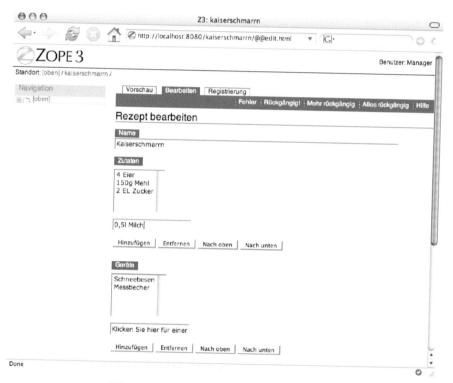

Fig. 9.1. A recipe's edit form in German.

Example 9.3.1 Internationalized schema (`interfaces.py`)

```
1   from zope.interface import Interface
2   from zope.schema import List, Text, TextLine, Int
3   from zope.i18nmessageid import MessageFactory
4   _ = MessageFactory('worldcookery')
5
6   class IRecipe(Interface):
7       """Store information about a recipe.
8       """
9
10      name = TextLine(
11          title=_(u"Name"),
12          description=_(u"Name of the dish"),
13          required = True
14          )
15
16      ingredients = List(
17          title=_(u"Ingredients"),
18          description=_(u"List of ingredients necessary for this recipe."),
19          required=True,
20          value_type=TextLine(title=_(u"Ingredient"))
21          )
22
23      tools = List(
24          title=_(u"Tools"),
25          description=_(u"List of necessary kitchen tools"),
26          required=False,
27          value_type=TextLine(title=_(u"Tool"))
28          )
29
30      time_to_cook = Int(
31          title=_(u"Time to cook"),
32          description=_(u"Necessary time for preparing the meal described,
                        "
33                          "in minutes."),
34          required=True
35          )
36
37      description = Text(
38          title=_(u"Description"),
39          description=_(u"Description of the recipe"),
40          required=True
41          )
```

9.3.2 Page Templates

Page Templates typically contain many strings that need to be internationalized. Similar to *TAL* and *METAL* which are used to modify the XML output
tree, a third command set in another namespace[3] is used to tag internationalized values. The namespace prefix here is i18n by convention. The following
list gives an overview over the i18n command set in Page Templates:

translate tells the TAL interpreter to translate the contents of the element, using for a message id either an explicitly given one or the existing
element contents. Examples:

```
<h1 i18n:translate="heading-objective">The objective
</h1>
```

```
<p i18n:translate="">The goal of the World Cookery
website is to provide a place for hobby cooks to
share their favourite recipes.</p>
```

```
<div tal:content="view/label">Label inserted and
translated here</div>
```

For the heading, an explicit message id is given, heading-objective.
For the paragraph, the paragraph contents will be used as the message
id. In both cases, the element contents serve as default fallback values
when translation fails.

The last example above does not look like translation is involved, but
it might very well be. When the TAL interpreter encounters a Message
object (we assume view/label resolves to one), it translates it automatically. Hence, i18n:translate is really only required for user messages
that are defined in the template itself, provided that i18n messages are
correctly defined in the corresponding Python code.

domain sets the translation domain for the current element and all child
elements. Examples:

```
<div i18n:domain="worldcookery">
  <span i18n:translate="">This is looked up in the worldcookery
  domain.</span>
  <span i18n:translate="" i18n:domain="zope">This is not.</span>
</div>
```

attributes specifies which attributes, whether static or dynamically inserted, are to be translated. As with tal:attributes, several entries
are separated by semicolon. Specifying a message id is optional. Example:

---

[3] http://xml.zope.org/namespaces/i18n

```
<form>
  <input type="text" name="field"
         tal:attributes="title widget/label" />
  <input type="submit" title="Save form data"
         value="Save"
         i18n:attributes="title; value button-save" />
</form>
```

In this example the first form element, a text input box, receives a dynamically set attribute, `title`. Assuming that `widget/label` yields a `Message` object, it will be translated automatically.

The second form element, a submit button, demonstrates the usage of `i18n:translate` for static attributes. The message id for `title` is the value itself, the message id for `value` is explicitly set to `button-save`. In both cases, the static attribute contents is assumed as the default fallback value when translation fails.

name marks an element as a variable placeholder. Like in messages generated in Python code, Page Template messages often need the placeholder functionality too. Example:

```
<p i18n:translate="time-report">
  It takes
  <span tal:replace="context/time_to_cook"
        i18:name="time_to_cook" />
  minutes to cook
</p>
```

This would be the TAL equivalent of

```
>>> time_report = _(u'time-report',
...       u"It takes ${time_to_cook} minutes to cook",
...       mapping={'time_to_cook': 45})
```

as covered in Section 9.2.

With this we can now internationalize our Page Templates. So far, we only wrote three: the one used to display recipes (`browser/recipeview.pt`), the one used for editing recipes (`browser/form.pt`) and the one used for the dynamic sequence widget (`browser/widget.pt`). Example 9.3.2 and Example 9.3.3 show internationalized versions of two of them. Internationalizing the form template is left up to you as an exercise. Even after inserting i18n markup, the Page Templates are still valid XML documents and can still be viewed in a browser directly off of the file system.

9.3.3 ZCML

The least problematic part of the whole internationalization process is ZCML configuration. Because of the way the configuration machinery works, it

Example 9.3.2 Internationalized View Page Template
(browser/recipeview.pt)

```
1  <html xmlns="http://www.w3.org/1999/xhtml"
2        xmlns:tal="http://xml.zope.org/namespaces/tal"
3        xmlns:i18n="http://xml.zope.org/namespaces/i18n"
4        i18n:domain="worldcookery">
5  <head>
6    <title tal:content="context/name/title">recipe name goes here</title>
7  </head>
8  <body>
9
10   <h2 tal:content="context/name/title">recipe name goes here</h2>
11
12   <table>
13     <tbody>
14       <tr>
15         <td i18n:translate="">Time needed for preparation:</td>
16         <td i18n:translate="">
17             <tal:var replace="context/time_to_cook"
18                      i18n:name="time_to_cook">xyz</tal:var> mins
19         </td>
20       </tr>
21
22       <tr>
23         <td i18n:translate="">Ingredients:</td>
24         <td>
25           <ul>
26             <li tal:repeat="ingredient context/ingredients"
27                 tal:content="ingredient">ingredients go here</li>
28           </ul>
29         </td>
30       </tr>
31
32       <tr>
33         <td i18n:translate="">Needed kitchen tools:</td>
34         <td>
35           <ul>
36             <li tal:repeat="tool context/tools"
37                 tal:content="tool">tools go here</li>
38           </ul>
39         </td>
40       </tr>
41
42     </tbody>
43   </table>
44
45   <p tal:content="structure view/renderDescription">
46     Longer description goes here.
47   </p>
48
49 </body>
50 </html>
```

Example 9.3.2 (continued)

---

3. For XML validity we need to define the namespace of the i18n command set. The prefix used is i18n by convention.

4. Because all of the messages in this Page Template should be part of the worldcookery domain, we set it at the topmost place.

15, 23, and 33. As stated previously, the i18n:translate attribute invokes translation of the elements contents. Here we leave the attribute value empty, so the implied message id is the element contents itself.

17–18. This is a good example of placeholders within translation messages in Page Templates. The actual time that is necessary to prepare a dish is inserted into the message, thus requires a named placeholder. This is accomplished with the i18n:name attribute.

---

knows what values are expected for which directive parameters. That means that there is no need to specify what needs to be translated and what not— ZCML already knows! The only thing left for us to do is set a translation domain. Because we have not done this, Zope has warned us before with a message similar to the following:

```
.../zope/configuration/fields.py:380: UserWarning: You did not
specify an i18n translation domain for the 'title' field in
.../worldcookery/browser/configure.zcml
```

That means we have used configuration directives that take translatable strings but do not know in which domain they should be translated. That can easily be fixed by setting the domain on the configuration context of the corresponding file, meaning the configure document element of a ZCML file or a context higher up in the ZCML tree. In our case, it would make sense to add it to the topmost ZCML file of our package, configure.zcml so that all included files, such as browser/configure.zcml inherit the setting. Simply replace the opening document element tag with the following:

```
<configure
    xmlns="http://namespaces.zope.org/zope"
    i18n_domain="worldcookery"
    >
...
```

Now, the ZCML interpreter knows in which domain translation messages are to be created and the extractor utility can correctly extract the messages. This will be, among others, the subject of the next section.

Finally, it is possible to explicitly specify a message id in ZCML, too. Here, we have to rely on a special syntax because everything needs to be

Example 9.3.3 Internationalized widget template (`browser/widget.pt`)

```
1   <div xmlns:tal="http://xml.zope.org/namespaces/tal"
2       xmlns:i18n="http://xml.zope.org/namespaces/i18n"
3       i18n:domain="worldcookery">
4
5   <script type="text/javascript" src="sequence.js"
6           tal:attributes="src context/++resource++sequence.js">
7   </script>
8
9   <p tal:define="form_value view/_getFormValue">
10    <input type="hidden" name="foo.marker" id="foo.marker"
11          tal:define="marker string:${view/name}.marker"
12          tal:attributes="name marker; id marker" />
13    <tal:loop tal:repeat="item form_value">
14      <input type="hidden" name="foo" id="value.0.foo" value="item"
15            tal:condition="item"
16            tal:attributes="name string:${view/name};
17                            id string:value.${repeat/item/index}.${view/
                                name};
18                            value item" />
19    </tal:loop>
20    <input type="hidden" id="foo" tal:attributes="id view/name" />
21    <select id="select.foo" size="5"
22            tal:attributes="id string:select.${view/name};
23                            size python:min(max(len(form_value), 5), 12)">
24      <tal:loop tal:repeat="item form_value">
25        <option tal:condition="item" tal:content="item"
26              tal:attributes="value item">item</option>
27      </tal:loop>
28    </select>
29  </p>
30
31  <p>
32    <input type="text" id="input.foo"
33          tal:attributes="id string:input.${view/name}"
34          value="Click here to add an item" onfocus="this.value=''"
35          i18n:attributes="value" />
36  </p>
37  <p>
38    <button
39        type="button" onclick="sequenceAddItem('foo')"
40        tal:attributes="onclick string:sequenceAddItem('${view/name}')"
41        i18n:translate="button-add">
42      Add
43    </button>
44    <button
45        type="button" onclick="sequenceRemoveItem('foo')"
46        tal:attributes="onclick string:sequenceRemoveItem('${view/name}')"
47        i18n:translate="button-remove">
48      Remove
49    </button>
```

Example 9.3.3 (continued)

```
50    <button
51       type="button" onclick="sequenceMoveItem('foo', -1)"
52       tal:attributes="onclick string:sequenceMoveItem('${view/name}', -1)
                "
53       i18n:translate="button-move-up">
54      Move Up
55    </button>
56    <button
57       type="button" onclick="sequenceMoveItem('foo', 1)"
58       tal:attributes="onclick string:sequenceMoveItem('${view/name}', 1)"
59       i18n:translate="button-move-down">
60      Move Down
61    </button>
62  </p>
63  </div>
```

35. Translating the default value of a text input box in a form is the typical example for i18n:attributes; even the examples earlier on introduced it this way. Here we see a perfect application of this example.

41, 47, 53, and 59. Since the button labels are only one or two words each and often do not provide enough context to ensure a unique translation, we use explicit message ids here just to be sure.

---

contained in the attribute value; the explicit message id, if given, is included in square brackets before the message text:

```
[label-edit] Edit
```

This will set the message id explicitly to label-edit while retaining the message text and default translation as Edit. In the special case that a leading word enclosed in square brackets is intended to be part of the message text and not the message id, prepend the attribute value with an empty set of square brackets, like so:

```
[] [top]
```

To ensure proper translation of our application, we can now specify some explicit message ids for some configuration values. Example 9.3.4 lists an internationalized version of browser/configure.zcml. Note that not all string parameters passed to a ZCML directive can be translated text. Typically only those that will appear in a browser presentation, such as form labels, menu entry titles, etc.

Example 9.3.4 Internationalized configuration file
(`browser/configure.zcml`)

```
1   <configure
2       xmlns="http://namespaces.zope.org/zope"
3       xmlns:browser="http://namespaces.zope.org/browser"
4       >
5
6     <browser:page
7         for="worldcookery.interfaces.IRecipe"
8         name="index.html"
9         class=".recipe.ViewRecipe"
10        permission="zope.View"
11        />
12
13    <configure package="zope.app.preview" i18n_domain="zope">
14      <browser:page
15          for="worldcookery.interfaces.IRecipe"
16          name="preview.html"
17          template="preview.pt"
18          permission="zope.ManageContent"
19          menu="zmi_views" title="Preview"
20          />
21    </configure>
22
23    <browser:page
24        for="worldcookery.interfaces.IRecipe"
25        name="edit.html"
26        class=".recipe.RecipeEditForm"
27        permission="zope.ManageContent"
28        menu="zmi_views" title="[label-edit] Edit"
29        />
30
31    <adapter
32        factory=".recipe.form_template"
33        for=".recipe.RecipeEditForm"
34        name="worldcookery.form"
35        />
36
37    <browser:addMenuItem
38        title="[label-recipe] Recipe"
39        factory="worldcookery.Recipe"
40        view="worldcookery.Recipe"
41        permission="zope.ManageContent"
42        />
43
44    <browser:page
45        for="zope.app.container.interfaces.IAdding"
46        name="worldcookery.Recipe"
47        class=".recipe.RecipeAddForm"
48        permission="zope.ManageContent"
49        />
```

Example 9.3.4 (continued)

```
50    <adapter
51        factory=".recipe.form_template"
52        for=".recipe.RecipeAddForm"
53        name="worldcookery.form"
54        />
55
56    <browser:resource name="sequence.js" file="sequence.js" />
57
58  </configure>
```

13. Because the preview page comes from a Zope package and the configuration directive we used, including the title, is generic to the preview page, we tell ZCML to use the zope domain. That way, it will use the translation that is already available in Zope's message catalogs, which means one message less for us to translate.

28 and 38.   Where messages might be ambiguous, such as for short labels and menu entry titles, we provide an explicit message id using the square bracket syntax.

Summary

- In Python, a message factory, named _ (underscore) by convention, is used to create message objects. It is important that messages are created from string constants, not from possibly dynamic variables so that the extractor utility can pick them up.
- In Page Templates, inserted Message objects are translated automatically. A third command set is used to identify translatable text occurring within a template. The contents of an element or an attribute can be translated, with or without an explicitly given message id. Placeholder functionality is also available.
- ZCML directives already know which values are translatable messages. The ZCML interpreter only needs to know which translation domain they belong to. Once set, the domain setting is inherited in included files until overridden.

9.4 Message catalogs

We have now successfully made our application aware of translation. Only a few files had to be changed and most of the changes were small adjustments. Thanks to the internationalization framework Zope provides, writing translatable software requires very little overhead. What we have not done yet is to add the translations. Often developers do not provide translations themselves but acquire them from professional translators. Therefore, the developers need to tell the translators what is to be translated. Then they also need to integrate a translated set of messages back into the application so that automatic translation can do its job.

The translation system in Zope uses a well known backend for retrieving translations, the *GNU gettext* system. The *gettext* library provides access to message ids and their message strings stored in files called *message catalogs*. Message catalogs are plain text files but the library itself can only work with a binary representation of the files. You will need the *gettext utilities*, the msgfmt program in particular, to compile the text files to the binary catalogs. The *gettext utilities* can be retrieved from the GNU project homepage[4]; packages for your operating system might also exist.

The extractor utility

As mentioned earlier, Zope comes with an extractor utility called i18nextract (usually available from an instance's bin directory) which can extract all messages from Python code, Page Templates and ZCML files. It writes the result into a message catalog *template* (file extension .pot). i18nextract takes the following arguments:

-p, --path specifies the path of the package to be searched. All Python modules, ZCML files and Page Templates in this package and subpackages are searched for messages.

-d, --domain specifies the translation domain for which the message catalog is to be created. Only messages from this domain will be included in the catalog template, except for the ones found in Python code; messages found in Python code are included regardless of their domain (this is a limitation of the extracting algorithm). If not set, the domain defaults to zope, thus needs to be given for all third-party packages.

-o specifies a directory *within* the given package where the catalog template file is to be written to. It is a convention that all internationalization-related files of a package reside in a subdirectory called locales. The filename of the catalog template will be <domain>.pot. If this option is not specified, the extractor writes the file to the current directory.

By passing the right arguments to those parameter options, we obtain the template file for message catalogs, locales/worldcookery.pot:

---

[4] GNU project homepage <http://www.gnu.org/software/gettext/>

```
~/Zope3Instance$ bin/i18nextract -p lib/python/worldcookery \
                 -d worldcookery -o locales
base path: '~/Zope3Instance/lib/python/worldcookery'
search path: '~/Zope3Instance/lib/python/worldcookery'
domain: 'worldcookery'
output file: '~/Zope3Instance/lib/python/worldcookery/locales/
              worldcookery.pot'
```

This generated catalog template contains all the messages we have defined in the source code throughout our package. The syntax follows the *gettext* message catalog syntax. In the template file, the message string is simply left empty. This is what an entry in the file looks like:

```
#: lib/python/worldcookery/browser/widget.pt:33
#. Default: "Add"
msgid "button-add"
msgstr ""
```

You can now give the catalog template to a translator who will translate each message by filling in the translation for the empty message string. This can be achieved with a simple text editor or a specialized tool, like *KBabel*[5] and *gtranslator*[6] which are available for Unix/X11 systems and *poEdit*[7] which is available for all major platforms. Using such a tool is recommended because these tools are capable of writing non-ASCII text (usually in UTF-8) and ensure that the syntax of the catalog files is still valid.

Message catalogs in their text version have the file extension .po. When we retrieve such a file from a translator, we have to install it in the locales directory and compile it. The *gettext* system expects a subdirectory of locales for each language that is available. So, if we had a Spanish translation, we would create a directory called es inside locales. In that directory, we create another directory called LC_MESSAGES in which we put our Spanish message catalog file, worldcookery.po. We then have to compile it to its binary version as *gettext* only works with the compiled catalogs. This is achieved with the msgfmt program of the *gettext utilities*. Compiled catalogs carry the .mo file extension:

```
.../locales/es/LC_MESSAGES$ msgfmt -o worldcookery.mo worldcookery.po
```

Note that the translation tools mentioned above often aid the translator here, for example *poEdit* automatically compiles message catalogs upon saving. For a detailed description of the *gettext* system and the *gettext utilities*, please refer to the *gettext manual* [6].

As a final step, we need to tell the translation machinery where to find the translations we provided. We do that using a ZCML directive called registerTranslations of the http://namespaces.zope.org/i18n

---

[5] KBabel homepage <http://kbabel.kde.org/>

[6] gtranslator homepage <http://gtranslator.sourceforge.net/>

[7] poEdit homepage <http://poedit.sourceforge.net>

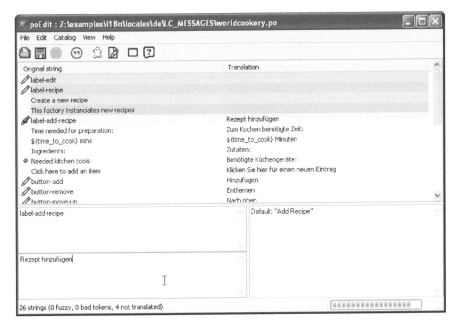

Fig. 9.2. Translating the `worldcookery` domain to German with *poEdit*.

namespace. Change the document element of `configure.zcml` to the following:

```
<configure
    xmlns="http://namespaces.zope.org/zope"
    xmlns:i18n="http://namespaces.zope.org/i18n"
    i18n_domain="worldcookery"
    >
```

and insert the following line somewhere in the file:

```
<i18n:registerTranslations directory="locales" />
```

Zope will then pick up the message catalogs that you can provide under `locales/<language>/LC_MESSAGES` as compiled *gettext* files. The filenames *must* be of the form `<domain>.mo`. You can check whether Zope has found the message catalogs in a ZMI screen in the process management area (see Figure 9.3).

Finally be aware that the fact that English is the default language of our application is unknown to Zope. It will therefore also try to find message catalogs for English if an English "translation" is requested. If those catalogs do not exist, Zope may display websites in a different language than English, if a user's preferred languages list other languages than English. To make Zope aware that English is supported by the application, we provide an *empty*

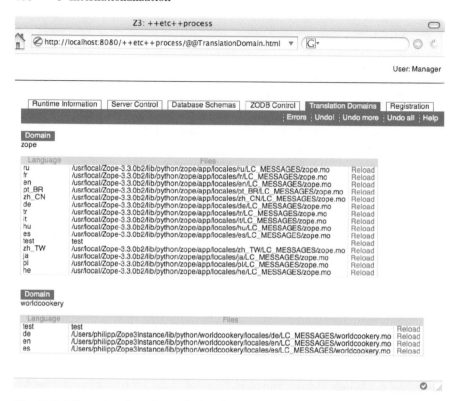

Fig. 9.3. File system-based translation domains can be reloaded on the fly through the ZMI.

message catalog in `locales/en/LC_MESSAGES`. Simply copying over the POT file is perfectly sufficient for that.

Summary

- Translation messages are stored in message catalogs, one for each translation domain and language.
- Zope comes with an automatic extractor utility that extracts messages from Python code, Page Templates and ZCML files and writes them into a message catalog template file.
- Zope uses the *GNU gettext* system as a backend for retrieving translation messages. The *gettext utilities* are needed to compile message catalogs from their editable text format to the required binary format.
- The compiled message catalogs are managed in a standard *gettext* directory structure below a directory usually called `locales`.

Flashback

Internationalization support was initially implemented in Zope 3 and then backported to Zope 2. One of the results of these efforts was *Placeless Translation Service* (PTS), the most common Zope 2-only solution to allow translated Page Templates and messages in Python code. While PTS has a few features that Zope 3's message catalogs do not yet have (such as automatic compilation of gettext catalogs and the collection of missing messages in a message catalog), the whole i18n framework from Zope 3 is much more flexible. Since every message catalog is its own utility, it would not be difficult to provide a custom implementation with the missing features.

Rocky says...

Java developers will find the use of the GNU gettext system slightly more complicated than using property files as resource bundles. But the extra flexibility will be well worth becoming familiar particularly since there are a plethora of tools available already. In addition, the use of the GNU gettext system spans across many platforms and programming languages ensuring a high level of support.

9.5 Localization

Internationalization is not simply a matter of translating everything literally. Different countries have different cultural backgrounds. This can mean differences in calendars and dates on one hand and numbers and currencies on the other. Some examples:

Calendars
In the western Christian societies, the Gregorian calendar[8] is predominant, whereas in Islamic countries, the Islamic calendar[9] is used. *1 Muharram AH 1423* and *16 March 2002* are the same day, but in different calendars. Even within the Gregorian calendar there are subtle differences between different societies. In the United States, a date is commonly given in the order of *Month/Day/Year* and the week starts on Sunday. In Europe, on the other hand, the week starts on Monday and dates are given in the form of *Day/-Month/Year* while in Asia you often see *Year-Month-Day*.

---

[8] Named after Pope Gregory XIII, who introduced it in 1582; superseded the Julian calendar of the Roman empire.

[9] A pure lunar calendar counting the years since the prophet Muhammad emigrated to Medina.

Numbers

In the Anglo-Saxon world, numbers and currencies are also written differently than in Europe. Decimal numbers in Europe use a *comma* for the decimal separator and commonly a *dot* for the thousand separator. In English-speaking countries, it is the opposite way. Furthermore, the position of the currency symbol changes. A million dollars are commonly written as *$1,000,000*, whereas in Europe a million euros would be written as *1.000.000 €*.

Localization

Adjusting an application to pick up these internationalization issues is commonly referred to as *localization* (l10n). There are many subtle differences that would be impossible to take care of manually. Fortunately, Zope provides a rich localization API as part of the `zope.i18n.locales` package. Central to the API design are *locale objects*. A *locale* represents the localization aspect of a particular language or region and is referred to by the typical two letter code combinations. For example, `es` stands for the Spanish locale, `es-ES` for Spanish in Spain and `es-MX` for Spanish in Mexico.

Just like translation, localization is a pure presentation matter. What is stored in a database are floating point numbers and `datetime` objects. They contain the abstract values. When presenting those values to a user, such as in form of an HTML page, you will have to make sure to apply the right formatting. Formatting is conveniently done by formatters which are retrieved from the locale object. The locale object, on the other hand, is usually retrieved from the request because formatting is part of the presentation.

Numbers

As a simple example, we shall look at a Page Template that has to display different kinds of numbers in a localization-sensible environment. Because our *World Cookery* application does not need to deal with numbers or dates, it is difficult to provide an example in the context of this application. To try the localization features of Page Templates out we can use the persistent, content space-based *ZPT Page*, which is perfect for trying out features like this. Go to an arbitrary folder in the ZMI and add a *ZPT Page* by clicking on the corresponding entry in the *Add* menu on the left. For the source of the template, enter the code listing shown in Example 9.5.1 and provide a name for the object on the bottom, for example `locales.html`. After you have saved, click on the *Preview* tab to see the result of the localization. You should be shown something similar to Figure 9.4, depending on your browser's locale.

Dates and times

To demonstrate the localization of date and time values we will use the interactive interpreter shell. The reason is `date` or `datetime` objects are involved and these cannot be created as easily in web-based *ZPT Pages*. First create

Example 9.5.1 Demonstration of localization in a Page Template
(`locales.html`)

```
1  <html>
2  <head>
3    <title>L10n formatting examples</title>
4  </head>
5
6  <body tal:define="locale request/locale">
7
8  <p>
9    The number pi has the value of
10   <span tal:define="pi          modules/math/pi;
11                     formatter python:locale.numbers.getFormatter('decimal
                                ')"
12         tal:replace="python:formatter.format(pi)">3.14</span>
13 </p>
14
15 <p>
16   The speed of light is
17   <span tal:define="c          python: 3e8;
18                     formatter python:locale.numbers.getFormatter('
                                scientific')"
19         tal:replace="python:formatter.format(c)">3*10^8 m/s</span>
20   metres per second.
21 </p>
22
23 <p>
24   In order to be a millionaire, you need possess
25   <span tal:define="million    python:1e6;
26                     formatter python:locale.numbers.getFormatter('
                                currency')"
27         tal:replace="python:formatter.format(million)">$1,000,000</span>.
28 </p>
29
30 </body>
31 </html>
```

6. The preferred locale of the browser is available as an attribute on the request.

11, 18, and 26. In order to format numbers, one has to retrieve a *formatter* from
      the `numbers` attribute of the locale object. There are four different categories
      of formatters:

*   `decimal`
*   `percent`
*   `scientific`
*   `currency`

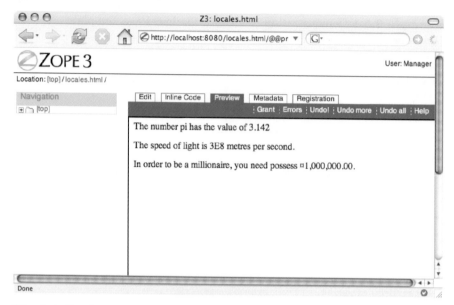

Fig. 9.4. Rendering locale-sensitive information with Page Templates (here in the English/U.S.A. locale).

a `datetime` object. We can use the convenient class method `utcnow` to create an object that reflects today's date and the current time:

```
$ python
>>> from datetime import datetime
>>> now = datetime.utcnow()
>>> now
datetime.datetime(2004, 7, 23, 15, 46, 36, 911803)
```

Now we can acquire different locales, for example one for English and one for German:

```
>>> from zope.i18n.locales import locales
>>> english = locales.getLocale('en')
>>> german = locales.getLocale('de', 'DE')
```

Similar to number formatting, we have to retrieve formatters from the locale's `dates` attribute. As with number formatters, there are again different categories:

- `date`
- `time`
- `dateTime`

So if we wanted to format the `datetime` object we just created with today's date and the current time, we would probably want to the use the `dateTime` formatter:

```
>>> formatter = english.dates.getFormatter('dateTime')
>>> formatter.format(now)
u'Jul 23, 2004 3:46:36 PM'                                    ▼
```

In a German environment, the same date would be printed differently:

```
>>> formatter = german.dates.getFormatter('dateTime')
>>> formatter.format(now)
u'23.07.2004 15:46:36'                                        ▼
```

Dates can be written in different forms; one could spell out the name of the month or just use the numbers, for example. We can use one of the following identifiers to set the length of a date format:

- short
- medium
- long
- full

For example, you could print all of the available date and time information, including the time zone by acquiring the formatter that produces output in the full length:

```
>>> formatter = english.dates.getFormatter('dateTime', length='full')
>>> formatter.format(now)
u'Friday, July 23, 2004 3:46:36 PM +000'
>>> formatter = german.dates.getFormatter('dateTime', length='full')
>>> formatter.format(now)
u'Freitag, 23. Juli 2004 15:46 Uhr +000'                      ■
```

Localized times and dates are already translated, so there is no need to invoke the translation machinery for this.

Summary

- Internationalization not only includes the translation of static text, but also the localization (l10n) of regional information such as numbers, dates and times.
- Zope's localization API comes in form of *locale* objects which represent the formatting of numbers, dates, and times for a language and a region.
- Formatting of localization-sensible values is achieved through formatter objects which are acquired from the locale object; different formatters exist for different formatting categories and presentation lengths.

Using Zope 2

The Zope 2 request object does not (yet) support all of the Zope 3 request API, for example the `locale` attribute. You will have to look up the locale object manually in Zope 2, like this:

```
>>> from zope.i18n.interfaces import IUserPreferredLanguages
>>> from zope.i18n.locales import locales
>>> languages = IUserPreferredLanguages(request)
>>> langs = languages.getPreferredLanguages()
>>> if langs:
...     parts = (langs[0].split('-') + [None, None])[:3]
... else:
...     parts = (None, None, None)
...
>>> locale = locales.getLocale(*parts)
```

The `IUserPreferredLanguages` adapter used here will be discussed in detail in Chapter 11.

Rocky says...

Fortunately the `zope.i18n.locales` API is similar enough to `java.util.Locale` that Java developers should have little difficulty understanding how to use l10n in Zope. Although the much more flexible manner in which to retrieve a locale object will be a welcome addition.

10

Customizing a Site's Layout

Our application lets us do quite a lot already with a small amount of code. We can add and edit recipes to the object database where they are persisted and later displayed to the visitor. It's time to start thinking about the appearance of the overall application. Fortunately, Zope lets us worry about this independently of component code. That means we can delay the layout of the application for as long as we wish. We could hire a designer to do the layout for us, we only need to integrate the design into the application. This chapter shows you how to do that.

Using Zope 2

Everything covered in this chapter also applies to recent Zope 2 versions, of course only when Zope 3-style views are used. Note that systems like the CMF have created bridges from the Zope 3 skinning technology to their own skinning system. Therefore, adjusting the layout of such an application typically does not involve any of the steps presented here, except for the ones shown in Section 10.2.

10.1 Layers and skins

Views determine how objects are represented. In most cases, browser views might present the different aspects of a particular component (e.g. display, edit, add functionality), but they still want to use a common design. It is usually necessary to present the whole web application in a common design. Sometimes two separate designs within the application are required, for example one for visitors and one for editors. In Zope jargon the look of a site, its layout or design, is called a *skin*. In other systems, the same concept is sometimes called a *theme*. You can imagine skins as wallpapers that give the naked objects an appearance, or as wrapping papers that wrap dull boxes to make them look pretty.

Experience has shown that skins have to provide a lot of basic infrastructure that is common to all of them. In order to be able to share this common groundwork, skins are often broken down into *layers*. A skin then is essentially a combination of layers. That way, skins can share those layers that provide the basic functionality they need and then provide their specific custom look and feel on top of that.

Layers

In Chapter 7 we learned that views are multi-adapters for the object they present and the request. Hence we get different views for different types of requests. Layers use exactly this behaviour by marking the request with additional interfaces: they are marker interfaces extending IBrowserRequest, either directly or indirectly by extending other layers.

Let us take the IWorldCookerySkin interface from Example 10.1.1. It extends IBrowserRequest, albeit indirectly through another layer interface called IDefaultBrowserLayer. It is therefore by definition a layer (do not be irritated by its name for now).

Example 10.1.1 Defining a skin interface (`skin/interfaces.py`)

```
1  from zope.publisher.interfaces.browser import IDefaultBrowserLayer
2
3  class IWorldCookerySkin(IDefaultBrowserLayer):
4      """Skin for the WorldCookery application"""
```

To understand how layers work we shall now register a browser view, though we will not register it for IBrowserRequest but for IWorldCookerySkin. For the view itself we can take anything, such as the simple browser page from Chapter 7:

```
$ python
>>> from zope.component import provideAdapter
>>> from zope.publisher.interfaces.browser import IBrowserPage
>>> from worldcookery.interfaces import IRecipe
>>> from worldcookery.skin.interfaces import IWorldCookerySkin
>>> from worldcookery.browser.recipe import ViewRecipe
>>> provideAdapter(
...     ViewRecipe,
...     adapts=(IRecipe, IWorldCookerySkin),
...     provides=IBrowserPage,
...     name=u'index.html'
... )
```

▼

Now, when taking a simple test request, we will see that the view cannot be found, simply because that request object does not provide the required `IWorldCookerySkin`. The error typically thrown when component lookup fails is `ComponentLookupError`:

```
>>> from worldcookery.recipe import Recipe
>>> from zope.publisher.browser import TestRequest
>>> from zope.component import getMultiAdapter
>>> kebab = Recipe()
>>> request = TestRequest()
>>> getMultiAdapter((kebab, request), name=u'index.html')
Traceback (most recent call last):
  ...
zope.component.interfaces.ComponentLookupError:
   ((<worldcookery.recipe.Recipe object at 0x146ce30>,
     <zope.publisher.browser.TestRequest instance URL=...>),
     <InterfaceClass zope.interface.Interface>, u'index.html')
```

▼

Of course, it is not difficult to get rid of this error. We must only make sure the request is marked with our layer interface:

```
>>> from zope.interface import alsoProvides
>>> alsoProvides(request, IWorldCookerySkin)
>>> getMultiAdapter((kebab, request), name=u'index.html')
<worldcookery.browser.recipe.ViewRecipe object at 0x2313650>
```

■

As you can see, by marking the request with additional layers you can change view lookup behaviour, depending on which views are registered for which layers. With layers, for example, you can override views defined in other layers, depending on which layer takes precedence on the request. This is decided based on the order of the interfaces that are provided by the request.

Skins

Layers are usually grouped in skins, as we initially discussed. Skins are also interfaces and they inherit from all the layers they group. That means, they also indirectly extend `IBrowserRequest` and are by definition also layers. In fact, the decision whether something is just a layer or already a skin is quite arbitrary. For example, you could group several skins together and create a skin based on that.

Now, there *is* a small difference between layers and skins: skins have a human-readable name and provide `IBrowserSkinType`. The name is important for the users as they will perhaps get to choose the different designs or themes of a page; showing them the dotted name of the layer interface would surely be out of question. The `IBrowserSkinType` interface is important to Zope as it will find skins by that interface.

With `IWorldCookerySkin` we have a layer interface, now we only need to give it a name and let it provide `IBrowserSkinType` to turn it into a skin. In order to do that, we will use `interface` ZCML directive which we already know from Chapter 5. The listing is shown in Example 10.1.2. Note we are using a yet another subpackage of the `worldcookery` package to place the components related to the *WorldCookery* skin. That means we have to make sure we load the subpackage's configuration, too. Add the following line near the bottom of `configure.zcml`:

```
<include package=".skin" />
```

Example 10.1.2 Register a layer interface as a skin
(`skin/configure.zcml`)

```
1    <configure xmlns="http://namespaces.zope.org/zope">
2
3      <interface
4          interface=".interfaces.IWorldCookerySkin"
5          type="zope.publisher.interfaces.browser.IBrowserSkinType"
6          name="WorldCookery"
7          />
8
9    </configure>
```

5. By marking the layer interface with this interface type we tell Zope to treat it as a skin (e.g. include it in a list of skins that is offered to the user).

6. Here we set the human-readable name under which the layer will be known as a skin. In contrast to the dotted name of the layer, this name can easily be shown to users and appear in URLs.

The `interface` directive will not only apply the interface type to the layer interface, it will also make it available as a utility. That means we can lookup skin interfaces as simple utilities using their human-readable name instead of their dotted name:

```
$ bin/debugzope
>>> from zope.component import getUtility
>>> from zope.publisher.interfaces.browser import IBrowserSkinType
>>> getUtility(IBrowserSkinType, name=u'WorldCookery')
<InterfaceClass worldcookery.skin.interfaces.IWorldCookerySkin>    ∎
```

Using skins

You may be wondering *How do skins and layers end up on the request?* There are several possibilities. The easiest way to just try out a skin without changing a lot of configuration is to use the `++skin++` traversal namespace. For

example, we can view Zope's Management Interface using the *WorldCookery*
skin by opening the following URL in our browser:

```
http://localhost:8080/++skin++WorldCookery/
```

Of course, this will look really basic because we haven't actually provided
our own skin macro for our skin yet.

We can also make the *WorldCookery* skin the default skin from now on and
prevent visitors from having to type in the long and complicated URL above.
To do that we can use the `browser:defaultSkin` directive. However,
`zope.app` already sets this value to *Rotterdam* which is the default skin for
the Zope Management Interface. If we were to use this directive again, we
would get a configuration conflict. To avoid that, we need make sure that
when we use the directive, it overrides `zope.app`'s value.

ZCML provides such an override mechanism through the `includeOverrides`
directive. This directive works like the `include` directive which we already
know, except that the ZCML statements in the included files are able to override any directives on the same level as (or below) the `includeOverrides`
statement. In practice, an instance's `etc/site.zcml` includes the `etc/`
`overrides.zcml` file and files from the `etc/package-includes` directory ending in `-overrides.zcml` through the overrides mechanism. Any
directive in these files will be able to override anything else (because `site.`
`zcml` is the root of the ZCML execution tree).

For the *World Cookery* application we install a `worldcookery-overrides.`
`zcml` snippet in `etc/package-includes` with the following contents:

```
<include package="worldcookery" file="overrides.zcml" />
```

This will load the `overrides.zcml` file from the `worldcookery` package
already in overrides mode, because the snippet itself is loaded in overrides
mode. The contents of `overrides.zcml` is shown in Example 10.1.3.

Example 10.1.3 Overriding Zope's default skin (`overrides.zcml`)

```
1   <configure
2       xmlns="http://namespaces.zope.org/zope"
3       xmlns:browser="http://namespaces.zope.org/browser"
4       >
5
6     <browser:defaultSkin name="WorldCookery" />
7
8   </configure>
```

Table 10.1. Layers and skins defined in Zope packages

Interface	Skin name	Description
zope.publisher.interfaces.browser.IDefaultBrowserLayer	-	If not specified otherwise, all views are registered for this layer. Always put this layer in your skin definition so that view lookup will work as expected.
zope.app.basicskin.IBasicSkin	Basic	Extremely rudimentary skin only based on IDefaultBrowserLayer.
zope.app.rotterdam.Rotterdam	Rotterdam	Zope's standard skin.
zope.app.debugskin.IDebugLayer	-	Provides views for exceptions to improve error debugging.
zope.app.debugskin.IDebugSkin	Debug	Identical to the Rotterdam skin except that exceptions are displayed with their traceback, as provided by IDebugLayer.
zope.app.tree.browser.IStaticTreeLayer	-	Provides a static navigation tree, in contrast to Rotterdam's dynamic tree which requires ECMAScript.
zope.app.tree.browser.IStaticTreeSkin	StaticTree	Identical to Rotterdam except that the dynamic navigation tree is replaced by a static version, as provided by IStaticTreeLayer.

Summary

- Skins determine the look and feel of an application.
- Skins are groupings of layers or other skins, both are interfaces directly or indirectly extending `IBrowserRequest`. Skins have a human-readable name and provide `IBrowserSkinType`.
- By registering views for a certain layer (instead of the default one, `IDefaultBrowserLayer`), a skin may change view lookup behaviour and allow views to be customized.
- A skin other than the default skin can be invoked using the `skin` traversal namespace (for example `++skin++WorldCookery`); the default skin can be changed in an override ZCML directive.

Flashback

The concept of skins was first introduced to Zope in the *Content Management Framework* (CMF) and is extensively used in CMF-based applications such as *Plone* and *CPS*. As in Zope 3, CMF skins are defined as an ordered list of layers. However, CMF layers are not abstract markers as they are in Zope 3; they are not interfaces. They exist as subfolders of the `portal_skins` tool object in which the view objects, such as Page Templates or Python Scripts are located. That, of course, makes it much easier to see all things that are available in a certain layer.

The fact that both skins and layers are marker interfaces for the browser request in Zope 3 gives us several advantages, though. First, a layer can be a skin at the same time and a layer can already group other layers. Second, views for a particular layer can come from many different packages. In the CMF, each *Product* would typically register its own layer and change all skins to include it upon installation. That is not necessary anymore. In Zope 3, views are registered for `IDefaultBrowserLayer` by default anyway, meaning no layer needs to be specified upon registration unless actually wanted.

10.2 Page Template macros

When presenting data to a browser, views within one skin generally share a lot of common markup. For example, views in the ZMI always have the same basic HTML structure, only a few parts are unique to each view, most significantly the body of the view. Obviously, we would only want to define the general HTML structure once and reuse it everywhere. Page Templates allow us to do that using *macros*.

A macro is a piece of HTML markup that is meant to be reused in other Page Template views. Markup within macros is not limited to static HTML but can contain regular TAL statements. Those parts of a macro that can change with each view are called *slots*. Macros and slots in Page Templates are defined using the *Macro Expression Template Attribute Language* (METAL). METAL works like TAL in the sense that it uses attributes in a special namespace[1] for commands. It defines the following commands:

`define-macro` defines the markup tree starting below the current element as a macro.

`define-slot` defines the markup tree starting below the current element as a slot.

`use-macro` inserts the contents of a macro into the current template.

`extend-macro` must be used in combination with `define-macro` and allows the newly defined macro to inherit the extended macro's slots.

`fill-slot` fills a slot of the current macro with contents.

For more information, please refer to the METAL specification [8].

As an example, consider a simple macro that applies a certain formatting to arbitrary text. To save the time of writing a file system-based template and registering it via ZCML, we can simply create a *ZPT Page* in the ZMI. ZPT Pages are persistent Page Templates that are added like regular content objects. They allow quick mock-ups of Page Templates without the extra hassle of configuration. Simply go to an arbitrary folder in the ZMI and add a *ZPT Page* by clicking on the corresponding entry in the *Add* menu on the left hand side. Enter the following source code and give the object the name `macro.html`:

```
<html xmlns:metal="http://xml.zope.org/namespaces/metal"
      metal:define-macro="page_with_text">
<head>
  <title metal:define-slot="title">title</title>
</head>
<body>
  <p style="font-weight:bold;">
    <span metal:define-slot="text" />
  </p>
</body>
</html>
```

As you can see, in this Page Template there is a macro that is called page_with_text and starts with the html element. There are two slots

---

[1] http://xml.zope.org/namespaces/metal

in the macro that allow views to fill in custom information: `title` for the page's title and `text` for the text that is to be displayed. We can now provide a simple Page Template-based view that uses the macro. Add another ZPT Page called `page.html` in the same folder with the following source code:

```
<div xmlns:metal="http://xml.zope.org/namespaces/metal"
     metal:use-macro="context/macro.html/macros/page_with_text">
<title metal:fill-slot="title">Hello world!</title>
<span metal:fill-slot="text">Hello world!</span>
</div>
```

This page's markup structure has little to do with the one above. It is not even valid HTML as far as the structure is concerned. However, all that matters is that the macro from above is used. All markup that occurs within a use-macro is ignored and superseded by the macro itself, unless a slot is filled. If you open the preview of `page.html` in your browser now, you will see the following HTML being presented:

```
<html>
<head>
  <title>Hello World!</title>
</head>
<body>
  <p style="font-weight:bold;">
    <span>Hello world!</span>
  </p>
</body>
</html>
```

As you can see, the result has the markup structure of the macro but the slots contain data from the view.

Macros as part of a skin

In the quick demonstration above, the macro was exposed by the ZPT Page under the `macros` attribute. We could reference the macro by giving the path of the template containing it. This is not practical for macros that are part of a Zope skin. These are exposed through a special view called `standard_macros`. Every Zope skin should provide at least the following macros through this view:

page provides markup structure for a regular page without management capabilities (a regular browser page).

view is the macro for an object view as part of the ZMI. These pages are typically also registered in the `zmi_views` browser menu.

dialog, addingdialog allow pages to display themselves as dialogs or special variants of dialogs. These pages typically have little framework around the main content. In Rotterdam, they are identical to page.

By convention, these macros provide at least the following set of standard slots:

title allows the Page Template to insert a custom title element into the HTML header.

headers can be used for additional HTML headers to be inserted into the page, such as references to CSS or JavaScript files as well as meta tags.

body denotes the slot of the main page content which all Page Templates should fill.

Knowing this, we can revise the Page Template we use for displaying recipes. Example 10.2.1 shows a revised recipeview.pt now using the page macro provided by the current Zope skin. When you now view a recipe, compare the result as shown in Figure 10.1 with the way it looked before we involved the macro (Figure 7.3).

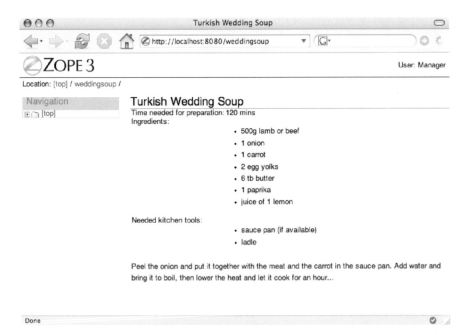

Fig. 10.1. Displaying a recipe with a template using a standard Zope skin macro.

Example 10.2.1 View Page Template using a standard Zope skin macro
(`browser/recipeview.pt`)

```
1   <html xmlns="http://www.w3.org/1999/xhtml"
2         xmlns:tal="http://xml.zope.org/namespaces/tal"
3         xmlns:i18n="http://xml.zope.org/namespaces/i18n"
4         xmlns:metal="http://xml.zope.org/namespaces/metal"
5         metal:use-macro="context/@@standard_macros/page"
6         i18n:domain="worldcookery">
7   <head>
8     <title metal:fill-slot="title"
9            tal:content="context/name/title">recipe name goes here</title>
10  </head>
11  <body>
12  <div metal:fill-slot="body">
13
14    <h2 tal:content="context/name/title">recipe name goes here</h2>
15
16    <table>
17      <tbody>
18        <tr>
19          <td i18n:translate="">Time needed for preparation:</td>
20          <td i18n:translate="">
21            <tal:var replace="context/time_to_cook"
22                     i18n:name="time_to_cook">xyz</tal:var> mins
23          </td>
24        </tr>
25
26        <tr>
27          <td i18n:translate="">Ingredients:</td>
28          <td>
29            <ul>
30              <li tal:repeat="ingredient context/ingredients"
31                  tal:content="ingredient">ingredients go here</li>
32            </ul>
33          </td>
34        </tr>
35
36        <tr>
37          <td i18n:translate="">Needed kitchen tools:</td>
38          <td>
39            <ul>
40              <li tal:repeat="tool context/tools"
41                  tal:content="tool">tools go here</li>
42            </ul>
43          </td>
44        </tr>
45
46      </tbody>
47    </table>
```

Example 10.2.1 (continued)

```
48    <p tal:content="structure view/renderDescription">
49      Longer description goes here.
50    </p>
51
52  </div>
53  </body>
54  </html>
```

4. All macro-related commands are contained in this namespace which is abbreviated with the `metal` prefix by convention.

5. Since this Page Template is not a management screen or exposes any other kind of management facility, the `page` macro is to be used. It is acquired by means of the special `standard_macros` view.

8–9. One of the slots that the `page` macro provides for customization is the `title` slot. It allows overriding Page Templates to set the title of the HTML page.

12 and 53. Templates using the `page` macro are supposed to fill the `body` slot with the main contents of the page. Here we basically wrap the essential recipe display in a `fill-slot` command.

Summary

- Page Templates can inherit the markup structure of other Page Templates through *macros*. *Slots* allow the insertion of content into the provided structure.
- The common layout of browser pages in Zope is provided by a few skin macros, most importantly the `page` macro.
- Skin macros are looked up through a special view called `standard_macros`.

10.3 Custom skins

In Section 10.1 we created a layer based on the default layer and registered it as a skin. This skin does not do much yet because the infrastructure that it inherits from the default layer is very rudimentary. Skins on top of the default layer have to provide all of the necessary Page Template macros, CSS stylesheets, images, etc. to influence the layout of the overall application. We will do this in a very basic way in this section, and defer more advanced skinning techniques until the next section.

Skin macros

Skin macros determine the common structure of all pages within a skin. They take care of producing the HTML header and common elements of HTML body, such as logos, global navigation, etc. In the previous section we have already seen the effect the page macro in this respect. Now we will provide our own very basic implementation of this macro as shown in Example 10.3.1. All that this Page Template does is define the page macro and some of the most common slots, as well as adding a *World Cookery* logo to all pages.

Now we need to make our page macro available to all other browser pages. Before we can do that, we must understand how skin macros are looked up. We have already seen in Example 10.2.1 that this happens through a special view called standard_macros. This view looks up macros from a set of Page Template views. It also typically deals with macro aliases (for example when the view macro is in fact just an alias to the page macro). We will therefore also have to provide the standard_macros view and tell it to look up macros from our new Page Template. Example 10.3.2 shows a browser view that provides access to our page macro as well as a custom version of the standard_macros view.

Both the standard_macros view and the template defining the page macro need to be registered now. There is no magic to that, both are simply defined as browser views. Example 10.3.3 shows a revised version of skin/configure.zcml.

Stylesheets, images and other resources

Skins typically need to load a lot of additional files to go with the HTML markup. Common examples are Cascading Stylesheets (CSS), images, ECMAScripts, etc. Since these are typically static and do not present a particular type of object, they are not views. They are really more like auxiliary data that needs to be loaded together with the website. These types of components are called *resources*.

Resources can be referenced in Page Templates using the ++resource++ traversal namespace:

```
<img tal:attributes="src context/++resource++worldcookery.png" />
```

When included like this, resources will in fact render themselves as a URL under which they will be available. This URL will typically be based on the nearest *site* (see Chapter 18 for more information on sites) so that their URL remains the same throughout the whole application. That way browsers and HTTP proxies can easily cache them. If you have not defined any sites, the root folder will be the URL base. The URL of the resource in the example above will then look like this:

```
http://localhost:8080/@@/worldcookery.png
```

Example 10.3.1 A custom page macro (`skin/worldcookery.pt`)

```
1   <html xmlns="http://www.w3.org/1999/xhtml"
2         xmlns:tal="http://xml.zope.org/namespaces/tal"
3         xmlns:metal="http://xml.zope.org/namespaces/metal"
4         metal:define-macro="page">
5   <head>
6     <title metal:define-slot="title">World Cookery</title>
7     <link rel="stylesheet" type="text/css" href="worldcookery.css"
8           tal:attributes="href context/++resource++wc/worldcookery.css" />
9     <link rel="icon" type="image/png" href="favicon.png"
10          tal:attributes="href context/++resource++wc/icon.png" />
11    <metal:slot define-slot="headers" />
12  </head>
13
14  <body>
15    <div id="logo">
16      <img src="worldcookery.png" alt="World Cookery"
17           tal:attributes="src context/++resource++wc/worldcookery.png" />
18    </div>
19
20    <div id="content">
21      <metal:slot define-slot="body">
22        The body goes here
23      </metal:slot>
24    </div>
25  </body>
26  </html>
```

7–8. A custom HTML structure is likely to require custom CSS as well. Therefore we load a stylesheet here which we will yet have to write and register as a resource (see below).

11.   Here we define the `headers` slot, one of the slots that skin macros should carry by convention. Note that when a whole element is in either the `tal` or `metal` namespaces, it is stripped from the output. TAL or METAL attributes in such elements do not have to carry the namespace prefix. For example,

```
<metal:macro define-macro="page">...</metal:macro>
```

is equivalent to

```
<span metal:define-macro="page" tal:omit-tag="">...</span>
```

21–23.   Finally, we have to provide the most important slot, body, for pages to fill.

As we have already seen in Chapter 8 when registering an ECMAScript file for the dynamic sequence widget, single browser resources are registered using the `browser:resource` ZCML directive. For the *WorldCookery* skin

Example 10.3.2 A custom `standard_macros` view
(`skin/standardmacros.py`)

```
1   from zope.publisher.browser import BrowserView
2   from zope.app.pagetemplate import ViewPageTemplateFile
3   from zope.app.basicskin.standardmacros import StandardMacros as
        BaseMacros
4
5   class WorldCookeryMacros(BrowserView):
6
7       template = ViewPageTemplateFile('worldcookery.pt')
8
9       def __getitem__(self, key):
10          return self.template.macros[key]
11
12  class StandardMacros(BaseMacros):
13      macro_pages = ('worldcookery_macros',)
```

5–1.   This browser view provides access to the custom page macro. Note the use
of `BrowserView` instead of `BrowserPage` as a base class: this view is not
meant to be published.

1 and 12.   Zope provides a base implementation of the `standard_macros` view
which we can simply subclass here.

13.   The base class already takes care of the actual macro look-up. We have to
provide it with a list of Page Template views to look for the macro. We only
have the Page Template from Example 10.3.1 which we will register under the
name `worldcookery_macros`.

we want to register a whole bunch of resources at once, for example the logo
and the CSS file that we are already referencing in our custom page macro
(Example 10.3.1). This is done with the `browser:resourceDirectory`
directive which registers a directory as a resource. See Example 10.3.4 for a
demonstration. In this example we also provide an icon for recipes.

Conclusion

We can now restart Zope and see our new skin in action. Since we made the
WorldCookery skin the default skin earlier, all browser pages will by default
use our skin macro. As you will notice, our custom skin macro does shockingly
little. For example, the menus and tabs that appear in the Rotterdam skin
are now gone. Any serious attempt at implementing a custom skin therefore
has to take care of including these and other common elements. The next
section of this chapter covers Zope technology that allows us to implement
complex skins with such elements easily.

Example 10.3.3 Registering the custom macro views
(`skin/configure.zcml`)

```
1   <configure
2       xmlns="http://namespaces.zope.org/zope"
3       xmlns:browser="http://namespaces.zope.org/browser"
4       >
5
6     <interface
7         interface=".interfaces.IWorldCookerySkin"
8         type="zope.publisher.interfaces.browser.IBrowserSkinType"
9         name="WorldCookery"
10        />
11
12    <browser:view
13        for="*"
14        name="worldcookery_macros"
15        class=".standardmacros.WorldCookeryMacros"
16        permission="zope.View"
17        layer=".interfaces.IWorldCookerySkin"
18        />
19
20    <browser:view
21        for="*"
22        name="standard_macros"
23        class=".standardmacros.StandardMacros"
24        permission="zope.View"
25        allowed_interface="zope.interface.common.mapping.IItemMapping"
26        layer=".interfaces.IWorldCookerySkin"
27        />
28
29  </configure>
```

12 and 20. The macro views do not need to be publishable. They only need to be available for look up, e.g. from a Page Template. Hence we use the `browser:view` directive here instead of `browser:page`.

13 and 21. All skin-related views should always be registered for *any* object which is expressed through an asterisk (*).

17 and 26. Of course we register the skin-related views for the `IWorldCookerySkin` layer, using the `layer` argument. This argument is available on nearly all `browser` directives.

Fig. 10.2. a) Logo for the *World Cookery* application (`skin/wc/worldcookery.png`). **b**) Icon for recipe objects (`skin/wc/icon.png`).

Example 10.3.4 Registering resources and icons
(`skin/configure.zcml`)

```
1     ...
2     <browser:resourceDirectory
3         name="wc"
4         directory="wc"
5         layer=".interfaces.IWorldCookerySkin"
6         />
7
8     <browser:icon
9         name="zmi_icon"
10        for="worldcookery.interfaces.IRecipe"
11        file="wc/icon.png"
12        layer=".interfaces.IWorldCookerySkin"
13        />
14    ...
```

8–13. Icons are not exactly resources. They are more like views because they
       are registered for a specific interface. Icons used by the ZMI carry the name
       zmi_icon. Custom UIs might use different icon names.

Summary

- Skin macros provide the common HTML markup (header and common elements of the body) for browser pages. The Page Templates
  that define them are registered as browser views for all objects (⋆).
- The standard_macros browser view looks up skin macros from
  the Page Template views that define the macros. The view also takes
  care of macro aliases.
- Files that are not views but still part of a skin (e.g. CSS, images,
  ECMAScripts) are called *resources*. They are registered using the
  browser:resource directive.

10.4 Content providers and viewlets

The skin macro we created in the previous section is admittedly very simple, too simple for a content management application such as *World Cookery*. Here are some things that it is missing and that might be worth adding to the skin:

- navigation capabilities, for example in the form of a navigation tree or breadcrumbs
- login status and a link to a login/logout page
- the *Add* menu for content editors
- the ZMI tabs and action menus

These are only some items that the *Rotterdam* skin has by default. You can probably think of other page elements, e.g. search boxes, copyright notices in the page footer, etc. Instead of modifying the skin macro to include all of these things, we want to try a more flexible approach in this section.

Content providers

We have noticed that pages in a web application are typically composed of many different elements. Most of them occur on every page so that the layout of the overall application is the same. One way to ensure this is to include them all in the skin macro. That, however, would not only make the skin macro grow quite large, it would also make it difficult to disable or exchange certain elements of the skin on certain pages.

For example, the *Add* menu is a typical skin element, but it makes only sense in the context of folder-like objects where you can actually add subobjects. In another example, some pages might need to include some ECMAScript or additional CSS files while the rest of the pages do not. How would the skin macro know when to include the *Add* menu or when to include the additional resources?

A *content provider* is a component that represents a page element. Essentially, that means a content provider represents a snippet of HTML, whether it is part of the HTML header (e.g. including ECMAScript or CSS) or part of the body (e.g. the *Add* menu). Like views, content providers are named multi-adapters. Unlike views, however, they adapt *three* objects:

- the object that is being viewed
- the request that invoked the view
- the view

This way, different or no content providers can be found depending on the viewed object *and* depending on the view. For example, a content provider that includes special ECMAScript for only certain pages would then only be registered for those pages.

Content providers provide `IContentProvider` from the `zope.contentprovider` package. They can be looked up in Python code like any other multi-adapter:

```
>>> getMultiAdapter((context, request, view), IContentProvider,
...                  name=u"worldcoookery.Logo")
```

Notice that the tuple of adapted objects now contains three objects.

Usually, though, content providers are looked up from Page Templates. After all, they typically return HTML content. In Page Templates they are looked up using the `provider` expression:

```
<img tal:replace="structure provider:worldcookery.Logo" />
```

Notice that we use the `structure` modifier here because the content provider returns HTML markup that should be inserted verbatim.

Viewlets and viewlet managers

We could now create content providers for each of the page elements that we want to add. We could then refer to each content provider in the skin macro using the `provider` expression. The advantage gained in this would be the flexibility of registering different content providers for different objects and/or views.

We are still left with one problem, though: What happens when we want to *add* a totally new page element? We would write a new content provider, but we would also have to modify the skin macro to have the provider included. It would be much nicer if the skin macro would not have to be modified.

The solution is to abstract certain regions in a skin macro. For example, ECMAScript and CSS declarations all occur in one place, the HTML header. Instead of including every single content provider that has to do with ECMAScript or CSS declarations, we can include one central content provider that is responsible for this region. This content provider will then find all the "little" content providers that want to be included in this region. These "little" content providers are called *viewlets*, while the one aggregating them in a region is called a *viewlet manager*.

Let us now define a couple of regions in our skin macro that will be filled with viewlets: a *headers* region where viewlets can insert additional references to CSS and ECMAScript files, a *toolbar* region that can contain menus similar to menus in a desktop application, and a *sidebar* region for additional content boxes on the side. There are three steps to defining a region (in other words, a viewlet manager):

1. Defining a marker interface for the viewlet manager that will identify it when it has to look up its viewlets. Example 10.4.1 shows the ones we create for the *WorldCookery* skin.
2. Registering a viewlet manager for its marker interface. The viewlet manager will also get a name with which it can be looked up as a content

provider (viewlet managers are content providers!). Example 10.4.2 shows the viewlet manager registrations in our skin.

3. Referencing the viewlet manager in the skin macro. This is done with the `provider` expression, as for any other content provider. The name of the content provider is, of course, in fact the name of the viewlet manager that was registered in the previous step. Example 10.4.3 shows the modified skin macro of our skin.

Example 10.4.1 Defining marker interfaces for viewlet managers (`skin/interfaces.py`)

```
1  from zope.publisher.interfaces.browser import IDefaultBrowserLayer
2  from zope.viewlet.interfaces import IViewletManager
3
4  class IWorldCookerySkin(IDefaultBrowserLayer):
5      """Skin for the WorldCookery application"""
6
7  class IHeaders(IViewletManager):
8      """Viewlets for the HTML header"""
9
10 class IToolbar(IViewletManager):
11     """Viewlets for the toolbar (e.g. tabs and actions)"""
12
13 class ISidebar(IViewletManager):
14     """Viewlets for the sidebar (e.g. add menu)"""
```

2. We are defining marker interfaces for viewlet managers, hence we use `IViewletManager` as a base interface.

Writing viewlets

So far so good. From an end-user point of view the skin has not changed. We have the viewlet managers, but we do not yet have the corresponding viewlets.

Viewlets are content providers, therefore they can be implemented like any other multi adapter in Python (for example like browser pages). However, since viewlets typically return HTML snippets, they are often just implemented using a Page Template that is registered directly using the `browser:viewlet` ZCML directive as a shortcut.

All of the viewlets in the *WorldCookery* skin are implemented in pretty much the same manner. We shall therefore only cover one of the simpler ones, namely the one providing the login/logout links in the toolbar (more advanced viewlets will be covered in the coming chapters). Example 10.4.4

Example 10.4.2 Registering viewlet managers as named content providers (`skin/configure.zcml`)

```
1    ...
2    <browser:viewletManager
3        name="worldcookery.Headers"
4        provides=".interfaces.IHeaders"
5        layer=".interfaces.IWorldCookerySkin"
6        permission="zope.View"
7        />
8
9    <browser:viewletManager
10       name="worldcookery.Toolbar"
11       provides=".interfaces.IToolbar"
12       layer=".interfaces.IWorldCookerySkin"
13       permission="zope.View"
14       />
15
16   <browser:viewletManager
17       name="worldcookery.Sidebar"
18       provides=".interfaces.ISidebar"
19       layer=".interfaces.IWorldCookerySkin"
20       permission="zope.View"
21       />
22   ...
```

3, 10, and 17. Since viewlet managers are content providers, they will be registered with a name with which they can later be looked up, e.g. using the `provider` expression in Page Templates.

4, 11, and 18. Each viewlet manager can be identified with its marker interface. Viewlets will then be registered for this particular viewlet manager using the marker interface as an identifier.

shows the simple Page Template that renders the viewlet. Along with it we want to provide CSS specific to that viewlet. Resources that go along with viewlets need to be registered twice: once as a resource and once as a viewlet for the HTML header. Example 10.4.5 shows the configuration that is necessary to hook it all up.

The viewlets that render the other menus (ZMI actions and tabs) are pretty similar to the login/logout viewlet and are not shown here. Chapter 13 will demonstrate how a custom menu is defined and presented in a viewlet. More complicated viewlets than the ones we have written so far can be implemented in Python. Chapter 14 will show how to do that.

Example 10.4.3 Including viewlet managers as content providers in the skin macro (skin/worldcookery.pt)

```
 1  <metal:block xmlns:metal="http://xml.zope.org/namespaces/metal"
 2                  metal:define-macro="page">
 3  <!DOCTYPE html PUBLIC "-//W3C//DTD XHTML 1.0 Transitional//EN"
 4              "http://www.w3.org/TR/xhtml1/DTD/xhtml1-transitional.dtd">
 5  <html xmlns="http://www.w3.org/1999/xhtml"
 6        xmlns:tal="http://xml.zope.org/namespaces/tal">
 7  <head>
 8    <title metal:define-slot="title">World Cookery</title>
 9    <link rel="stylesheet" type="text/css" href="worldcookery.css"
10          tal:attributes="href context/++resource++wc/worldcookery.css" />
11    <link rel="icon" type="image/png" href="favicon.png"
12          tal:attributes="href context/++resource++wc/icon.png" />
13    <metal:slot define-slot="headers" />
14    <tal:providers replace="structure provider:worldcookery.Headers" />
15  </head>
16
17  <body>
18    <div id="toolbar" tal:content="structure provider:worldcookery.Toolbar
          ">
19      The toolbar goes here
20    </div>
21
22    <div id="visualContentWrapper">
23      <div id="sidebar" tal:define="sidebar provider:worldcookery.Sidebar"
24            tal:condition="sidebar" tal:content="structure sidebar">
25        The sidebar goes here
26      </div>
27
28      <div id="content">
29        <metal:slot define-slot="body">
30          The body goes here
31        </metal:slot>
32      </div>
33
34    </div>
35  </body>
36  </html>
37  </metal:block>
```

14, 18–20, and 23–26.   Here we insert the output from each viewlet manager using the standard way to look up content providers in Page Templates. Viewlets for the HTML header will be inserted right below the head element while the toolbar and sidebar live in their own div elements.

Example 10.4.4 Viewlet rendering the login/logout links
(`skin/login.pt`)

```
1  <div id="login_logout" i18n:domain="zope">
2    <h1 i18n:translate="">User:</h1>
3    <span tal:replace="request/principal/title">user name</span>
4    <tal:block replace="structure context/@@login_logout" />
5  </div>
```

4. This viewlet is as simple as it is because it can rely on the login_logout view
   that is made available by Zope's authentication machinery. This view already
   takes care of deciding whether a user is logged in or not. It also renders the
   appropriate links to the login or logout page. All we need to do here is wrap it
   in a div.

Custom viewlet managers

By default, viewlet managers will use Python's cmp mechanism on the viewlet
objects to order them. Given that viewlets usually do not provide a custom
__cmp__ method, the order that they may appear in is rather arbitrary. While
the order of the viewlets may sometimes not be important, it is in many cases
desirable to specify a concrete order, for example in our skin's toolbar region.
In such a case it is a good idea to provide a custom viewlet manager that
sorts viewlets according to the desired criteria. Example 10.4.6 shows the
implementation of a viewlet manager that sorts viewlets according to their
name (the name they have as named adapters).

Now we can give the toolbar viewlets new names that reflect their desired position in the toolbar, e.g. 10login, 20logo, 30actions, etc.
We only need to specify that our custom viewlet manager is to be used
for the toolbar region. We do that with the class parameter of the
browser:viewletManager directive.

Summary

- Exchangeable page elements can be rendered by content providers.
  These are multi-adapters for the object that is displayed, the request
  and the view that displays the object.
- Content providers are looked up by name, typically from a Page
  Template using the provider expression.
- Many content providers for the same page region (viewlets) can be
  grouped by a viewlet manager. The viewlet manager acts as a content
  provider itself and looks up all the viewlets associated with it.

Example 10.4.5 Configuring the login/logout viewlet
(`skin/configure.zcml`)

```
1     ...
2     <browser:viewlet
3         name="login"
4         for="*"
5         manager=".interfaces.IHeaders"
6         template="login.pt"
7         layer=".interfaces.IWorldCookerySkin"
8         permission="zope.View"
9         />
10
11    <browser:viewlet
12        name="login.css"
13        for="*"
14        manager=".interfaces.IHeaders"
15        class=".resourceviewlet.LoginCSSViewlet"
16        layer=".interfaces.IWorldCookerySkin"
17        permission="zope.View"
18        />
19    ...
```

2–9.   This directive hooks up the template in Example 10.4.4 as a viewlet. Note that the viewlet is registered for all objects (*) and that it will appear in the toolbar viewlet manager. Of course, it is just a matter of changing this configuration to let it appear in some other place.

11–18.   In addition to configuring the CSS file that goes along with this viewlet, login.css, as a resource, we also have to make sure it is included in the HTML header. We do that by registering a viewlet for the respective viewlet manager. Instead of naming a template, this viewlet comes from a class, LoginCSSViewlet which is defined as follows:

```
from zope.viewlet.viewlet import CSSViewlet
LoginCSSViewlet = CSSViewlet('wc/login.css')
```

Rocky says...

Those Java developers who are familiar with Java portlets based on JSR 168 [7] will have little difficulty understanding viewlets. While some of the terms have different names, the technology is conceptually the same.

Example 10.4.6 Custom viewlet manager that sorts viewlets according to their names (`skin/manager.py`)

```
1  from zope.viewlet.manager import ViewletManagerBase
2
3  class SortingViewletManager(ViewletManagerBase):
4
5      def sort(self, viewlets):
6          return sorted(viewlets)
```

1 and 3. We can use the regular viewlet manager implementation as a base class. It already does all the work for us, we only have to override its `sort` method to do our custom sorting.

5–6. The base class calls the `sort` method with an iterable containing tuples of the form `(name, viewlet)`. Arbitrary iterables can easily be sorted using Python's built-in `sorted` function. The tuples will be sorted first according to the name, then according to the viewlet object, which is a result of regular tuple sorting semantics.

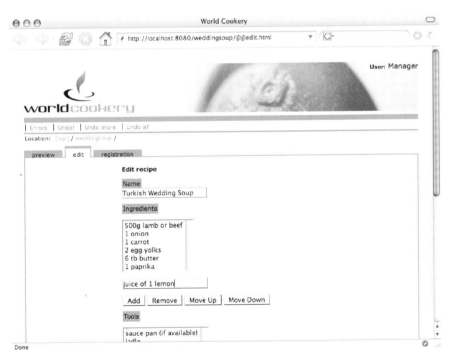

Fig. 10.3. A recipe's edit form displayed in the *WorldCookery* skin.

11

Adapters

One of the major concepts behind Component Architecture is to divide different types of functionality into different components in order to keep the amount of functionality provided by a single component small. Its strength lies in combining these components into a powerful application. In Chapter 2, *adapters* were defined as components that allow you to extend the functionality of existing components. Adapters play a *major* role in Component Architecture and in Zope 3, the software based on it.

Adapters are useful when a component needs to work with a certain framework. Instead of requiring the objects the framework works with to provide a certain API, the framework usually tries to adapt the object to one of its own APIs. If an adapter exists for the object, then the framework can work with the object through the adapter. This chapter will demonstrate implementing adapters. Because adapters are an integral part of the Component Architecture, they will frequently appear in later chapters.

We have already worked with a framework using adapters: the Zope publisher. Views are named adapters that add presentation functionality to the objects they present.

11.1 Size

A common task in a user or management interface is to display the size of stored objects. Zope has its own API to handle size information, formalized in the `ISized` interface provided by the `zope.size` package. No object is required to implement this interface directly, though. You usually provide an adapter to it.

Adapters convert ("adapt") one or more objects, each identified by interfaces or class, into another. In this case, we want to adapt an `IRecipe` object into one that provides `ISized`. Adapters are typically simple classes. An adapter factory for a class is the `__init__` method. It needs to take as many arguments as objects are adapted. In case of single adaption, it is a common convention to name this argument context and store it as the context attribute on the adapter object.

Even though it might seem a little awkward to compute a size of a recipe, we shall provide a size adapter here. The reason is that this is a very common and simple adapter for a content component and serves well as an example. The ISized interface only expects two relatively simple methods. Example 11.1.1 shows the implementation for recipes.

As with any other type of component, we need to configure the adapter now. This is easily achieved with the adapter ZCML directive. Add the following line to configure.zcml:

```
<adapter factory=".size.RecipeSize" />
```

This directive is simple because a lot of information is already stored inside the adapter implementation, for example which interface is adapted and which provided.

Testing

We can now test the adapter on the interactive interpreter shell. First, we create a recipe object and provide some initial data:

```
$ python
>>> from worldcookery.recipe import Recipe
>>> falafel = Recipe()
>>> falafel.name = u"Falafel"
>>> falafel.ingredients = [u"beans", u"peas", u"garlic"]        ▼
```

Before we can look up the adapter, we need to register it using the registration API from zope.component. Then we can adapt our recipe object to ISized. This is achieved by calling the interface with the object as an argument. Think of this as a type casting known in other programming languages. We "cast" (read: adapt) the recipe object to ISized:

```
>>> from zope.component import provideAdapter
>>> from worldcookery.size import RecipeSize
>>> provideAdapter(RecipeSize)
>>> from zope.size.interfaces import ISized
>>> size = ISized(falafel)                                      ▼
```

Note that if falafel had already provided ISized, the adapter call would have returned falafel identically.

We now have an object that provides ISized, so we can call the two methods promised by this interface. Of course, we know that this is really our adapter for the recipe object, so we know what output to expect. To enable the variable interpolation for the message id the sizeForDisplay returns, we have to use the familiar translate function:

Example 11.1.1 Adapter to display a recipe's size (`size.py`)

```
1   from zope.interface import implements
2   from zope.component import adapts
3   from zope.size.interfaces import ISized
4   from zope.i18nmessageid import MessageFactory
5   _ = MessageFactory('worldcookery')
6   from worldcookery.interfaces import IRecipe
7
8   class RecipeSize(object):
9       implements(ISized)
10      adapts(IRecipe)
11
12      def __init__(self, context):
13          self.context = context
14
15      def sizeForSorting(self):
16          """Compute a size for sorting"""
17          chars = 0
18          chars += len(self.context.name)
19          chars += sum(map(len, self.context.tools))
20          chars += sum(map(len, self.context.ingredients))
21          chars += len(self.context.description)
22          return ('byte', chars)
23
24      def sizeForDisplay(self):
25          """Generate a displayable size report"""
26          unit, chars = self.sizeForSorting()
27          return _('${chars} characters', mapping={'chars': chars})
```

9. Once created, the adapter is supposed to provide `ISized`. The easiest way to ensure this is by having the class implement it.

10. This lets us declare what kind of object this adapter adapts. This information is not strictly necessary nor always sensible to provide (e.g. with browser views), though it is useful for the Component Architecture, for example when registering the adapter.

12–13. A factory that instantiates an adapter takes exactly one argument, the object that is to be adapted. Most of the time, an adapter's factory is the class's __init__ method. The object that is to be adapted should then be stored on the adapter as the `context` attribute so that the methods of the adapter have access to it.

15–22. This method is used by management views and similar facilities when objects are to be sorted by size. Because objects may not necessarily be able to tell their size in a uniform way, e.g. number of bytes, different basic units are supported:

Example 11.1.1 (continued)

- `'byte'` for file-like objects,
- `'item'` for objects that contain a number of items, such as containers,
- `'line'` for textual components, like objects holding plain text or source code.

For our recipe, we simply add the length of all strings that are stored inside the recipe and return that as the number of bytes. This, of course, can only serve as a rough estimate, because the size of a Unicode encoded into a string varies depending on the encoding you choose.

24–27. This method is supposed to generate a small message that can be used when displaying the size of objects. This message, of course, needs to be an i18n message so that it can be translated. Then we simply let the sizeForSorting method compute the number of characters and fill the placeholder value on the message.

```
>>> size.sizeForSorting()
('byte', 22)
>>> from zope.i18n import translate
>>> translate(size.sizeForDisplay())
u'22 characters'
```

To prove that the adapter is indeed working within the Zope application server, we can go to the Zope management interface and view the contents of a folder that contains one or more recipes. A recipe's size in characters should now be shown in the *Size* column of the folder listing, as shown in Figure 11.1.

Summary

- Object listings frequently need to list the size of objects. The zope.size package provides a small general framework for this problem.
- The functionality of providing the size of an object is implemented as an adapter from an interface the object provides to ISized.
- Adapter factories take a single argument, context, the object that is to be adapted.
- Objects are adapted to a particular interface by calling the interface with the object as an argument, making adaptation syntactically similar to type casting.

Fig. 11.1. The *Contents* screen in the ZMI uses `ISized` adapters to display the size of objects.

11.2 File representation

Apart from publishing objects to web browsers over HTTP, Zope knows a variety of other protocols, such as WebDAV, XML-RPC and FTP. WebDAV and XML-RPC are covered in Chapter 13, FTP is subject of this section. As the name already suggests, the *file transfer protocol* (FTP) is about files (and directories). Zope, however, does not work with simple files, it works with objects. The different aspects of objects are easy to communicate to a browser through different views, as we have seen. An FTP client still expects a structure of simple files and directories. How can we connect both sides?

A Zope developer with the experience of this chapter and the previous ones, already knows the answer—adapters! Not unlike in the previous section, a Zope package provides a collection of interfaces that make up a file representation API. Using this API, other components such as generic FTP views can adapt objects so that they are representable as files or directories. The file contents or directory listings can then be sent to the client which does not know that it is looking at objects; it only sees files.

The `zope.filerepresentation` package defines the following API interfaces:

IReadFile represents an object as a readable file. Methods allow access to the contents of the file representation and its size.

IWriteFile represents an object as a writable file. The `write` method allows writing data to the file.

IReadDirectory represents an object as a readable directory. Methods allow the retrieval of a list of objects contained in the directory and can be represented as files or directories themselves. The methods are identical to `IReadContainer` of the `zope.app.container` package.

IWriteDirectory represents an object as a writable directory. Objects can be added to the directory through file and directory factories. The methods are identical to `IWriteContainer` of the `zope.app.container` package.

IFileFactory creates a new object in a container based on file contents and content type information.

IDirectoryFactory creates a new object in a container when the client wishes to create a directory. This usually, but not necessarily results in creating a container-like object.

By providing adapters to the appropriate interfaces above, we can easily enable file representation for our content components, thus allowing access through FTP. When we provide adapters for `IReadFile` and `IFileFactory`, we will also be able to issue an HTTP *PUT* request to save the object data.

A limited example

The way we defined the recipe content type in `IRecipe` makes it hard to find a sensible file representation for recipe objects. If one really wanted a one-to-one relationship between recipe objects and their file representations, one would have to to find a way to encode all data stored in a recipe in a text file, for example using XML, and to decode that data again. Given the right tools, this is quite possible, but out of the scope of this chapter.

As a demonstration of the file representation API, we will only provide adapters that allow us to edit a recipe's *description* as a normal text file. That means we will have to write adapters that provide `IReadFile` and `IWriteFile`. Additionally, we can write a factory that creates new recipes when an FTP or WebDAV client uploads a text file that ends in `.recipe`. Example 11.2.1 shows the code for the three adapters.

File factories are adapters for containers in which they should be responsible for creating new objects. When a file is uploaded to a container, the FTP or WebDAV view tries to turn it into an object by acquiring an `IFileFactory` adapter. However, the type of the file that is uploaded can be anything, an image, a text file or something else. Obviously, one would want different file factories for each type of object that can be created. Which factory is chosen is determined by the extension of the file that is uploaded. The appropriate factory adapter is then looked up *by name* which corresponds to the extension of the file. Example 11.2.2 shows the configuration for the factory adapter which is registered as a *named adapter*, as well as configuration directives for the read and write adapters.

Testing

Just like the size adapter, we can test the file representation adapters in the interactive interpreter shell. Let us first create a recipe object through a file factory. In order to acquire the factory, we need a folder object since we registered the factory as an adapter for folders. We can throw the folder away afterwards. Even though the factory is an adapter, we cannot look it up by calling the interface anymore because that will not take the adapter name into account. We need to use `getAdapter` from `zope.component` now:

```
$ bin/debugzope
>>> from zope.app.folder import Folder
>>> from zope.filerepresentation.interfaces import \
...     IReadFile, IWriteFile, IFileFactory
>>> from zope.component import getAdapter
>>> folder = Folder()
>>> factory = getAdapter(folder, IFileFactory, ".recipe")        ▼
```

Now we can call the factory with some made-up data. We expect to get a recipe object back, of course, and that the recipe's description equals to the data we passed to the factory.

```
>>> data = "Add spices to the water and bring it to boil. " \
...        "Then add the couscous."
>>> couscous = factory("couscous", "text/plain", data)
>>> couscous
<worldcookery.recipe.Recipe object at 0x27d9770>
>>> couscous.name
'Couscous'
>>> couscous.description
u'Add spices to the water and bring it to boil. Then add the
couscous.'                                                       ▼
```

Now we can get a file representation for the recipe again and read its data. Note that the file representation returns a string object, not a Unicode object, since only the former can be written to a file stream.

Example 11.2.1 Adapters for file representation
(`filerepresentation.py`)

```
1   from zope.interface import implements
2   from zope.component import adapts
3   from zope.filerepresentation.interfaces import IReadFile, IWriteFile
4   from zope.filerepresentation.interfaces import IFileFactory
5   from worldcookery.recipe import Recipe
6   from worldcookery.interfaces import IRecipe
7
8   class RecipeReadFile(object):
9       implements(IReadFile)
10      adapts(IRecipe)
11
12      def __init__(self, context):
13          self.context = context
14          self.data = self.context.description.encode('utf-8')
15
16      def read(self):
17          return self.data
18
19      def size(self):
20          return len(self.data)
21
22  class RecipeWriteFile(object):
23      implements(IWriteFile)
24      adapts(IRecipe)
25
26      def __init__(self, context):
27          self.context = context
28
29      def write(self, data):
30          self.context.description = data.decode('utf-8')
31
32  class RecipeFactory(object):
33      implements(IFileFactory)
34
35      def __init__(self, context):
36          self.context = context
37
38      def __call__(self, name, content_type, data):
39          recipe = Recipe()
40          recipe.name = name.title()
41          recipe.description = data.decode('utf-8')
42          return recipe
```

16–20. The interface requires us to provide `read` and `size` methods for the data
which in this case is the description text of the recipe. In the `IRecipe` schema,
we defined `description` as text which means it is a Unicode string. However,
we have to return a string here, so we encode the data to UTF-8, an encoding
that can handle the whole Unicode range. This data is pre-computed in the
constructor of the adapter.

Example 11.2.1 (continued)

29–30. The IWriteFile adapter is even easier to implement, we just have to provide a write method. As much as we encoded Unicode to UTF-8 in the IReadFile adapter, we have to *decode* incoming strings with it to obtain a Unicode object.

38–42. File factory adapters have to be callable which we accomplish here by providing a __call__ method. In that we create a new recipe object, store the data we are given from the caller and return it. The object will then be added to the container the factory adapter was acquired for.

```
>>> readfile = IReadFile(couscous)
>>> readfile.size()
68
>>> readfile.read()
'Add spices to the water and bring it to boil. Then add the
couscous.'
```
▼

Finally, we can adapt the recipe object to a writable file and store new data on it. The recipe will be changed accordingly, of course:

```
>>> writefile = IWriteFile(couscous)
>>> writefile.write("Couscous consists of grains made from semolina.")
>>> couscous.description
u'Couscous consists of grains made from semolina.'
```
■

To see the file representation in action, you can also use an FTP client to connect to Zope and retrieve a recipe's description as a file or upload an existing text file to a recipe. In order to do that, you first need to enable Zope's FTP server in your instance's etc/zope.conf. The respective entry might look like this:

```
<server ftp>
  type FTP
  address 8021
</server>
```

When adding new files to a folder via FTP, you can give them the .recipe extension and the files will be turned into Recipe objects thanks to our IFileFactory adapter. Not only the generic FTP views use the file representation adapters, though. The WebDAV view for the HTTP *PUT* command uses file factories as well, so you could also try adding a recipe with a WebDAV client.

Example 11.2.2 Configuring file representation adapters
(`configure.zcml`)

```
1    ...
2    <adapter
3        factory=".filerepresentation.RecipeReadFile"
4        permission="zope.View"
5        />
6
7    <adapter
8        factory=".filerepresentation.RecipeWriteFile"
9        permission="zope.ManageContent"
10       />
11
12   <adapter
13       factory=".filerepresentation.RecipeFactory"
14       for="zope.app.folder.interfaces.IFolder"
15       name=".recipe"
16       permission="zope.ManageContent"
17       />
18   ...
```

4, 9, and 15. The directive we use to configure the file representation adapters looks, of course, the same way as with the size adapter. However, since these adapters serve in the context of FTP and WebDAV views and modify objects, we need to make sure their usage is restricted to users with correct permissions.

14. `IFileFactory` adapters are registered for containers in which they should be responsible for creating new objects. In our case, we want to be able to add new recipes to folder objects so we register the adapter for the folder interface.

15. File factory adapters are an example of *named adapters* because there exist more than one of them. In this case, different factories are responsible for different file extensions which are also the names of the adapters. Here we make our factory responsible for all files with the `.recipe` extension.

Summary

- Zope has built-in support for the file-based protocols FTP and Web-DAV.
- Objects can be represented as files using adapters, allowing them to be read and written through file-based protocols.
- File factories create new objects based on file data. They are named adapters registered for the type of container the file is supposed to be created in.

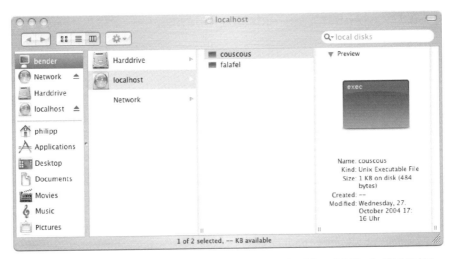

Fig. 11.2. A Zope folder with recipes mounted under Mac OS X via WebDAV.

Flashback

Adapters are a truly innovative concept and a significant advance over Zope 2. In versions of Zope prior to Zope3, it is very difficult (and nearly impossible) to extend the functionality of existing components. To make an object FTP or WebDAV-aware in Zope 2, you have to provide special methods, such as `manage_FTPget`, `PUT`, or `PUT_factory` directly in the object's implementation; the same goes for providing size information. In Zope 3, it is a simple matter of providing the right adapters. Adapters and views even allow us to seamlessly integrate components that originally were not even designed to work in Zope, something that is nearly impossible in Zope 2. This is a big deal because it helps us reduce duplication and re-inventions of the wheel.

The file factory idea, on the other hand, is not that new and already exists in a similar way in the CMF. There, the *Content Type Registry* tool inside the CMF site matches file extensions, file names or MIME types with content type factories which are invoked when a file is created through FTP or WebDAV inside a CMF site. By using adapters for this functionality, Zope 3 makes the creation of objects based on a file representation much more flexible because each factory can decide what kind of object is to be created based on the given circumstances (container, name, and MIME type).

11.3 Customizing an existing adapter

Zope has many components that provide some particular default behaviour.
Especially when the policy induced by these components should be exchangeable, the functionality is factored out into a separate, exchangeable component which usually is either an adapter or a utility. It is often necessary to
replace an existing component with a custom one to achieve a different behaviour from the application. In some cases, such as with browser skins, you
are *supposed* to customize the default components.

In Chapter 9, we learned that Zope automatically deduces the preferred
language from an HTTP header sent by the browser in the request. Browsers
either allow setting a list of preferred languages or they acquire the value from
the locale setting of the environment they are running in. In either case, the
preferred language the browser exposes to Zope might not match the user's
preferences at all. Just the fact that somebody is using a computer running a
German version of Microsoft Windows would not necessarily mean that that
person would also prefer to operate our web application in German.

If we want to allow users to choose the language they are viewing the
web application in, we would have to change the language deducing behaviour of Zope. We do this by changing the `IUserPreferredLanguages`
adapter for the request. Zope provides the default adapter which inspects
the `Accept-Language` HTTP header in the `zope.publisher.browser`
module. We will override it with our own one which should give a user-editable
setting (in the form of a form variable or a browser cookie) precedence over
the HTTP header. In case such a value is absent, the expected behaviour
of evaluating the HTTP header will still be intact. Since most adapters are
implemented with classes, we can subclass the existing adapter, thus inheriting the existing functionality. Example 11.3.1 demonstrates the brevity of
the adapter code.

Overriding existing configuration

Because Zope already defines an adapter from `IBrowserRequest` to
`IUserPreferredLanguages`, we cannot simply register our own adapter
in `configure.zcml`. We want our adapter to *override* the existing one,
hence we have to make another entry in `overrides.zcml` file. Its contents
is shown in Example 11.3.2, including the setting of the default browser skin
as introduced in Chapter 10.

You can now open a browser page in Zope and append `?ZopeLanguage=es`
to the URL, for example. This will cause our custom adapter to find the necessary form variable in the request and thus let the whole page appear in
Spanish. Note that due to our custom adapter inheriting from the simple
`BrowserLanguages` class, the `++lang++` namespace adapter no longer
works (as it requires a more sophisticated `IUserPreferredLanguages`
adapter).

Example 11.3.1 A custom preferred languages adapter
(`browser/adapter.py`)

```
1  from zope.publisher.browser import BrowserLanguages
2
3  class BrowserFormLanguages(BrowserLanguages):
4
5      def getPreferredLanguages(self):
6          langs = super(BrowserFormLanguages, self).getPreferredLanguages()
7          form_lang = self.request.get("ZopeLanguage", None)
8          if form_lang is not None:
9              langs.insert(0, form_lang)
10         return langs
```

6. Using the super functionality, we retrieve the language values from the base class's implementation of getPreferredLanguages.

7. Here we retrieve possible language values from the request which could either be sent by the browser as a form variable or a cookie under the name ZopeLanguage. If we retrieve a valid value (in other words, not None), we put at the top of the list of preferred languages, telling the negotiator that this would then be the most preferred language.

Example 11.3.2 Overriding an existing adapter configuration with a custom one (`overrides.zcml`)

```
1  <configure
2      xmlns="http://namespaces.zope.org/zope"
3      xmlns:browser="http://namespaces.zope.org/browser"
4      >
5
6    <browser:defaultSkin name="WorldCookery" />
7
8    <adapter
9        factory="worldcookery.browser.adapter.BrowserFormLanguages"
10       />
11
12 </configure>
```

In conclusion, this example is probably one of the best ones to demonstrate the Component Architecture at work. We changed the behaviour of one of Zope's core frameworks by writing only third party software and three lines of configuration! Keep in mind, though, that this is not just a consequence of the Component Architecture itself. It is possible to write code that makes use of the Component Architecture in a way that would still make that code hard to customize. Zope 3 has been written from ground up to be based on customizable components. The functionality of extracting preferred languages from a request did not *have* to be an adapter. However using an adapter gave us maximum flexibility. Try to follow Zope's rule and factor out additional functionality into separate components as soon as possible. It will be easier when the time comes for you to adjust or customize your own code.

Summary

- The translation machinery uses an adapter to retrieve a list of preferred languages from the browser request.
- Zope's default implementation for such an adapter interprets the values sent by most of today's browser in the `Accept-Language` HTTP header.
- By overriding the adapter with a custom one, it is possible to adjust the existing behaviour or change it altogether.

Using Zope 2

When the Zope 3 i18n machinery is used in Zope 2, it will also use an `IUserPreferredLanguages` adapter to determine the target language. When the Zope 3 i18n machinery is used exclusively, the default language adapter which inspects the HTTP headers as discussed above usually suffices. However, when an application uses the Zope 3 machinery for some i18n domains and an older Zope 2 solution for others, both systems need to come to the same conclusion regarding the preferred language. The Five product therefore provides two compatibility adapters:

- `Products.Five.i18n.PTSLanguages` for compatibility with Placeless Translation Service
- `Products.Five.i18n.LocalizerLanguages` for compatibility with Localizer

Automated Testing

In the introduction, Zope was advertised as a product that makes it easy to do Quality Assurance. So far, we have not done much to demonstrate that. That is mostly because we were busy exploring the Component Architecture. Now it is time to start thinking about measures that ensure not only a good development process but also a high-quality software product.

12.1 Introduction

As an application grows it takes an increasingly large amount of time to do manual testing. There comes a moment when you would like to automate your tests so that the computer can test the application for you.

Traditionally, automatic tests come under the following categories:

Unit tests isolate a specific component and test only this component's functionality. This is the most common and most effective kind of test because environmental circumstances do not influence the functionality of the component and its testing.

Relying on other components for testing means that any potential bugs these components contain would let the test fail, even if the component that was to be tested was fine. Unit tests avoid these dependencies; if a component has to rely on other components because of its nature (for example adapters or views), it is common practice to write *mock objects* that pretend to be the necessary components while in fact they are very simple implementations.

Integration tests make sure that component interaction works as expected. While unit tests cover the individual component's responsibility, integration tests cover a whole set of components integrated into an application sub-process. Often, integration tests only make sense when you already have done unit tests of the components that are interacting. If you do not have unit tests and an integration test fails, you will not be able to tell whether it failed because of one of the components made the test fail, or whether it failed because the integration was not working.

Integration tests in Zope are sadly called *functional tests*, making it difficult to differentiate them from real functional tests.

Functional tests treat an application like black box and do not take implementation details into account. They see what the user sees and exercise everything a user would do with the application, ideally through the user interface itself. In a case of a web application, the test could simply pretend to be a web browser operated by a user, for example.

Functional tests are independent of the development platform and programming language of the application, especially in the case of web applications. There are numerous web testing kits for functional testing web applications available, the most popular probably being Selenium.[1]

The right philosophy

Having automatic tests is not a guarantee for a higher quality software product per se. Test cases can be ineffective and thus useless if they do not cover realistic circumstances. On the other hand, tests that do not exercise possible edge-cases may easily hide bugs. Within the Zope community, the following testing philosophy has proven to be quite successful to circumvent such cases:

- Each time a change is made to the application, the whole test suite is run to check whether the whole application is still working.
- When a new feature is added, a test case has to be written that makes sure that all of the new functionality is covered by tests. That not only ensures that the code works right now but also in the future.
- When a bug is found in spite of automatic tests and a bugfix is applied, the tests covering that particular feature should be revised and extended to exercise the action that led to the discovery of the bug. This ensures that the bugfix actually does what it is intended to do.

It is the correct combination of leveraging the given tools and a solid philosophy that makes up good Quality Assurance. In this chapter we look at the Quality Assurance tools Zope provides us with. As for the philosophy, you will have to find one that suits best you, your team and the software you are developing. This is sadly beyond the scope of this chapter, but further reading is encouraged, such as [26].

---

[1] Selenium website <http://www.openqa.org/selenium>

12.2 Unit tests

As mentioned, unit tests are the most common type of test, however, they are not a feature of Zope. Python comes with unit test support in the `unittest` module, a contribution from the *PyUnit* project. It manages tests by grouping them in different levels:

- A *test* is a minimal, atomic test for one particular functionality of a component.
- A *test case* is a group of the tests that test the functionality of one particular component.
- A *test suite* is a collection of test cases, usually the ones from the module or package.

Because the other types of tests that will be introduced in this chapter rely on the infrastructure provided by the `unittest` module, these categories also apply to them.

In the test infrastructure based on the `unittest` module, test cases are classes that derive from `unittest.TestCase`. Every method on such a class that begins with `test` is a test and will be called when the test case is executed. Furthermore, `TestCase` provides a number of useful methods for asserting values and other circumstances. Consider a very simple test case typed in at the interactive interpreter shell:

```
python
>>> import unittest
>>> class SimpleTestCase(unittest.TestCase):
...        def test_one_plus_one(self):
...                self.assertEqual(1 + 1, 2)
...                self.failIfEqual(1 + 1, 3)
...
>>> unittest.main()
.
----------------------------------------------------------------------
Ran 1 test in 0.002s

OK
```

For general information about *PyUnit* and its `unittest` module, please consult the *PyUnit* website[2]. We will cover the Zope-specific parts of unit tests next.

Unit testing a component

We could write a unit test for the `Recipe` class now. However, it provides almost no functionality other than being persistent and providing some default values.

---
[2] PyUnit project website <http://pyunit.sourceforge.net>

Let us look at an example that has functionality worth testing. The adapters we wrote in the previous chapter are perfect for this. Example 12.2.1 shows a unit test for the ISized adapter. Note that unit tests typically go into a tests.py module or, if there are many tests that should be split up into their own modules, a tests package.

To run the unit test, simply execute the test_size.py file as a Python script from the command line. Make sure that both the Zope 3 libraries and the instance's library directory are in your *python path*:

```
~/Zope3Instance$ export PYTHONPATH=./lib/python:
                 /usr/local/Zope-3.x.y/lib/python
~/Zope3Instance$ python lib/python/worldcookery/tests/test_size.py
..
----------------------------------------------------------------------
Ran 2 tests in 0.078s

OK
```

On Windows, the commands look slightly different, but the outcome is the same:

```
C:\Zope3Instance> set PYTHONPATH=.\lib\python
C:\Zope3Instance> python lib\python\worldcookery\tests\test_size.py
..
----------------------------------------------------------------------
Ran 2 tests in 1.192s

OK
```

As the test framework reports both tests are passing. The adapter is working correctly, just like we expected, of course.

Summary

- Unit tests are based on *PyUnit*, Python's unit test implementation which is provided in the unittest module.
- Test cases are classes inheriting from unittest.TestCase whose methods begin with test are the tests of the test case.
- The setUp and tearDown methods can be used to provide initialization and clean up for every test within a test case.

Flashback

Compared to Zope 2, testing in Zope 3 has become both more sophisticated and much easier. That is because the Zope 3 developers have made software testing part of the development cycle from the very beginning.

Example 12.2.1 Unit test for the size adapter (tests/test_size.py)

```
1   import unittest
2   from zope.i18n import translate
3   from worldcookery.recipe import Recipe
4   from worldcookery.size import RecipeSize
5
6   class RecipeSizeTestCase(unittest.TestCase):
7
8       def setUp(self):
9           self.recipe = recipe = Recipe()
10          recipe.name = u"Fish and Chips"
11          recipe.ingredients = [u"Fish", u"Potato chips"]
12          recipe.description = u"Fish and Chips is a typical British dish."
13          self.size = RecipeSize(recipe)
14
15      def test_size_for_sorting(self):
16          unit, size = self.size.sizeForSorting()
17          self.assertEqual(unit, 'byte')
18          self.assertEqual(size, 71)
19
20      def test_size_for_display(self):
21          msg = self.size.sizeForDisplay()
22          self.assertEqual(u"71 characters", translate(msg))
23
24  def test_suite():
25      suite = unittest.TestSuite()
26      suite.addTest(unittest.makeSuite(RecipeSizeTestCase))
27      return suite
28
29  if __name__ == '__main__':
30      unittest.main()
```

8–13. A test case's setUp method is called before each test is executed. It can be used to instantiate test objects, for instance a Recipe object and a size adapter for that recipe.

15–18 and 20–22. With the recipe object and the size adapter already instantiated in setUp, the actual tests are quite simple. We provide a test for each method the ISized interface promises and test the behaviour of each method independently.

24–30. At last, the "boiler plate" code at the bottom allows us to run the tests from the command line and independently from the test runner while providing the test runner with a test suite when running the test as part of a large test run.

In Zope 2, one can easily write unit tests for a component using the
ZopeTestCase package. While it is not mandatory to use it when testing
Zope 2 components, it is very convenient as many Zope 2 objects need
a lot of machinery in place in order to function properly. The degree
of dependency on other objects is very high in Zope 2, mostly due to
implicit acquisition. For this reason most unit tests for Zope 2 software
use *ZopeTestCase*. The problem with this is that these tests are never
real unit tests because they depend on too much Zope infrastructure. In
fact, *ZopeTestCase* loads almost a whole Zope instance with a volatile
ZODB database instance to execute the tests. Thus they should probably
be considered integration tests, not unit tests.

Zope 3 on the other hand is as light-weight as you want it to be.
For simple components, a special test setup is not even required. For
components requiring Component Architecture functionality, tests can
use the `PlacelessSetup` mix-in class which only sets up basic services.
As you can see, testing is one of the places where Zope 3's modularity
pays off since you only have to load as much as you need and not the
whole thing.

Rocky says...

Java developers should instantly recognize this path to software quality.
Using *PyUnit* for writing python tests will be second nature to those
accustomed with *JUnit* for which it was modelled after.

12.3 Doctests

While unit tests provide a good way to test a component's functionality, they
have obvious deficiencies. To the Python programmer they feel unnatural to
write. For instance you have to call various methods for test assertions. In this
respect the *PyUnit* package cannot deny its descent from the Java world. To
a Python programmer, it feels much more natural to play with components
on the interactive interpreter shell first and see if the component behaves as
expected. If you look back, you can see that this is exactly what we have
been doing! What could be more natural than to use the interpreter itself as
a test harness?

The idea behind *doctests* includes another aspect. A unit test is most
often the first piece of code in which the component is used to its full extent.
For someone who wants to know how a component behaves, a unit test is
generally a good place to find out. The problem is the way we wrote the
unit tests in the previous section. They are quite hard to read and maybe

even difficult to find. Doctests solve both these problems. Doctests allow you to test a component while documenting it in a way another developer can understand. That is, they allow you to both document a component and provide a test at the same time.

The right place for documentation

Python has a very neat way of providing documentation inside code—*docstrings*. We have already used them in interfaces. Docstrings were invented so that developers can document components in a uniform way. Since doctests are understood as a type of component documentation, their place is in the component's docstring, as their name suggests. Example 12.3.1 shows the modified size adapter now carrying a docstring with a doctest.

To run the doctest, we need to provide some Python code so that we can run it. We already provide this in terms of the *PyUnit* infrastructure. Example 12.3.2 shows a listing of a test module that creates a test suite necessary for running the doctest in the test runner or from the command line. To run the doctest directly, we simply execute this module from the command line:

```
~/Zope3Instance$ python lib/python/worldcookery/tests/
                 test_size_doctest.py

.
-------------------------------------------------------------------------
Ran 1 test in 0.337s

OK
```

Looking at Example 12.3.1, doctests should seem familiar. We have exercised tests with components on the interactive interpreter shell before, only those tests were done for our sake, not for the component's sake. We now know that the doctest philosophy does not make that distinction. Whatever is documentation for us is a test for the component.

Doctests from text files

Most times, component documentation is too extensive to fit into a single docstring so one would rather provide a separate text file. By using `DocFileSuite` instead of `DocTestSuite` it is possible to generate a test suite from a text file instead of docstrings. The structure of that file corresponds to the structure of regular docstring-based doctests. Example 12.3.3 exercises a test on the file representation adapters that were introduced in Section 11.2. If you go back to these pages, you will see that the file-based test does exactly what we did on the interactive interpreter shell to test the adapters, including the explanations in between.

Just like a regular doctest, a file-based test should be turned into a test suite object so that we can execute it. Note that the tests in the file do not

Example 12.3.1 The size adapter with a *doc test* (`size.py`)

```
1   from zope.interface import implements
2   from zope.component import adapts
3   from zope.size.interfaces import ISized
4   from zope.i18nmessageid import MessageFactory
5   _ = MessageFactory('worldcookery')
6   from worldcookery.interfaces import IRecipe
7
8   class RecipeSize(object):
9       """Provide size functionality for recipes
10
11      For a demonstration of this adapter, consider the following
12      recipe object, providing some demo data:
13
14        >>> from worldcookery.recipe import Recipe
15        >>> recipe = Recipe()
16        >>> recipe.name = u"Fish and Chips"
17        >>> recipe.ingredients = [u"Fish", u"Potato chips"]
18        >>> recipe.description = u"Fish and Chips is a typical British dish
             ."
19
20      Now we instantiate the adapter.  For sorting, the adapter computes
21      a recipe's size in the 'bytes' unit (number of characters):
22
23        >>> size = RecipeSize(recipe)
24        >>> size.sizeForSorting()
25        ('byte', 71)
26
27      It also provides a message id for displaying size in a UI.  In
28      order to display the message correctly, we have to set up some
29      basic services so we can use the translation facilities:
30
31        >>> from zope.i18n import translate
32        >>> translate(size.sizeForDisplay())
33        u'71 characters'
34      """
35      implements(ISized)
36      adapts(IRecipe)
37
38      def __init__(self, context):
39          self.context = context
40
41      ...
```

9–34. The docstring of the adapter class now contains explanation of what it does and how it can be used. Code demonstrations are inserted as if they were printouts from the interactive interpreter. The doctest machinery parses the doctest, executes those statements, and compares their return values with the expected return values that are printed out in the doctest. To make the doctest easier to follow, we explain what we are doing in the test after every few lines.

Example 12.3.2 Test module for running doc tests
(tests/test_size_doctest.py)

```
1  import unittest
2  from doctest import DocTestSuite
3
4  def test_suite():
5      return unittest.TestSuite((DocTestSuite('worldcookery.size'),))
6
7  if __name__ == '__main__':
8      unittest.main(defaultTest='test_suite')
```

2 and 5. We return a test suite which we create from a *doctest suite*. The
DocTestSuite class takes as an argument the dotted path of the module that
is supposed to contain components that have doctests. If not given, the current
module is assumed which is always useful when providing doctests external to
the module of the actual component.

handle any form of test setup such as the necessary adapter registration. This
will have to be handled by the test module, too. Example 12.3.4 shows how
to do it.

Summary

- Regular unit tests tend to be unnatural to write and are also difficult
  for other developers to understand.
- *Doctests* cope with this problem by being both documentation for,
  and testing of, a component.
- Doctests can be located in a component's docstring, though generally
  they are placed in text files due to their length. Verbatim output of
  interactive interpreter sessions is used as both documenting demonstration and as test code at the same time.

12.4 Running tests

So far we have written only a few test cases. More tests will follow in this
and later chapters as we extend the application. Calling each test individually
takes time and when dealing with a large number of test cases, it is easy to
forget to run a few. To solve this problem, Zope is equipped with a *test
runner* program. This program automatically finds test suites in source code
packages and runs them. It can be found in a Zope instance under bin/
test.

Example 12.3.3 Text file-based test for file representation adapters (`filerepresentation.txt`)

```
1    =========================================
2    File representation adapters for recipes
3    =========================================
4
5    Let us first create a recipe object through a file factory.  In order
6    to acquire the factory, we need a folder object since we registered
7    the factory as an adapter for folders.  We can throw the folder away
8    afterwards.  Even though the factory is an adapter, we cannot look it
9    up by calling the interface anymore because that will not take the
10   adapter name into account.  We need to use ``getAdapter`` from
11   ``zope.component`` now:
12
13      >>> from zope.app.folder import Folder
14      >>> from zope.filerepresentation.interfaces import \
15      ...      IReadFile, IWriteFile, IFileFactory
16      >>> from zope.component import getAdapter
17      >>> folder = Folder()
18      >>> factory = getAdapter(folder, IFileFactory, ".recipe")
19
20   Now we can call the factory with some made-up data.  We expect to get
21   a recipe object back, of course, and that the recipe's description
22   equals to the data we passed to the factory.
23
24      >>> data = "Add spices to the water and bring it to boil. " \
25      ...          "Then add the couscous."
26      >>> couscous = factory("couscous", "text/plain", data)
27      >>> couscous # doctest: +ELLIPSIS
28      <worldcookery.recipe.Recipe object at ...>
29      >>> couscous.name
30      'Couscous'
31      >>> couscous.description
32      u'Add spices to the water and bring it to boil. Then add the couscous.'
33
34   Now we can get a file representation for the recipe again and read its
35   data.  Note that the file representation returns a string object, not
36   a Unicode object, since only the former can be written to a file stream.
37
38      >>> readfile = IReadFile(couscous)
39      >>> readfile.size()
40      68
41      >>> readfile.read()
42      'Add spices to the water and bring it to boil. Then add the couscous.'
43
44   Finally, we can adapt the recipe object to a writeable file and store
45   new data on it.  The recipe will be changed accordingly, of course:
46
47      >>> writefile = IWriteFile(couscous)
48      >>> writefile.write("Couscous consists of grains made from semolina.")
49      >>> couscous.description
50      u'Couscous consists of grains made from semolina.'
```

Example 12.3.4 Test module for running the text file-based file representation tests (`tests/test_filerepresentation.py`)

```
1   import unittest
2   from doctest import DocFileSuite
3
4   import zope.component.testing
5   from zope.app.folder.interfaces import IFolder
6   from zope.filerepresentation.interfaces import IReadFile, \
7       IWriteFile, IFileFactory
8
9   from worldcookery.interfaces import IRecipe
10  from worldcookery.filerepresentation import RecipeReadFile, \
11      RecipeWriteFile, RecipeFactory
12
13  def setUp(test):
14      zope.component.testing.setUp(test)
15      zope.component.provideAdapter(RecipeReadFile)
16      zope.component.provideAdapter(RecipeWriteFile)
17      zope.component.provideAdapter(RecipeFactory, adapts=(IFolder,),
18                                    name='.recipe')
19
20  def test_suite():
21      return unittest.TestSuite((
22          DocFileSuite('filerepresentation.txt',
23                       package='worldcookery',
24                       setUp=setUp,
25                       tearDown=zope.component.testing.tearDown),
26          ))
27
28  if __name__ == '__main__':
29      unittest.main(defaultTest='test_suite')
```

2 and 22–25. Instead of `DocTestSuite` we now use `DocFileSuite` which creates a test suite from a regular text file whose name we pass in as the first parameter. The `package` parameter specifies the Python package in which the text file can be found, while the optional `setUp` and `tearDown` parameters can be used to pass in initialization and a cleanup functions. For initialization, we provide our own `setUp` function while the one provided by `zope.component.testing` suffices for cleanup.

13–18. The `setUp` function will be called by the test suite before the file test is executed. We use it to initialize the Component Architecture by calling `zope.component`'s `setUp` function and to register the adapters that we want to test.

When looking for tests to run, the test runner searches for `tests.py` modules or for modules below `tests` packages. Within each of those modules, it executes the `test_suite` function to obtain a `TestSuite` object (or a derivative, in case of doctests). It then uses the test suite to execute the tests.

The test runner offers a variety of options, such as different report facilities and a choice of types of test to include in a test run.

Program synopsis

```
bin/test [options] [module filter] [test filter...]
```

Parameters

Test searching and filtering

-s package, --package package, --dir package searches for tests only in the specified Python package. This is useful for limiting the search scope of the test runner, thus limiting the number of tests to be run. Package names have to be give as dotted names. This option can be specified more than once.

--m filter, --module filter filters module names by applying a regular expression in search mode. The regular expression is evaluated against dotted names module names. A leading exclamation mark (*!*) negates the expression. This option can be specified more than once; tests from modules matching any of the specified filters will be executed.

--t filter, --test filter filters tests (method names of test case classes) by applying a regular expression in search mode. Otherwise works like the module filter (see above).

-u, --unit runs only the unit tests and ignores any tests on layers (see Section 12.5 for more on testing layers).

-f, --non-unit runs all tests other than unit tests, meaning all tests that are on layers (see Section 12.5 for more on testing layers).

-a level, --at-level level runs the tests at a given level. All tests at a level above the specified one are not run. Level 0 runs all tests, the default is level 1. Configuration file setting: LEVEL.
The level of a test is determined by an optional `level` attribute on the `TestCase` derivative class.

--all runs tests at all levels. This is a shortcut for -a 0.

Reporting

-p, --progress shows the running progress in percent.

-v, --verbose switches to verbose output. With one -v, a dot is printed
for each test. With -vv the name of each test is printed. If no -v is
specified at all, no output is given while running the tests, except when
errors occur.
The behaviour changes slightly when specified together with -p. With
-p and -v, the percent indicator and the test name is printed. With -p
and -vv, the test name is not truncated to fit into 80 columns.

-1 reports only the first failure in a doctest.

--ndiff, --udiff, --cdiff reports doctest failures as normal diff, uni-
fied diff or context diff.

Execution modes

-D, --post-mortem loads the Python Debugger (pdb) when a test failure
occurs.

-N n, --repeat n repeats the selected tests *n* times.

-k, --keepbytecode prevents the test runner from deleting stale bytecode
before running tests.

Examples

The following command runs all tests found in the worldcookery package.
Since we have not yet written any integration tests, only the four unit tests
from the previous sections will be run:

```
~/Zope3Instance$ bin/test -v -s worldcookery
Running tests at level 1
Running unit tests:
  Running:
....
  Ran 4 tests with 0 failures and 0 errors in 0.036 seconds.
```

The following command makes sure that only unit tests are run (in case
integration tests were there). It also sets the output to the highest verbosity.
Notice the different types of tests (docfile, doctest, regular unit test):

```
~/Zope3Instance$ bin/test -u -vv -s worldcookery
Running tests at level 1
Running unit tests:
```

```
  Running:
/Users/philipp/instances/wc33/lib/python/worldcookery/
    filerepresentation.txt
test_size_for_display (worldcookery.tests.test_size.
                      RecipeSizeTestCase)
test_size_for_sorting (worldcookery.tests.test_size.
                      RecipeSizeTestCase)
RecipeSize (worldcookery.size)
  Ran 4 tests with 0 failures and 0 errors in 0.039 seconds.
```

The following command narrows the test search down to unit tests in the worldcookery package whose names contain "size" or "Size". Of course, we expect the two unit test and the doc test to be executed:

```
~/Zope3Instance$ bin/test -vv -s worldcookery -t [sS]ize
Running tests at level 1
Running unit tests:
  Running:
test_size_for_display (worldcookery.tests.test_size.
                      RecipeSizeTestCase)
test_size_for_sorting (worldcookery.tests.test_size.
                      RecipeSizeTestCase)
RecipeSize (worldcookery.size)
  Ran 3 tests with 0 failures and 0 errors in 0.021 seconds.
```

Summary

- Running tests individually from their modules can be tiresome when a large number of tests are involved
- Zope's test runner automatically finds tests and executes them, making automatic testing very easy.
- Various options control the amount and type of tests that are found, the way they are run and the way output is presented.

Using Zope 2

Recent Zope 2 releases also ship with the Zope 3 test runner. It can be invoked from a Zope 2 instance with the bin/zopectl test command.

12.5 Integration tests

As mentioned earlier, in the Zope world functional tests are really integration tests. Functional tests would treat Zope like a black box. "Functional tests" in Zope, however, do not simulate a browser client program and connect through the HTTP port. They only simulate the necessary objects, such as the browser request. That means, they are more like integration tests. Zope's "functional tests" are still a good way to test behaviour not covered by unit tests, such as all view-related actions. The reaction of a button clicked in an HTML form cannot be covered by unit tests, but by integration or functional tests.

As a simple demonstration, we shall provide an integration test for the `IUserPreferredLanguages` adapter we wrote in Section 11.3, as this is a component that other components rely on and it itself relies on a request environment. That means it can pretty much only be tested with an integration test. Example 12.5.1 shows the code listing of the test case. Note that integration tests are placed in a package called `ftests` ("*functional tests*") by convention.

Test layers

You might have noticed that the integration test does not register the mock objects that it makes use of. If it were a unit test, we should expect that it would do this in `setUp` and `tearDown` methods. In integration tests, however, a clean up of registered mock objects such as utilities and adapters would mean that the whole adapter and utility registries would have to be wiped. The whole testing harness would have to be set up and torn down for every single test. While this is not a problem in unit tests, it would mean terrible performance in integration tests where the test harness is basically the whole application configuration.

Zope's test runner deals with this problem by putting different types of tests on different layers. Unit tests are executed without a layer. As mentioned already, they handle their setup and clean-up individually. Integration tests, however, are executed in the context of a layer that does the setup and clean-up. Tests of a particular layer are run together and are generally not expected to do setup or clean-up. For integration tests that generally means that mock objects should be avoided if possible. After all, an integration test tries to test the application as a whole. If mock objects are necessary, they should be registered on the layer level.

The layer that integration tests are executed under simply loads the whole Zope 3 ZCML configuration tree. Therefore, the easiest way to register mock objects for integration tests is via ZCML. Example 12.5.2 lists the additional configuration needed for the test setup. To have it loaded for integration tests (and not for normal operations), we add another package include file called `worldcookery-ftesting.zcml` to our instance's `etc/package-includes` directory with the following line:

```
<include package="worldcookery" file="ftesting.zcml" />
```

Example 12.5.1 Integration test for the alternate
IUserPreferredLanguages adapter (`ftests/test_adapter.py`)

```
 1  import unittest
 2
 3  from zope.i18n import translate
 4  from zope.i18n.interfaces import ITranslationDomain
 5  from zope.i18n.simpletranslationdomain import SimpleTranslationDomain
 6  from zope.i18nmessageid import MessageFactory
 7  _ = MessageFactory('worldcookery_test')
 8  from zope.publisher.browser import BrowserPage
 9  from zope.app.testing.functional import BrowserTestCase
10
11  messages = {('es', u'msg'): u"Eso es un mensaje",
12              ('de', u'msg'): u"Dies ist eine Nachricht"}
13  wc_test = SimpleTranslationDomain('worldcookery_test', messages)
14
15  class TestPage(BrowserPage):
16
17      def __call__(self):
18          msg = _(u'msg', u"This is a message")
19          return translate(msg, context=self.request)
20
21  class LanguageAdapterTestCase(BrowserTestCase):
22
23      def test_default(self):
24          response = self.publish('/@@testpage')
25          self.assertEqual(response.getBody(), u"This is a message")
26
27      def test_http_header(self):
28          response = self.publish('/@@testpage',
29                                  env={"HTTP_ACCEPT_LANGUAGE": 'de'})
30          self.assertEqual(response.getBody(), u"Dies ist eine Nachricht")
31
32      def test_browser_form(self):
33          response = self.publish('/@@testpage', form={"ZopeLanguage": 'es
34          '})
34          self.assertEqual(response.getBody(), u"Eso es un mensaje")
35
36      def test_form_overrides_header(self):
37          response = self.publish('/@@testpage', form={"ZopeLanguage": 'es
38          '},
38                                  env={"HTTP_ACCEPT_LANGUAGE": 'de'})
39          self.assertEqual(response.getBody(), u"Eso es un mensaje")
40
41  def test_suite():
42      suite = unittest.TestSuite()
43      suite.addTest(unittest.makeSuite(LanguageAdapterTestCase))
44      return suite
45
46  if __name__ == '__main__':
47      unittest.main()
```

Example 12.5.1 (continued)

11–13. For the test setup, we need to provide some translations of the message that the above view is going to return and register them in a translation domain object as a utility.

15–19. In order to test the effects of the adapter, we need a simple view that returns a short, predictable i18n message, such as the one we see here.

9 and 21. Zope's "functional" test cases inherit from `BrowserTestCase`, meaning a browser request environment is simulated.

24, 28–29, 33, and 37–38. In a unit test, we would test the adapter directly. In this integration test, we simulate a browser request by calling the `publish` method which is inherited from `BrowserTestCase`. It takes the relative URL of the page to be virtually published as well as the following optional keyword parameters:

`basic` can be a string holding fictitious authentication information, e.g. `"mgr:mgrpw"` as defined in `etc/ftesting.zcml` in your Zope instance.

`form` can be a dictionary holding simulated data from an HTML form, in other words, simulated HTTP GET or POST parameters.

`env` can be a dictionary holding additional HTTP headers. Here, the `HTTP_ACCEPT_LANGUAGE` header is obviously of interest to us since it simulates the preferred language of the user's operating system or browser preferences.

That will take care of *World Cookery's* `ftesting.zcml` file. Since the adapter is loaded in `overrides.zcml`, we also need to adjust `etc/overrides_ftesting.zcml` to include the following line:

```
<include files="package-includes/*-overrides.zcml" />
```

To run the integration test, we use the test runner:

```
~/Zope3Instance$ bin/test -fs worldcookery
Running zope.app.testing.functional.Functional tests:
  Set up zope.app.testing.functional.Functional in 14.115 seconds.
  Ran 4 tests with 0 failures and 0 errors in 0.500 seconds.
Tearing down left over layers:
  Tear down zope.app.testing.functional.Functional ... not supported
```

Functional doctests

Regular integration tests are tedious to write because they need to simulate browser request or other types of user interaction. Doing that from a Python

---

Example 12.5.2 Configuration file for integration tests (`ftesting.zcml`)

```
1   <configure
2       xmlns="http://namespaces.zope.org/zope"
3       xmlns:browser="http://namespaces.zope.org/browser"
4       >
5
6     <utility
7         component="worldcookery.ftests.test_adapter.wc_test"
8         name="worldcookery_test"
9         />
10
11    <browser:page
12        for="zope.app.folder.interfaces.IRootFolder"
13        name="testpage"
14        class="worldcookery.ftests.test_adapter.TestPage"
15        permission="zope.Public"
16        />
17
18  </configure>
```

---

program is not only difficult, it also requires some insights into the way Zope's publishing works.

To cope with that problem, Zope allows us to write integration tests as doctests ("functional doctests"). These are very explicit with respect to the client emulation because they are essentially literal recordings of HTTP sessions (request and response output).

Of course, it is very unlikely that one writes down a whole HTTP session down in a file (though it is of course possible). Instead, we can rely on a much simpler way of creating functional doctests. The Python program *tcpwatch*[3] can interact as an intermediary between a web browser and a web server and save the server/client communication of a whole HTTP session to log files. The `dochttp` program which comes with Zope can convert these log files into a doctest text file.

To create a functional doctest by "recording" an HTTP session, do the following:

1. Create a temporary directory where tcpwatch can write the log files to, for example `/tmp/tcpwatch` or `C:\temp\tcpwatch` on Windows. Then start the tcpwatch program with appropriate parameters:

   ```
   ~/tcpwatch$ python tcpwatch.py -L 9080:8080 -s -r /tmp/tcpwatch
   Forwarding :9080 -> :8080
   Recording to directory /tmp/tcpwatch/.
   ```

---

[3] Shane Hathaway's website <http://hathawaymix.org/Software/TCPWatch> or Zope CVS repository <http://cvs.zope.org/Packages/tcpwatch/>

This will let tcpwatch listen on port 9080 and forward all requests to port 8080 which it is assumed that your Zope instance is listening to. In case it is listening to a different port or that port 9080 is already taken for something else you will have to adjust the command line.

2. In case your tests involve components that are security protected (all management and editing views generally are), it is recommended to create a manager principal with the login name mgr and password mgrpw. This account is setup by the functional test setup machinery and only available during tests. However, since we are trying to make a test from a regular HTTP session recording, we need to simulate things like user authentication.

   To configure the manager test principal, add the following lines to your instance's etc/principals.zcml file:

   ```
   <principal
       id="zope.test_manager"
       title="Functional Test Manager"
       login="mgr"
       password="mgrpw"
       />
   ```

3. Now open the pages you want to test in a web browser. Be careful to tcpwatch's port and not Zope's port directly; otherwise the session will not be recorded. When asked for authentication, login with the mgr account. Everything you do with your browser now will be recorded. You therefore should try to pay attention not to open too many pages that are not related to the test, even though these unnecessary steps can be deleted later.

   When you have completed testing the application through the browser, quit tcpwatch by hitting **Ctrl–C**.

4. The temporary directory that was used to store tcpwatch's recordings in should now contain several files, one for each request and one for each response that was made. The dochttp.py Python script can now be used to convert these files into a doctest file:

   ```
   ~/Zope3Instance$ python /usr/local/Zope-3.x.y/lib/python/zope/
   app/tests/dochttp.py /tmp/tcpwatch > lib/python/.../test.txt
   ```

   On Windows, you need to adjust the command to the different installation and logging directories:

   ```
   C:\Zope3Instance> python C:\Python24\Lib\site-packages\zope\app\
   tests\dochttp.py C:\temp\tcpwatch > lib\python\...\test.txt
   ```

5. As one of the last steps, edit the generated doctest file. Add your test specific comments and get rid of request/response pairs that are irrelevant to the test. Finally, create a test module that instantiates a test suite so that the test is executable.

As an example for a functional doctest, the integration test for the IUserPreferredLanguages adapter was converted to a doctest. It was created in the above described manner using tcpwatch and then edited to include a few explaining comments. It not only can now serve as another test for the component, it is also a very clear piece of documentation of the component for anyone familiar with the HTTP protocol. Example 12.5.3 lists the doctest file whereas Example 12.5.4 shows the module for the test suite instantiation. To run the functional test, we again use the test runner.

Test browser

Functional doctests as we just introduced them are a good way to simulate an HTTP client. However, if you want to describe and test typical browser behaviour, they can become inconvenient. For example, submitting HTML forms or dealing with cookies involves rather unreadable HTTP data. A carbon copy of the raw HTTP request and response is also not the ideal form to test for user interface behaviour, such as correct hyperlinks, form submit buttons etc.

To better simulate a web browser, Zope offers a *test browser*. This component available from zope.testbrowser lets you write functional tests that exercise an application from a browser point of view, rather than from an HTTP client's point of view. There are two flavours of the test browser available:

zope.testbrowser.browser.Browser opens real HTTP connections and can therefore be used for real functional testing against live systems. This variant of the test browser allows one to write tests much like with Selenium or similar frameworks, except that the tests will be executed in Python and not as JavaScript in a web browser. If you have many functional tests, this will make a big difference concerning the execution speed of the tests.
This flavour of the test browser is obviously not tied to the Zope application server at all. It can be used to test any web application, whether Zope-based or not. Test browser is also separately available for this reason, e.g. as a package from the Python Cheese Shop.[4]

zope.testbrowser.testing.Browser interfaces with the Zope 3 publisher instead of opening HTTP connections. Hence it can be used for integration tests in Zope, much like the http function in the functional doctests we have had so far.

The API of both test browser variants is exactly the same. This makes it easy to switch a functional test to an integration test and vice versa.

---

[4] Cheese Shop page for Zope's test browser <http://cheeseshop.python.org/pypi/ZopeTestbrowser>

Example 12.5.3 Functional doctest for the `IUserPreferredLanguages` adapter (`browser/adapter.txt`)

```
1   ===============================================
2   Form variable-based browser language adapter
3   ===============================================
4
5   The ``IUserPreferredLanguages`` adapter provided by the ``adapter.py``
6   module allows the preferred language to be specified in a request form
7   variable in addition to the HTTP headers.
8
9   Without any language specification, the default translation (English)
10  is returned:
11
12      >>> print http(r"""
13      ... GET /@@testpage HTTP/1.1
14      ... """)
15      HTTP/1.1 200 Ok
16      Content-Length: 17
17      Content-Type: text/plain;charset=utf-8
18      <BLANKLINE>
19      This is a message
20
21  When the `Accept-Language` HTTP header is provided, the adapter works
22  like the default one:
23
24      >>> print http(r"""
25      ... GET /@@testpage HTTP/1.1
26      ... Accept-Language: de
27      ... """)
28      HTTP/1.1 200 Ok
29      Content-Length: 23
30      Content-Type: text/plain;charset=utf-8
31      <BLANKLINE>
32      Dies ist eine Nachricht
33
34  The innovation is that when a request variable, e.g. from a GET form,
35  is provided, it influences the target translation language, too:
36
37      >>> print http(r"""
38      ... GET /@@testpage?ZopeLanguage=es HTTP/1.1
39      ... """)
40      HTTP/1.1 200 Ok
41      Content-Length: 17
42      Content-Type: text/plain;charset=utf-8
43      <BLANKLINE>
44      Eso es un mensaje
```

Example 12.5.3 (continued)

```
45  Note that the request variable takes precedence over any HTTP header:
46
47  >>> print http(r"""
48  ... GET /@@testpage?ZopeLanguage=es HTTP/1.1
49  ... Accept-Language: de
50  ... """)
51  HTTP/1.1 200 Ok
52  Content-Length: 17
53  Content-Type: text/plain;charset=utf-8
54  <BLANKLINE>
55  Eso es un mensaje
```

12, 24, 37, and 48.   The http function is the key to functional doctests. It simulates a browser request and is the equivalent of the publish method of regular functional test cases. It is always available as a global function in doctests without having to be imported. It returns a response object that, when printed, outputs the body of Zope's response to the fictitious browser.

18, 31, 43, and 55.   In an HTTP response, a blank line is used to mark the boundary between the response header and body. However when occurring in a doctest, a blank line would be misinterpreted as a boundary between two paragraphs in the text file. The doctest interpreter lets us use a special marker, <BLANKLINE>, to match blank lines in test output therefore.

Example 12.5.4 Test module for running the functional doctest (ftests/ test_adapter_doctest.py)

```
1  import unittest
2  from zope.app.testing.functional import FunctionalDocFileSuite
3
4  def test_suite():
5      return FunctionalDocFileSuite('adapter.txt',
6                                    package='worldcookery.browser')
7
8  if __name__ == '__main__':
9      unittest.main(defaultTest='test_suite')
```

2 and 5–6.   In total analogy to DocFileSuite, FunctionalDocFileSuite makes a functional doctest out of a text file. Both test suite constructors are identical in other respects, for example parameters.

As with traditional functional doctests, there is also a convenient way to record test browser tests using the *browser test recorder*.[5] This test recorder is written in ECMAScript and, as its name suggests, works from within the browser. Due to the ECMAScript security model, the test recorder has to be loaded from the same website that you want to record tests for. When installed and configured as a package in your Zope instance (see Chapter 3 for instructions on installing additional packages in instances), you can access the test recorder via a resource URL, usually

```
http://localhost:8080/@@/recorder/index.html
```

The handling of the test recorder is quite easy. After entering a URL to start with, the recording is started with the *Go* button. The browser will then load the first page in the lower frame. You can now start working with the application. Once you are done, *Stop Recording* will stop the recording process and show you the list of steps that you performed during the recording. It can then create either one of the functional test formats for you. It is also possible to add comments during a recording. They will be inserted into the test transcript.

Figure 12.1 shows a recording of the add form we implemented in Chapter 8. The resulting doctest is shown in Example 12.5.5. Obviously it was modified and enhanced here and there after the recording, most importantly the browser variant for Zope 3 integration tests was imported. The overall structure comes from the recording, though. The module for the test suite is the same as for classical functional doctests, as it was described in Example 12.5.4.

Summary

- In Zope 3, integration tests are called "functional tests". They test whether a component integrates correctly with others by simulating user behaviour.
- Classic integration test cases inherit from `BrowserTestCase` which most importantly provides the `publish` method for simulating the publishing of a browser request.
- Functional doctests provide a way to spell out integration tests as doctests. They can easily be generated from a HTTP client session recorded by *tcpwatch*.
- The test browser provides an alternate way to spell functional doctests (and real black box tests!) that test web applications from a web browser point of view. Such tests can easily be recorded from within a browser using the browser test recorder.

---

[5] Python Cheese Shop page for the browser test recorder <http://cheeseshop.python.org/pypi/zope.testrecorder>

Example 12.5.5 Integration test for the recipe add form, using the test browser (`browser/addform.txt`)

```
1    ==============================
2    Adding recipes through the web
3    ==============================
4
5    Let us take a browser and open the recipe add form:
6
7       >>> from zope.testbrowser.testing import Browser
8       >>> browser = Browser()
9       >>> browser.addHeader('Authorization', 'Basic mgr:mgrpw')
10      >>> browser.open('http://localhost/+/worldcookery.Recipe=fishnchips')
11
12   In that form we fill all form elements with some typical recipe data:
13
14      >>> browser.getControl('Name').value = 'Fish and Chips'
15      >>> browser.getControl('Time to cook').value = '20'
16      >>> browser.getControl('Description').value = \
17      ...     "Fish and Chips is a typical British dish."
18
19   After filling the form we submit it by clicking the ``Add`` button:
20
21      >>> browser.getControl('Add').click()
22
23   We have now been redirected to the containing folder.  Its *Contents*
24   listing now mentions our recipe:
25
26      >>> print browser.url
27      http://localhost/@@contents.html
28      >>> link = browser.getLink('fishnchips')
29      >>> print link.url
30      http://localhost/fishnchips/@@SelectedManagementView.html
31
32   We can also look at the recipe now and verify that the data we entered
33   above has been saved properly:
34
35      >>> browser.open('http://localhost/fishnchips')
36      >>> '<h2>Fish And Chips</h2>' in browser.contents
37      True
38      >>> '20 mins' in browser.contents
39      True
40      >>> '<p>Fish and Chips is a typical British dish.</p>' in browser.
            contents
41      True
```

7. We are using the test browser variant for Zope 3 integration tests.

9. This lines demonstrates how the browser can be configured to send additional HTTP headers (e.g. HTTP basic authorization).

Example 12.5.5 (continued)

14–17. Here we add some sample data into the form fields. Due to the fact that our custom sequence widget facilitates ECMAScript, the test browser cannot use it properly. Hence we have to omit the corresponding fields from test here. This demonstrates the limits of the programmable test browser nicely. It just *emulates* browser behaviour in Python, it does not remote control a real browser like Selenium does.

14–17 and 21. Notice how we are accessing controls such as form fields and buttons through their user-visible labels (e.g. *Name*), not their HTML IDs (e.g. field.name). After all, a user accessing a web site through a regular browser would do the same. More important, a wrong label would mean broken functionality from a user point of view, even if the form element carries the correct HTML ID. Hence, a good functional test should exercise as much user behaviour as possible.

Fig. 12.1. Using the browser test recorder to record a functional test for the recipe add form.

Using Zope 2

Integration tests in Zope 2 are typically implemented using `ZopeTestCase`. Like Zope 3's integration tests, ZopeTestCase loads the whole Zope configuration (except the servers) before running the tests. Unlike Zope 3, it does not use test layers and does not achieve the same isolation between tests that layers guarantee. ZopeTestCase provides the following classes, all available for import from the `Testing.ZopeTestCase` package:

`ZopeTestCase` is a general base class for ZopeTestCase-based tests that are implemented like classical Python unit tests.

`ZopeDocTestSuite`, `ZopeDocFileSuite` equip doctests with the necessary ZopeTestCase setup.

`FunctionalTestCase` is the ZopeTestCase equivalent of Zope 3's `BrowserTestCase` and works very similarly.

`FunctionalDocTestSuite`, `FunctionalDocFileSuite` are the ZopeTestCase versions of the functional doctest fixtures available in Zope 3. Like their Zope 3 equivalents, they provide a global `http` function that simulates HTTP connections.

While useful for integration tests, ZopeTestCase is discouraged for regular unit tests.

The test browser is also available in recent Zope 2 versions. The variant that opens real HTTP connections works with Zope 2 (as it does with any other HTTP server), a version for integration tests in Zope 2 is provided by the `Products.Five.testbrowser` package. Other than the different import path, it behaves like the Zope 3 version used in our examples.

13

Advanced Views

By now you probably understand what Steve Alexander meant when he defined Zope as a platform that "manages complexity in gluing software components together". Since we originally wrote the `Recipe` class in Chapter 5, we have not changed it at all, but look where we are now thanks to adapters!

In Chapter 7 and Chapter 8 we added through-the-web adding, editing, and displaying functionality to recipes by implementing appropriate browser pages. That was relatively easy to do because the adding and editing views are auto-generated and the displaying is handled by a Page Template. In this chapter, we will explore views in general. We will see how to write browser views that do not return HTML and how to write views for other HTTP protocols.

13.1 Browser pages with non-HTML content

Browser pages do not necessarily need to return HTML or even XML. Browsers can load binary content from an HTTP server and either display directly through the use of plug-ins, or save the data as a file. In this section we will discuss the necessary steps when returning binary data to the browser, especially large amounts. We will do this using a common case, namely server-side generation of PDF files, as an example. For that we will use the *ReportLab* library, a third-party package that allows the creation of PDF files from Python code, as well as *PIL/Imaging*, a third-party package that allows image manipulation from Python code and is used by ReportLab. See *Installing necessary third-party libraries* for installation instructions.

Installing necessary third-party libraries

The *ReportLab* library is a third-party library for creating PDF files from Python, while the *PIL/Imaging* library is a third-party library for image manipulation from Python. Both are freely available as open source

---

software under BSD-style licenses. You maybe obtain source packages or Windows binaries from the ReportLab Open Source website[1] and the PythonWare website[2], respectively.

Installing from source (Unix)

The source installation of ReportLab follows the standard *distutils* procedure as known from most other Python libraries. Extract the source archive in an arbitrary directory and run the following commands:

```
reportlab-1_xx/reportlab$ python setup.py build
reportlab-1_xx/reportlab$ python setup.py install
```

This will first compile the extension modules and then install it in the Python's `site-packages` directory so that it is available for import. Note that you will most likely need administrator rights to issue the second command. Alternatively, you can install the library into your home directory or another place where you have write permissions. Issue `python setup.py install --help` for further information.

The installation of PIL/Imaging is almost identical. Only here you will first have to compile the `libImaging` library manually. To do that enter the following commands after extracting the source archive:

```
Imaging-1.x.y$ cd libImaging
Imaging-1.x.y/libImaging$ ./configure
Imaging-1.x.y/libImaging$ make
```

When that has successfully completed, run the standard *distutils* procedure like with ReportLab above:

```
Imaging-1.x.y/libImaging$ cd ..
Imaging-1.x.y$ python setup.py build
Imaging-1.x.y$ python setup.py install
```

Windows

The installation of Imaging/PIL is nearly identical to the installation of Zope 3 on Windows. The binary PIL download contains an automatic installer which will detect a valid Python installation and install itself into its library path automatically.

Installing the ReportLab package requires a bit more manual interaction. You will have to download both the source archive as well as the Windows binary archive which only contains the binary shared libraries. Extract the source archive and copy the `reportlab` directory to your Python's `site-packages` directory, e.g. `C:\Python23\Lib\site-packages`. Then extract the archive containing the binary shared libraries. The files contained should have the file extension `pyd`. Copy them to your Python's `DLL` directory, e.g. `C:\Python23\DLL`. ReportLab is now installed.

Our goal is to generate a PDF file from a recipe object. We therefore need to first generate the PDF data and then serve it to the browser from a browser page. Since the PDF generation is independent from the browser page, we can factor it out to a separate component. First we define an interface, IPDFPresentation, that describes a PDF representation of an object. This interface is shown in Example 13.1.1. As the documentation of this interface states, PDF data should be stored in a file object. Hence the API that is described by IPDFPresentation is a subset of Python's file API.

Example 13.1.1 Interface for PDF representation (pdf/interfaces.py)

```
1   from zope.interface import Interface
2   from zope.schema import Bytes
3   from zope.i18nmessageid import MessageFactory
4   _ = MessageFactory('worldcookery')
5
6   class IPDFPresentation(Interface):
7       """Present objects as PDF in a file object
8       """
9       def read(size=-1):
10          """Read data from file"""
11
12      def tell():
13          """Return the file's current position"""
14
15      def seek(offset, whence=0):
16          """Set the file's current position"""
```

The PDF representation of a recipe will be handled by an adapter. This adapter will take a recipe object and a request; it will return a file object that holds the PDF data. Adapting the request in addition to the recipe object is necessary for translation. Example 13.1.2 shows this adapter while Example 13.1.3 shows some general purpose functions for PDF generation that could be reused when PDF data has to be generated elsewhere.

Since ReportLab is not a part of Zope itself, the library's functionality cannot be explained here in detail. The examples in this chapter are as simple as possible to merely demonstrate the principle of non-HTML, Python-implemented browser pages. For a complete reference, please refer to the *ReportLab User Guide* [21] and the *ReportLab API Reference* [20].

Example 13.1.2 and Example 13.1.3 nicely demonstrate how easily one can use third-party libraries within Zope. Zope allows you to take advantage of the numerous open source Python libraries. The *Python Cheese Shop*[4] has a catalog of most of the freely available Python packages. If you are looking for a certain tool set outside of Zope's traditional focus you might find useful libraries there.

---

[4] Python Cheese Shop website <http://cheeseshop.python.org/>

Example 13.1.2 Adapter that provides PDF representation of recipes
(pdf/recipe.py)

```
1  from tempfile import TemporaryFile
2  from reportlab.platypus import SimpleDocTemplate, Paragraph
3
4  from zope.interface import implementer
5  from zope.component import adapter
6  from zope.publisher.interfaces import IRequest
7  from zope.i18n import translate
8
9  from worldcookery.interfaces import IRecipe
10 from worldcookery.pdf.common import getStyleSheet, writeDocument
11 from worldcookery.pdf.interfaces import IPDFPresentation
12
13 @adapter(IRecipe, IRequest)
14 @implementer(IPDFPresentation)
15 def recipeToPDF(context, request):
16     # this translates AND encodes to utf-8
17     def _(msg, mapping=None):
18         return translate(msg, domain='worldcookery', mapping=mapping,
19                          context=request).encode('utf-8')
20
21     title = ('<para spaceBefore="20" spaceAfter="40">%s</para>'
22              % context.name.encode('utf-8'))
23     description = ('<para spaceBefore="15">%s</para>'
24                    % context.description.encode('utf-8'))
25     ingr = [ingr.encode('utf-8') for ingr in context.ingredients]
26     tools = [tool.encode('utf-8') for tool in context.tools]
27     time_to_cook = _(u'${time_to_cook} mins',
28                      mapping={'time_to_cook': context.time_to_cook})
29
30     # create the document structure
31     style = getStyleSheet()
32     doc_structure = [
33         Paragraph(title, style['title']),
34         Paragraph(_(u"Name of the dish:"), style['h3']),
35         Paragraph(context.name.encode('utf-8'), style['Normal']),
36         Paragraph(_(u"Ingredients:"), style['h3']),
37         Paragraph(', '.join(ingr), style['Normal']),
38         Paragraph(_(u"Needed kitchen tools:"), style['h3']),
39         Paragraph(', '.join(tools), style['Normal']),
40         Paragraph(_(u"Time needed for preparation:"), style['h3']),
41         Paragraph(time_to_cook, style['Normal']),
42         Paragraph(description, style['Normal']),
43         ]
44
45     tempfile = TemporaryFile()
46     writeDocument(tempfile, doc_structure)
47     return tempfile
```

Example 13.1.2 (continued)

13–15. So far our adapters were always classes. This adapter here happens to be implemented as a function. After all, adapter factories only need to be callables that take the objects that are to be adapted and return the result. A function serves this requirement equally well. Note that we can use decorators to declare which kinds of objects the adapter adapts and what it adapts to, similar to the `adapts` and `implements` declarations on a class level.

By the way, adapter factories can indicate that adaption has failed by returning None. The adapter machinery will treat this as a failed adapter lookup. If such behaviour is wanted from an adapter factory, it can obviously not be done by writing a class because classes always return something when they are called.

17–19. Translatable strings in this PDF need to be translated. Unlike with ZPTs where translations happens automatically once a string is marked as an i18n message, we need to perform translation manually when creating the PDF. Also, ReportLab does not work directly with Unicode objects but accepts only UTF-8 which is why we have to encode all Unicode objects in UTF-8 beforehand. This function will take care of both. Note that its awkward naming is due to the convention that translatable messages should be marked with an underscore so that the extraction utility can detect them.

45–47. In order to fulfil the contract of `IPDFPresentation`, we return a file object. Since the file will most likely be thrown away later, we use a temporary file.

Returning large amounts of binary data to the browser

Now that we can render PDF from recipes, we want to return this data to the browser. PDF files can be quite large. We want to make sure that while Zope is streaming the data to the client, application resources such as database connections will not be blocked for the whole time. The Zope publisher allows browser pages to return Unicode strings when small amounts of data is involved. For large amounts of data, browser pages can return a file object. The publisher will then end the transaction, thus freeing all application resources, and stream the data from the file to the client. Note that for this to work, only real file objects (or temporary files created via the Python `tempfile` package) will work, objects with a file-like interface such as `StringIO` will not.

Fortunately, we have already designed our PDF adapter to save its data into a temporary file. Hence we can simply return this file object to the publisher, as the publisher already knows what to do with it. Note that Python's temporary files will automatically be deleted when their file objects are garbage collected. Example 13.1.4 shows the browser page responsible for returning PDF to the browser.

Example 13.1.3 Common functions for generating *World Cookery* PDF documents (pdf/common.py)

```
1   import os.path
2   from reportlab.pdfbase import pdfmetrics
3   from reportlab.pdfbase.ttfonts import TTFont
4   from reportlab.platypus import Image, SimpleDocTemplate
5   from reportlab.lib import styles, units, pagesizes
6
7   def getStyleSheet():
8       fonts = {'LuxiSans': 'luxisr.ttf',
9                'LuxiSansOblique': 'luxisri.ttf',
10               'LuxiSansBold': 'luxisb.ttf',
11               'LuxiSansBoldOblique': 'luxisbi.ttf'}
12      for name, fn in fonts.items():
13          filename = os.path.join(os.path.dirname(__file__), fn)
14          pdfmetrics.registerFont(TTFont(name, filename))
15
16      stylesheet = styles.getSampleStyleSheet()
17      stylesheet['Normal'].fontName = 'LuxiSans'
18      stylesheet['title'].fontName = 'LuxiSansBold'
19      stylesheet['h1'].fontName = 'LuxiSansBold'
20      stylesheet['h2'].fontName = 'LuxiSansBold'
21      stylesheet['h3'].fontName = 'LuxiSansBoldOblique'
22      return stylesheet
23
24  def writeDocument(stream, structure):
25      logofile = os.path.join(os.path.dirname(__file__), 'worldcookery.png
            ')
26      logo = Image(logofile, 2060.0*units.inch/600, 651*units.inch/600)
27      doc = SimpleDocTemplate(stream, pagesize=pagesizes.A4)
28      doc.build([logo] + list(structure))
```

8–14. Zope 3 uses Unicode strings everywhere to support internationalization properly. The standard PDF fonts as required by the specification do not support Unicode. The ReportLab library however supports Unicode in conjunction with TrueType fonts. So, in order to allow Unicode in our PDF document, we register such a TrueType font including its bold and italic variants[3]

25–26. This creates an image object of the World Cookery logo which is most likely to be used in all World Cookery PDF documents. Thus it makes sense to define it here in a central place.

Conditional configuration

Now we only need to register the adapter and the browser page. There is nothing new for us in this, Example 13.1.5 lists the two necessary ZCML directives.

Example 13.1.4 Browser page returning PDF data (`pdf/browser.py`)

```
1   from zope.traversing.api import getName
2   from zope.component import getMultiAdapter
3   from zope.publisher.browser import BrowserPage
4   from worldcookery.pdf.interfaces import IPDFPresentation
5
6   class PDFView(BrowserPage):
7
8       def __call__(self):
9           filename = getName(self.context) + '.pdf'
10          response = self.request.response
11          response.setHeader('Content-Disposition',
12                             'attachment; filename=%s' % filename)
13          response.setHeader('Content-Type', 'application/pdf')
14          return getMultiAdapter((self.context, self.request),
15                                 IPDFPresentation)
```

9–13. Here we set the right content type for the binary data in the response headers. Additionally, we suggest a filename (the object name of the recipe) in case the user wants to save the PDF on disk. This is also done by setting appropriate HTTP response headers. The response can be retrieved from the request.

Example 13.1.5 Configuring the PDF browser page (`pdf/configure.zcml`)

```
1   <configure
2       xmlns="http://namespaces.zope.org/zope"
3       xmlns:browser="http://namespaces.zope.org/browser"
4       >
5
6     <adapter factory=".recipe.recipeToPDF" />
7
8     <browser:page
9         for="worldcookery.interfaces.IRecipe"
10        name="pdf"
11        class=".browser.PDFView"
12        permission="zope.View"
13        />
14
15  </configure>
```

Since we chose to put all PDF-related components in the `worldcookery.pdf` subpackage, we must not forget to include its configuration in `configure.zcml`:

```
<include package=".pdf" />
```

That would, of course, require that the ReportLab library was installed on all systems where the *World Cookery* application was deployed, because the worldcookery.pdf package depends on ReportLab.

Fortunately, ZCML allows us to apply conditions to directives. The directive will only be executed when the condition evaluates to true. Conditions can be specified using the zcml:condition attribute. These conditions consist of two parts, a verb and an argument. There are currently four supported verbs:

have, not-have take one argument, a feature name, and check whether this feature is available or not available, respectively. Features can be defined with the meta:provides directive. By enabling or disabling features, one can easily enable or disable one or more ZCML directives and thus enable or disable certain application functionality.

installed, not-installed take one argument, a Python package name, and check whether this package is available or not available, respectively. If the package cannot be imported, the condition evaluates to false.

The installed verb fits our case perfectly. The include directive with an appropriate condition therefore looks like this:

```
<include package=".pdf"
         xmlns:zcml="http://namespaces.zope.org/zcml"
         zcml:condition="installed reportlab"
         />
```

Summary

- Browser pages can return non-HTML data to the client, though they should set the appropriate HTTP response headers.
- Returning large amounts of data to the client without blocking application resources can be done efficiently by writing it to a (temporary) file and returning that file to the publisher.
- It is easy to use third-party Python libraries such as ReportLab in Zope. The Python Cheese Shop website has a catalog with most of the freely available ones.
- Conditions on ZCML directives, specified using the zcml:condition attribute, will let the directive only be executed when the condition evaluates to true.

Using Zope 2

Working with non-HTML data works very similar in Zope 2. You will also have to set the appropriate HTTP response headers. Re-

Fig. 13.1. A PDF viewer showing a PDF document generated by the World Cookery application.

turning large amounts of data without blocking application resources is done in a very similar way. You first write the data to a (temporary) file on the filesystem. Then you open the file with `ZPublisher.Iterators.filestream_iterator` and return it to the publisher. This is a subclass of the built-in `file` class that handles iteration over binary data more efficiently.

Rocky says...

Those developing with J2EE should notice that streaming content with Zope is conceptually similar to streaming content with Servlets. Getting a request/response pair and feeding back the data is a very common pattern. The major difference is the use of python `file` objects instead of `java.io` for the actual objects being passed to the response.

13.2 Browser menus

Menus are a concept known from graphical user interfaces (GUIs). They allow the user to choose items from a list of options. When an option is selected, an action is carried out. Zope has a feature called *browser menus*. Like regular menus, they are context-sensitive lists of options that a user can choose from, only that these options are other browser pages that one can open. Browser menus do not have to look like menus known from regular GUI applications. Their look is determined by how they are rendered in HTML and how that HTML is styled using stylesheets.

Zope makes use of browser menus in various places. The ZMI itself frequently presents us with three browser menus: the tabs for different ZMI object management screens (zmi_views), general management screens (zmi_actions), and the list of content objects that are addable to a folder. The entries in these menus point to other browser pages, in most of the above cases management screens. As you can see, we chose to display these all of them quite differently in our skin, even though they are all browser menus.

A custom menu

As an example for a custom browser menu we shall provide a menu that lists alternative views for an object. In the case of recipes we want it to list the PDF view we wrote above as an alternative view.

First, we need to define our own browser menu which we will call alternate_views. This, of course, is done in ZCML (see Example 13.2.1). We will also have to modify the configuration of the PDF browser page so that it is registered with this menu (see Example 13.2.2).

Example 13.2.1 Defining a browser menu (`browser/configure.zcml`)

```
1    ...
2    <browser:menu
3        id="alternate_views"
4        title="Menu containing a list of alternative views for an object"
5        />
6    ...
```

2–5. Browser menus are defined with the browser:menu directive. They are later looked up by their *id*. The *title* parameter merely exists for documentation purposes.

Example 13.2.2 Adding the PDF browser page to the browser menu
(`pdf/configure.zcml`)

```
1  <configure
2      xmlns="http://namespaces.zope.org/zope"
3      xmlns:browser="http://namespaces.zope.org/browser"
4      >
5
6    <adapter factory=".recipe.recipeToPDF" />
7
8    <browser:page
9        for="worldcookery.interfaces.IRecipe"
10       name="pdf"
11       class=".browser.PDFView"
12       permission="zope.View"
13       menu="alternate_views" title="PDF"
14       />
15
16  </configure>
```

13. Adding browser pages to browser menus is no news for us. We have done so previously with the adding and editing forms as well as the preview page in Chapter 7.

Now we want to show the list of alternate views somewhere. The best way to do that without modifying either the skin macro or the Page Template that displays recipes is to write a viewlet. Example 13.2.3 shows the Page Template that renders the viewlet, Example 13.2.4 shows its registration.

Example 13.2.3 Viewlet rendering the `alternate_views` menu (`skin/alternateviews.pt`)

```
1  <div id="alternate_views" class="box" i18n:domain="worldcookery">
2    <h1 i18n:translate="">Also viewable as:</h1>
3    <ul>
4      <li tal:repeat="item context/@@view_get_menu/alternate_views">
5        <a href=""
6           tal:attributes="href item/action; title item/description"
7           tal:content="item/title">alternate view</a>
8      </li>
9    </ul>
10 </div>
```

4. Menus can be accessed from Page Templates via the `view_get_menu` view. We can then iterate over the menu items and display them in a bullet-point list.

Example 13.2.4 Registering the alternate views viewlet
(skin/configure.zcml)

```
1      ...
2      <browser:viewlet
3          name="alternate_views"
4          for="worldcookery.interfaces.IRecipe"
5          manager=".interfaces.ISidebar"
6          view="worldcookery.browser.recipe.ViewRecipe"
7          template="alternateviews.pt"
8          layer=".interfaces.IWorldCookerySkin"
9          permission="zope.View"
10         />
11     ...
```

4–6. Note how we register this viewlet: it will only be available when viewing
recipe objects, it will appear in the sidebar, and it will only appear there when
the ViewRecipe browser page is active (this is the default view for recipes,
index.html). After all, offering alternate display views when the user is in
an edit form does not make much sense. Note that this again demonstrates the
flexibility of viewlets: we can make viewlets appear for just one view or for a
group of views.

When we now display a recipe, we are offered a PDF document as an
alternative form of viewing a recipe (see Figure 13.2). If you want, you can
write yet another browser page that displays recipes, perhaps in plain text or
reStructuredText, and register this view in our alternate_views menu.

Summary

- Browser menus provide lists of browser pages based on context, permission and other filter options.
- When registered, browser pages can optionally be listed in a browser
  menu.
- Browser menus can be accessed from Page Templates using the
  view_get_menu view.

Using Zope 2

Browser menus are also available in Zope 2 and work pretty much the
same way there. They can also be accessed the same way, through the
view_get_menu view.

Fig. 13.2. A browser menu offering alternative views for a recipe.

The CMF has a system similar to browser menus called *actions*. Recent CMF versions allow you to specify Zope 3-style browser menu items that will then appear as action items in the CMF. That way you can register your browser pages in exactly the same way as you would do in Zope 3 and still be compatible with the CMF's action system.

13.3 Other HTTP protocols

The HTTP protocol is not only used by browsers, it can also be used to edit and modify remote resources via the *Distributed Authoring and Versioning* protocol, commonly called *DAV* or *WebDAV* [17]. It enhances the set of HTTP's methods such as GET and POST with a number of methods allowing content editing and versioning. This makes it the number one alternative to FTP in web publishing environments.

There is also the XML-RPC [28] protocol. This is a remote procedure protocol based on HTTP and XML. Its almost simplistic approach to remote procedures makes it easy to implement in any kind of environment with any kind of programming language, provided XML and HTTP libraries are available. Zope has built-in support for both these HTTP subprotocols. It is a just a matter of wiring your components up to it.

Before we can start though, we must understand how Zope decides whether an incoming HTTP connection is to be treated as a browser request, an XML-RPC call or a WebDAV request. The request object is instantiated by the publication machinery. The publication will decide which request factory to use based on

- the HTTP method (GET, POST, etc.),
- the content type of the request,
- whether the factory can handle a request given the request environment (also known as the CGI environment),
- and the priority with which the request factory was registered (factories with higher priorities will be used first).

Zope's default publication comes with request factories that will instantiate the following kinds of requests (listed in order of their priority):

SOAP requests will be created for HTTP POST methods when the content type of the request is text/xml and the request environment contains a HTTP_SOAPACTION variable.

XML-RPC requests will be created for HTTP POST methods when the request's content type is text/xml.

Browser requests are created for the HTTP GET, POST and HEAD methods and all content types.

HTTP/WebDAV requests are created in all other cases.

New request factories can be registered with the publisher ZCML directive. They must implement IPublicationRequestFactory from the zope.app.publication package.

13.3.1 WebDAV

In Zope WebDAV is treated like HTTP because it is essentially HTTP with extra methods. WebDAV requests are therefore represented as regular HTTP requests. Views for WebDAV and HTTP views are implemented the same way.

In contrast to browser views whose names are exposed in the URL to which the client browser either sends a GET or POST request, HTTP views are named after the HTTP method they are supposed to handle. Therefore, when a DAV client issues a PROPFIND request on an object, the Zope publisher will look up a view for this object called PROPFIND. It will then call the PROPFIND method on this view.

DAV support in Zope 3 is still in its early stages. As of this release, the zope.app.http and zope.app.dav packages provide views for the following HTTP methods:

OPTIONS This view gives information about which HTTP methods are allowed on an object by checking if the necessary views can be looked up.

PUT This view uses the file representation adapter for IWriteFile or, in case a new object is uploaded, for IFileFactory to save incoming data. We already implemented file representation adapters in Chapter 11, so recipes will automatically support this view.

DELETE This is a view on containers, for example folders, allowing contained objects to be deleted. To do that, it uses a file representation adapter for IWriteDirectory. Containers and their file representation adapters will be covered in Chapter 15.

MKCOL This also is a view on containers and can be used to create sub-containers (in DAV lingo, collections). It uses the file representation adapters IWriteDirectory IDirectoryFactory to create and store a new container. Containers and their file representation adapters will be covered in Chapter 15.

PROPFIND This view returns metadata associated with an object to a DAV client using annotation adapters. Metadata using annotations will be covered in Chapter 14.

PROPPATCH This view sets metadata associated with an object to a DAV client using annotation adapters.

As you can see, moving/renaming (MOVE) and copying (COPY) objects through DAV is not supported out-of-the-box yet, neither is locking (LOCK, UNLOCK).

Apart from the incomplete WebDAV implementation, it is also very difficult to support a wide range of DAV clients at the same time because they differ quite radically from each other.

Summary

- In Zope 3, WebDAV requests are identical to HTTP requests.
- HTTP/WebDAV views are looked up and published differently to browser pages. Instead of looking up a named page, a view with the name of the request method is looked up and a method with the name of the request method is called.
- It is uncommon to write HTTP/WebDAV views yourself. Zope provides a number of views for HTTP methods that make use of adapters where per-component customization is needed.

Using Zope 2

As of this writing, Zope 2 has a much better WebDAV implementation than Zope 3. It is not only more complete (it supports locking, for example), it is also more robust with respect to different client behaviour. Zope 2 applications often communicate with Microsoft Windows' Web Folders, for example, which provide a way to mount a WebDAV resource as a Windows drive.

13.3.2 XML-RPC

XML-RPC allows us to remote control a Zope application. Client implementations for this protocol exist for many programming languages, allowing simple data exchange between heterogeneous environments. For this to work properly, XML-RPC is limited to the following data types:

- Boolean (in Python `bool`),
- integer (in Python `int`),
- double (in Python `float`),
- string (in Python `str`, `unicode`),
- array (in Python `list`, `tuple`),
- struct (in Python `dict`),
- date and time (in Python `xmlrpclib.DateTime`),
- binary data (in Python `xmlrpclib.Binary`).

Zope makes the implementation of XML-RPC views very easy. Our goal is obviously to be able to retrieve and change information about recipes. For this we need to write two views which we conveniently combine in one view class as shown in Example 13.3.1. The ZCML configuration for these two views is shown in Example 13.3.2. Note that we are again using a subpackage, (`worldcookery.xmlrpc`), for XML-RPC-specific components, just like we put browser components in the `worldcookery.browser` subpackage. Therefore, do not forget to include the following line in `configure.zcml`:

```
<include package=".xmlrpc" />
```

A Python client

To test these views, we need an XML-RPC client that communicates with them. Fortunately Python's standard library includes a module for XML-RPC communication, `xmlrpclib`, that allows us to easily write a client program in Python. Example 13.3.3 shows the listing of a small Python program that can be used to retrieve and display the information of a recipe via XML-RPC. To do so now, issue the following command on your command line:

```
.../xmlrpc/demo$ ./displayrecipe.py http://localhost:8080/miso
```

or if you are on Windows:

```
...\xmlrpc\demo> python displayrecipe.py http://localhost:8080/miso
```

XML-RPC is called a *remote* procedure protocol for a good reason. It means you are not limited to a locally running server when issuing procedure calls.

The example client program presented here is obviously very limited. It does not check whether the given URL is well-formed, it does not catch any exceptions occurring when connecting to the remote server or when issuing the remote procedure call. It also does not handle authentication. Furthermore and most importantly, it does call the second view we configured, the `edit` XML-RPC method. Do not worry about not being able to test it, though. There is a functional doctest in the `xmlrpc/README.txt` file which exercises both the `info` and `edit` methods. Only it's sheer length prevents this file from being printed here as a listing.

As an optional exercise, you may write a small application that retrieves a recipe's data, lets you edit it (e.g. in a file using a regular text editor program) and saves the data back to the recipe.

A Java client

It was mentioned earlier that XML-RPC allows client-server communication in a heterogeneous environment. Many other web solutions are based on languages like Java, Perl or PHP. All of these have support for XML-RPC, too, which means you can exchange data between systems written in these languages and Zope very easily. For a demonstration, consider the Java program `DisplayRecipe` in the `xmlrpc/demo` directory. It uses the Xml-Rpc library from the Apache project which is freely distributable under the

Example 13.3.1 XML-RPC view class for retrieving/editing information of recipes (`xmlrpc/recipe.py`)

```
1   from zope.schema import getFields
2   from zope.app.publisher.xmlrpc import XMLRPCView
3   from worldcookery.interfaces import IRecipe
4
5   def to_unicode(string):
6       if isinstance(string, unicode):
7           return string
8       return string.decode('utf-8')
9
10  class RecipeView(XMLRPCView):
11
12      def info(self):
13          return dict((field, getattr(self.context, field))
14                      for field in getFields(IRecipe))
15
16      def edit(self, info):
17          context = self.context
18          context.name = to_unicode(info['name'])
19          context.ingredients = \
20              [to_unicode(ingr) for ingr in info['ingredients']]
21          context.tools = [to_unicode(tool) for tool in info['tools']]
22          context.time_to_cook = info['time_to_cook']
23          context.description = to_unicode(info['description'])
24
25          return "Object updated successfully"
```

2 and 10.   Just like `zope.publisher.browser` provides a base class for browser views (`BrowserView`), a base class for XML-RPC views is also provided.

13–14.   Since we have to wrap the information contained in a recipe in XML-RPC-compatible data types, we simply ask the `IRecipe` schema for its fields, get the data from the object's attributes according to those fields, and return it in a dictionary, a data type that XML-RPC can handle.

5–8.   When saving data back on the recipe object, we need to make sure that we assign Unicode objects, not just regular strings. Otherwise we would invalidate the schema. XML-RPC itself only knows the string data type. `xmlrpclib` converts strings that contain non-ASCII characters to Unicode objects automatically. This function takes care of pure ASCII strings, thus always ensuring a Unicode object.

25.   At the end of every XML-RPC method, we must not forget to always return some value compatible with XML-RPC data types. By default, if a Python method or function does not have a `return` statement, it returns None. XML-RPC does not support such a null value and a lacking `return` statement might lead to a failure[5].

Example 13.3.2 Configuration of XML-RPC views
(`xmlrpc/configure.zcml`)

```
1  <configure
2     xmlns="http://namespaces.zope.org/zope"
3     xmlns:xmlrpc="http://namespaces.zope.org/xmlrpc"
4     >
5
6     <xmlrpc:view
7         for="worldcookery.interfaces.IRecipe"
8         class=".recipe.RecipeView"
9         methods="info"
10        permission="zope.View"
11        />
12
13    <xmlrpc:view
14        for="worldcookery.interfaces.IRecipe"
15        class=".recipe.RecipeView"
16        methods="edit"
17        permission="zope.ManageContent"
18        />
19
20 </configure>
```

9 and 16. XML-RPC views are configured with `xmlrpc:view` which works similar to `browser:page`. The difference lies in the `methods` parameter which specifies a list of method names of the view class. For each name in that list, an XML-RPC view will be registered under that name. Since we want different permissions for the `info` and `edit` views, we have to use the `xmlrpc:view` directive twice.

Apache Software License [1]. A compiled package can be obtained from its website.[6]

In order to run the program, you need a Java 2 Runtime Environment (J2RE) version 1.5, which can be downloaded for many operating system from Sun's Java website,[7] and version 3.0 of Apache's XmlRpc library. In order for the Java Virtual Machine to find the XmlRpc library, we have to set the `CLASSPATH` environment variable (it corresponds to Python's `PYTHONPATH` variable) to include all of the library's JAR files. Assuming that the Java Virtual Machine (the `java` program) is in your `PATH` environment variable, enter the following command on the command line:

`.../xmlrpc/demo$` **java DisplayRecipe http://localhost:8080/miso**

The command is the same on Unix and on Windows. When issued, the output should be identical to the output of the Python program.

---

[6] Apache XmlRpc package website <http://ws.apache.org/xmlrpc/>
[7] Sun Java website <http://java.com>

Example 13.3.3 Retrieving a recipe's information via XML-RPC in a Python program (`xmlrpc/demo/displayrecipe.py`)

```python
#! /usr/bin/env python
"""%(script)s -- retrieves and displays information about a recipe via
    XML-RPC

Usage: python %(script)s URL-of-a-recipe-object
"""
import sys
import xmlrpclib

def heading1(string):
    return "=" * len(string) + "\n" + string + "\n" + "=" * len(string)

def heading2(string):
    return string + "\n" + "-" * len(string)

def itemizedlist(list):
    bulletpoints = ["* " + item.encode('utf-8') for item in list]
    return '\n'.join(bulletpoints)

def main():
    if len(sys.argv) < 2:
        print >>sys.stderr, __doc__ % {'script': sys.argv[0]}
        sys.exit(1)

    recipe_url = sys.argv[1]
    server = xmlrpclib.Server(recipe_url)
    info = server.info()

    print heading1(info['name'].encode('utf-8'))
    print
    print "Time needed for preparation: %s mins" % info['time_to_cook']
    print
    print heading2("Ingredients:")
    print
    print itemizedlist(info['ingredients'])
    print
    print heading2("Needed kitchen tools:")
    print
    print itemizedlist(info['tools'])
    print
    print info['description'].encode('utf-8')

if __name__ == "__main__":
    main()
```

7. XML-RPC support is provided by the `xmlrpclib` module. It is part of Python's standard library and does not have to be downloaded.

Example 13.3.3 (continued)

25. A server providing XML-RPC functionality is represented using the `xmlrpclib.Server` class.

26. A remote procedure is simply invoked as if it were a method on the server object. Here we obtain a recipe's data in a dictionary (sent as an XML-RPC "struct" over the wire). Note that `xmlrpclib` converts strings with non-ASCII strings into Unicode objects, so before outputting to the console we need to encode all strings, preferably in UTF-8.

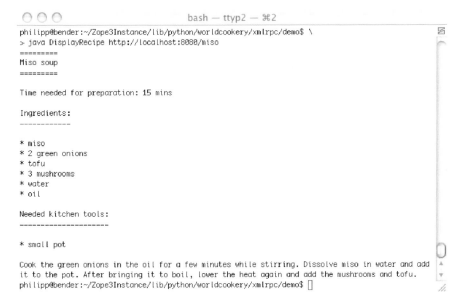

```
bash — ttyp2 — ⌘2

philipp@bender:~/Zope3Instance/lib/python/worldcookery/xmlrpc/demo$ \
> java DisplayRecipe http://localhost:8080/miso
=========
Miso soup
=========

Time needed for preparation: 15 mins

Ingredients:
------------

* miso
* 2 green onions
* tofu
* 3 mushrooms
* water
* oil

Needed kitchen tools:
---------------------

* small pot

Cook the green onions in the oil for a few minutes while stirring. Dissolve miso in water and add
it to the pot. After bringing it to boil, lower the heat again and add the mushrooms and tofu.
philipp@bender:~/Zope3Instance/lib/python/worldcookery/xmlrpc/demo$ []
```

Fig. 13.3. Java client program retrieving recipe data from the Zope server via XML-RPC.

Summary

- XML-RPC is a simplistic protocol for remote procedure calls. It is based on HTTP and uses XML for the data payload.
- XML-RPC is limited to the most basic data types, thus allowing the data exchange between heterogeneous environments.
- Using XML-RPC is a standard technique for exchanging data in a heterogeneous web service environment.
- Zope has built-in support for XML-RPC views. Python comes with a library for building XML-RPC clients.

Rocky says...

Java developers will appreciate the inclusion of an XML-RPC API right in the Python standard library. This puts the transparent use of XML-RPC in Python closer to the transparency offered by *RMI* in Java.

14

Metadata

An important aspect of many web applications, especially content management systems (CMS), is the storage of primary data. However the extra or secondary data associated with objects, generally called *metadata*, also plays an important role. Common examples of metadata include:

- information about the creator, author, or editor of a document,
- time and date of the creation or last modification of an object,
- state of a document in an organizational workflow.

Zope handles metadata very well and supports important standards out-of-the-box. We will see how to use them in this chapter.

14.1 Annotations

Our recipe class knows how to store information about recipes. It does not know how to store metadata and we would really like to keep it that way. After all, metadata is just data that is *associated* with primary data, it is not part of the primary data.

In order to allow us to store metadata without modifying our recipe component, Zope employs a system called annotation. As this is again functionality that the original component does not provide, you can bet that adapters are involved.

In annotations, we must distinguish the following two concepts:

IAnnotations Despite the confusing plural form, an IAnnotations adapter is a singular object with a dictionary-like interface that can store metadata. This adapter persistently associates metadata with content objects such as our recipes.

Often a simple IAnnotations adapter is used that stores the metadata container on a special attribute of the object itself (see below), but this should not be assumed. Simply adapt the object to IAnnotations, and trust that you have a persistent store of metadata associated with the object.

IAnnotatable Zope needs to determine if an object has an IAnnotations adapter very frequently, which means it needs to be done very quickly. Rather than trying to adapt each object to IAnnotations and reacting to success or failure, Zope uses an optimization. It requests that objects "promise" to be adaptable to IAnnotations.

They do this by declaring to be annotatable, by providing IAnnotatable from the zope.annotation package. This interface does not promise any additional functionality expressed in methods or attributes. It is an implied contract, a *marker interface*. The implied contract is that it is possible to get an annotations adapter for any annotatable object.

Now the only question remaining is where is metadata stored? Obviously, the annotations adapter has to take care of that. It would be no other component's responsibility. Because there are different ways of storing metadata, some of them appropriate for persistent objects, some of them not, there can be no general annotations adapter.

However, Zope would not be Zope if it did not already provide a built-in solution. Most objects in Zope are persisted in the ZODB. Its persistency machinery automatically stores objects and their attributes in the database. The *attribute annotations* adapter makes use of this by storing an object's annotations in an __annotations__ attribute on the object. Objects can decide whether they want to allow that by providing IAttributeAnnotatable, a subinterface of IAnnotatable. The adapter is registered for IAttributeAnnotatable.

Trying out annotations

For a demonstration, consider the following interactive interpreter session. After initializing Zope, we create a bare recipe object and try to adapt it. It obviously fails because it is not marked annotatable.

```
$ bin/debugzope
>>> class Recipe(object):
...     pass
...
>>> meatloaf = Recipe()
>>> from zope.annotation.interfaces import IAnnotations
>>> annotations = IAnnotations(meatloaf)
Traceback (most recent call last):
  ...
TypeError: ('Could not adapt', <__main__.Recipe object at 0x35c4f0>,
<InterfaceClass zope.annotation.interfaces.IAnnotations>)          ▼
```

However, we can instantly make it annotatable by directly providing IAttributeAnnotatable on it. This marks it as annotatable and allows us to adapt it to IAnnotations:

```
>>> from zope.interface import alsoProvides
>>> from zope.annotation.interfaces import IAttributeAnnotatable
>>> alsoProvides(meatloaf, IAttributeAnnotatable)
>>> annotations = IAnnotations(meatloaf)                              ▼
```

The annotations adapter behaves like a standard mapping object, such as a dictionary. Since there are different types of metadata, storing data directly in this mapping is strongly discouraged. The convention is to store an additional mapping under a key, usually the name of the software's Python package, and to store that metadata in that second mapping. World Cookery-specific metadata, for example, would be the cook who first invented the dish:

```
>>> annotations['worldcookery'] = {}
>>> annotations['worldcookery']['cook'] = \
...      u"Philipp von Weitershausen"                                 ▼
```

Similarly, Dublin Core metadata is stored using the zope.app.dublincore. ZopeDublinCore key, rating meta-data with the worldcookery.rating key (more on those later). This way different metadata will not conflict.

When we provided IAttributeAnnotatable on the recipe object, we not only made it annotatable; we also explicitly allowed annotations to be stored on the object as an attribute. The following lines reveal that this has indeed happened:

```
>>> meatloaf.__annotations__
<BTrees._OOBTree.OOBTree object at 0x28a3a50>
>>> dict(meatloaf.__annotations__)
{'worldcookery': {'cook': u'Philipp von Weitershausen'}}             ■
```

For objects persisted in the ZODB, attribute annotations are a care-free and easy solution, because they are persisted with the object automatically. There are circumstances, however, when it is not good to use attribute annotations, for example when content objects are generated from data coming from the file-system or an SQL database. Then, attribute annotation data would not be stored automatically which is why you would have to handle annotations differently in those cases.

In any case, it should not matter to the components storing metadata. All they care about is getting an annotations adapter to store the metadata. Where it is stored does not matter to them.

Annotations per class

Obviously we would like to allow annotations on all recipe objects, so having the class implement IAttributeAnnotatable sounds like a reasonable thing to do. However, it is not common to add such a statement to the

Python code directly. The `Recipe` class as a content object only cares to implement those interfaces that require implementation, such as `IRecipe`.

`IAttributeAnnotatable`, however, is a marker interface promising an abstract contract. Whether or not this promise should be given is more of a configuration issue than an implementation issue. Therefore, the implementation of `IAttributeAnnotatable` is generally expressed in a class's configuration, as shown by Example 14.1.1.

Example 14.1.1 Making recipes annotatable through attribute annotations (`configure.zcml`)

```
1    ...
2    <class class=".recipe.Recipe">
3      <implements
4          interface="zope.annotation.interfaces.IAttributeAnnotatable"
5          />
6      <require
7          permission="zope.View"
8          interface=".interfaces.IRecipe"
9          />
10     <require
11         permission="zope.ManageContent"
12         set_schema=".interfaces.IRecipe"
13         />
14   </class>
15     ...
```

3–5. Classes can be made to implement interfaces in addition to the ones they already implement from their source code. This is done with the `implements` subdirective of the `class` directive. This directive only makes sense for marker interfaces. Otherwise classes could promise to implement certain interfaces when in fact they do not. `IAttributeAnnotatable` is the most common interface this directive is used for.

Summary

- As it is not part of an object's primary data, metadata should be managed and possibly stored separately from the content objects it is associated with.
- Zope 3 uses annotation adapters as metadata storage; an annotation adapter manages all metadata associated with a particular object.
- For persistent objects, attribute annotations is the preferred way to handle annotations. On objects marked as attribute-annotatable the

annotations adapter stores metadata in a hidden attribute on the object, thus letting it to be persisted with the object.

- Different software packages should use different annotation keys to distinguish their metadata and avoid conflicts and ambiguities.

Rocky says...

Java developers should not confuse Zope 3's implementation and use of metadata with `java.jmi`. Zope's metadata and annotations are more about enhancing user generated content, not about defining extra attributes of Python code.

14.2 The Dublin Core

A de facto industry standard in the field of metadata is the *Dublin Core* [5], [16]. It defines a set of information that is generally found useful in document-oriented systems, high-level Internet protocols such as WebDAV, and data exchange formats such as RSS. Here are the metadata categories for resources as defined by the Dublin Core:

Title provides a human-readable and meaningful name for the resource. Most of the time, even in Zope, documents are referred to by their filename or name within their container which is not always meaningful to a person.

Creator states a person or organization responsible for the content of the resource.

Subject contains a list of keywords thematically describing the contents of the resource.

Description is usually a short abstract of what the resource depicts.

Publisher states a person or organization responsible for making the resource available.

Contributor lists possible contributors to the contents of the resource.

Date can be one or more dates representing an important event in the resource's life-cycle. Most of the time, a creation date and modification dates are recorded.

Type gives information about what kind of information the resource contains. This may include general categories or even genres.

Format informs readers and editors about the data format that the information is stored and presented in. This would most typically be a MIME type identifier.

Identifier gives a unique and unambiguous reference to the resource. This can be anything within a system of unique identifiers, such as an ISBN number, a URI, or even an IP address or telephone number.

Source is a list of resources from which the current resource was derived from.

Language states the language the resource's text is written and presented in.

Relation can contain a list of identifiers with which the resource stands in relation to. The type of relation is arbitrary and up to the application to fill with a meaning.

Coverage defines the scope of the resource.

Rights gives information about intellectual rights, copyrights, etc. regarding the resource.

All Dublin Core elements support multiple values. This obviously only makes sense for a few of them, such as *Subject, Contributor,* and *Rights.* Other properties, such as *Date* and *Relation,* only make sense when treated with qualifiers that tell the application which date and what kind of a relation are meant. Zope supports the Dublin Core standard to its full extent, but the general interfaces are designed for every-day use-cases, thus simplifying the unnecessary complexity.

Zope's support for Dublin Core resides in the zope.dublincore package. At the heart of this package is the ZopeDublinCore adapter, an adapter for annotatable objects that allows you to work with Dublin Core properties without having to go through annotations, even though the properties are stored in annotations, of course. Key interfaces are IZopeDublinCore for property read access and IWriteZopeDublinCore for write access, respectively.

Trying it out in the interpreter shell

Again we want to demonstrate how the Dublin Core adapter works with an example from the interactive interpreter shell:

```
$ bin/debugzope
>>> class Recipe(object):
...     pass
...
>>> fried_chicken = Recipe()                                    ▼
```

Since the object is not annotatable, we cannot adapt it to the Dublin Core interface.

```
>>> from zope.dublincore.interfaces import IWriteZopeDublinCore
>>> dc = IWriteZopeDublinCore(fried_chicken)
Traceback (most recent call last):
  ...
TypeError: ('Could not adapt', <__main__.Recipe object at 0x227fc30>,
<InterfaceClass zope.dublincore.interfaces.IWriteZopeDublinCore>)  ▼
```

However, after marking it attribute-annotatable, the adaption works. We can successfully assign Dublin Core metadata, more importantly without going through annotations:

```
>>> from zope.interface import alsoProvides
>>> from zope.annotation.interfaces import IAttributeAnnotatable
>>> alsoProvides(fried_chicken, IAttributeAnnotatable)
>>> dc = IWriteZopeDublinCore(fried_chicken)
>>> dc.title = u'Fried chicken'                                 ▼
```

Of course, the metadata still ends up in the annotations as the following look behinds the scenes reveals:

```
>>> dict(fried_chicken.__annotations__)
{'zope.app.dublincore.ZopeDublinCore': <zope.dublincore.
annotatableadapter.ZDCAnnotationData object at 0x29036b0>}    ■
```

We see that the Dublin Core adapter in fact stores its data under the `zope.dublincore.ZopeDublinCore` annotation key. How and in what format is secondary. We will not have to worry about ever having to work with this manually.

Metadata automation

Zope does a lot more for us when our objects are annotatable than just providing the Dublin Core adapter. As you may have noticed, recipes now have a new management tab, *Metadata* (see Figure 14.1). It allows content editors to edit the most basic metadata, namely title and description.

The *Metadata* ZMI view also reveals automatically computed metadata:

- creation date,
- date of last modification,
- and the user name of the creator.

Fig. 14.1. Zope provides a form for all annotatable objects in which basic Dublin Core metadata can be edited.

If you add a new recipe to a folder, you will see that these values has automatically been computed and annotated to the object. We will learn in Chapter 16 how this works, for now it is just important to know that Zope does this.

Dublin Core is not only used within a document or resource management system, it also comes into action when data is interchanged. As mentioned above, the WebDAV protocol allows a client program to query object metadata using the PROPFIND method. Zope's central view implementation for PROPFIND builds upon annotations and annotation-related adapters such as Dublin Core, thus allowing client programs to query Dublin Core and other metadata directly though WebDAV.

Permissions

Viewing and changing Dublin Core properties is protected by special permissions:

`zope.app.dublincore.view` is required from all principals when accessing Dublin Core metadata. Like `zope.View`, it is granted to anonymous by default.

`zope.app.dublincore.change` is required for changing Dublin Core properties.

An example in Page Templates

Since Zope's Dublin Core solution is integrated, most of your work with the Dublin Core is in presentation components, such as Page Templates. Here is a simple example to demonstrate how to access Dublin Core metadata in ZPT. After this we will look at how to use the Dublin Core adapter in Python.

In order not to over-complicate things, we will simply write a small viewlet that shows when a particular object was created and when it was last modified. Example 14.2.1 shows its source code. Its registration in ZCML shall be omitted here as it looks like any other viewlet registration we have done so far. Just note that we will register this viewlet for objects providing `IAnnotatable`, as the Dublin Core metadata will likely be available for such objects.

An example in Python

As an example for working with the Dublin Core adapter from Python, let us extend the XML-RPC view class from the previous chapter to provide another method for Dublin Core metadata retrieval. Example 14.2.2 shows the modified XML-RPC view class whereas Example 14.2.3 displays the little change necessary in order to configure the additional view method.

Since we already wrote an XML-RPC client in Chapter 13, consider it an optional exercise to write one for the new view method. The functional doctest in `xmlrpc/README.txt` was updated, so the functionality of the view is ensured either way.

Summary

- The Dublin Core specification describes a set of metadata commonly associated with resources in document management systems.

Example 14.2.1 Accessing Dublin Core metadata from Page Templates
(`skin/metadata.pt`)

```
1  <div id="metadata" class="box" i18n:domain="worldcookery"
2       tal:define="created context/zope:created;
3                   modified context/zope:modified;
4                   formatter python:request.locale.dates.getFormatter('
                        dateTime')"
5       tal:condition="python:created or modified">
6    <h1 i18n:translate="heading-about">About this item</h1>
7
8    <p i18n:translate="" tal:condition="created">
9      Created on
10     <span i18n:name="created_date"
11           tal:replace="python:formatter.format(created)" />
12   </p>
13
14   <p i18n:translate="" tal:condition="modified">
15     Last modified on
16     <span i18n:name="modified_date"
17           tal:replace="python:formatter.format(modified)" />
18   </p>
19 </div>
```

2–3.   Apart from traversal to attributes or dictionary keys, ZPT's path expressions can make use of *namespace adapters*. These are special traversing adapters for the TALES expressions that allow accessing additional information, such as metadata. The zope namespace adapter provides access to the most basic set of Dublin Core metadata, such as *Title*, *Created Date*, and *Modified Date*. The latter two are accessed here.

4, 11, and 17.   Note that we have a textbook example of localization here. The created and modified dates are localization-sensitive values. As discussed in Chapter 9, we acquire a date formatter from the request's locale and format the dates so they will be displayed according to local conventions.

- Zope's Dublin Core support lies mainly in an adapter provided by the `zope.dublincore` package.
  Since it is metadata, the adapter stores Dublin Core information in annotations.
- Zope also provides automated metadata updating facilities that are triggered when objects are added and/or modified.
- In Page Templates, the zope TALES namespace adapter provides access to basic Dublin Core fields.

Example 14.2.2 Enhanced XML-RPC view class providing a view method for metadata retrieval (`xmlrpc/recipe.py`)

```python
1   import time
2   import xmlrpclib
3   from zope.schema import getFields
4   from zope.dublincore.interfaces import IZopeDublinCore
5   from zope.app.publisher.xmlrpc import XMLRPCView
6   from worldcookery.interfaces import IRecipe
7
8   def to_unicode(string):
9       if isinstance(string, unicode):
10          return string
11      return string.decode('utf-8')
12
13  class RecipeView(XMLRPCView):
14
15      def info(self):
16          return dict((field, getattr(self.context, field))
17                      for field in getFields(IRecipe))
18
19      def dublincore_info(self):
20          dc = IZopeDublinCore(self.context)
21          info = dict((field, getattr(dc, field))
22                      for field in getFields(IZopeDublinCore))
23          for name in ('effective', 'created', 'expires', 'modified'):
24              if info[name]:
25                  epochtime = time.mktime(info[name].timetuple())
26                  info[name] = xmlrpclib.DateTime(epochtime)
27              else:
28                  info[name] = ''
29          return info
30
31      def edit(self, info):
32          context = self.context
33          context.name = to_unicode(info['name'])
34          context.ingredients = \
35              [to_unicode(ingr) for ingr in info['ingredients']]
36          context.tools = [to_unicode(tool) for tool in info['tools']]
37          context.time_to_cook = info['time_to_cook']
38          context.description = to_unicode(info['description'])
39
40          return "Object updated successfully"
```

20–22.   After adapting the recipe object to `IZopeDublinCore`, we use the same trick as in the `info` method to populate a dictionary with values from the instance attributes, this time from the adapter.

Example 14.2.2 (continued)

23–38.   As specified by the IZopeDublinCore interface, the date values are stored
as datetime objects, a data type that xmlrpclib cannot serialize[1]. To ensure
proper data exchange between Zope and the XML-RPC client, we have to
convert datetime objects into xmlrpclib.DateTime objects. Values that
are None are converted to empty strings.

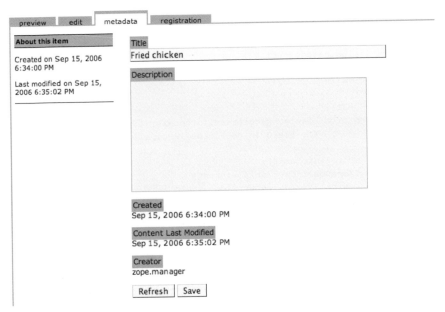

Fig. 14.2. Showing created and last modified dates in a sidebar viewlet.

Flashback

In Zope 2, the Content Management Framework (CMF) first introduced
Dublin Core support, mainly through a set of interfaces. CMF content
classes can choose to implement these to signal to the rest of application that they supported Dublin Core methods. This is by far the most
prominent usage of interfaces in a Zope application prior to Zope 3.

The CMF also provides an implementation of these interfaces,
DefaultDublinCoreImpl, that content classes can inherit from to
gain Dublin Core functionality. The obvious difference to Zope 3 here
is, again, that extra functionality like handling metadata, especially a
certain kind like Dublin Core, is constrained to external components like

Example 14.2.3 Adding another XML-RPC view method to the configuration (`xmlrpc/configure.zcml`)

```
1  <configure
2      xmlns="http://namespaces.zope.org/zope"
3      xmlns:xmlrpc="http://namespaces.zope.org/xmlrpc"
4      >
5
6      <xmlrpc:view
7          for="worldcookery.interfaces.IRecipe"
8          class=".recipe.RecipeView"
9          methods="info dublincore_info"
10         permission="zope.View"
11         />
12
13     <xmlrpc:view
14         for="worldcookery.interfaces.IRecipe"
15         class=".recipe.RecipeView"
16         methods="edit"
17         permission="zope.ManageContent"
18         />
19
20  </configure>
```

9. By adding the `dublincore_info` method to this list it will be registered as an XML-RPC view, protected with the `zope.View` permission like the `info` method.

---

adapters. This makes Zope 3 much more flexible, since the an adapter can easily be exchanged—a base class cannot.

Finally, Zope 3 absolutely surpasses the CMF's metadata model by offering a totally generic solution: annotations. They not only allow us to associate information useful to humans but also application-relevant data, such as workflow states, revision control status, etc.

14.3 Custom metadata

It is often necessary to store custom metadata. Experience shows that advanced and complex applications always require at least one or two fields more than the Dublin Core standard provides. This is far from being a tragedy, since we can simply write adapters to store the custom metadata in annotations.

As a simple example for such a component, consider an online rating system through which visitors of the *World Cookery* website can rate recipes according to how good they found the dish or the recipe description. Again, the rating information is not part of the actual recipe data schema. Since it is clearly metadata, it belongs in an annotation.

Interfaces

First, we will have to define two interfaces (see Example 14.3.1). IRatable is a marker interface identifying objects that can be rated. It extends the IAnnotatable marker interface to express the dependency on annotations. The second interface, IRating, describes the actual rating API, gathering rating information and performing ratings. An adapter for ratable objects will provide this interface.

Example 14.3.1 Interfaces for the simple rating system (interfaces.py)

```
 1   ...
 2   from zope.schema import Float
 3   from zope.annotation.interfaces import IAnnotatable
 4
 5   class IRatable(IAnnotatable):
 6       """Marker interface that promises that an implementing object maybe
 7       rated using ``IRating`` annotations.
 8       """
 9
10   class IRating(Interface):
11       """Give and query rating about objects, such as recipes.
12       """
13
14       def rate(rating):
15           """Rate the current object with `rating`.
16           """
17
18       averageRating = Float(
19           title=_(u"Average rating"),
20           description=_(u"The average rating of the current object"),
21           required=True
22           )
23
24       numberOfRatings = Int(
25           title=_(u"Number of ratings"),
26           description=_(u"The number of times the current has been rated"),
27           required=True
28           )
```

An adapter

In analogy to the IZopeDublinCore adapter, we now provide the IRating adapter for ratable objects. It will store all rating information in the ratable object's annotations, thus providing a frontend to this particular type of metadata through the IRating interface. Example 14.3.2 shows the source code.

Example 14.3.2 Adapter providing rating functionality based on annotations (rating.py)

```
1  from persistent.dict import PersistentDict
2  from persistent.list import PersistentList
3  from zope.interface import implements
4  from zope.component import adapts
5  from zope.annotation.interfaces import IAnnotations
6  from worldcookery.interfaces import IRating, IRatable
7
8  KEY = "worldcookery.rating"
9
10 class Rating(object):
11     implements(IRating)
12     adapts(IRatable)
13
14     def __init__(self, context):
15         self.context = self.__parent__ = context
16         annotations = IAnnotations(context)
17         mapping = annotations.get(KEY)
18         if mapping is None:
19             blank = {'average': 0.0, 'ratings': PersistentList()}
20             mapping = annotations[KEY] = PersistentDict(blank)
21         self.mapping = mapping
22
23     def rate(self, rating):
24         ratings = self.mapping['ratings']
25         ratings.append(float(rating))
26         self.mapping['average'] = sum(ratings)/len(ratings)
27
28     @property
29     def averageRating(self):
30         return self.mapping['average']
31
32     @property
33     def numberOfRatings(self):
34         return len(self.mapping['ratings'])
```

8. As mentioned earlier in this chapter, annotations are stored under a certain key so that different sets of metadata do not conflict. The string here defines the key used for storing rating information. By making this a de facto string constant, we avoid potential typos when using the key later.

Example 14.3.2 (continued)

15. Since this is a trusted adapter, it will be security-proxied. In that case it is a good idea to fill the __parent__ attribute with the context object so that the security machinery can look up local grants (in case they exist) by walking up the parent hierarchy.

16–17.   Like the Dublin Core adapter, we read and write to and from annotations. Therefore we get yet another adapter, the annotations adapter. From it we acquire a mapping object for storing rating data in. The IAnnotations interface requires the annotations adapter to behave like a mapping object itself.

19–20.   In case the mapping object cannot be acquired, it means that this adapter is invoked on this particular object instance for the first time. We thus provide a default mapping with a zero average and an empty list. Since the annotations are likely to be persisted, we have to be careful that we comply with the rules of persistency. To be safe, we use PersistentDict and PersistentList instead of their non-persistent flavours.

For configuration, we will not only have to configure the adapter, but we will also have to make the Recipe class ratable so that the adapter works on it. Example 14.3.3 shows how configure.zcml needs to be enhanced.

As usual, we can now test the adapter on the command line. Consider a recipe:

```
$ bin/debugzope
>>> class Recipe(object):
...        pass
...
>>> hamburgers = Recipe()                                              ▼
```

In order to mark it ratable, it also needs to be annotatable, for example attribute-annotatable:

```
>>> from zope.annotation.interfaces import IAttributeAnnotatable
>>> from worldcookery.interfaces import IRatable
>>> from zope.interface import alsoProvides
>>> alsoProvides(hamburgers, IAttributeAnnotatable, IRatable)          ▼
```

Now we can rate the object using the IRating adapter:

```
>>> from worldcookery.interfaces import IRating
>>> rating = IRating(hamburgers)
>>> rating.rate(1)    # I don't like hamburgers
>>> rating.rate(9)    # I like hamburgers                              ▼
```

Example 14.3.3 Configuring the rating adapter and making recipes ratable
(`configure.zcml`)

```
1     ...
2     <class class=".recipe.Recipe">
3       <implements
4           interface="zope.annotation.interfaces.IAttributeAnnotatable
5                       .interfaces.IRatable"
6           />
7       <require
8           permission="zope.View"
9           interface=".interfaces.IRecipe"
10          />
11      <require
12          permission="zope.ManageContent"
13          set_schema=".interfaces.IRecipe"
14          />
15    </class>
16
17    ...
18
19    <adapter
20        factory=".rating.Rating"
21        trusted="true"
22        />
23
24    <class class=".rating.Rating">
25      <require
26          permission="zope.View"
27          interface=".interfaces.IRating"
28          />
29    </class>
30    ...
```

3–6. We want recipes to be ratable, we therefore add `IRatable` to the list of
additional interfaces the `Recipe` class should implement.

21. Like all other components invoked through user-interaction, adapters have to
respect security-protected methods and attributes. That is usually not a problem because the object's attributes that the adapter works with should have
security declarations that requires a permission from the user. The problem
is that this mechanism does not work with attribute annotations because the
__annotations__ attribute is hardly ever configured with security declarations.
After all, the classes are not supposed to know about it.

The solution here is to mark this adapter as *trusted*. This will prevent any
security checks when the adapter accesses attributes on the object, it will have
free access. In return, the adapter itself will be security proxied and needs
security declarations (see below).

Example 14.3.3 (continued)

24–29. Since the IRatable adapter is a trusted adapter, it itself rather than the
adapted object will be security proxied. That means the adapter implementation (the Rating class) now needs security declarations as well, otherwise
other components could not use it.

Example 14.3.4 Docfile test for the rating adapter (rating.txt)

```
 1  ===============
 2  Rating objects
 3  ===============
 4
 5  The rating system allows users to rate objects on a continuous scale
 6  (a discrete scale can be enforced by a view).  We distinguish
 7  *ratable* objects which have to annotatable and implement ''IRatable'
 8  on one hand and the ''IRating'' adapter for ratable objects which the
 9  rating of the latter on the other hand.
10
11  Consider a simple object, e.g. a recipe:
12
13     >>> from worldcookery.recipe import Recipe
14     >>> hamburgers = Recipe()
15
16  In order to mark it ratable, it also needs to annotatable, for example
17  attribute-annotatable:
18
19     >>> from zope.annotation.interfaces import IAttributeAnnotatable
20     >>> from worldcookery.interfaces import IRatable
21     >>> from zope.interface import alsoProvides
22     >>> alsoProvides(hamburgers, IAttributeAnnotatable, IRatable)
23
24  Now we can rate the object using the ''IRating'' adapter:
25
26     >>> from worldcookery.interfaces import IRating
27     >>> rating = IRating(hamburgers)
28     >>> rating.rate(1)    # I don't like hamburgers
29     >>> rating.rate(9)    # I like hamburgers
30
31  Of course, the adapter also tells about the average rating and number
32  of ratings that have been issued yet:
33
34     >>> rating.averageRating
35     5.0
36     >>> rating.numberOfRatings
37     2
```

Of course, the adapter also tells about the average rating and number of ratings that have been issued yet:

```
>>> rating.averageRating
5.0
>>> rating.numberOfRatings
2
```

This small interpreter session makes a nice doctest if slightly modified. Example 14.3.4 shows the listing of a docfile test, serving as a test and documentation for the rating system at the same time. Example 14.3.5 contains the mandatory test suite and initialization routines as shown in Chapter 12.

Example 14.3.5 Test suite and initialization routines for the rating docfile test (`tests/test_rating.py`)

```
1  import unittest
2  from doctest import DocFileSuite
3
4  import zope.component.testing
5  from zope.annotation.attribute import AttributeAnnotations
6  from worldcookery.rating import Rating
7
8  def setUp(test):
9      zope.component.testing.setUp(test)
10     zope.component.provideAdapter(AttributeAnnotations)
11     zope.component.provideAdapter(Rating)
12
13 def test_suite():
14     return unittest.TestSuite((
15         DocFileSuite('rating.txt',
16                     package='worldcookery',
17                     setUp=setUp,
18                     tearDown=zope.component.testing.tearDown),
19         ))
20
21 if __name__ == '__main__':
22     unittest.main(defaultTest='test_suite')
```

"Persistent" adapters

As you may have noticed from the pattern of Zope's Dublin Core adapter and our rating adapter, annotations effectively allow you to implement "persistent" adapters. This doesn't mean that the adapter objects themselves are persisted. Rather, the adapters draw all their values from the object's persistent annotations. Adapting the same object over and over will always yield the same values. To the user of the adapter it seems as if the adapter itself is persistent.

Browser views

As with the Dublin Core, an adapter by itself is not helpful for the user. A visitor of the *World Cookery* website wants to rate objects through a web browser. That means we have to provide browser access to the rating system.

Once again we can make this functionality available through a viewlet and have it appear every time we view a ratable object. Such a viewlet, however, would have to be slightly more complicated than the ones we have implemented so far. It would not only render itself, it would also have to take input and do something with this input. Such functionality cannot be handled by a Page Template alone. We will have to implement this viewlet in Python. Example 14.3.6 shows the viewlet class that makes the rating functionality available as part of the skin. Example 14.3.7 shows the Page Template that goes with the viewlet, Example 14.3.8 demonstrates how a viewlet that implemented in Python is registered.

Example 14.3.6 Viewlet for rating functionality implemented in Python (skin/rating.py)

```
1  from zope.viewlet.viewlet import ViewletBase
2  from zope.app.pagetemplate import ViewPageTemplateFile
3  from worldcookery.interfaces import IRating
4
5  class RatingViewlet(ViewletBase):
6
7      def update(self):
8          rating = self.request.form.get('worldcookery.rating')
9          if rating is not None:
10             IRating(self.context).rate(rating)
11
12     render = ViewPageTemplateFile('rating.pt')
13
14     def rating(self):
15         return IRating(self.context)
16
17     ratingChoices = (1, 2, 3, 4, 5)
```

1 and 5. Viewlets can choose to subclass the optional base class `ViewletBase`. Much like base classes such as `BrowserPage`, this base class merely provides an object constructor (`__init__`).

7–12. Viewlets need to have two methods, `update` and `render`. In the former, viewlets can prepare (e.g. compute) some data that they will later need for rendering themselves. The `update` methods of all viewlets in a viewlet manager will be called first. Here we use this method to inspect the request for a rating that may have been submitted from the form that appears when the viewlet is

Example 14.3.6 (continued)

rendered. A viewlet is rendered by invoking its `render` method. Here we again implement this method by pointing to a Page Template, whose source code is shown in Example 14.3.7.

Example 14.3.7 Page Template rendering the rating viewlet (`skin/rating.pt`)

```
1   <div id="ratings" class="box" i18n:domain="worldcookery">
2     <h1 i18n:translate="heading-ratings">Ratings</h1>
3
4     <p i18n:translate=""
5        tal:define="rating view/rating;
6                    average rating/averageRating;
7                    votes rating/numberOfRatings;
8                    formatter python:request.locale.numbers.getFormatter('
                       decimal')">
9        This recipe has received an average rating of
10       <strong tal:content="python:formatter.format(average, '###0.0')"
11               i18n:name="rating">0.0</strong>
12       (<strong i18n:name="votes" tal:content="votes">12</strong> votes).
13     </p>
14
15     <form action="" tal:attributes="action request/getURL" method="post">
16       <p i18n:translate="">Rate this recipe:</p>
17       <select name="worldcookery.rating:float">
18         <option tal:repeat="rating view/ratingChoices"
19                 tal:attributes="value rating"
20                 tal:content="rating">rating</option>
21       </select>
22       <input type="submit" value="Rate" i18n:attributes="value rate-button"
               />
23     </form>
24   </div>
```

5 and 18. From the viewlet instance we acquire the rating adapter instance and a list of possible ratings.

8 and 10. Here we have an another example of localization. The average rating is obviously a floating point number, which is localization-sensitive too. Again, we acquire a number formatter from the request's locale to format the number according to a pattern. Here, it makes sense to round to the first digit after the dot.

8. Since the viewlet itself will take care of processing the rating input in its `update` method, we set the form action to whatever the current URL is. That way we can ensure that the same page will be shown again and that the rating viewlet will be invoked.

Example 14.3.8 Configuration for rating viewlet
(`skin/configure.zcml`)

```
1     ...
2     <browser:viewlet
3         name="rating"
4         for="worldcookery.interfaces.IRatable"
5         manager=".interfaces.ISidebar"
6         class=".rating.RatingViewlet"
7         layer=".interfaces.IWorldCookerySkin"
8         permission="zope.View"
9         />
10    ...
```

6. As you now can see we refer to our viewlet class via the `class` parameter. With
   the previous viewlets we simply used the `template` parameter to refer to a
   Page Template.

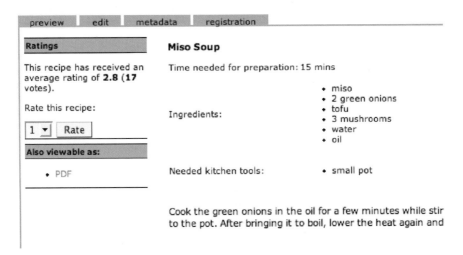

Fig. 14.3. Viewlet allowing the user to rate a recipe.

Summary

- Sometimes, custom metadata outside of the already supported Dublin Core needs to be associated with objects.
- It is recommended to abstract custom metadata—including the functionality to change it—in an interface, such as `IRating` in the example.
- Instead of directly reading and writing annotated data, an adapter for the abstract metadata interface takes care of storing the annotated data, like the `IRating` adapter does in the example.

15

Containers

When we created recipes with the web interface, we simply added them to the database root, the root folder. Folders are special content components because they contain other content components. They are *content containers*. Containment is an important concept in Zope and containers are important components. They occur everywhere, not only where content components are involved.

After introducing the basic concepts and necessary interfaces, this chapter explains common uses of containers, such as containment constraints and names of contained objects.

15.1 Object hierarchies and traversal

We are used to putting things into hierarchies. On the file system, for example, we use directories to group files and other directories. Then we end up with file paths such as

```
Documents/Recipes/Spain/Tapas.doc
```

We can have the same kind of paths in URLs, e.g.

```
http://worldcookery.com/recipes/spain/tapas/edit.html
```

How does Zope find `tapas` and `edit.html`, and what does `recipes/spain` represent?

Traversal

The Zope publisher breaks URLs like the one above into segments. It then tries to find objects corresponding to these segments. This process is called *traversal*. It is like a walk through an object hierarchy, similar to walking through a directory hierarchy on the file system.

Traversal of URL paths is handled by `IPublishTraverse` adapters. For any given object, its `IPublishTraverse` adapter knows how to traverse to the "next" object. This is pretty easy for most objects because they do not contain other objects. Hence the next object can only be a view. Take recipes, for example. When you see a URL like

```
http://worldcookery.com/gazpacho/edit.html
```

You know that `edit.html` will be a view for `gazpacho` (it could be the browser form we wrote in Chapter 8). That is why we can write `edit.html` instead of `@@edit.html` because it is unambiguous (you can only traverse to views from recipes anyways).

The story is different for objects that reference or contain other objects. Here it would be good to let traversal find the subobjects. Objects that contain other objects therefore need their custom `IPublishTraverse` adapter which tells the publisher how to get at the contained objects.

Containers

In Python, a common way to reference other objects while giving them names is to use dictionaries. In the context of creating object hierarchies in Zope, we call those *containers*. Anything that can be used like a dictionary can essentially serve as a container.

The only restriction is that the keys by which objects are looked up from a container have to be strings or Unicode objects. Also, a simple dictionary does not suffice most of the time. A container for persistent objects, for example, should most probably be persistent itself, and containers that anticipate lots of subobjects will want to use the BTree mechanism discussed in Chapter 6. Zope comes with a very generic container implementation called *folders* which both is persistent and uses BTrees.

The whole container API is described in the `IContainer` interface which is a combination of the `IReadContainer` and `IWriteContainer` interfaces, all provided by the `zope.app.container.interfaces` module. As the names suggest, `IReadContainer` describes methods for read access whereas `IWriteContainer` contains the API for write access. As we will see later, this distinction makes security configuration very easy.

Containers obviously have a custom `IPublishTraverse` adapter which will traverse to the objects in a container. The adapter uses standard dictionary access to do that. Since contained objects can potentially have any name, object lookup and view lookup may collide. Would `container/index.html` refer to the `index.html` object inside the container or the `index.html` view of the container? As we already know, Zope avoids this conflict by prepending view names with `@@`.

If you would like to avoid `@@`, you just have to ensure that container names and view names do not collide. You can do this with a strict naming convention for view names (e.g. they always end in `.html`) and a name chooser for containers that ensures that the names of contained objects do not conflict with the naming convention for view names (e.g. it would disallow object names ending in .html). We will cover name choosers later this chapter in Section 15.4.

Traversal in Page Templates

It is important to note that the traversal of URL paths is fundamentally different from the evaluation of TALES path expressions, even though they look similar at first sight. Path expressions can allow you to access any attribute of an object and, if the object behaves like a dictionary, any key in the mapping. Of course, they can also access views (e.g. the standard_macros view).

URL traversal on the other hand is limited to what IPublishTraverse adapters allow. This is much less than what path expressions can access. For example, you can access attributes of recipes from Page Templates (e.g. context/time_to_cook), but you could not simply enter http://localhost:8080/recipe/time_to_cook in your browser and see the attribute's value displayed.

Summary

- Traversal is the process of breaking URL paths into segments and associating objects with each segments. The latter is done by IPublishTraverse adapters.
- The default IPublishTraverse adapter looks up views for objects. It does not traverse to attributes of objects.
- The typical model for creating objects that contain or refer to other objects is containers. Containers behave very much like dictionaries, their API is the same.
- URL traversal is not to be confused with the evaluation of TALES path expressions. Both have different scopes (especially with respect to what is available) and different behaviour.

Using Zope 2

At first sight, Zope 2 has a simpler approach to traversal. Essentially, Zope 2's publisher traverses objects through attribute access. That means any attribute of an object is potentially accessible via URL traversal (unless security forbids it). It also means that Zope 2's equivalent to containers, *object managers*, do not use the mapping API for looking up and storing objects, but simple attribute access and assignment.

Objects can still influence the way the publisher will traverse them. In older versions of Zope 2 the publisher will check whether objects have a __bobo_traverse__ method and call it. Recent versions of Zope 2 also support the IPublishTraverse adapter, which is the preferred way to customize traversal due to its compatibility with Zope 3.

Rocky says...

Java web developers will probably notice here how different URL traversal in J2EE is compared to Zope. In Zope you must think of URL segments as objects. There is no (standard) configuration option for mapping a request handler to an arbitrary URL.

15.2 Containment and location

Containers know which objects they contain. But how can objects that are contained know *that* they are contained and *where*? We will answer this question now.

Location

Objects that are contained in a container normally have no idea that they are contained. Most of the time, they do not even need to know. However, components operating on the object might need to know whether an object is contained, and if so, which container it is contained in and by which name it is known to the container. A commonly used component of this kind is the absolute_url or IAbsoluteURL view. It needs to know the name of the object it is supposed to compute the URL for as well as the names of all parent objects in order to compute the full URL.

The Zope framework that allows such parent relations is the *location* framework provided by the zope.location package. The ILocation interface is what ties everything together. If a component provides ILocation, it promises to provide the following attributes:

- __parent__ (its container),
- __name__ (its name in the container).

If these attributes are not None, then the object is *locatable*, meaning it is part of a hierarchy and can be found via traversal through this hierarchy.

As a demonstration we will use the interactive interpreter shell as usual. A simplistic object will serve as a locatable. A class exactly like this is provided by the zope.location package as a potential base class. We will define it here ourselves for demonstration purposes, though:

```
$ python
>>> from zope.location.interfaces import ILocation
>>> from zope.interface import implements
>>>
>>> class Location(object):
...     implements(ILocation)
...     __name__ = __parent__ = None
...                                                              ▼
```

Instances of this class are potentially locatable. They are not *actually* locatable, of course, as long as the name and parent attributes are None. As an example we create three instances of which one is always the parent object of the next one, like grandfather, father, and son. The locate function can be used to wire the location information into potentially locatable objects. It is a shorter spelling of assigning the __name__ and __parent__ attributes:

```
>>> son = Location()
>>> father = Location()
>>> grandfather = Location()
>>>
>>> from zope.location import locate
>>> locate(son, father, name=u"son")
>>> locate(father, grandfather, name=u"father")
>>> grandfather.__name__ = u"grandfather"                       ▼
```

Note that the parent of a locatable object does not necessarily have to be a container. Locatability makes no assumptions about the parent object. As you can see, the signature of the locate function is

```
locate(object, parent, name=None)
```

The *name* parameter is optional.

A function of locatability is a walkable hierarchy of object ancestors. An object's parent can have a parent itself and so forth. The LocationIterator makes this sequence of parents iterable, for example in a simple loop:

```
>>> from zope.location import LocationIterator
>>> for obj in LocationIterator(son):
...     print obj.__name__
...
son
father
grandfather                                                     ■
```

Since the grandfather object was not assigned a parent, the iteration stops there.

Containment

Containment is just another aspect of locatability. It is locatability from a container's point of view. Locatability by itself expresses mere parent-child relationships. Containment adds the notion of being contained in a Zope container.

Whether or not an object is contained is expressed through the IContained interface which is provided by the zope.app.container package. This is a marker interface that extends ILocation. Any contained object is therefore locatable.

Imagine a simple container such as SampleContainer from the zope.app.container.sample module. We can easily store potentially locatable objects on it by using standard dictionary syntax. This time we will resort to the simple Location class as it is provided by zope.location to save typing:

```
$ python
>>> from zope.app.container.sample import SampleContainer
>>> from zope.location import Location
>>> container = SampleContainer()
>>> container[u'gazpacho'] = gazpacho = Location()          ▼
```

Now we would also like to express the containment relation between this object and its container. That includes making the container the parent of this object. To do that we have to use the contained function instead of locate:

```
>>> from zope.app.container.contained import contained
>>> contained(gazpacho, container, name=u'gazpacho')
<zope.location.location.Location object at 0x134ff90>      ▼
```

As you can see, the signature of the contained function is exactly like the one for locate. They are also now marked as *contained*, meaning they now provide IContained:

```
>>> from zope.app.container.interfaces import IContained
>>> IContained.providedBy(gazpacho)
True                                                       ▼
```

Last but not least it should be mentioned that adding the object to the container and making it contained can be combined in one step by using the setitem function:

```
>>> chorizo = Location()
>>> from zope.app.container.contained import setitem
>>> setitem(container, container.__setitem__, u'chorizo', chorizo)
>>> IContained.providedBy(chorizo)
True
>>> chorizo.__parent__ is container
True
>>> chorizo.__name__
u'chorizo'
>>> container[u'chorizo'] is chorizo
True                                                       ▼
```

The syntax of the `setitem` function differs from one of `locate` and `contained`:

```
setitem(container, setitem_method, name, object)
```

What about non-locatable objects?

So far we have only added locatable objects to containers. They can easily be made contained because they already have `__name__` and `__parent__` attributes. Setting these attributes and marking them with `IContained` is just a formality.

Not all objects are locatable, though. As a matter of fact most are not locatable, including instances of our `Recipe` class. The containment machinery cannot assign the `__name__` and `__parent__` attributes by force either. It might simply not be allowed by the class and result in an `AttributeError`.

Zope's answer to this problem are *contained proxies*. Like security proxies, they wrap an object almost transparently. While security proxies protect the wrapped object against forbidden access, contained proxies add containment functionality to non-locatable objects. In other words, they make it look like the object had `__name__` and `__parent__` attributes without actually modifying it.

The containment machinery will make use of contained proxies transparently. That means it finds out automatically when an object needs to be wrapped in one and when not. As we have seen above, it does not wrap objects that are already locatable. Let us repeat the above experiment with an object that is *not* locatable such as a regular recipe object:

```
>>> from worldcookery.recipe import Recipe
>>> paella = Recipe()
>>> setitem(container, container.__setitem__, u'paella', paella)    ▼
```

At first, the contained object looks like a regular recipe object. But a closer look reveals that it now has `__name__` and `__parent__` attributes. The `type` function discovers the real nature of this object—a proxy wrapping a recipe object:

```
>>> container[u'paella']
<worldcookery.recipe.Recipe object at 0x795b30>
>>> container[u'paella'].__name__
u'paella'
>>> container[u'paella'].__parent__ is container
True
>>> type(container[u'paella'])
<class 'zope.app.container.contained.ContainedProxy'>          ▼
```

As we expect, the original object has not been modified. It does not have the containment-relevant attributes that the proxied one had:

```
>>> paella.__name__
Traceback (most recent call last):
  ...
AttributeError: 'Recipe' object has no attribute '__name__'
>>> paella.__parent__
Traceback (most recent call last):
  ...
AttributeError: 'Recipe' object has no attribute '__parent__'        ∎
```

Summary

- The relationship between an object and its parent in an object hierarchy can be expressed through the location machinery by providing
  ILocation.
- Containment is locatability in the context of containers; it is expressed through IContained.
- When located in a container, locatable objects are marked as contained; non-locatable objects are proxied so that they comply with
  the containment machinery.

Flashback

Zope 2 does not have a system of containment per se. It does have a
mighty, powerful and quite intriguing acquisition system which can wrap
objects that are acquired so that they gain acquisition information. In
other words, if an object is acquired from its containing object manager,
then this object manager is its acquisitional parent. However, if the object
is acquired from a different object over several hierarchy levels, then
whichever object is last in the traversal chain becomes the acquisitional
parent. Thus the acquisitional parent is dynamic and depends on the
acquisition context. Containment relations are not expressed explicitly.

Zope 3 content objects do not have to have identifiers (IDs). Whether
or not objects have identifiers or names is a containment issue, it does
not have to be an issue of the object. That is why Zope 3 abolishes the
mandatory Zope 2 *ID* that objects have to provide in order to function
within a Zope object manager. Objects *can* have names in Zope 3, but
those are assigned and managed by the container without any implications for the object itself, unless the object explicitly wants to be involved
by providing ILocation.

15.3 Containment constraints

Apart from the general containment relations introduced above, it is also often necessary to implement constraints on what a container can contain, and in which type of container an object may be contained. As with any type of constraint, containment constraints are expressed in interfaces. They are not managed by the containers to ensure light-weight container implementations. Instead, a general machinery takes care of them, much like with containment relations.

In Example 15.3.1, we define a new interface, IRecipeContainer. It describes a container that only holds recipe objects, while we changed IRecipe to extend already known IContained interface with a constraint for the parent object.

Example 15.3.1 Containment constraints expressed in interfaces (interfaces.py)

```
1  from zope.interface import Interface
2  from zope.schema import List, Text, TextLine, Int
3  from zope.i18nmessageid import MessageFactory
4  _ = MessageFactory('worldcookery')
5  from zope.app.container.interfaces import IContainer, IContained
6  from zope.app.container.constraints import contains, containers
7
8  class IRecipe(IContained):
9      """Store information about a recipe.
10     """
11     containers('worldcookery.interfaces.IRecipeContainer')
12
13  ...
14
15  class IRecipeContainer(IContainer):
16     contains('worldcookery.interfaces.IRecipe')
```

5 and 8. IRecipe now extends the IContained interface to indicate that recipes can be located in containers. This requires recipes to have __name__ and __parent__ attributes.

11 and 16. contains and containers allow you to model containment hierarchies. The former will constrain the allowed types of objects in a container while the latter will limit the types of containers that an object can be added to. Note that both functions take either interfaces or strings containing interfaces' dotted import paths. That is to avoid problems with circular references (e.g. when a container can also contain objects of its own kind). Here the IRecipeContainer is not yet defined when IRecipe is declared, which is why we use strings.

Container implementation

As mentioned before, containers are simple mapping objects which makes implementing their API a trivial task. To make life even easier, SampleContainer is a container implementation that can serve as a base class for custom container implementations. If persistency is needed, BTreeContainer is an alternative. The general content container Folder is an option when containment constraints are not the primary goal of the component in question.

Example 15.3.2 shows the trivial implementation of IRecipeContainer. Containment-relevant statements were made in the interface which only leaves us with the usual security declarations in configure.zcml (shown in Example 15.3.3).

Example 15.3.2 Simple container implementation for recipes (folder.py)

```
1  from zope.interface import implements
2  from zope.app.container.btree import BTreeContainer
3  from worldcookery.interfaces import IRecipeContainer
4
5  class RecipeFolder(BTreeContainer):
6      implements(IRecipeContainer)
```

Testing the container

As usual we will take the time to test the component on the interpreter shell. This will also help us understand how constraints are checked. We instantiate our recipe folder:

```
$ python
>>> from worldcookery.folder import RecipeFolder
>>> folder = RecipeFolder()                                    ▼
```

The checkObject function can now check constraints. As we expect, an error is raised trying to check an object that does not provide IRecipe:

```
>>> from zope.app.container.constraints import checkObject
>>> tortillas = object()
>>> checkObject(folder, u'tortillas', tortillas)
Traceback (most recent call last):
  ...
zope.app.container.interfaces.InvalidItemType:
(<worldcookery.folder.RecipeFolder object at 0x367130>,
 <object object at 0x354448>,
 (<InterfaceClass worldcookery.interfaces.IRecipe>,))      ▼
```

Example 15.3.3 Mandatory security declarations for the recipe folder
(`configure.zcml`)

```
1    ...
2    <class class=".folder.RecipeFolder">
3      <implements
4          interface="zope.annotation.interfaces.IAttributeAnnotatable"
5          />
6      <require
7          permission="zope.View"
8          interface="zope.app.container.interfaces.IReadContainer"
9          />
10     <require
11         permission="zope.ManageContent"
12         interface="zope.app.container.interfaces.IWriteContainer"
13         />
14   </class>
15   ...
```

8 and 12.   Now we see that two interfaces, one that contains method definitions
relevant for read access and one with write access, pays off for security declarations. Instead of listing the relevant attributes we simply refer to the interfaces.

Passing an object that *does* provide `IRecipe` will make `checkObject` execute without error:

```
>>> from zope.interface import implements
>>> from worldcookery.interfaces import IRecipe
>>> class Recipe(object):
...     implements(IRecipe)
...
>>> sangria = Recipe()
>>> checkObject(folder, u'sangria', sangria)
>>>
```

However, a container that is not a recipe container will not be acceptable:

```
>>> from zope.app.container.sample import SampleContainer
>>> container = SampleContainer()
>>> checkObject(container, u'sangria', sangria)
Traceback (most recent call last):
 ...
zope.app.container.interfaces.InvalidContainerType:
(<zope.app.container.sample.SampleContainer object at 0x142ff10>,
 (<InterfaceClass worldcookery.interfaces.IRecipeContainer>,))
```

As usual, this interpreter session was added as a docfile test (`folder.
txt`). Listing this file again here would be redundant.

Adjusting to IContained

In Example 15.3.1 we changed the contract of the IRecipe interface by letting it extend IContained. This has two implications. Firstly, recipes now have to provide __name__ and __parent__ attributes. Secondly, the automated add and edit forms will have to omit the fields from IContained because they are not set through forms but by the container machinery.

Example 15.3.4 shows the trivial but necessary change for the Recipe class. The __name__ and __parent__ attributes should default to None to indicate that a recipe has no name or container by default. Note that this is the first time we have to modify the Recipe class since Chapter 6!

Example 15.3.4 Providing default attributes for IContained fields in the Recipe class (recipe.py)

```
1   from persistent import Persistent
2   from zope.interface import implements
3   from worldcookery.interfaces import IRecipe
4
5   class Recipe(Persistent):
6       implements(IRecipe)
7
8       __name__ = __parent__ = None
9
10      name = u''
11      ingredients = []
12      tools = []
13      time_to_cook = 0
14      description = u''
15   ...
```

Example 15.3.5 shows the change to the automated forms to make them work with contained objects.

Browser configuration

As with recipes we also need to provide some browser-relevant configuration so that we can use the recipe folder immediately in the ZMI. Example 15.3.6 declares an entry in the browser *Add* menu for it and configures container-typical browser views. The latter are conveniently configured with one directive that registers the following views:

- The contents page (@@contents.html) which is the first management screen for folders and other containers. This provides a detailed object listing, as well as functionality like copy and paste.

Example 15.3.5 Omitting `IContained` fields in the automated add and edit forms (`browser/recipe.py`)

```
1   ...
2   class RecipeEditForm(EditForm):
3       form_fields = Fields(IRecipe).omit('__parent__', '__name__')
4       form_fields['ingredients'].custom_widget = DynamicSequenceWidget
5       form_fields['tools'].custom_widget = DynamicSequenceWidget
6       label = _(u"Edit recipe")
7
8       template = NamedTemplate('worldcookery.form')
9
10  class RecipeAddForm(AddForm):
11      form_fields = Fields(IRecipe).omit('__parent__', '__name__')
12      form_fields['ingredients'].custom_widget = DynamicSequenceWidget
13      form_fields['tools'].custom_widget = DynamicSequenceWidget
14      label = _(u"Add recipe")
15
16      template = NamedTemplate('worldcookery.form')
17
18      def create(self, data):
19          recipe = createObject(u'worldcookery.Recipe')
20          applyChanges(recipe, self.form_fields, data)
21          return recipe
22  ...
```

3 and 11.   By omitting __parent__ and __name__ from the form fields we make sure that the form will not try to render widgets for them. There are no widgets defined for them anyways, the form would therefore break terribly if we did not exclude them here.

- The index view (`@@index.html`) which either redirects to an object inside the container called `index.html` or, if that does not exist, displays a list of contained objects similar to the contents page.
- The adding view (`+`) which is responsible for producing add forms (such as the ones registered with `browser:addform`), checking containment constraints (using `checkObject` like shown above) and adding created objects to the container.

When you now go the Zope Management Interface, you will see that you cannot add *Recipe* objects to regular folders anymore. Instead, you have to create a recipe folder, in which you may add recipes.

Summary

- The container machinery allows constraints to be specified on containers and contained objects. Constraints may specify that a

Example 15.3.6 Browser configuration for the recipe folder
(`browser/configure.zcml`)

```
1    ...
2    <browser:addMenuItem
3        title="Recipe Folder"
4        class="worldcookery.folder.RecipeFolder"
5        permission="zope.ManageContent"
6        />
7
8    <browser:containerViews
9        for="worldcookery.interfaces.IRecipeContainer"
10       contents="zope.ManageContent"
11       index="zope.View"
12       add="zope.ManageContent"
13       />
14   ...
```

8–13. This directive defines the common browser views necessary to make containers work in the ZMI in one statement. We are only required to give the
permissions for the different views it registers.

---

given object can only be added in a given type of container or,
conversely, that a given container can only hold a given type of
object. As with any type of constraint, containment constraints are
specified in interfaces.

- Extending an interface to extend IContained changes its contract
  and requires subsequent changes in its implementations and other
  components that use the interface, e.g. browser forms.
- Container implementations are trivial and can rely on common base
  classes most of the time.
- Security declarations, browser menu configuration, and browser
  icons for containers are configured like with any other content object;
  common container views can be registered with a combined directive.

15.4 Names of contained objects

It is not always acceptable to allow arbitrary names for objects inside containers. Zope allows containers to influence names of contained objects in
either one of two ways:

- The object name is entered by the user and post-validated. This is the
  default.

- The object name is computed and cannot be influenced by the user.

In both cases it is usually not the container itself that pre-computes or post-validates names. It is an adapter that adapts containers to the INameChooser interface. This interface describes two methods, checkName and chooseName, which are called according to the either one of the above described cases.

Whether a container chooses names or not

How does Zope decide whether a container pre-computes names or not? The answer is simple: It assumes that all regular containers allow arbitrary names and that a mere validation of the name entered by the user is sufficient, unless a name was not entered by the user.

Now if the container provides IContainerNamesContainer, a marker interface derived from IContainer, then it is assumed that it wants to choose its own names. In this case, the add form does not include an input field for the object name and the container adding view calls the chooseName method of the INameChooser adapter. The adapter is also consulted when objects are moved and renamed.

Choosing names

In our *World Cookery* application, we have a redundancy of names already. Recipes have a name attribute which is documented in the IRecipe schema and as contained objects they have names inside the container. Why not synchronize these names and make recipe's names automatically their names inside the container?

In order to let recipes' container names be synchronized with their name attribute we need to do two things: First, we need to provide a custom INameChooser adapter that computes a recipe's container name from its actual name. Example 15.4.1 shows how to implement this adapter.

Secondly, we need to declare RecipeFolder as an IContainerNames Container. This is best done in ZCML (Example 15.4.2) since we are dealing with a marker interface. In the same listing we also register the INameChooser adapter.

Tests

No component shall be left untested, especially when it is one that can be tested so easily from the interpreter shell. To keep things simple we instantiate the INameChooser adapter manually. This way we do not have to load site configuration:

```
$ python
>>> from worldcookery.folder import RecipeFolder, RecipeNameChooser
>>> folder = RecipeFolder()
>>> chooser = RecipeNameChooser(folder)                          ▼
```

Example 15.4.1 Recipe folder with name chooser adapter (`folder.py`)

```
1   from zope.interface import implements
2   from zope.component import adapts
3   from zope.exceptions.interfaces import UserError
4   from zope.i18nmessageid import MessageFactory
5   _ = MessageFactory('worldcookery')
6
7   from zope.app.container.btree import BTreeContainer
8   from zope.app.container.contained import NameChooser
9   from worldcookery.interfaces import IRecipeContainer
10
11  class RecipeFolder(BTreeContainer):
12      implements(IRecipeContainer)
13
14  class RecipeNameChooser(NameChooser):
15      adapts(IRecipeContainer)
16
17      def checkName(self, name, object):
18          if name != object.name:
19              raise UserError(_(u"Given name and recipe name do not match
                    !"))
20          return super(RecipeNameChooser, self).checkName(name, object)
21
22      def chooseName(self, name, object):
23          name = object.name
24          self.checkName(name, object)
25          return name
```

8, 14, and 20.   A default name chooser adapter for standard `IContainers` is already provided by the `zope.app.container.contained` module. It makes
sense to subclass it here because it already implements checks for invalid
characters in containers and non-emptiness. That is why we delegate to its
`checkName` method after performing a check against the recipe's name.

15.   `INameChooser` adapters are adapters for containers. Since this adapter is
specific to recipes, we declare it to only adapt `IRecipeContainer`.

3 and 19.   The `INameChooser` interface requires us to raise `UserError` if the
validation of a name fails. User errors (and other exceptions providing
`IUserError`) are displayed to the user (as opposed to system errors). That
is why we have to mark the error message as an i18n message id to allow
translation.

Example 15.4.2 Enabling the name chooser adapter (`configure.zcml`)

```
1    ...
2    <class class=".folder.RecipeFolder">
3      <implements
4          interface="zope.annotation.interfaces.IAttributeAnnotatable
5                      zope.app.container.interfaces.IContainerNamesContainer
                        "
6          />
7      <require
8          permission="zope.View"
9          interface="zope.app.container.interfaces.IReadContainer"
10         />
11     <require
12         permission="zope.ManageContent"
13         interface="zope.app.container.interfaces.IWriteContainer"
14         />
15   </class>
16
17   <adapter factory=".folder.RecipeNameChooser" />
18   ...
```

5. Like `IAttributeAnnotatable`, `IContainerNamesContainer` is a marker interface and therefore best set in ZCML. Whether or not the `INameChooser` adapter is enabled is a configuration issue anyway.

A blank recipe object has an empty name (this is the class default), which is not acceptable for a container name:

```
>>> from worldcookery.recipe import Recipe
>>> tapas = Recipe()
>>> tapas.name
u''
>>> chooser.chooseName(u'', tapas)
Traceback (most recent call last):
  ...
zope.exceptions.interfaces.UserError:
An empty name was provided. Names cannot be empty.
```
▼

When we now provide a name that is acceptable for container names (the restrictions for container names are minimal), we see that the name chooser adapter chooses a name for us (the recipe's name). When checking a name, it expectedly accepts the recipe's name while rejecting anything else with a user error:

```
>>> tapas.name = u"Tapas"
>>> chooser.chooseName(u'', tapas)
u'Tapas'
>>> chooser.checkName(tapas.name, tapas)
```

```
True
>>> chooser.checkName(u'Tasty tapas', tapas)
Traceback (most recent call last):
  ...
zope.exceptions.interfaces.UserError:
Given name and recipe name do not match!
```
▼

As mentioned, the restrictions on container names are minimal. An important one is that it may not be empty. Apart from that, characters critical to traversal (+, @, and /) may not occur either:

```
>>> tapas.name = u'Tapas with/without olives'
>>> chooser.checkName(tapas.name, tapas)
Traceback (most recent call last):
  ...
zope.exceptions.interfaces.UserError:
Names cannot begin with '+' or '@' or contain '/'
```
▼

This test can also be found in the recipe folder docfile test (folder.txt).

When we now restart Zope to add a recipe to a recipe folder, we will not be asked for the object name anymore. The INameChooser adapter will choose the name from the recipe name.

In case you are wondering whether Unicode with mixed case and possibly contained spaces and other non-alphanumeric characters is such a good idea for container names, do not worry. Unicode is very much allowed in URLs and is encoded using UTF-8. Unlike other systems, Zope has always valued human-readable URLs very highly, which is why you will rarely see Zope applications with URLs that are composed of numbers and other cryptic, human-unfriendly characters.

Summary

- Container names can be influenced through either post-validation of a user-provided name or pre-computation of a name without user influence.
- Names are validated and/or computed by an INameChooser adapter for the container.
- Container names can hold any Unicode characters except those relevant to traversal (+, @, and /); names may not be empty.

Using Zope 2

Add forms and the adding view in Zope 2 will also adapt object managers to INameChooser to validate names of objects. Other Zope 2 machinery that does not stem from Zope 3 technology will not be aware of name chooser adapters, however.

15.5 File representation

In Chapter 11 where we initially covered file representation adapters, we did not have a custom container for recipes. Before, recipes were added to regular folders, now they can only be contained in IRecipeContainers. That means we have to at least adjust the configuration of the recipe file factory which until now was registered for IFolder.

File representation adapters for containers are fortunately quite easy. Of course, containers are represented as directories, not as files most of the time. The corresponding file representation interfaces IReadDirectory and IWriteDirectory extend IReadContainer and IWriteContainer, respectively,   unchanged. In other words, a container is usually its own file representation adapter, unless it is supposed to do something additional to delegate between file representations and the container. That we do not consider necessary here and therefore save ourselves the work of defining file representation adapters.

One item on the list remains, though. As much as there exists a file factory that creates objects when files are uploaded there exists a directory factory that creates sub-containers in containers when a directory is created over WebDAV or FTP. In our case, recipe folders may not contain any other object than recipe objects; that implies that they cannot contain subfolders, which means we should disallow the creation of subcontainers.

Example 15.5.1 shows a simple directory factory that raises an error when invoked. The necessary configuration including the change to the registration of the recipe file factory is listed in Example 15.5.2. The doctest that was provided in Chapter 12 was also updated and can be read for documentation purposes in Example 15.5.3, along with its test module in Example 15.5.4.

Example 15.5.1 Directory factory disallowing subcontainers in recipe folders (filerepresentation.py)

```
1   ...
2   from worldcookery.interfaces import IRecipeContainer
3
4   class RecipeFactory(object):
5       implements(IFileFactory)
6       adapts(IRecipeContainer)
7
8       def __init__(self, context):
9           self.context = context
```

Example 15.5.1 (continued)

```
10      def __call__(self, name, content_type, data):
11          recipe = Recipe()
12          recipe.name = name.title()
13          recipe.description = data.decode('utf-8')
14          return recipe
15
16  from zope.filerepresentation.interfaces import IDirectoryFactory
17  from zope.exceptions.interfaces import UserError
18
19  class RecipeDirectoryFactory(object):
20      implements(IDirectoryFactory)
21      adapts(IRecipeContainer)
22
23      def __init__(self, context):
24          self.context = context
25
26      def __call__(self, name):
27          raise UserError(u"Cannot create subfolders in recipe folders.")
```

6. Now we declare this file factory just for recipe containers, as recipes may not be created outside them. Hence a recipe factory for containers other than `IRecipeContainer` would not make sense.

Example 15.5.2 ((Re-)configuring file and directory factories for recipe folders (`configure.zcml`))

```
1   ...
2   <adapter
3       factory=".filerepresentation.RecipeFactory"
4       permission="zope.ManageContent"
5       />
6
7   <adapter
8       factory=".filerepresentation.RecipeDirectoryFactory"
9       permission="zope.ManageContent"
10      />
11  ...
```

2–5. Now that recipes are the only objects allowed inside `IRecipeNameContainer`, we can safely assume it to be the only file factory registered for this container. That means we do not have to register it as a named adapter (where the name was the file extension) anymore. The name parameter is missing from the directive.

Example 15.5.3 Doctest for file representation adapters of the new recipe folder (`filerepresentation.txt`)

```
1   ========================================
2   File representation adapters for recipes
3   ========================================
4
5   Let us first create a recipe object through a file factory.  In order
6   to acquire the factory, we need a folder object since we registered
7   the factory as an adapter for folders.  We can throw the folder away
8   afterwards.  Even though the factory is an adapter, we cannot look it
9   up by calling the interface anymore because that will not take the
10  adapter name into account.  We need to use ``getAdapter`` from
11  ``zope.component`` now:
12
13      >>> from worldcookery.folder import RecipeFolder
14      >>> from zope.filerepresentation.interfaces import \
15      ...     IReadFile, IWriteFile, IFileFactory
16      >>> from zope.component import getAdapter
17      >>> folder = RecipeFolder()
18      >>> factory = IFileFactory(folder)
19
20  Now we can call the factory with some made-up data.  We expect to get
21  a recipe object back, of course, and that the recipe's description
22  equals to the data we passed to the factory.
23
24      >>> data = "Add spices to the water and bring it to boil. " \
25      ...        "Then add the couscous."
26      >>> couscous = factory("couscous", "text/plain", data)
27      >>> couscous # doctest: +ELLIPSIS
28      <worldcookery.recipe.Recipe object at ...>
29      >>> couscous.name
30      'Couscous'
31      >>> couscous.description
32      u'Add spices to the water and bring it to boil. Then add the couscous.'
33
34  Now we can get a file representation for the recipe again and read its
35  data.  Note that the file representation returns a string object, not
36  a Unicode object, since only the former can be written to a file stream.
37
38      >>> readfile = IReadFile(couscous)
39      >>> readfile.size()
40      68
41      >>> readfile.read()
42      'Add spices to the water and bring it to boil. Then add the couscous.'
43
44  Finally, we can adapt the recipe object to a writeable file and store
45  new data on it.  The recipe will be changed accordingly, of course:
46
47      >>> writefile = IWriteFile(couscous)
48      >>> writefile.write("Couscous consists of grains made from semolina.")
49      >>> couscous.description
50      u'Couscous consists of grains made from semolina.'
```

Example 15.5.3 (continued)

```
51  Note that it is not possible to create subfolders in a recipe folder.
52  Doing so raises a ''UserError'':
53
54      >>> from zope.filerepresentation.interfaces import IDirectoryFactory
55      >>> factory = IDirectoryFactory(folder)
56      >>> factory(u"subfolder")
57      Traceback (most recent call last):
58      ...
59      UserError: Cannot create subfolders in recipe folders.
```

Example 15.5.4 Test suite for file representation adapters of the new recipe folder (`tests/test_filerepresentation.py`)

```
1   import unittest
2   from doctest import DocFileSuite
3
4   import zope.component.testing
5   from zope.filerepresentation.interfaces import IReadFile, \
6       IWriteFile, IFileFactory
7
8   from worldcookery.interfaces import IRecipe
9   from worldcookery.filerepresentation import RecipeReadFile, \
10      RecipeWriteFile, RecipeFactory, RecipeDirectoryFactory
11
12  def setUp(test):
13      zope.component.testing.setUp(test)
14      zope.component.provideAdapter(RecipeReadFile)
15      zope.component.provideAdapter(RecipeWriteFile)
16      zope.component.provideAdapter(RecipeFactory)
17      zope.component.provideAdapter(RecipeDirectoryFactory)
18
19  def test_suite():
20      return unittest.TestSuite((
21          DocFileSuite('filerepresentation.txt',
22                       package='worldcookery',
23                       setUp=setUp,
24                       tearDown=zope.component.testing.tearDown),
25          ))
26
27  if __name__ == '__main__':
28      unittest.main(defaultTest='test_suite')
```

Summary

- The file representation interfaces for directories are identical to the corresponding container interfaces; a container can therefore be its own file representation adapter.
- Directory factories create sub-containers when a directory is created through WebDAV or FTP.

16

Events

A key concept of the Component Architecture is *events*. In many applications, it is necessary to trigger certain operations in particular circumstances. Zope provides a flexible and efficient event system that makes the implementation of such event-triggered components as well as the triggering itself very easy.

Using Zope 2

Everything discussed in this chapter also applies to recent Zope 2 versions where the Zope 3 event system, especially object events, has replaced an older notification systems. However, many Zope 2 applications do not make use of the Zope 3 event system yet. For backward compatibility, Zope 2 object managers also send a number of additional events (see Table 16.1) that are unknown in Zope 3.

16.1 Introduction

Components can inform other components that something has happened by sending an event. Events are simple objects that indicate what has happened. Components that react upon events are called *event subscribers*.

Events are sent by calling the `notify` function from the `zope.event` package. This function simply broadcasts the event to a list of subscribers without any filtering. The `zope.component` package inserts a subscriber into that list that itself broadcasts the event to a special type of adapters, *subscription adapters*.

Subscription adapters for event filtering

Usually, when adapting an object, the result is either one object (the adapter) or no object (when an adapter cannot be found). With subscription adapters, *all* adapters that match the criteria will be returned. This can be used to find and filter subscribers for a particular event. In other words, `zope.component`'s event subscriber broadcasts the event by finding all subscription adapters for it. Actually, it looks up special subscription adapters called *handlers* because their "factories" are not expected to return anything.

In this process, regular adapter semantics also apply. That means the interfaces that the event provides are used to filter the event subscribers. That way, a subscriber registered for `Interface` will be called for all events, whereas a subscriber listening to a specific interface will only be invoked when an event with this interface is broadcast.

An example

To understand how the event system works we will use the trusty interpreter shell again. As an example event consider the circumstance that a meal has been cooked is ready for serving now. The event that would be sent out in such a case is described by the simple interface we now define:

```
$ python
>>> from zope.interface import Interface, Attribute
>>> class IDinnerIsDone(Interface):
...     recipe = Attribute("Recipe")
...
>>>                                                      ▼
```

The `recipe` attribute will hold the recipe that was cooked for dinner. An implementation of this interface is of course quite simple:

```
>>> from zope.interface import implements
>>> class DinnerIsDone(object):
...     implements(IDinnerIsDone)
...     def __init__(self, recipe):
...         self.recipe = recipe
...
>>>                                                      ▼
```

Now we need a subscriber that is called whenever this event occurs. We just learned that we can implement subscribers as subscription adapters. Actually, we just have to implement a handler which is similar to a subscription adapter but not required to return anything, in contrast to a real adapter factory. That means we can use a simple function to implement the subscriber. The argument of the function is of course the object that is to be adapted, the event. Our subscriber tells the family that dinner is ready and informs them of the meal that is served:

```
>>> from zope.component import adapter
>>> @adapter(IDinnerIsDone)
... def tellFamily(event):
...     print "Dinner is ready! We're having a " \
```

```
...         "delicious %s!" % event.recipe.name
...
>>>
```
▼

The only thing that is left now is registering it as an event handler:

```
>>> from zope.component import provideHandler
>>> provideHandler(tellFamily)
```
▼

Now our event subscriber is registered as a handler. We should try sending the event now. As mentioned above, sending out events is quite simple. We just have to call the notify function from the zope.event package with the event object as parameter:

```
>>> from worldcookery.recipe import Recipe
>>> cordon_bleu = Recipe()
>>> cordon_bleu.name = u"Cordon bleu"
>>>
>>> from zope.event import notify
>>> notify(DinnerIsDone(cordon_bleu))
>>>
```
▼

As you can see, nothing happened. That is because the zope.component event listener has not been added to the list of subscribers and therefore could not dispatch to our handler. Importing the zope.component.event module will take care of this. When sending out an instance of DinnerIsDone now, we will see that the tellFamily subscriber is called:

```
>>> import zope.component.event
>>> notify(DinnerIsDone(cordon_bleu))
Dinner is ready! We're having a delicious Cordon bleu!
```
■

Note that importing zope.component.event to enable the dispatch to handlers is only necessary in isolated environments such as the interpreter shell. In a Zope application, this module is already imported by a lot of Zope core modules.

Synchronous execution

It is worth noting that event subscribers and the handlers registered in the adapter registry are invoked *synchronously*. This is necessary because subscribers usually perform actions that require the presence of authentication credentials; these are only available through the security interaction (see Chapter 22) during the request processing. This means that the active Zope thread will be blocked if a subscriber is doing some time-consuming data processing. It is important, therefore, not to perform such operations in a (regular) event subscriber.

More on subscription adapters

As mentioned before, the event system uses a special kind of subscription adapters, handlers, because their adapter "factories" (the event subscribers) are not expected to return anything. When regular adapter factories return nothing (None), the Component Architecture thinks the adaption has failed. That is why it makes a special case out of subscription adapters that are used as event handlers.

It should also be mentioned that neither subscription adapters nor handlers can be registered with names yet (as named adapters). This lack does not affect standard event subscriber usage of subscription adapters, but can affect other uses of the subscription adapter components.

Summary

- Zope allows components to notify other components of certain circumstances by sending events.
- Events are objects that carry as much information as needed to describe the event.
- The zope.event package broadcasts events to a list of subscribers. The zope.component package has a subscriber that dispatches these events to subscription adapters.
- Subscription adapters can usually be implemented as simple callables (e.g. functions) that take the event object as an argument.
- Event notification is *synchronous*!

Rocky says...

The firing and consumption of events can roughly be compared to using java.util.Observer and java.util.Observerable, although Zope's events are much higher level and richer in functionality. You should consider making use of IObjectModifiedEvent and IObjectCreatedEvent to manage the life cycles of objects.

16.2 Object events

A commonly used set of events are *object events*. These are events that can be triggered when certain operations are performed on a particular object, such as creation and modification. Table 16.1 gives an overview over the types of events that Zope sends out, including the object events.

Table 16.1. Common event types in Zope

Interface	Package	Description
IObjectEvent	zope.component	Indicates that something has happened to an object. More detailed specification by subinterfaces.
IRegistrationEvent	zope.component	Sent when the component registration status of an object changes.
IRegistered	zope.component	Sent when an object is registered with any of the component registries.
IUnregistered	zope.component	Sent when an object is unregistered with any of the component registries.
IObjectCreatedEvent	zope.lifecycleevent	Sent when an object has been created.
IObjectCopiedEvent	zope.lifecycleevent	Indicates that an object has been copied.
IObjectModifiedEvent	zope.lifecycleevent	Triggered when an object has been modified.
IObjectMovedEvent	zope.app.container	Indicates that an object has been moved to a different container or renamed within the same container.
IObjectAddedEvent	zope.app.container	Sent when an object has been added to a container.
IObjectRemovedEvent	zope.app.container	Indicates that an object has been removed from a container.
IContainerModifiedEvent	zope.app.container	Sent when a container object has been modified, e.g. an object has been added or removed from the container or subobjects were reordered.
IObjectClonedEvent	OFS (Zope 2 only)	Sent after an object has been cloned and the clone has been added to its object manager (IObjectCopiedEvent in contrast is sent directly after the object has been duplicated).

Table 16.1. (continued)

Event	Module	Description
IObjectWillBeMovedEvent	OFS (Zope 2 only)	Sent before an object is moved.
IObjectWillBeAddedEvent	OFS (Zope 2 only)	Sent before an object is added to an object manager.
IObjectWillBeRemovedEvent	OFS (Zope 2 only)	Sent before an object is removed from an object manager.
IPrincipalCreated	zope.app.authentication	Sent when a principal object is created.
IAuthenticatedPrincipalCreated	zope.app.authentication	Indicates that a principal has been created by way of an authentication operation.
IFoundPrincipalCreated	zope.app.authentication	Indicates that a principal has been created by a way of a search operation
IIntIdAddedEvent	zope.app.intid	Sent when an object is registered with an IIntIds utility and has received a unique integer id.
IIntIdRemovedEvent	zope.app.intid	Sent when an object is removed from the IIntIds utility.
IDatabaseOpenedEvent	zope.app.appsetup	Indicates that a ZODB instance has been opened.
IDatabaseOpenedWithRootEvent	zope.app.appsetup	Indicates that a ZODB instance with a root object has been opened.
IProcessStartingEvent	zope.app.appsetup	Triggered when the Zope process is starting up.
IBeforeTraverseEvent	zope.app.publication	Triggered before each traversal step.
IEndRequestEvent	zope.app.publication	Indicates the end of a request.
IMailEvent	zope.sendmail	Generic mail event.
IMailSentEvent	zope.sendmail	Sent when an email has been sent successfully.
IMailErrorEvent	zope.sendmail	Indicates that an email cannot be delivered.

Zope acts and reacts

We are not dealing with any events in our sample application, yet they are sent. The automatically generated add and edit forms, for example, send out IObjectAddedEvent and IObjectModifiedEvent events. The setitem function from the previous chapter sends out IObjectAddedEvent or IObjectMovedEvent, respectively, depending on whether an object is newly added to a container or whether it is moved from another container. IObjectMovedEvent is also sent when an item is renamed within the same container. The copy/paste/move machinery from zope.copypastemove sends an IObjectCopiedEvent event when an object is duplicated.

Zope does not only send out events; some components have subscribed to certain events. For example, the Dublin Core machinery has a subscriber to the IObjectCreatedEvent and IObjectModifiedEvent events that updates the Creator, Creation Date, and Modification Date Dublin Core properties of the object.

Sending object events

Code that does something to objects (e.g. modify them, add them to containers, etc.) also has the responsibility to send the corresponding events. The automated add and edit forms already do most of the work for us here. We just have to make sure that we send events when we modify objects ourselves, for example in the ratings adapter from Chapter 14. The adapter modifies an object's annotations which means it should send an IObjectModifiedEvent event.

Example 16.2.1 shows the necessary modifications to the ratings adapter. As you can see, sending events is as trivial as it was in the interpreter session in the last section. Example 16.2.2 demonstrates how to check for events in tests.

Subscribing to object events

You can subscribe to object events like you subscribe to any other type of event. Then your subscriber would be called for every occurrence of such an event, regardless of the object that the event is sent for.

It is also possible to subscribe to object events of only specific objects, for example when you are only interested in the IObjectModifiedEvent of recipes. The zope.component.event module has a subscriber registered that dispatches all object events to subscription *multi*-adapters of the object and the event. With this you only have to register the subscriber for the interface of the object and the event's interface, e.g. IRecipe and IObjectModifiedEvent.

In our example we want to register a subscriber to IObjectModified Event to update the a recipe's Dublin Core metadata. The idea is to synchronize the *Title* property of Dublin Core and the recipe's name. Currently we

Example 16.2.1 Sending out an object event in the ratings adapter
(`rating.py`)

```
1   from persistent.dict import PersistentDict
2   from persistent.list import PersistentList
3   from zope.interface import implements
4   from zope.component import adapts
5   from zope.annotation.interfaces import IAnnotations
6   from zope.event import notify
7   from zope.lifecycleevent import ObjectModifiedEvent, Attributes
8   from worldcookery.interfaces import IRating, IRatable
9
10  KEY = "worldcookery.rating"
11
12  class Rating(object):
13      implements(IRating)
14      adapts(IRatable)
15
16      def __init__(self, context):
17          self.context = self.__parent__ = context
18          annotations = IAnnotations(context)
19          mapping = annotations.get(KEY)
20          if mapping is None:
21              blank = {'average': 0.0, 'ratings': PersistentList()}
22              mapping = annotations[KEY] = PersistentDict(blank)
23          self.mapping = mapping
24
25      def rate(self, rating):
26          ratings = self.mapping['ratings']
27          ratings.append(float(rating))
28          self.mapping['average'] = sum(ratings)/len(ratings)
29          info = Attributes(IRatable, 'averageRating', 'numberofRatings')
30          notify(ObjectModifiedEvent(self.context, info))
31
32      @property
33      def averageRating(self):
34          return self.mapping['average']
35
36      @property
37      def numberOfRatings(self):
38          return len(self.mapping['ratings'])
```

7 and 29–30. The `zope.lifecycleevent` package also provides implementations for all object event interfaces. They are instantiated with the object in question as parameter and a description object that indicates which fields of which schema have changed. Note that the object itself does not have to provide the schemas in this case. Here the object modified event is to be interpreted in terms of the adapter to the schema (because rating the object changes the values of the `IRating` adapter).

Example 16.2.2 Testing whether object events are being sent
(`rating.txt`)

```
1   ==============
2   Rating objects
3   ==============
4
5   The rating system allows users to rate objects on a continuous scale
6   (a discrete scale can be enforced by a view).  We distinguish
7   *ratable* objects which have to annotatable and implement ``IRatable`
8   on one hand and the ``IRating`` adapter for ratable objects which the
9   rating of the latter on the other hand.
10
11  Consider a simple object, e.g. a recipe:
12
13    >>> from worldcookery.recipe import Recipe
14    >>> hamburgers = Recipe()
15
16  In order to mark it ratable, it also needs to annotatable, for example
17  attribute-annotatable:
18
19    >>> from zope.annotation.interfaces import IAttributeAnnotatable
20    >>> from worldcookery.interfaces import IRatable
21    >>> from zope.interface import alsoProvides
22    >>> alsoProvides(hamburgers, IAttributeAnnotatable, IRatable)
23
24  Now we can rate the object using the ``IRating`` adapter:
25
26    >>> from worldcookery.interfaces import IRating
27    >>> rating = IRating(hamburgers)
28    >>> rating.rate(1)   # I don't like hamburgers
29    >>> rating.rate(9)   # I like hamburgers
30
31  Of course, the adapter also tells about the average rating and number
32  of ratings that have been issued yet:
33
34    >>> rating.averageRating
35    5.0
36    >>> rating.numberOfRatings
37    2
38
39  Since the adapter changes the object's annotations to store rating
40  information, we expect that an ``IObjectModifiedEvent`` event is sent:
41
42    >>> from zope.component.eventtesting import getEvents
43    >>> from zope.lifecycleevent.interfaces import IObjectModifiedEvent
44    >>> events = getEvents(IObjectModifiedEvent)
45    >>> len(events)
46    2
47    >>> for event in events:
48    ...      print event.object is hamburgers
49    ...
50    True
51    True
```

Example 16.2.2 (continued)

42 and 44. `getEvent` returns a list of events that were sent out. The query can
be narrowed down by providing an event type interface. `getEvent` only works
with a proper test setup from `zope.component.eventtesting`, (as demonstrated in Example 16.2.4, for example).

Example 16.2.3 A subscriber that updates a recipe's Dublin Core Title
property (`dublincore.py`)

```
1   from zope.component import adapter
2   from zope.dublincore.interfaces import IWriteZopeDublinCore
3   from zope.lifecycleevent.interfaces import IObjectModifiedEvent
4   from worldcookery.interfaces import IRecipe
5
6   @adapter(IRecipe, IObjectModifiedEvent)
7   def updateRecipeDCTitle(recipe, event):
8       """Update a recipe's Dublin Core Title property with its name
9
10      Consider a simple recipe object with a name:
11
12        >>> from worldcookery.recipe import Recipe
13        >>> noodles = Recipe()
14        >>> noodles.name = u"Noodles"
15
16      In order for Dublin Core to work we need it to be annotatable:
17
18        >>> from zope.interface import alsoProvides
19        >>> from zope.annotation.interfaces import IAttributeAnnotatable
20        >>> alsoProvides(noodles, IAttributeAnnotatable)
21
22      It does not have a title yet:
23
24        >>> dc = IWriteZopeDublinCore(noodles)
25        >>> dc.title
26        u''
27
28      Now we send out the event and, voila!, the title has been set:
29
30        >>> from zope.event import notify
31        >>> from zope.lifecycleevent import ObjectModifiedEvent
32        >>> notify(ObjectModifiedEvent(noodles))
33        >>> dc = IWriteZopeDublinCore(noodles)
34        >>> dc.title
35        u'Noodles'
36      """
37      dc = IWriteZopeDublinCore(recipe)
38      dc.title = recipe.name
```

Example 16.2.3 (continued)

6–7. Object event subscribers take two arguments, the object that the event is being sent for and the event object itself. They are also declared as subscribers for the combination of those two interfaces (content type, event type).

---

have a redundancy in these properties and there is no reason why these should not contain the same information. The subscriber that does this is ridiculously short in its implementation. Just two lines are necessary (Example 16.2.3).

The doctest for the subscriber and the corresponding test suite module (Example 16.2.4) take up much more lines than the actual implementation, though. It also took substantially longer to write. While it might seem irritating, sometimes even frustrating for the developer to spend more code and time on automated testing, it is an investment that will pay off when a bug in the application has be to chased down, and any software developer knows that software is *never* bug-free.

Example 16.2.4 Test suite setup for the object event subscriber doctest
(tests/test_dublincore.py)

```
1  import unittest
2  from doctest import DocTestSuite
3
4  import zope.component.testing
5  import zope.component.eventtesting
6  from zope.annotation.attribute import AttributeAnnotations
7  from zope.dublincore.interfaces import IWriteZopeDublinCore
8  from zope.dublincore.annotatableadapter import ZDCAnnotatableAdapter
9  from worldcookery.dublincore import updateRecipeDCTitle
10
11 def setUp(test):
12     zope.component.testing.setUp(test)
13     zope.component.eventtesting.setUp(test)
14     zope.component.provideAdapter(AttributeAnnotations)
15     zope.component.provideAdapter(ZDCAnnotatableAdapter,
16                                   provides=IWriteZopeDublinCore)
17     zope.component.provideHandler(updateRecipeDCTitle)
18
19 def test_suite():
20     return unittest.TestSuite((
21         DocTestSuite('worldcookery.dublincore',
22                      setUp=setUp,
23                      tearDown=zope.component.testing.tearDown),
24         ))
25
26 if __name__ == '__main__':
27     unittest.main(defaultTest='test_suite')
```

Example 16.2.4 (continued)

---

13. Apart from the usual `zope.component.testing` test setup we also need to set up some event-related test fixtures. Without those, object event subscribers and helpers such as `getEvent` would not work.

17. Subscribers are registered with `provideHandler`.

Last but not least we need to register the subscriber. This is done via the `subscriber` ZCML directive which registers event subscribers and subscription adapters. Event subscribers are registered with the `handler` argument:

```
<subscriber handler=".dublincore.updateRecipeDCTitle" />
```

Other than that the `subscriber` directive can be used much like `adapter` directive.

Summary

- Object events are sent out to notify subscribers when something has happened to an object.
- Object event subscribers are registered for the event type and the type of the object that the event is sent for.
- Components that perform actions on objects are responsible for sending the appropriate events.
- Zope's automation frameworks such as the form and container machineries send out appropriate events that one can subscribe to.

16.3 Sending emails for event notification

As a more advanced use case of object events we will now cover email notification. This will not only get us more comfortable with events in general, as a by-product we will also learn about the email machinery of Zope. Email notification is a very typical use case of object events because it actually involves notifying real users and not just other components that are part of an application.

In our example application, we will allow users to subscribe to certain recipes with their email address. This information will be stored in the recipe's annotations. The interface that describes how to access to this annotation data and the adapter providing this interface are shown in Example 16.3.1 and Example 16.3.2, respectively. Because we are creating the email-specific

Example 16.3.1 Interface for managing email subscriptions to objects (`mail/interfaces.py`)

```
1   from zope.interface import Interface
2   from zope.schema import Tuple, TextLine
3   from zope.i18nmessageid import MessageFactory
4   _ = MessageFactory('worldcookery')
5
6   class IMailSubscriptions(Interface):
7
8       subscribers = Tuple(
9           title=_(u"Subscribers"),
10          description=_(u"Email addresses of subscribers"),
11          value_type=TextLine(title=_(u"Subscriber")),
12          readonly=True
13          )
14
15      def subscribe(email):
16          """Subscribe an email address to the notifications"""
17
18      def unsubscribe(email):
19          """Unsubscribe an email address"""
```

Example 16.3.2 Adapter that keeps email subscriptions to an object in its annotations (`mail/annotations.py`)

```
1   from persistent.list import PersistentList
2   from zope.interface import implements
3   from zope.event import notify
4   from zope.component import adapts
5   from zope.annotation.interfaces import IAnnotatable, IAnnotations
6   from zope.lifecycleevent import ObjectModifiedEvent, Attributes
7   from worldcookery.mail.interfaces import IMailSubscriptions
8
9   KEY = "worldcookery.subscriptions"
10
11  class MailSubscriptionAnnotations(object):
12      implements(IMailSubscriptions)
13      adapts(IAnnotatable)
14
15      def __init__(self, context):
16          self.context = context
17          annotations = IAnnotations(context)
18          emails = annotations.get(KEY)
19          if emails is None:
20              emails = annotations[KEY] = PersistentList()
21          self.emails = emails
```

Example 16.3.2 (continued)

```
22      @property
23      def subscribers(self):
24          return tuple(self.emails)
25
26      def subscribe(self, email):
27          if email not in self.emails:
28              self.emails.append(email)
29              info = Attributes(IMailSubscriptions, 'subscribers')
30              notify(ObjectModifiedEvent(self.context, info))
31
32      def unsubscribe(self, email):
33          if email in self.emails:
34              self.emails.remove(email)
35              info = Attributes(IMailSubscriptions, 'subscribers')
36              notify(ObjectModifiedEvent(self.context, info))
```

components in a subpackage to the worldcookery package, do not forget
to include into the main configure.zcml file the following line:

```
<include package=".mail" />
```

The email subscription adapter is quite similar to the rating adapter we
wrote in Chapter 13. Like the rating adapter, we configure it as a trusted
adapter and provide security settings for the adapter class, as shown in Example 16.3.3.

Example 16.3.3 Configuring the email subscription adapter
(mail/configure.zcml)

```
1   <configure
2       xmlns="http://namespaces.zope.org/zope"
3       >
4
5     <adapter
6         factory=".annotations.MailSubscriptionAnnotations"
7         trusted="true"
8         />
9
10    <class class=".annotations.MailSubscriptionAnnotations">
11      <require
12          permission="zope.View"
13          interface=".interfaces.IMailSubscriptions"
14          />
15    </class>
16
17  </configure>
```

Sending emails

Now we can write subscribers that send out emails when object events are invoked for recipes. We could do this by simply using Python's `smtplib` package. Zope's `zope.sendmail` package provides a few additional features, though:

Pluggable mail delivery via `IMailDelivery` utilities. Zope comes with two implementations of such a utility that are both transaction-aware. That way emails will be discarded and not actually delivered when the transaction is aborted after the application has sent the emails. One implementation, direct delivery, keeps the emails in memory until the transaction is committed while the other one, queued delivery, writes emails to a *Maildir* [9] directory and uses a separate thread to send them. The latter is much more efficient when sending large emails or large amounts of emails.

Pluggable `IMailer` utilities. These utilities are responsible for sending out the emails when the delivery utility wants them to. Zope comes with a default implementation that sends emails via SMTP. If you need to send emails through another system, you would only have to implement a new mailer utility. Since the configuration of the mailer utility is done through ZCML (including the mail server in case of the SMTP mailer), applications are easily deployable in different environments without code changes.

Example 16.3.4 shows the event subscribers that send out emails for the different events. Note that this example only creates emails with English text for simplicity's sake. An internationalized example might want to take the preferences of the email subscribers into account, thus requiring a more complicated set of data to be stored in annotations. The recipe contents, though, can obviously still be in any language; in fact, the emails are sent out in UTF-8, thus compatible with any language in the Unicode specification.

Testing

Instead of going through an interactive interpreter session now we will just write a doctest. I am sure that by now you should be comfortable enough with the interpreter to do your own tests with components.

In the test setup we need to provide the necessary components that the subscription adapter and the event subscriber functions expect. That includes the `IAnnotations` adapter, the subscriptions adapter itself, and also a mail delivery utility of which we simply provide a dummy implementation that prints the email message to the shell. That makes it easy for us writing the doctest and for others reading it as a piece of documentation. The test setup is shown in Example 16.3.7, the actual doctest text file is listed in Example 16.3.6.

Example 16.3.4 Object event subscribers for recipes that send out notification emails (`mail/recipe.py`)

```
1   import email.Charset
2   email.Charset.add_charset('utf-8', email.Charset.SHORTEST, None, None)
3   from datetime import datetime
4   from email.MIMEText import MIMEText
5
6   from zope.component import getUtility, adapter
7   from zope.sendmail.interfaces import IMailDelivery
8   from zope.lifecycleevent.interfaces import IObjectModifiedEvent
9   from zope.app.container.interfaces import IObjectAddedEvent
10  from zope.app.container.interfaces import IObjectRemovedEvent
11
12  from worldcookery.interfaces import IRecipe
13  from worldcookery.mail.interfaces import IMailSubscriptions
14
15  @adapter(IRecipe, IObjectAddedEvent)
16  def notifyAdded(recipe, event):
17      return emailNotifications(recipe, "added")
18
19  @adapter(IRecipe, IObjectModifiedEvent)
20  def notifyModified(recipe, event):
21      return emailNotifications(recipe, "modified")
22
23  @adapter(IRecipe, IObjectRemovedEvent)
24  def notifyRemoved(recipe, event):
25      return emailNotifications(recipe, "removed")
26
27  def _messageBody(recipe):
28      body = u"""Name: %(name)s
29
30  Time to cook: %(time_to_cook)s
31
32  Ingredients:
33  %(ingredients)s
34
35  Necessary Kitchen Tools:
36  %(tools)s
37
38  %(description)s"""
39      return body % {
40          'name': recipe.name,
41          'time_to_cook': recipe.time_to_cook,
42          'ingredients': '\n'.join(u'- ' + ingr for ingr in recipe.
                ingredients),
43          'tools': '\n'.join(u'- ' + tool for tool in recipe.tools),
44          'description': recipe.description
45          }
```

Example 16.3.4 (continued)

```
46  def emailNotifications(recipe, action):
47      subscriptions = IMailSubscriptions(recipe, None)
48      if subscriptions is None or not subscriptions.subscribers:
49          return
50      subject = "'%s' was %s" % (recipe.name, action)
51      message = MIMEText(_messageBody(recipe).encode('utf-8'), 'plain', '
            utf-8')
52      message['Subject'] = subject
53      message['From'] = 'notify@worldcookery.com'
54      message['To'] = ', '.join(subscriptions.subscribers)
55      message['Date'] = datetime.now().strftime('%a, %d %b %Y %H:%M:%S %z')
56      mailer = getUtility(IMailDelivery, 'worldcookery')
57      mailer.send("notify@worldcookery.com", subscriptions.subscribers,
58                    message.as_string())
```

1–2. We use components provided by the email package from Python's standard library to generate MIME messages. A small glitch in this package lets messages encoded in UTF-8 normally be re-encoded in base64. The second line here overrides this so that messages encoded in UTF-8 are sent out in their original encoding.

4 and 52–56. To create an email document according to the email specification [19] [18] and the MIME standard [15] we use Python's MIMEText class. It represents text email messages and instantiated with the message body as an encoded string, the text minor type (plain, html, etc.), and the encoding used. It also allows us to conveniently set MIME headers using a regular mapping API. At last, the as_string method can be used to retrieve the text representation of MIMEText objects.

15–25. The subscriber functions for the three object events we choose to subscribe to simply delegate the work to the emailNotifications function.

57–59. Email delivery is handled by *named* IMailDelivery utilities. It is generally a good idea to configure a mail delivery for each package. Here we use the utility named worldcookery which is configured in Example 16.3.5. Delivery utilities have a send method which takes the *from* and *to* addresses as well as the message text as arguments.

Example 16.3.5 Configuring email event subscribers and mail sender utilities (`mail/configure.zcml`)

```
1   <configure
2        xmlns="http://namespaces.zope.org/zope"
3        xmlns:mail="http://namespaces.zope.org/mail"
4        >
5
6    ...
7
8    <mail:smtpMailer
9         name="worldcookery"
10        hostname="localhost"
11        port="25"
12        />
13
14   <mail:queuedDelivery
15        name="worldcookery"
16        permission="zope.SendMail"
17        queuePath="mail-queue"
18        mailer="worldcookery"
19        />
20
21   <subscriber handler=".recipe.notifyAdded" />
22   <subscriber handler=".recipe.notifyModified" />
23   <subscriber handler=".recipe.notifyRemoved" />
24
25   </configure>
```

3. Configuration directives regarding the mail framework are available under the `http://namespace.zope.org/mail` namespace, typically bound to the `mail` prefix.

8–12. Configuring mail delivery utilities in Zope takes two configuration directives, one for the delivery utility (see below) and one for the mailer utility which actually takes care of the mail transport. Here we simply configure the standard SMTP mailer to use a mail server on the local machine.

14–19. This directive configures the `IMailDelivery` utility. It is named `worldcookery` and uses the mail transport utility configured above. The `queuePath` argument specifies a file-system path for the *Maildir* directory that shall contain the queued emails.

Example 16.3.6 Doctest for the mail subscription machinery
(`mail/emailsubscriptions.txt`)

```
1   ==================
2   Email subscriptions
3   ==================
4
5   Using the event subscribers in this package, Zope can send out
6   notification emails when an object has changed, for example for a
7   recipe:
8
9      >>> from worldcookery.recipe import Recipe
10     >>> cordon_bleu = Recipe()
11     >>> cordon_bleu.name = u'Cordon bleu'
12     >>> cordon_bleu.time_to_cook = 45
13     >>> cordon_bleu.ingredients = [u'Ham', u'Cheese', 'Filet']
14     >>> cordon_bleu.tools = [u'Tooth picks']
15     >>> cordon_bleu.description = u'Hmm, cordon bleu!'
16
17  The recipients of such noficiation emails are stored in annotations.
18  We therefore have to make the object attribute annotatable:
19
20     >>> from zope.interface import alsoProvides
21     >>> from zope.annotation.interfaces import IAttributeAnnotatable
22     >>> alsoProvides(cordon_bleu, IAttributeAnnotatable)
23
24  Without any subscribers, there will be no email sent, though:
25
26     >>> from zope.event import notify
27     >>> from zope.lifecycleevent import ObjectModifiedEvent
28     >>> notify(ObjectModifiedEvent(cordon_bleu))
29
30  We first have to subscribe to the object (upon which a notification
31  email is already sent):
32
33     >>> from worldcookery.mail.interfaces import IMailSubscriptions
34     >>> subscriptions = IMailSubscriptions(cordon_bleu)
35     >>> subscriptions.subscribe('chicken@worldcookery.com')
36     Content-Type: ...
37     ...
38
39  When we now send out an object modified event, the email subscriber
40  will send out an email that looks like this:
41
42     >>> notify(ObjectModifiedEvent(cordon_bleu))
43     Content-Type: text/plain; charset="utf-8"
44     MIME-Version: 1.0
45     Content-Transfer-Encoding: 7bit
46     Subject: 'Cordon bleu' was modified
47     From: notify@worldcookery.com
48     To: chicken@worldcookery.com
49     Date: ...
```

Example 16.3.6 (continued)

```
50    <BLANKLINE>
51    Name: Cordon bleu
52    <BLANKLINE>
53    Time to cook: 45
54    <BLANKLINE>
55    Ingredients:
56    - Ham
57    - Cheese
58    - Filet
59    <BLANKLINE>
60    Necessary Kitchen Tools:
61    - Tooth picks
62    <BLANKLINE>
63    Hmm, cordon bleu!
```

Example 16.3.7 Test suite for the mail subscription tests (mail/tests.py)

```
1   import unittest
2   from doctest import DocFileSuite, ELLIPSIS
3
4   import zope.component.testing
5   import zope.component.eventtesting
6   from zope.interface import implements
7   from zope.sendmail.interfaces import IMailDelivery
8   from zope.annotation.attribute import AttributeAnnotations
9
10  from worldcookery.mail.recipe import notifyModified
11  from worldcookery.mail.annotations import MailSubscriptionAnnotations
12
13  class DummyMailDelivery(object):
14      implements(IMailDelivery)
15      def send(self, fromaddr, toaddr, msg):
16          print msg
17
18  def setUp(test):
19      zope.component.testing.setUp(test)
20      zope.component.eventtesting.setUp(test)
21      zope.component.provideAdapter(AttributeAnnotations)
22      zope.component.provideAdapter(MailSubscriptionAnnotations)
23      zope.component.provideUtility(DummyMailDelivery(), name='worldcookery
            ')
24      zope.component.provideHandler(notifyModified)
25  def test_suite():
26      return unittest.TestSuite((
27          DocFileSuite('emailsubscriptions.txt',
28                       setUp=setUp,
29                       tearDown=zope.component.testing.tearDown,
30                       optionflags=ELLIPSIS),
31          ))
32
33  if __name__ == '__main__':
34      unittest.main(defaultTest='test_suite')
```

Example 16.3.7 (continued)

13–16 and 23.   As a mail delivery utility we register a dummy implementation that simply prints the message text to the console.

2 and 31.   Doctests allow several options to be set by using binary flags. The ELLIPSIS flag tells the doctest parser to interpret a set of triple dots (. . .) as an ellipsis. This is frequently needed in functional doctests when large HTTP return messages are to be shortened in the test. Here we use them to elide the time and date of the created email message (see line 49 as well as lines 36 and 37 of the doctest, Example 16.3.6).

Browser views

Last but not least we need to implement a browser form that lets users sign up for email notification. With our experience in Page Templates and Python-implemented browser views this should be simple task. Note that for now we will not take care of security. Anybody with the permission to view the subscription page can subscribe to an object with any email address; anybody can also unsubscribe any email address.

The HTML form for email subscription (Example 16.3.8) simply contains a text input box that lets users enter an email address. Two buttons, *Subscribe* and *Unsubscribe* lead to views that handle subscription and unsubscription, respectively.

Example 16.3.8 Page Template with email subscription form (mail/subscribe.pt)

```
1   <html xmlns="http://www.w3.org/1999/xhtml"
2         xmlns:tal="http://xml.zope.org/namespaces/tal"
3         xmlns:metal="http://xml.zope.org/namespaces/metal"
4         xmlns:i18n="http://xml.zope.org/namespaces/i18n"
5         metal:use-macro="context/@@standard_macros/page"
6         i18n:domain="worldcookery">
7   <head>
8     <title metal:fill-slot="title" i18n:translate="">
9     Subscribe to
10    <tal:var i18n:name="obj_title" tal:replace="context/zope:title">
11      obj_title
12    </tal:var>
13    </title>
14  </head>
15  <body>
16  <div metal:fill-slot="body">
```

Example 16.3.8 (continued)

```
17    <h2 i18n:translate="">
18      Subscribe to
19      <em i18n:name="obj_title" tal:replace="context/zope:title">obj_title
          </em>
20    </h2>
21
22    <p i18n:translate="">
23      Using this form you can change the status of your email
24      subscription to
25      <em i18n:name="obj_title" tal:content="context/zope:title">obj_title
          </em>.
26      Enter your email address in the field below and click the
27      <em>Subscribe</em> button to subscribe; to unsubscribe, click the
28      <em>Unsubscribe</em> button.
29    </p>
30
31    <form action="" method="post"
32          tal:attributes="action context/@@absolute_url">
33      <p>
34        <label for="email" i18n:translate="">Email address:</label>
35        <input id="email" name="email" type="text" />
36      </p>
37      <p>
38        <input type="submit" name="@@subscribe:method" value="Subscribe"
39               i18n:attributes="value button-subscribe" />
40        <input type="submit" name="@@unsubscribe:method" value="Unsubscribe
               "
41               i18n:attributes="value button-unsubscribe" />
42      </p>
43    </form>
44
45  </div>
46  </body>
47  </html>
```

33, 39, and 41. Each button invokes a different view. Like Zope 2's ZPublisher, Zope 3's publishing machinery allows to mark form names as names of views that shall be invoked by appending `:method`. The actual action of the form has to be the URL of the object whose views shall be invoked. This is totally transparent to the views. In this example, the *Subscribe* button invokes the `@@subscribe` view, the *Unsubscribe* button the `@@unsubscribe` view.

Going beyond the examples

If you want to experiment more with email notifications and how components work together, try to combine the PDF generation and the mail framework. Why not send out generated PDFs as attachments? Or if that is too heavy for you on the network bandwidth or the user's mailboxes, HTML emails gen-

Example 16.3.9 Browser pages for subscribing/unsubscribing email addresses to an object (`mail/browser.py`)

```
1  from zope.publisher.browser import BrowserView
2  from worldcookery.mail.interfaces import IMailSubscriptions
3
4  class MailSubscriptionView(BrowserView):
5
6      def subscribe(self, email):
7          subscriptions = IMailSubscriptions(self.context)
8          subscriptions.subscribe(email)
9          self.request.response.redirect('.')
10
11     def unsubscribe(self, email):
12         subscriptions = IMailSubscriptions(self.context)
13         subscriptions.unsubscribe(email)
14         self.request.response.redirect('.')
```

1 and 4. For convenience we simply put the implementations of the two browser pages on one class and use `BrowserView` for the base class. These pages will be registered with the `browser:pages` directive (see Example 16.3.10).

Fig. 16.1. Notification email sent by the World Cookery application.

Example 16.3.10 Combined browser page configuration
(mail/configure.zcml)

```
1   <configure
2       xmlns="http://namespaces.zope.org/zope"
3       xmlns:mail="http://namespaces.zope.org/mail"
4       xmlns:browser="http://namespaces.zope.org/browser"
5       >
6
7     ...
8
9     <browser:pages
10        for="worldcookery.interfaces.IRecipe"
11        class=".browser.MailSubscriptionView"
12        permission="zope.ManageContent"
13        >
14      <browser:page
15          name="subscribe"
16          attribute="subscribe"
17          />
18      <browser:page
19          name="unsubscribe"
20          attribute="unsubscribe"
21          />
22      <browser:page
23          name="subscribe.html"
24          template="subscribe.pt"
25          menu="alternate_views" title="Mail subscriptions"
26          />
27    </browser:pages>
28
29  </configure>
```

9–27. When several browser pages are to be registered for one interface with a
common permission and possibly using the same class, the browser:pages
directive allows one to group browser:page directives and thus avoid repetition.

25. We add the email subscription form page to the menu of alternate views. That
way a link to it will show up when displaying recipes.

---

erated by Page Templates could jazz the simple text email up, too. Maybe
implement both and let the user choose between plain text, HTML and PDF?
Just do not forget that the event subscribers are invoked synchronously and
creating a PDF will probably take considerable time. An asynchronous approach as with email delivery is advised.

Summary

- Object events are a typical use case for notification via emails.
- Zope's email framework supports pluggable `IMailDelivery` utilities which accept emails from an application. The default implementations are transaction-aware, the recommended queued delivery implementation avoids storing emails in memory and sends them in a separate thread.
- Zope's email framework also supports pluggable `IMailer` utilities which take care of the actual email transportation. The default implementation transport emails via SMTP.

Part III

Expert

17

Sources and Vocabularies

In Chapter 4, we introduced a variant of interfaces that allow easy data modelling: schemas. Schemas are composed of fields which describe constraints on certain data values, such as the type, the length, size or range of the value stored. In this chapter we will learn about another constraint: value sets.

> **Using Zope 2**
>
> Everything discussed in this chapter also applies to Zope 2.

17.1 Sources

Constraining just the type of an object is often not enough. Sometimes you would like to allow only values from a certain set. Storing the name of a week day, for example, means storing a Unicode string that can only be either one of seven values. Any text that is not the name of a week day would be illegal, even if it was of the type Unicode string. The constraint is a *limited value set*.

Limited value sets

Constraints involving value sets, whether limited or not, are expressed through the `Choice` field. Let us pick up the example of storing the name of a week day, for example in a schema for a university lecture (they probably do not occur on a Sunday):

```
$ python
>>> from zope.interface import Interface
>>> from zope.schema import Int, Choice
>>> class ILecture(Interface):
```

```
...      period = Int(title=u'Period')
...      weekday = Choice(
...          title=u'Weekday',
...          values=[u'Monday', u'Tuesday', u'Wednesday',
...                  u'Thursday', u'Friday', u'Saturday']
...      )
...
```
▼

The values parameter tells the Choice field which exact set of values is allowed. Note that Choice does not learn anything about the type of the values and it does not need to. It will only check whether possible field values are part of the set or not:

```
>>> ILecture['weekday'].validate(u'Wednesday')
```
▼

That value is accepted since the validate did not raise an exception. It will raise ConstraintNotSatisfied if it finds an invalid value:

```
>>> ILecture['weekday'].validate(u'Sunday')
Traceback (most recent call last):
  ...
zope.schema._bootstrapinterfaces.ConstraintNotSatisfied: Sunday
```
∎

Arbitrary value sets with sources

It is rare that one deals with limited and static value sets. Most of the time, value sets are dynamic and not limited. For example, take an instant messenger application that allows users to send messages to one of their buddies. The recipient of such a message would have to be a buddy from a user's buddy list. This list obviously varies from user to user and its length is arbitrary. How would you express such a constraint? The answer to that is *sources*. Sources express dynamic and possibly context-sensitive value sets. By specifying a source instead of a static set of values in the Choice schema field, you can express a dynamic value constraint.

Implementing simple sources is quite easy. The source API is expressed in the ISource interface from the zope.schema package. According to this interface, sources only have to be able to tell you whether an item is in the set or not. In other words, they have to support Python's in operator which means they need to have a __contains__ method. Sources do not need to be able to list all the items in their dynamic value set. Sometimes that is not even possible, only finding out whether a particular item is in the set is possible.

A very simplistic implementation of a buddy source could look like this:

```
$ python
>>> from zope.schema.interfaces import ISource
>>> from zope.interface import implements
>>> class BuddySource(object):
```

```
...        implements(ISource)
...        def __contains__(self, buddy):
...            return buddy in (u'Max', u'Greg', u'Tony')
...                                                            ▼
```

This source does not give us any advantage over the static value set we used in the weekdays example. The important part, however, is that we have now factored the decision whether somebody is a valid recipient or not out into a different component. It is no longer the schema's responsibility. This is how the source is hooked up in the schema, once again using a `Choice` field, but now with the `source` parameter:

```
>>> from zope.interface import Interface
>>> from zope.schema import Text, Choice
>>> class IInstantMessage(Interface):
...        recipient = Choice(
...            title=u"Recipient",
...            source=BuddySource()
...            )
...        message_text = Text(title=u"Message text")
...                                                            ■
```

The behaviour regarding valid and invalid items is the same as with static value sets specified in the `Choice` field.

Summary

- In many applications, only certain values from a defined value set are allowed for an object's attribute.
- Value sets, whether dynamic or static, are expressed through sources. Sources provide `ISource` and have to support the containment operator at a minimum.
- A value set constraint is expressed through the `Choice` field which either accepts a static list of acceptable values or a source (or a vocabulary name, see the next section below).

17.2 Vocabularies

Vocabularies are a particular type of sources. They are not as pure in concept as sources because they mix data with the way the data is presented in so-called terms (see below). For that and other reasons they are considered outdated and obsolete by some. Yet Zope continues to provide and use vocabularies in many places. They are also easier to use than sources in many respects, especially for simple dynamic value sets.

In vocabulary jargon, we distinguish the following terms:

Value is an object that is part of the vocabulary.

Term is an abstract object that a represents an object in the vocabulary. This layer of abstraction is necessary, because it is possible for objects of arbitrary types to be part of the same vocabulary. Terms are described by the `ITerm` interface.

Token is an ASCII-only string giving a term a unique identifier. The relation between terms and tokens has to be a one-to-one function. Tokens are necessary to uniquely identify terms in encoding-sensitive environments such as browser views and the file system. Terms that have tokens provide the `ITokenizedTerm` interface which extends `ITerm`. Vocabularies indicate that they support tokenized terms by providing `IVocabularyTokenized` apart from `IVocabulary`.

Title gives terms a name for presentation purposes. This is an optional feature, but useful when a list of terms are to be displayed in a user interface. Tokens are usually too cryptic to serve this purpose, nor do they support translation. Titles are often i18n messages. Terms that have a title indicate it by providing `ITitledTokenizedTerm`.

A vocabulary has to provide `IBaseVocabulary` at a minimum. It extends `ISource` and therefore requires vocabularies to support the in operator. In addition to that, it requires each vocabulary to have a `getTerm` method that fetches a term object for a specific value inside the vocabulary.

`IBaseVocabulary` does not require iterability and can therefore be used for cases where the exact set of values cannot be determined or would be very expensive to compute, e.g. the set of user accounts in a system with a large user base. Many vocabularies, however, especially the ones that are used in schemas for automated browser forms, represent finite and iterable sets. Such vocabularies provide `IVocabulary` which extends `IBaseVocabulary` with iteration capabilities.

Simple vocabularies

Both `ITerm` and `IVocabulary` are interfaces that are easy to implement. The requirements on vocabularies and their terms are very light from the Zope side. The difficult part about implementing vocabularies is the modelling of real data or relationships.

For simple use cases where a list of values is already available, `SimpleVocabulary` from the `zope.schema.vocabulary` module can be used as a vocabulary implementation. It can easily be tried out on the interpreter shell. When a sequence of values is already available, the `fromValues`

class method can be used to create a vocabulary, for example from a list of
numbers:

```
$ python
>>> numbers = range(10)
>>> from zope.schema.vocabulary import SimpleVocabulary
>>> vocab = SimpleVocabulary.fromValues(numbers)                    ▼
```

As with sources, one of the minimum requirements of vocabularies is that they
allow a containment check using the in operator. As expected, the integer 1
is contained in the vocabulary, but 10 is not.

```
>>> 1 in vocab
True
>>> 10 in vocab
False                                                              ▼
```

Since they are created from an iterable sequence, simple vocabularies are
always iterable. Elements of the iteration are the term objects:

```
>>> for term in vocab:
...     print term.value,
...
0 1 2 3 4 5 6 7 8 9                                                ▼
```

Terms of `SimpleVocabulary` possess tokens which are computed by converting values to strings. Since we did not associate titles with the items in
the vocabulary, titles are not available:

```
>>> one = vocab.getTerm(1)
>>> one.value
1
>>> from zope.schema.interfaces import ITokenizedTerm
>>> ITokenizedTerm.providedBy(one)
True
>>> one.token
'1'
>>> from zope.schema.interfaces import ITitledTokenizedTerm
>>> ITitledTokenizedTerm.providedBy(one)
False                                                             ▼
```

It is generally not a good idea to trust `SimpleVocabulary` with generating tokens. First, not everything converts to a string uniquely, if at all.
Second, a string object can still contain non-ASCII characters which are not
allowed in tokens. Therefore, it is better to either provide the tokens yourself
or a custom and fail-safe routine that produces unique ASCII tokens.

A `SimpleVocabulary` instance with custom tokens can be instantiated
using the `fromItems` class method. It accepts nested sequences like a dictionary's `items` method generates:

```
>>> numbers = {
...        'zero': 0,
...        'one': 1,
...        'two': 2,
...        'three': 3,
...        'four': 4,
...        'five': 5,
...        'six': 6,
...        'seven': 7,
...        'eight': 8,
...        'nine': 9
... }
>>> vocab = SimpleVocabulary.fromItems(numbers.items())
>>> 1 in vocab
True
>>> 10 in vocab
False
>>> one = vocab.getTerm(1)
>>> one.token
'one'                                                      ▼
```

Vocabulary terms can be re-identified by their given token, as long as the vocabulary implements IVocabularyTokenized, which SimpleVocabulary does:

```
>>> from zope.schema.interfaces import IVocabularyTokenized
>>> IVocabularyTokenized.providedBy(vocab)
True
>>> two = vocab.getTermByToken('two')
>>> two.value
2                                                          ■
```

Utility vocabularies

Zope itself makes use of vocabularies in a few places, for example when a site administrator chooses a permission by which a component is protected through the ZMI. Here it is obviously desirable to only list valid permissions and to double-check the form values when they are submitted. Thus, a vocabulary is used.

As discussed before, small software components like permissions and factories are registered as named utilities. Their type is identified by the interface they provide. This way, a generic utility vocabulary can be used to query named utilities of a certain type. Using the right interfaces, the utility vocabulary can be used to query permissions, factories, interfaces, content types, and more. See Table 17.1 for a list of utility vocabularies provided by Zope.

Let us look up one of those vocabularies. Vocabularies are not registered as utilities for IVocabulary directly. Instead, their constructors are regis-

Table 17.1. Default vocabularies for certain types of named utilities and other components

Name	Values	Tokens	Package
`Cache Names`	IDs of cache utilities providing `ICache`.	Same as values	`zope.app.cache`
`Interfaces`	All registered interfaces (providing `IInterface`).	Dotted name of the interfaces	`zope.app.component`
`Content Types`	Content type interfaces (providing `IContentType`).	Dotted name of the interfaces	`zope.app.content`
`Object Interfaces`	Interfaces that the current context object provides.	Dotted name of the interfaces	`zope.app.interface`
`SourceTypes`	Factory name of a text source factory.	Same as the value	`zope.app.renderer`
`Permissions`	Permission objects providing `IPermission`.	Permission ids	`zope.app.security`
`Permission Ids`	IDs of permission objects	Same as value	`zope.app.security`
`Role Ids`	IDs of role objects	Same as value	`zope.app.securitypolicy`
`Connection Names`	Names of database connection utilities providing `IZopeDatabaseAdapter`.	Same as value	`zope.app.sqlscript`
`Mail Delivery Names`	Names of mail delivery utilities providing `IMailDelivery`.	Same as value	`zope.sendmail`

tered for `IVocabularyFactory`. The reason is that utilities are context-dependent and are always instantiated with the current context. Let us take the permissions vocabulary, for example.

```
$ bin/debugzope
>>> from zope.component import getUtility
>>> from zope.schema.interfaces import IVocabularyFactory
>>> permissions_factory = getUtility(
...     IVocabularyFactory, u"Permissions")
```

We can now instantiate the vocabulary, passing None as context. A quick check verifies that we are indeed dealing with a utility vocabulary. As a final demonstration, we can iterate over the vocabulary's terms to see that the terms' tokens are the permission ids while the values are, of course, the permission objects themselves:

```
>>> permissions = permissions_factory(None)
>>> permissions
<zope.app.component.vocabulary.UtilityVocabulary object at 0x2883950>
>>> for term in permissions:
...     print term.token, term.value
...
zope.AddImages <Permission object at 0x2ca1d30>
zope.AddSQLScripts <Permission object at 0x2ca1b50>
zope.ManageApplication <Permission object at 0x2ca1c90>
...
```

Summary

- Vocabularies deal with abstractions of the actual values called *terms*. Each term can be represented uniquely by a *token*.
- Simple   vocabularies   are   easily   implemented   using `SimpleVocabulary` from the `zope.schema.vocabulary` module.
- Zope itself provides and uses a number of vocabularies, most importantly *utility vocabularies* which lists registered utilities.

17.3 Using vocabularies

In actual applications, vocabularies typically obtain their values from a few places. If you are building an application for component management (for example like the ZMI), you would probably use utility vocabularies a lot. It is also quite common to store sets of allowed values for a certain field in the annotations of the object or one of its containers. This is quite easy and practical, and expresses the tight relationship between the vocabulary as metacontent or metadata, and the actual content.[1]

In the *World Cookery* example application, we will use a different approach. We suppose that the list of kitchen tools that can be added to a recipe will find its values in a vocabulary. The values in this vocabulary will be defined site-wide, and is thus not dependent on the location of the recipe within the site. Therefore, we will use a utility that provides the vocabulary values. Where these come from is only a question of which utility we wire in. This allows us to easily provide a different implementation of the utility. In the next chapter, we will see how to do this customization based on a site-based configuration within a particular Zope instance.

Making the schema ready for vocabularies

First, we change the IRecipe schema so that values for the tools field are taken from a vocabulary. As before, this is done using the Choice field, but this time we do not give it a list of values or a source instance; instead, we provide a vocabulary (factory) name. Example 17.3.2 shows the modified IRecipe schema.

Now we have to provide the vocabulary we refer to in the schema. As we want the vocabulary to retrieve the actual values from a utility, we have to provide such a utility as well. The interface that the utility provides can be as simple as IKitchenTools shown in Example 17.3.1.

Example 17.3.1 Interface for the kitchen tools utility (interfaces.py)

```
1   ...
2
3   from zope.schema import Iterable
4
5   class IKitchenTools(Interface):
6
7       kitchen_tools = Iterable(
8           title=_(u"Kitchen tools"),
9           description=_(u"A list of valid kitchen tools"),
10          )
```

---

[1] As an optional exercise, try to re-implement the vocabulary that is introduced in this section as an annotations-based one. Store the annotations on the object containing the recipe and provide a browser view for editing the vocabulary items.

Example 17.3.2 Recipe schema with a `Choice` field (`interfaces.py`)

```
1   from zope.interface import Interface
2   from zope.schema import List, Text, TextLine, Int, Choice
3   from zope.i18nmessageid import MessageFactory
4   _ = MessageFactory('worldcookery')
5   from zope.app.container.interfaces import IContainer, IContained
6   from zope.app.container.constraints import contains, containers
7
8   class IRecipe(IContained):
9       """Store information about a recipe.
10      """
11      containers('worldcookery.interfaces.IRecipeContainer')
12
13      name = TextLine(
14          title=_(u"Name"),
15          description=_(u"Name of the dish"),
16          required = True
17          )
18
19      ingredients = List(
20          title=_(u"Ingredients"),
21          description=_(u"List of ingredients necessary for this recipe."),
22          required=True,
23          value_type=TextLine(title=_(u"Ingredient"))
24          )
25
26      tools = List(
27          title=_(u"Tools"),
28          description=_(u"List of necessary kitchen tools"),
29          required=False,
30          value_type=Choice(title=_(u"Tool"), vocabulary="Kitchen Tools"),
31          unique=True
32          )
33
34      time_to_cook = Int(
35          title=_(u"Time to cook"),
36          description=_(u"Necessary time for preparing the meal described,
                  "
37                          "in minutes."),
38          required=True
39          )
40
41      description = Text(
42          title=_(u"Description"),
43          description=_(u"Description of the recipe"),
44          required=True
45          )
```

30–31. Since we still want to allow the selection of multiple kitchen tools, we keep the List field. Values *inside* that list need to come from the vocabulary. To ensure that no value occurs twice in the list, we pass the unique parameter as True.

Providing the vocabulary and a utility implementation

As an implementation for this utility, we will provide one that reads values from a UTF-8 encoded text file, kitchentools.dat, in which the acceptable kitchen tools are listed line by line. Note that this is just a primitive sample implementation. As always, you can provide your own IKitchenTools utility that provides values from a different data source. In the next chapter, we will do so ourselves.

As for the vocabulary itself, we can rely on existing infrastructure. In the previous section, we saw how to create vocabularies from a set of existing values by using SimpleVocabulary. This approach fits here, too. See Example 17.3.3 for the utility implementation and the vocabulary factory.

Example 17.3.3 Implementation of the kitchen tool utility and the vocabulary factory (kitchentools.py)

```
1   import os.path
2   from zope.interface import implements, alsoProvides
3   from zope.component import getUtility
4   from zope.schema.interfaces import IVocabularyFactory
5   from zope.schema.vocabulary import SimpleVocabulary
6   from worldcookery.interfaces import IKitchenTools
7
8   class KitchenToolsFromFile(object):
9       """Kitchen tools utility that reads data from a file
10      """
11      implements(IKitchenTools)
12
13      @property
14      def kitchen_tools(self):
15          file_name = os.path.join(os.path.dirname(__file__), "kitchentools
                .dat")
16          for line in file(file_name):
17              if line.strip():
18                  yield line.strip().decode('utf-8')
19
20  def kitchenToolVocabulary(context):
21      utility = getUtility(IKitchenTools)
22      return SimpleVocabulary.fromValues(utility.kitchen_tools)
23  alsoProvides(kitchenToolVocabulary, IVocabularyFactory)
```

15. The utility reads its data from a file called kitchentools.dat in the same directory that the kitchentools.py module is located in.

16. In Python, file objects are iterators which allow one to easily iterate over the lines within the file (only in the case of text files, of course). This also works platform independently.

Example 17.3.3 (continued)

---

18. Instead of loading the whole file into memory at once, we return items only one by one using the `yield` keyword. That way this method will not return a list but an iterable generator object, still fulfilling the `IKitchenTools` interface which requires a simple iterable. Before items are yielded, they are stripped of whitespace and decoded from UTF-8, the encoding that the file is supposed to be encoded in.

Configuration

As always after we have implemented components, we need to register them. There is nothing particularly different about registering vocabulary factories. They are registered like any other named utility. Example 17.3.4 shows the necessary directives.

Example 17.3.4 Configuring the vocabulary and the related utility (`configure.zcml`)

```
1    ...
2    <utility factory=".kitchentools.KitchenToolsFromFile" />
3
4    <utility
5        component=".kitchentools.kitchenToolVocabulary"
6        name="Kitchen Tools"
7        />
8    ...
```

Before we can try out our vocabulary-based content type in the browser using add and edit forms, we must not forget to disable the custom widget we applied to the `tools` field (see Example 17.3.5). Zope provides a special widget for `Choice` fields and for `Choice` fields within sequences (`List` and `Tuple` fields). It presents us with a list of items in the vocabulary that we can choose from. In our case, we can select multiple items from the list (in some web browsers, you need to press down the **Ctrl** key in order to be able to select multiple items from the list).

Summary

- Vocabularies are looked up by looking up their factories as named utilities. Vocabulary factories provide `IVocabularyFactory`
- Zope provides special widgets for `Choice` fields that make custom widgets unnecessary.

Example 17.3.5 Updated browser form implementation
(`browser/recipe.py`)

```
1   ...
2   class RecipeEditForm(EditForm):
3       form_fields = Fields(IRecipe).omit('__parent__', '__name__')
4       form_fields['ingredients'].custom_widget = DynamicSequenceWidget
5       label = _(u"Edit recipe")
6
7       template = NamedTemplate('worldcookery.form')
8
9   class RecipeAddForm(AddForm):
10      form_fields = Fields(IRecipe).omit('__parent__', '__name__')
11      form_fields['ingredients'].custom_widget = DynamicSequenceWidget
12      label = _(u"Add recipe")
13
14      template = NamedTemplate('worldcookery.form')
15
16      def create(self, data):
17          recipe = createObject(u'worldcookery.Recipe')
18          applyChanges(recipe, self.form_fields, data)
19          return recipe
20  ...
```

Sites

In many content management applications, hierarchical structures play an important role for organizing content. Content structures like these can easily be modelled in Zope using the location and containment concepts we covered in Chapter 15. Zope not only allows you to put content in such structures, it also allows you to locally customize component registrations in *sites*.

18.1 Introduction

A Zope instance is typically used to serve one particular web application. Of course, one instance can serve different web sites that offer the same application, possibly in different variants (for example using different skins, different user databases, etc.). Our *World Cookery* website, for instance, could offer English recipes at http://worldcookery.com while German recipes are published under the subsite http://worldcookery.com/de/, http://www.de.worldcookery.com or even http://worldcookery.de.

A part of a Zope instance that contains such a subsite is simply called a *site*. Any object can be a site as long as it provides ISite. It makes most sense when containers are sites. The best example here is Zope's Folder content type. Folders are *possible sites* (they provide IPossibleSite) which means they can be turned into sites. The root folder of a ZODB instance is always a site. Sites can be nested.

Global vs. local

Components are registered with component registries. The components we have written so far were all registered with the *global* registry, either via ZCML or in unit tests via the zope.component registration API. Such global components are always available everywhere.

Local components, on the other hand, are components that are defined in a particular place—a site. They are registered with that site's component registry, also known as a *site manager*. Then they are only available within a site, which includes subobjects, of course. Local definitions of components can shadow global ones, thus allowing customization of component definitions at a site level. In the case of nested sites, component look-up cascades from the most local site up to the root folder site and ends with the global registry.

How are sites found?

Imagine the following URL path:

```
/worldcookery_site/italian/Spagetthi/@@edit.html
```

where `worldcookery_site` is a site, `italian` a recipe folder, `Spaghetti` a recipe and `edit.html` a view on the recipe. As the Zope publisher traverses each segment of this URL path, it detects sites with local component registries:

Nothing traversed yet The global component registry will be used for all component lookups because it is always available.

/ The default root object (the root folder) of a Zope database is a site. As traversal passes this object, it makes its site manager the active component registry. Component lookup will now first consult this site's site manager, then the global component registry.

`worldcookery_site` This object is also a site, thus its site manager now becomes the active component registry. Component lookup will now first be handled by this site's site manager, it will then try the site manager of the root folder and lastly consult the global component registry.

`italian/Spaghetti/@@edit.html` Traversal progresses normally now. Component lookup will cascade through the component registries as described in the previous step. This applies to adapter lookup (e.g. for the `edit.html`) view as well as utility lookup (e.g. translation domains for translating text in the `edit.html`) view.

Creating a site from a folder

The easiest way to create a site is to create a folder and turn it into a site. To do that, go to the ZMI and select *Folder* from the *Add* menu. Give the folder a name, for example `worldcookery_site`, then click on it to see its contents. The actions menu should now contain a *Make a site* entry. Clicking on this will turn the current folder into a site.

Fig. 18.1. Regular folders can easily be turned into a site using this link.

When turning folders into sites, Zope creates a new local component registry, the site manager. The site manager only has to be a component registry, but by default Zope uses an implementation that is also a container. That way we can put our local components in it. Though the site manager does not become a regular subobject of the folder, it is available via the Zope Management Interface as ++etc++site, as you can see from the URL of the site management page. When you are in a folder and want to get to the site manager, click on the *Manage Site* link from the actions menu.

Something else happens to a folder when it is turned into a site. As a regular folder it only provides IPossibleSite, indicating that it can be turned into a site at any time. After we have turned the folder into a site, it now provides ISite.

Local components

Local components are usually persistent objects. That means they have a lot in common with content objects: they are added to containers, managed through the web, and stored in the ZODB. Local components can be added anywhere, though it is common practice to keep them separate from the content objects. Since the site manager is a container, it is a good idea to add them in there. For example, let us add an *Error Logging Utility* to the site manager of worldcookery_site. We can give it any name in the container, such as error_log.

Just adding a component is not enough to make it active. As with global components, local components need to be registered before they are found. To register an object as a local utility, we have to go to its *Registration* tab and click on *Register this object*. We can then specify the interface the utility shall provide, a name if its a named utility (leave it empty of it is not) and an optional comment.

After registering the utility, it is now available in `worldcookery_site` and below. For example, try to provoke a `NotFound` error by typing an nonexistent URL into your browser that starts with the URL of `worldcookery_site`. You will see that our error logging utility will have logged the exception. For errors in different parts of the site, the error will show up in a different error log, e.g. the one defined in the root folder site.

Summary

- Sites allow the customization of global software components by using local, persistent components.
- Any object can be a site, though most of the time they are containers (e.g. folders). By default, the root folder of a ZODB instance is always a site.
- Sites are found during traversal. The site manager of the site that was traversed last becomes the active component registry.
- Global components are registered with a global component registry via ZCML or the `zope.component` API. Local components are registered with local component registries (*site managers*) that are associated with sites.

Flashback

The CMF was among the first Zope-based frameworks that introduced the concept of a *site*. A *CMF Site* object or a derivative always has to be the root of a CMF-based application. Persistent CMF components, *CMF Tools*, can be added within such a site and are a lot like Zope 3's local utilities. The difference to Zope 3 is that Zope 3 also knows global utilities.

Another major difference is that sites can be anywhere in the location hierarchy in Zope 3, that includes being nested in other sites.[1] Local components can also live anywhere within that site and do not have to share the same namespace with content objects, for example when they are added to the `++etc++site` site manager.

Finally, local components in Zope 3 are only active when they have been explicitly registered. That makes it possible to have two different implementations of the same utility in a site, but only allow one to be active at a time. This is not as easily possible with the CMF. The generic registration process with site managers also makes work-around solutions like the *QuickInstaller* tool for CMF unnecessary.

18.2 Local utilities

Local utilities are the most common type of local component because utilities, especially named utilities, are widely used throughout Zope. Thus, a lot of software behaviour can be influenced by registering local utilities. Good examples of local flavours of named utilities we already know are *factories* and *translation domains*.

Local utilities are easy to create. It is not much harder than writing a persistent content component. After all, utilities are meant to be small, useful components and Zope already gives us a lot of user interface help, such as browser menus and generated forms.

Let us write a local utility. A good candidate for a local utility is the kitchen tools utility from the last chapter. By offering a local flavour of this utility, site administrators can customize the allowed values for the Kitchen Tools vocabulary without having to edit the kitchentools.dat file on the file system. More importantly, different policies can be implemented for different parts in the application by using different sites with different instances of the local utility. One reason to do this might be a subsite that contains recipes in a different language. In this case, the kitchen tool names obviously need to be translated, too.

Writing a local utility

When we implement the local utility, we want to take advantage of automatic form generation as we do with content components. The IKitchenTools interface which describes the utility interface is not entirely sufficient for that because it merely declares the kitchen_tools field as an Iterable. It does not specify an exact type, it can therefore not be represented by a widget.

Example 18.2.1 shows the ILocalKitchenTools interface which extends IKitchenTools and declares the kitchen_tools field as a List. This has two implications: first, every utility that provides ILocalKitchenTools also provides IKitchenTools by interface inheritance. Secondly, a definite type information for the iterable attribute has been given so that a widget can easily be looked up.

The implementation of ILocalKitchenTools is just as easy to produce as the persistent version of the IRecipe implementation. Example 18.2.2 shows the enhanced kitchentools.py module. Note that in some cases, it is even possible to have just one implementation for a global and a local utility. The fact that the global utility would be registrable and persistent does not bother the global utility service.

As for the basic configuration, we only have to configure it like a regular content component; see Example 18.2.3. The configuration directives that actually allow us to manage the local utility using the web interface are obviously browser-specific directives.

Example 18.2.1 Interface for a local version of the kitchen tools utility
(`interfaces.py`)

```
1  ...
2  from zope.schema import Iterable
3
4  class IKitchenTools(Interface):
5
6      kitchen_tools = Iterable(
7          title=_(u"Kitchen tools"),
8          description=_(u"A list of valid kitchen tools"),
9          )
10
11 class ILocalKitchenTools(IKitchenTools, IContained):
12
13     kitchen_tools = List(
14         title=_(u"Kitchen tools"),
15         description=_(u"A list of valid kitchen tools"),
16         value_type=TextLine(title=_(u"Kitchen tool"))
17         )
```

11. Though it is not a strict requirement, it is a good idea to make persistent utilities contained objects, much as it is a good idea to do this with persistent content objects.

13–17. We redefine the `kitchen_tools` field by using a concrete type constraint (`List`) instead of a mere functionality constraint (`Iterable`). Also, we do not forget to specify the `value_type` of the items contained.

Browser configuration

Since local utilities are managed through the browser management interface, we will have to provide at least some minimal browser configuration for our kitchen tool utility. Again, the analogy to a content object works well. With the recipe content type we were not able to do much either until we configured both the entry in the browser *Add* menu and the automated add and edit forms. Let us do the same for the kitchen tools utility. Example 18.2.4 shows an edit form, Example 18.2.5 its configuration.

We are now ready to add the utility, edit its data and register it with a local site manager. Once you have done that, try adding a new recipe. You will see that the list of acceptable kitchen tools directly corresponds to the kitchen tools you set in the local utility, not to the global utility anymore. The best part is, it is totally transparent to the vocabulary! For all it knows, it is still looking up an `IKitchenTools` utility.

Example 18.2.2 Local kitchen tools utility implementation
(`kitchentools.py`)

```
1   import os.path
2   from persistent import Persistent
3   from zope.interface import implements, alsoProvides
4   from zope.component import getUtility
5   from zope.schema.interfaces import IVocabularyFactory
6   from zope.schema.vocabulary import SimpleVocabulary
7   from worldcookery.interfaces import IKitchenTools, ILocalKitchenTools
8
9   class KitchenToolsFromFile(object):
10      """Kitchen tools utility that reads data from a file
11      """
12      implements(IKitchenTools)
13
14      @property
15      def kitchen_tools(self):
16          file_name = os.path.join(os.path.dirname(__file__), "kitchentools
                .dat")
17          for line in file(file_name):
18              if line.strip():
19                  yield line.strip().decode('utf-8')
20
21  class LocalKitchenTools(Persistent):
22      """Local, persistent kitchen tools utility
23      """
24      implements(ILocalKitchenTools)
25
26      __name__ = __parent__ = None
27
28      kitchen_tools = []
29
30  def kitchenToolVocabulary(context):
31      utility = getUtility(IKitchenTools)
32      return SimpleVocabulary.fromValues(utility.kitchen_tools)
33  alsoProvides(kitchenToolVocabulary, IVocabularyFactory)
```

2 and 21. Local components are persistent because they need to be stored within the ZODB.

26. Since the `ILocalKitchenTools` interface extends `IContained`, we need to provide default `__parent__` and `__name__` attributes.

28. No further machinery is required on part of the local utility other than to fulfil the `ILocalKitchenTools` interface. We do that here by providing an empty list as a default for the `kitchen_tools` attribute.

Example 18.2.3 Basic configuration of a local utility class
(`configure.zcml`)

```
 1    ...
 2    <class class=".kitchentools.LocalKitchenTools">
 3      <implements
 4          interface="zope.annotation.interfaces.IAttributeAnnotatable"
 5          />
 6      <require
 7          permission="zope.Public"
 8          interface=".interfaces.IKitchenTools"
 9          />
10      <require
11          permission="zope.ManageContent"
12          set_schema=".interfaces.ILocalKitchenTools"
13          />
14    </class>
15    ...
```

3–5. It is always a good idea to make persistent content-like objects annotatable.
That way we get metadata like Dublin Core properties for free.

6–13. The security configuration for the local utility looks just like the one of any
other schema-based content type. Note that this analogy only works so well
in this case because the kitchen tools utility does not really do much, it really
looks a lot like content.

Example 18.2.4 Edit form for the kitchen tools utility (`browser/kitchentools.py`)

```
 1   from zope.formlib.form import EditForm, Fields
 2   from zope.formlib.namedtemplate import NamedTemplate
 3   from zope.i18nmessageid import MessageFactory
 4   _ = MessageFactory('worldcookery')
 5
 6   from worldcookery.interfaces import ILocalKitchenTools
 7   from worldcookery.browser.widget import DynamicSequenceWidget
 8
 9   class KitchenToolsEditForm(EditForm):
10       form_fields = Fields(ILocalKitchenTools).omit('__parent__', '__name__
               ')
11       form_fields['kitchen_tools'].custom_widget = DynamicSequenceWidget
12       label = _(u"Edit Kitchen Tools")
13
14       template = NamedTemplate('worldcookery.form')
```

Example 18.2.5 Browser configuration for the kitchen tools utility
(`browser/configure.zcml`)

```
1    ...
2    <browser:addMenuItem
3        class="worldcookery.kitchentools.LocalKitchenTools"
4        title="Kitchen tools"
5        permission="zope.ManageContent"
6        />
7
8    <browser:page
9        for="worldcookery.interfaces.ILocalKitchenTools"
10       name="edit.html"
11       class=".kitchentools.KitchenToolsEditForm"
12       permission="zope.ManageContent"
13       menu="zmi_views" title="[label-edit] Edit"
14       />
15
16   <adapter
17       factory=".recipe.form_template"
18       for=".kitchentools.KitchenToolsEditForm"
19       name="worldcookery.form"
20       />
21   ...
```

Summary

- Local utilities are the common form of local components, especially named utilities such as roles and translation domains.
- A local utility is often only a persistent re-implementation of an existing global implementation; sometimes one implementation can be used for both purposes.

18.3 Implementing sites

Zope allows us to easily turn folders into sites and register local components in them through its management interface. That way we can administer some parts of our web application through-the-web. However, creating or recreating the application this way involves a lot of steps. Let us write our own site implementation to automate these steps. That way we can influence what happens when a *WorldCookery* site is created. For example, we can make sure that all necessary local utilities are automatically created along with the site.

Since our site should contain subobjects, such as recipe folders and recipes, we will make it a container. For that we can rely on the convenient BTreeContainer implementation that we used in Chapter 15. In addition, we need to satisfy the IPossibleSite interface which requires us to implement two simple methods, getSiteManager and setSiteManager.

Why do we make the *WorldCookery* site only an IPossibleSite? Why not make it an ISite with a site manager right away? When site managers are created, they need to be able to walk up the object tree to find the next site manager, to ensure component lookup will cascade all the way to the global component registry. We therefore define *WorldCookery* sites as IPossibleSite objects and turn them into real sites *after* they have been added to a container. We will do that with a subscriber to IObjectAddedEvent.

In Example 18.3.1 we define an interface for *WorldCookery* sites, IWorldCookerySite as well as an interface for an event interface that will indicate when a new *WorldCookery* site has been created. In Example 18.3.2 we provide an implementation for these interfaces. The necessary configuration is shown in Example 18.3.3. The browser configuration is not explicitly shown as it is exactly the same as for the recipe folder that was implemented in Chapter 15.

Example 18.3.1 Interfaces for *WorldCookery* sites (`interfaces.py`)

```
1   ...
2   from zope.component.interfaces import IObjectEvent
3   from zope.app.component.interfaces import IPossibleSite
4
5   class IWorldCookerySite(IPossibleSite, IContainer):
6       """Site containing the WorldCookery application"""
7
8   class INewWorldCookerySiteEvent(IObjectEvent):
9       """Indicates that a new WorldCookery site has been created"""
```

Creating and registering local components

By sending an event when a new *WorldCookery* site object receives a site manager, we have created a hook for other parts of our application to create and register local components in the same process. For example, we can write a subscriber to this event which creates a local kitchen tools utility in each newly created *WorldCookery* site. Example 18.3.4 shows the code.

We then need to hook up the subscriber with the usual ZCML directive:

```
<subscriber handler=".kitchentools.createLocalKitchenTools" />
```

Example 18.3.2 Implementation of a *WorldCookery* site (`site.py`)

```
1  from zope.interface import implements
2  from zope.component import adapter
3  from zope.event import notify
4  from zope.app.container.btree import BTreeContainer
5  from zope.app.container.interfaces import IObjectAddedEvent
6  from zope.app.component.site import SiteManagerContainer,
       LocalSiteManager
7
8  from worldcookery.interfaces import IWorldCookerySite
9  from worldcookery.interfaces import INewWorldCookerySiteEvent
10
11 class NewWorldCookerySiteEvent(object):
12     implements(INewWorldCookerySiteEvent)
13
14     def __init__(self, site):
15         self.object = site
16
17 class WorldCookerySite(SiteManagerContainer, BTreeContainer):
18     implements(IWorldCookerySite)
19
20     def setSiteManager(self, sm):
21         super(WorldCookerySite, self).setSiteManager(sm)
22         notify(NewWorldCookerySiteEvent(self))
23
24 @adapter(IWorldCookerySite, IObjectAddedEvent)
25 def setSiteManagerWhenAdded(site, event):
26     site.setSiteManager(LocalSiteManager(site))
```

4 and 17. Like with the recipe folder we implemented in Chapter 15, we use
BTreeContainer as a base class to implement the container API.

6 and 17. SiteManagerContainer is a convenient base class that satisfies the
IPossibleSite interface. In other words, it provides the getSiteManager
and setSiteManager methods to contain and retrieve a site manager (hence
the name). There is not much magic in these methods, just a few sanity checks.
Inheriting them from a base class simply lets us save a few lines.

24–26. As soon as a *WorldCookery* site is added to a container, we can
turn it into a "real" site by setting a site manager. Anything that provides IComponentLookup from the zope.component package will do
here. If all we needed were persistent component registrations, for example, we could use PersistentComponents from the zope.component.
persistentregistry module. But we would also like this site manager to
be a container, that is why we take LocalSiteManager.

22. When a site manager is set and this possible site is turned into a real site,
we send an event that will allow us to instantiate and register some initial
components in the new site.

Example 18.3.3 Configuration for *WorldCookery* sites (`configure.zcml`)

```
 1    ...
 2    <class class=".site.WorldCookerySite">
 3      <implements
 4          interface="zope.annotation.interfaces.IAttributeAnnotatable"
 5          />
 6      <allow attributes="getSiteManager" />
 7      <require
 8          permission="zope.ManageServices"
 9          attributes="setSiteManager"
10          />
11      <require like_class=".folder.RecipeFolder" />
12    </class>
13
14    <subscriber handler=".site.setSiteManagerWhenAdded" />
15    ...
```

6–10. We have to provide security declarations for the IPossibleSite API. The getSiteManager method needs to be publicly available, while setSiteManager should require site manager privileges.

11. With this subdirective we tell the security machinery to protect all other attributes the same way as the recipe folder is protected.

Example 18.3.4 Creating a local kitchen tools utility programmatically (`kitchentools.py`)

```
 1    ...
 2    from zope.component import adapter
 3    from worldcookery.interfaces import INewWorldCookerySiteEvent
 4
 5    @adapter(INewWorldCookerySiteEvent)
 6    def createLocalKitchenTools(event):
 7        kitchentools = LocalKitchenTools()
 8        previous = getUtility(IKitchenTools)
 9        kitchentools.kitchen_tools = list(previous.kitchen_tools)
10
11        sm = event.object.getSiteManager()
12        sm['kitchentools'] = kitchentools
13        sm.registerUtility(kitchentools, ILocalKitchenTools)
```

7–9. Here we create the local utility. In addition to that we look up the *current* kitchen tools utility and copy its data into the new utility. That way recipes in the newly created site will not have to start out with an empty list of kitchen tools.

Example 18.3.4 (continued)

11–13.   Here we register the local utility with the site manager. All component registries need to provide IComponentRegistry which specifies the
component registration API. This includes the methods registerUtility,
registerAdapter, etc. which behave much like the convenience functions
provideUtility, provideAdapter, etc. from the zope.component package which we have already used in interpreter sessions and tests.

When you now go to the Zope Management Interface and add a *WorldCookery Site*, you will that it is not only a ready-made site, but that its site
manager also contains a registered local kitchen tools utility.

Testing

Let us produce a minimal test for this machinery in the debug shell. First we
instantiate a *WorldCookery Site* object and find that it does not have a site
manager yet:

```
$ bin/debugzope
>>> from worldcookery.site import WorldCookerySite
>>> worldcookery_site = WorldCookerySite()
>>> worldcookery_site.getSiteManager()
Traceback (most recent call last):
  ...
ComponentLookupError: no site manager defined
```
▼

However, after adding it to a folder hierarchy that has a root, we see that it
has a site manager:

```
>>> from zope.app.folder import rootFolder
>>> root = rootFolder()
>>> root[u'worldcookery_site'] = worldcookery_site
>>> sitemanager = worldcookery_site.getSiteManager()
>>> sitemanager
<LocalSiteManager ++etc++site>
```
▼

We can also verify whether the kitchen tools utility has been created:

```
>>> u'kitchentools' in sitemanager
True
```
▼

Let us now test local component lookup. First we modify the local kitchen
tools utility so we can distinguish it from the global one:

```
>>> kitchentools = sitemanager[u'kitchentools']
>>> kitchentools.kitchen_tools.append(u'Spoon')
```
▼

Without making worldcookery_site's site manager the current component registry, the global utility will be found. It does not have the new kitchen

tool. After setting the site (this is what normally happens during traversal), we get the local utility:

```
>>> from zope.component import getUtility
>>> from worldcookery.interfaces import IKitchenTools
>>> u'Spoon' in getUtility(IKitchenTools).kitchen_tools
False
>>> from zope.app.component.site import setSite
>>> setSite(worldcookery_site)
>>> u'Spoon' in getUtility(IKitchenTools).kitchen_tools
True
```

As usual, this interpreter session has been added as a doctest to the worldcookery package (see site.txt).

Summary

- The API of sites is determined by the IPossibleSite interface.
- The zope.app.component.site module provides convenient classes for (possible) sites and local site managers.
- Component registries such as local site managers provide IComponentRegistry and IComponentLookup from the zope.component package. The API defined by those is similar to one of zope.component itself.

19

Indexing and Searching

In previous chapters we have substantially extended the *World Cookery* application. The application is ready for hobby cooks from around the world to add their favourite recipes, but what about visitors who might be looking for a specific recipe? There is currently no easy way for visitors to search for recipes. The *World Cookery* application definitely needs a search feature.

This chapter looks at Zope's indexing and searching capabilities plus some facilities that help us work with persistent objects.

19.1 Indexing and object references

You can no doubt tell by now that the ZODB is very different from relational databases. Thanks to its object-oriented approach, we can transparently store content as objects and organize it in object hierarchies, for example using Zope's containers.

However there are some things that the ZODB does not give us. For example it does not give the ability to uniquely identify a certain database record as you can with primary keys in relational databases. It also provides no indexing and searching functionality. These things are the responsibility of the application using the ZODB.

In this section we will discuss the machinery that Zope employs in order to allow arbitrary data to be indexed and searched.

General restrictions for indices

Putting it simply, indices use large mappings that identify search terms with objects. That way, when you are searching for objects that match a certain search term, you can find them easily in the index's mapping by using the search term as a key. Such a mapping could be in its simplest form a Python dictionary or a BTree in case you want it to be persistent and memory-efficient for large amounts of data.

When the index maps search terms to objects, it should not hold an actual reference to the object, though, for several reasons:

- The index cannot make the assumption that it can actually hold on to the object forever. If a persistent object is deleted from the folder and the index is still holding on to it, it would never be deleted.
- The information that the object holds might not really be maintained in this object. For example, the object might not be persistently stored in the ZODB but in fact dynamically created in order to represent a file on file system or a record in a relational database. In that case, holding on to the object is meaningless because you would not be holding on to the actual data source. Information is bound to get out of sync this way.
- A search might yield many objects that match the search criteria. When those objects are persistent in the ZODB, they would all have to be loaded into memory, just to create a list of search results. Searches that yield lots of large objects could consume an enormous amount of memory this way.
- Indices and catalogs must sort objects and perform set operations on them. Sorting and set operations on heterogeneous collections are unreliable, error-prone, and inefficient. They need homogeneous collections, ideally of a type for which there are Python and Zope optimizations available, like integers.

Unique integer IDs

Since indices are not allowed to store direct object references, they need to store something else that uniquely identifies objects instead. For the last reason mentioned above, they store integers. Each object is uniquely identified with an *integer ID*. That way, the indices do not store the object, but an integer that represents it. Managing integers is far easier than managing object references: they do not produce any of the problems mentioned above and they can be processed very fast even when you have lots of them.

Now that indices do not have to worry about object references, something else has to do it for them. Something that manages a one-to-one mapping from objects to integers. This is the responsibility of the *integer ID utility*. It can give an object a unique ID, and it can look it up again with this ID. Of course, the ID is only unique within one integer ID utility.

By introducing integer IDs, we have only deferred the problem of direct object references from the indices to the integer ID utility. The benefit is that indices only have to deal with integers. We still have to solve the problem of getting a hold of object references without introducing any of the problems above.

Weak references

Python has the concept of a *weak reference*. A weak reference lets you hold on to an object without actually owning a reference to it. Consider the following example of a strong reference:

```
$ python
>>> class Coffee(object):
...     def __del__(self):
...             print "Coffee was drunken."
>>> strong_coffee = Coffee()                                ▼
```

Now we get a weak reference to it:

```
>>> import weakref
>>> weak_coffee = weakref.ref(strong_coffee)                ▼
```

We can always get to the object by calling the weak reference:

```
>>> weak_coffee() is strong_coffee
True                                                        ▼
```

However, a weak reference will not keep the referenced object from being garbage collected when all strong references have disappeared:

```
>>> del strong_coffee
Coffee was drunken.
>>> weak_coffee() is None
True                                                        ■
```

Note that Python's built-in weak references cannot be persisted in the ZODB. If you want to weakly reference a persistent object from another one, use the `persistent.wref.WeakRef` class instead of `weakref.ref`.

Key references

The integer ID utility obviously needs to employ something like weak references to avoid holding on to objects directly. The only problem with weak references is that they are only hashable when the referenced object is hashable. In order to store a weak reference to the object in the mapping, the integer ID utility really needs to be able to compute a hash for the object, though, even when the object does not support it. That is why the integer ID utility stores *key references* instead of direct or weak references.

Key references are similar to weak references, except they promise support for __hash__ and __cmp__. The former is needed for key references to be usable as mapping keys. The latter is necessary if the mapping is a BTree (which it will be in most cases) because BTrees require a total ordering for their keys. That means they need to be comparable with one another.

Key references are created by adapting the object to `IKeyReference` from the `zope.app.keyreference` package. Zope already has an adapter that produces key references for persistent objects. For other kinds of objects (e.g. ones from object-relational mappers) that need also integer IDs, you would have to provide your own adapter.

Summary

- Unlike most relational databases, the ZODB does not provide indexing features. Indexing is the responsibility of the application.
- Indices must not store direct references to the objects they refer to. Instead they have to reference the indexed objects in a weak fashion, for performance reasons they use integer IDs.
- The integer ID utility is responsible for providing a one-to-one relationship from objects to integer IDs. The integer ID utility may not hold direct references to objects, either.
- Key references allow mappings such as the integer ID utility to weakly reference arbitrary objects, even when they are not hashable.

Rocky says...

Weak references will be no stranger to Java developers. The only thing to watch out for is the slightly different API for retrieving the object that the weak reference points to. For Python this is simply done by calling the weak reference itself as though it were a function.

19.2 The catalog and its indices

Searches are parametrized by queries. For example, if you were looking for classical symphonies written by Ludwig van Beethoven, the query would say: Look for objects of type "classical symphony" *and* of composer "Ludwig van Beethoven." Queries specify the parameters of a search, their constraints and their logical operations.

Ideally you have an index for each parameter in the query. For example, if you had a list of all pieces of music indexed according to their composition types, it would be easy to find all symphonies. Likewise, if you had the same list indexed according to composers, it would be easy to find all of Beethoven's pieces. The result of the query would in this case be the cross-section of both lists.

As you can see from this example, we need specialized indices for each kind of query parameter that searches can have. If, for instance, we want to be able to search objects that were created before, after or at a certain date,

we would need an index of the objects' creation date before we could make
that search.

The catalog

The Beethoven example shows that different object properties can be indexed
and combined in searches and that each property requires its own index.
Zope manages those indices and queries in a utility called the *catalog*. The
catalog is a local utility providing ICatalog from the zope.app.catalog
package. It is a container for indices. When queried, the catalog will invoke
each contained index as specified by the query, and build the cross-section of
the result. The catalog is Zope's "search engine."

Adding a catalog is straight-forward. Simply select *Catalog* from the *Add*
menu and provide a name, e.g. catalog. Since a catalog is registered as
a local utility, the typical place to put a catalog is the site manager. After
adding it, it needs to be registered in order to become active, just like all
other local utilities.

Since the indices inside the catalog need to deal with integer IDs, we
always need to create an integer ID utility along with a catalog. Simply select
Unique Id Utility from the *Add* menu and provide a name, e.g. intids. Also
do not forget to register it as a utility.

You can test whether the integer ID utility is correctly set up by adding a
recipe somewhere in the site. Afterwards, go back to the management interface of the integer ID utility. You will see that the number of registered objects
has increased by one. That is because the integer ID utility has an event subscriber set up for IObjectAddedEvent that registers each newly added
objects with the integer ID utility. Similarly, on IObjectRemovedEvent,
the object is removed from the integer ID utility again.

Text index

It is very common to do full text searches on websites. This requires indexing
objects with a text index. Zope provides such a text index in the zope.
index.text package. In the ZMI the index is addable via the *Add* menu
inside a catalog.

Let us add such a text index and call it fulltext. The add form which
is shown next lets us configure the index. The settings are typical for an
attribute index. Attribute indices index a particular attribute of objects. We
can select the interface that the attribute is part of, enter the attribute's
name and select whether the attribute is callable (in other words, whether
it is a method or not). An attribute index will only index those objects
that are adaptable to the specified interface. That way, we could index the
description attribute of the Dublin Core adapter easily by selecting the
IZopeDublinCore interface from the list. The index will automatically
adapt to that interface.

A common interface to choose for full text indexing is ISearchableText from the zope.index.text package. It only requires a getSearchableText method. Let us choose this interface from the list, enter the name of this method and check the callable option (because it is a method). The index becomes active immediately after adding it.

Now we only need to add an ISearchableText adapter that extracts the text for the full text index from recipes. It probably makes most sense to include the recipe title and the recipe description but not the ingredients and kitchen tools in this text. Example 19.2.1 shows the adapter implementation accordingly. Of course, it is also registered in configure.zcml with the following directive:

```
<adapter factory=".search.RecipeSearchableText" />
```

Example 19.2.1 Searchable text adapter for recipes (search.py)

```
1  from zope.interface import implements
2  from zope.component import adapts
3  from zope.index.text.interfaces import ISearchableText
4  from worldcookery.interfaces import IRecipe
5
6  class RecipeSearchableText(object):
7      """Extract searchable text from a recipe
8
9      Consider a simple recipe with some data:
10
11      >>> from worldcookery.recipe import Recipe
12      >>> kashu_maki = Recipe()
13      >>> kashu_maki.name = u'California roll'
14      >>> kashu_maki.ingredients = [u'cucumber', u'avocado']
15      >>> kashu_maki.description = u'The maki roll is made inside-out.'
16
17      The searchable text only includes the name and the description,
18      but not the ingredients:
19
20      >>> RecipeSearchableText(kashu_maki).getSearchableText()
21      u'California roll: The maki roll is made inside-out.'
22      """
23      implements(ISearchableText)
24      adapts(IRecipe)
25
26      def __init__(self, context):
27          self.context = context
28
29      def getSearchableText(self):
30          return self.context.name + u': ' + self.context.description
```

Automatically creating catalog and indices

In the previous chapter we provided hooks for setting up local utilities in newly created *WorldCookery* sites. If we wanted all *WorldCookery* sites to ship with search functionality enabled by default, we should make sure that every new site also includes a catalog with a configured text index. Example 19.2.2 shows the event subscriber programmatically sets up what we just did via the ZMI. It is registered in `configure.zcml` with the following directive:

```
<subscriber handler=".search.setupCatalogAndIndices" />
```

Summary

- Each object property that shall be part of a search query must have a corresponding index.
- Indices are managed by Zope's "search engine", the catalog. The catalog is a local utility and a container of indices. It relays queries to its indices and builds the cross-section of the results.
- Attribute indices index attributes of objects or their adapters.
- Zope ships with a text index that can perform full text indexing of text attributes.

Flashback

Those who know Zope 2 and the CMF are familiar with the catalog's predecessor in Zope 2, *ZCatalog*. It has inspired Zope 3's catalog in many ways, both in terms of good patterns as well as lessons learned.

For example, the catalog machinery in Zope 3 has been split up into several components and made much more flexible. Managing integer IDs, for instance, has been factored out into a separate component, making this functionality accessible to other parts of the application as well. Moreover, objects no longer need to be aware of the fact that they are indexed, thanks to events and adapters. In Zope 2, they need to explicitly enable cataloguing support which usually happens by inheriting from the `CatalogAware` mix-in class.

At the time of this writing, Zope 3's catalog is not yet as rich in features as the ZCatalog. The ZCatalog comes with more indices than Zope 3 does and has better support for lazy evaluation of large searches. Especially its efficiency has made it an indispensable tool in larger Zope 2 applications, for example CMF-based portals.

Example 19.2.2 Creating a catalog with text index programmatically
(`search.py`)

```
1   ...
2   from zope.component import adapter
3   from zope.app.intid.interfaces import IIntIds
4   from zope.app.intid import IntIds
5   from zope.app.catalog.interfaces import ICatalog
6   from zope.app.catalog.catalog import Catalog
7   from zope.app.catalog.text import TextIndex
8   from worldcookery.interfaces import INewWorldCookerySiteEvent
9
10  @adapter(INewWorldCookerySiteEvent)
11  def setupCatalogAndIndices(event):
12      sm = event.object.getSiteManager()
13
14      intids = IntIds()
15      sm['intids'] = intids
16      sm.registerUtility(intids, IIntIds)
17
18      catalog = Catalog()
19      sm['catalog'] = catalog
20      sm.registerUtility(catalog, ICatalog)
21
22      fulltext = TextIndex(
23          interface=ISearchableText,
24          field_name='getSearchableText',
25          field_callable=True
26          )
27      catalog[u'fulltext'] = fulltext
```

14–16. Every catalog needs an integer ID utility, so before we even add the catalog
we add the integer ID utility and register it.

18–20. The catalog is added and registered like any other local utility.

22–27. Here we create the text index so that it is already configured for the
`ISearchableText` interface. At least we add it to the catalog which is a
regular container and takes indices as subobjects.

Rocky says...

The functionality of Zope's catalog can most easily be compared to the
popular Apache Lucene search engine library for Java. Although Java
developers should appreciate being able to use the components that make
up the Zope catalog (such as the Integer ID utility) individually.

19.3 Querying the catalog for searching

Now that our *WorldCookery* site has a catalog with a configured full text index, we can provide the necessary user interface components for finding recipes. At a minimum, we would like to have a search form that allows the user to enter a query as well as a view that calls the catalog with the query and displays the search results.

Querying the catalog

First we must find out how to query the catalog. Let us do that with a simple example on the interpreter shell. We create two recipes objects with some searchable data:

```
$ python
>>> from worldcookery.recipe import Recipe
>>> california_roll = Recipe()
>>> california_roll.name = u'California roll'
>>> california_roll.description = u'Sushi'
>>> futomaki = Recipe()
>>> futomaki.name = u'Futomaki'
>>> futomaki.description = u'Sushi'                          ▼
```

We also register the `ISearchableText` adapter for recipes that we wrote earlier this chapter.

```
>>> from worldcookery.search import RecipeSearchableText
>>> from zope.component import provideAdapter
>>> provideAdapter(RecipeSearchableText)                     ▼
```

Now we need to index these recipes. The catalog requires the integer ID utility which in turn requires key references. As key references for persistent objects only work when these objects have been stored in the database already, we create a dummy database now and store the two recipes in it:

```
>>> from ZODB.DemoStorage import DemoStorage
>>> from ZODB import DB
>>> db = DB(DemoStorage())
>>> conn = db.open()
>>> root = conn.root()
>>> root['california_roll'] = california_roll
>>> root['futomaki'] = futomaki
>>> import transaction
>>> transaction.commit()                                     ▼
```

We must also register the key reference adapter for persistent objects:

```
>>> from zope.app.keyreference.persistent import \
...     KeyReferenceToPersistent
>>> from persistent.interfaces import IPersistent
>>> provideAdapter(KeyReferenceToPersistent, adapts=[IPersistent])  ▼
```

The recipes are now ready to be registered with the integer ID utility. This is usually dealt with automatically for all newly added objects via an event subscriber. Here we have to do it manually.

```
>>> from zope.app.intid import IntIds
>>> from zope.app.intid.interfaces import IIntIds
>>> from zope.component import provideUtility
>>> intids = IntIds()
>>> provideUtility(intids, IIntIds)
>>> intids.register(california_roll)
1935376408
>>> intids.register(futomaki)
1935376409                                                            ▼
```

Finally, we set up a catalog with a full text index inside.

```
>>> from zope.app.catalog.catalog import Catalog
>>> catalog = Catalog()
>>> from zope.app.catalog.text import TextIndex
>>> from zope.index.text.interfaces import ISearchableText
>>> catalog['fulltext'] = TextIndex(
...     interface=ISearchableText,
...     field_name='getSearchableText',
...     field_callable=True
... )                                                                 ▼
```

Now we have all the machinery in place to index the two recipes. This is done by calling the index_doc method on the catalog:

```
>>> catalog.index_doc(intids.getId(california_roll),
...                   california_roll)
>>> catalog.index_doc(intids.getId(futomaki), futomaki)              ▼
```

Normally, an event subscriber to IObjectModifiedEvent automatically indexes objects when they are modified.

Now we can finally query the catalog. This can be done by calling the apply method with a dictionary that contains the query. Each dictionary key corresponds to the name of an index inside the catalog. The apply method will query each catalog with that value and return a cross-section of the indices' result sets. In our case, a query would produce:

```
>>> list(catalog.apply({'fulltext': u'Sushi'}))
[1935376408, 1935376409]                                             ▼
```

As you can see, the apply method only returns a list of integer IDs. If we wanted to get the actual objects of the search result set, we could use the searchResults method instead. It returns an iterable of matching objects. Each iteration will look up the next object in the query. Unconsumed iterations will therefore not look up objects for no reason.

```
>>> for result in catalog.searchResults(fulltext=u'Sushi'):
...     print result.name
```

```
...
California roll
Futomaki                                                                    ■
```

A search viewlet

Now that we know how to query the catalog, we can use this knowledge in a couple of browser view components that allow searching the *World Cookery* site. First we need a search form. We can put a very simple search form inside a sidebar viewlet, as Example 19.3.1 demonstrates. Its configuration is omitted here, as it is nearly identical to the configuration of previously covered viewlets.

Example 19.3.1 Viewlet providing a simple search form for full text search on the *World Cookery* site (`skin/search.pt`)

```
1  <div id="search" class="box" i18n:domain="worldcookery">
2    <h1 i18n:translate="heading-search">Search this site</h1>
3
4    <form action="@@search.html" method="post">
5      <p>
6        <input type="text" name="query" value="" size="12" />
7        <input type="submit" value="Find"
8               i18n:attributes="value find-button" />
9      </p>
10   </form>
11 </div>
```

Example 19.3.2 shows the browser page that reacts to the search and queries the catalog. The Page Template that it uses to display the search results is shown in Example 19.3.3. We also omit the registration of the this browser page, since it is trivial.

We can now issue simple full text searches from the search box that is available on every page in the *World Cookery* application. We have thus reached the goal of letting users find recipes more easily. Our very simple catalog setup with only one index cannot handle complex searches because Zope does not yet have indices for all the various fields (e.g. date index for creation and modification date) that would be needed. However, due to the flexible architecture of the catalog, custom and third-party indices can easily be plugged in.

Example 19.3.2 Browser page responsible for issuing the search query
(`browser/search.py`)

```
1   from zope.component import getUtility, queryMultiAdapter
2   from zope.publisher.browser import BrowserPage
3   from zope.dublincore.interfaces import IZopeDublinCore
4   from zope.index.text.interfaces import ISearchableText
5   from zope.traversing.browser import absoluteURL
6   from zope.app.catalog.interfaces import ICatalog
7   from zope.app.pagetemplate import ViewPageTemplateFile
8
9   class SearchPage(BrowserPage):
10
11      def update(self, query):
12          catalog = getUtility(ICatalog)
13          self.results = catalog.searchResults(fulltext=query)
14
15      render = ViewPageTemplateFile('search.pt')
16
17      def __call__(self, query):
18          self.update(query)
19          return self.render()
20
21      def getResultsInfo(self):
22          for obj in self.results:
23              icon = queryMultiAdapter((obj, self.request), name='zmi_icon
                      ')
24              if icon is not None:
25                  icon = icon()
26
27              title = None
28              dc = IZopeDublinCore(obj, None)
29              if dc is not None:
30                  title = dc.title
31
32              text = ISearchableText(obj).getSearchableText()
33              if len(text) > 100:
34                  text = text[:97] + u'...'
35
36              yield {'icon': icon, 'title': title, 'text': text,
37                     'absolute_url': absoluteURL(obj, self.request)}
```

11–13.   Querying the catalog from a browser page is straight-forward. First we look
it up as a utility, then we call its `searchResults` method.

21–37.   Here we prepare some information on each object from the search results for
presentation in the template. This includes the Dublin Core title property, an
excerpt from the searchable text and an icon. Note that we also ensure efficient
handling of large result sets by using the `yield` statement, only yielding one
item at a time.

Example 19.3.3 Page Template displaying search results
(`browser/search.pt`)

```
 1  <html xmlns="http://www.w3.org/1999/xhtml"
 2         xmlns:tal="http://xml.zope.org/namespaces/tal"
 3         xmlns:metal="http://xml.zope.org/namespaces/metal"
 4         xmlns:i18n="http://xml.zope.org/namespaces/i18n"
 5         metal:use-macro="context/@@standard_macros/page"
 6         i18n:domain="worldcookery">
 7  <head>
 8    <title metal:fill-slot="title" i18n:translate="">Search results</title>
 9  </head>
10  <body>
11  <div metal:fill-slot="body">
12
13    <h2 i18n:translate="">Search results</h2>
14
15    <p i18n:translate="">
16      The search returned
17      <span i18n:name="number" tal:replace="python:len(view.results)" />
18      result(s).
19    </p>
20
21    <tal:loop repeat="result view/getResultsInfo">
22      <h3><img src="" tal:replace="structure result/icon" />
23          <a href="" tal:attributes="href result/absolute_url"
24             tal:content="result/title">title</a></h3>
25      <p><td tal:content="result/text" /></p>
26      <hr />
27    </tal:loop>
28
29  </div>
30  </body>
31  </html>
```

Summary

- Doing searches on the catalog involves looking it up as a utility and calling its `searchResults` method. Each keyword parameter passes the query for an index in the catalog.
- The resulting object of a catalog query is an iterable of objects matching the query. Lazy evaluation inside the iterator ensure that only one object is looked up with the integer ID utility at a time.

19.4 Database generations

In the previous chapter we added code that allowed us to create local components along with a new *WorldCookery* site. We used this to automatically add
a kitchen tool utility to every new site manager. In this chapter, we extended
that so that newly created sites now feature an integer ID utility and a catalog with a configured text index. But what about the sites we have already
created? They do not benefit from the additional code in this chapter.

Zope solves this problem with *database generations*. Each generation describe the database schema of a particular version of an application. For example, the database schema of the *World Cookery* application changed from
the previous chapter to this chapter because newly created *WorldCookery*
sites now contain more local utilities than in the previous chapter. We need
a way to evolve from the previous schema to the current one.

Schema managers

Database generations and their evolution are handled by schema managers.
These are utilities that tell Zope which database generation the application
requires in its current version. The schema manager also knows how to evolve
from an older generation to a newer one. The evolving usually happens in evolution scripts. Let us write such a script to evolve from the previous chapter's
generation to the current one.

First, we create a subpackage to our `worldcookery` application called
`generations`. This package will contain the evolution scripts (we expect
that the upcoming chapters will require more database generations). Then
we need to provide the schema manager utility. We can use the generic implementation from the `zope.app.generations` package. It is shown in
Example 19.4.1.

Before we register this schema manager, we need to tell Zope that the
initial database generation is 0. This is very important because judging from
our schema manager, Zope would think that the current generation is 1.
Therefore, we first configure a schema manager that sets the current generation to 0, as shown in Example 19.4.2. Then we start Zope to have the
generation stored in the ZODB. We can assure ourselves that the current
database generation for the *World Cookery* application is indeed 0 by going
to the *Database Schemas* tab of the application process controller (*Manage
process*).

After having done this, we can enable the schema manager from Example
19.4.1. Visiting the *Database Schemas* tab again will allow us to evolve the
database schema, as shown in Figure 19.1. Of course, we first need to write
an evolution script.

Example 19.4.1 Database schema manager for the *World Cookery* application (generations/__init__.py)

```
1  from zope.app.generations.generations import SchemaManager
2
3  WorldCookerySchemaManager = SchemaManager(
4      minimum_generation=0,
5      generation=1,
6      package_name='worldcookery.generations'
7      )
```

4. The minimum generation specifies the lowest database generation that is absolutely needed to run the application. Upon startup, Zope will evolve the database to the minimum generation if necessary. All other generations need to be manually evolved. Since we have not yet had any previous generations, we can leave this at its default value, zero.

5. This parameter specifies the current generation of the application. This is generation 1, the generation of this chapter. Generation 0 is the generation of the previous chapter.

6. Here we specify the name of the package where the schema manager can find the evolution scripts. Evolution scripts have to be named evolveN.py where N is the generation that the script evolves to.

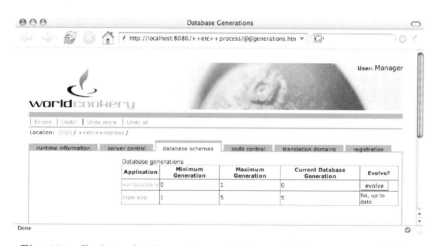

Fig. 19.1. Evolving database schemas in the application process controller.

Evolution scripts

Now we only need to provide the evolution script from generation 0 to 1. In generation 0, *WorldCookery* had no integer ID utility and catalog in their site

Example 19.4.2 Configuring database schema managers for the *World Cookery* application (`generations/configure.zcml`)

```
1   <configure xmlns="http://namespaces.zope.org/zope">
2
3     <utility
4         factory="zope.app.generations.generations.SchemaManager"
5         name="worldcookery"
6         />
7
8     <!-- Disable the utility above and enable this one in order to
9          evolve the database schema
10    <utility
11        component=".WorldCookerySchemaManager"
12        name="worldcookery"
13        />
14    -->
15
16  </configure>
```

3–6. This initial database manager is needed to set the initial database generation to 0. Leave this manager enabled and start Zope once. This will write the initial generation into the database.

10–13. After having set the initial generation in the database, disable the first schema manager and enable this one. You will then be able to evolve to generation 1, provided an evolution script exists.

---

manager. In generation 1 they do. Our evolution script therefore has to find all *WorldCookery* sites and add the catalog and integer ID utility if necessary. It should then also look for recipes and index them.

Summary

- Applications can track changes in their database schemas via generations. A generation corresponds to a database schema of a particular version of an application.
- Application-specific schema managers tell Zope the current database generation of the application. They also provide means to evolve the database from one generation to another.
- The generic schema manager implementation defers the database evolution to evolution scripts.
- The application process controller provides an overview over database generations. Evolution scripts can be invoked through its user interface.

Example 19.4.3 Evolution script for generation 1
(generations/evolve1.py)

```
1   from zope.component.interfaces import ObjectEvent
2   from zope.app.zopeappgenerations import getRootFolder
3   from zope.app.generations.utility import findObjectsProviding
4   from zope.app.intid import addIntIdSubscriber
5   from zope.app.catalog.catalog import indexDocSubscriber
6   from zope.app.component.site import setSite
7   from worldcookery.interfaces import IRecipe, IWorldCookerySite
8   from worldcookery.search import setupCatalogAndIndices
9
10  def evolve(context):
11      """Setup catalog and indices for fulltext search."""
12      root = getRootFolder(context)
13      for site in findObjectsProviding(root, IWorldCookerySite):
14          sm = site.getSiteManager()
15          if u'catalog' not in sm:
16              setupCatalogAndIndices(ObjectEvent(site))
17
18              setSite(site)
19              for recipe in findObjectsProviding(site, IRecipe):
20                  addIntIdSubscriber(recipe, ObjectEvent(recipe))
21                  indexDocSubscriber(ObjectEvent(recipe))
22              setSite(None)
```

10. Evolution scripts are supposed to have an `evolve` function. It takes one parameter, a context. The context provides access to the ZODB connection object via the `connection` attribute.

13. The `findObjectsProviding` function is a great helper to walk object hierarchies and find objects providing a certain interface along the way. Here we are looping through all *WorldCookery* site objects. Be aware that `findObjectsProviding` only walks container hierarchies, though. It does not find arbitrary objects (such as attributes of other objects), unless they are contained in a container.

16, 20, and 21. In order to provoke the necessary changes (adding the utilities and indexing of recipes), we directly call the subscribers that would normally have been invoked if the catalog had already been in place.

18 and 22. During the registration with the integer ID utility and the indexation of recipe objects, the newly created catalog and integer ID utility must be reachable with component lookup. We therefore tell the Component Architecture to take the site in question as the current site. That way, all component lookup will be directed to its site manager first.

20

Browser Sessions

In HTTP, the only way clients can interact with a server is through individual actions called requests. The web application cannot make any assumption about when or whether the client will send the next request or what that next request will entail. This makes HTTP a state-less protocol. A common technique to associate state on the server with HTTP clients are *sessions*. They are a pattern implemented by many web application servers in which arbitrary data that persists from request to request is associated with a client, independent of any user authorization. Zope provides flexible components to support this pattern.

20.1 Identifying clients

Browser cookies allow the web application to associate data with a particular client by having the client store the data. The client will then send that data with every subsequent request. However, the amount of data that can be effectively stored in a cookie is limited. When you need to associate larger amounts of data or more complex data, it is better to store it on the server.

Sessions allow you to temporarily store such data on the server side without requiring the user to authenticate first. However, this requires that clients can be identified uniquely so that each time the client sends a request, the same set of data is associated with it again. Zope does this by adapting the request to IClientId from the zope.app.session package. Client IDs only need to have a __str__ method. In other words, they must be equivalent to strings.[1]

There are several ways to identify clients that are used with varying success. The following data from a request can be used for identification:

---

[1] In other systems, the client ID is often referred to as the session ID.

IP addresses. Using the client's IP address for client identification is often
brittle because several clients could share the same IP address, for example when they are running on a multi-user system, or connecting through
an HTTP proxy or from a private network. This simple approach still is
useful sometimes, such as when building intranet applications. Intranets
usually operate in a private network where these problems are less likely
to occur.

URL elements. The application can create an identifier and assign it to the
client by creating URLs with the identifier in them. Many online shops
follow this approach because it works with most clients. There is no IP
address problem, nor is the approach dependent on browser cookies or
client-side features. The problem with this approach is that URLs become
less readable and harder to maintain. All URLs within the application
must be generated to contain the identifier. Furthermore, copy and past-
ing as well as bookmarking a URL introduces the risk of spoofing someone
else's session. Of course, the application could always double-check client
identifiers against another criterion such as the IP address. It should also
expire identifiers after a while.

Browser cookies. The application assigns a client identifier and stores it in a
cookie. This approach is the most straight-forward and the most transparent. However, it requires that the client supports cookies. Some older
or non-browser clients do not support cookies, and some browsers have
cookies switched off deliberately. Most browsers can be expected to support cookies without problems, though.

Client ID manager

Zope's default `IClientId` adapter defers the management of client IDs to a
utility providing `IClientIdManager`. The reason is that two of the three
client identification techniques discussed above require the client IDs to be
managed on the server side so that they can be expired. Such management
of client IDs is best done in a utility. Usually, a local utility is used because
different sites within the same Zope instance can then use different ways
of client identification. The `IClientId` adapter is still used for actually
retrieving the client ID, but the business logic is in the utility.

Let us look at a simple example. IP-based client identification seems simple enough to try it out on the interpreter prompt. First we register Zope's
standard `IClientId` adapter:

```
$ python
>>> from zope.app.session.session import ClientId
>>> from zope.component import provideAdapter
>>> provideAdapter(ClientId)                                    ▼
```

The adapter will defer to the `IClientIdManager` utility which we have to provide. This very simple utility just extracts the client's IP address from the request and returns it as the client identifier:

```
>>> from zope.app.session.interfaces import IClientIdManager
>>> from zope.interface import implements
>>> class IPClientIdManager(object):
...     implements(IClientIdManager)
...     def getClientId(self, request):
...         return request['REMOTE_ADDR']
...
>>> from zope.component import provideUtility
>>> provideUtility(IPClientIdManager())                          ▼
```

Now we can create a couple of test requests and see that our custom client identification mechanism correctly identifies clients based on their IP address:

```
>>> from zope.publisher.browser import TestRequest
>>> request1 = TestRequest(environ={'REMOTE_ADDR': '192.168.1.10'})
>>> request2 = TestRequest(environ={'REMOTE_ADDR': '192.168.1.20'})
>>> from zope.app.session.interfaces import IClientId
>>> IClientId(request1)
'192.168.1.10'
>>> IClientId(request2)
'192.168.1.20'                                                   ▼
```

A more sophisticated IP-based identification mechanism would perhaps combine the IP address with the HTTP *User-Agent* header to prevent two different client programs on the same system from being identified as one.

Zope provides a standard `IClientIdManager` implementation that performs identification based on browser cookies. It is a local utility so that different sites within a Zope instance can issue cookies with different prefixes and different lifetimes. To add this utility, select *Cookie Client Id Manager* from the *Add* menu. After adding it you can figure the utility by setting a prefix for the cookie name and the cookie life time in seconds. For our *World Cookery* application it seems sensible to choose `worldcookery` for the prefix. Session cookie lifetimes are typically chosen anywhere between 600 and 3600 seconds. Last but not least, the utility needs to be registered to be active.

Summary

- Sessions provide a way to associate larger or more complex amounts of data with a client than what is possible with browser cookies by storing data on the server side.
- Clients need to be identified uniquely so that data from previous requests can be associated with the same client again.

- Clients can be identified using various mechanisms, such as their IP address, explicit URL elements or browser cookies. The latter is most straight-forward with modern browser clients.
- Zope identifies clients by adapting the request to `IClientId`. Client IDs are equivalent to strings and can be converted to strings.
- Zope's default `IClientId` adapter defers to a (typically local) utility for `IClientIdManager`. The default implementation for that utility identifies clients via cookies.

Rocky says...

Developers using J2EE will probably notice a few more implementation details than they are accustomed to dealing with. Normally these details are only required when dealing with specific requirements. But the highly useful aspect here is that every aspect of session handling can be extended with reusable components independently from the rest of your application.

20.2 Storing session data

Applications use sessions to store data on the server side when the data they want to associate with clients is too complex to fit in a cookie. Such complex data can easily be stored in the database instead. Using the ZODB is especially tempting because it makes working with session data as flexible as working with any other type of data (such as content components). In addition, you have all the benefits you get from the ZODB such as transaction support.

Using the ZODB may become a problem when writes are too frequent. Normal websites have far more read transactions than write transactions. Modifying session data on every request would change that dramatically and might create scalability issues. If modifications to session data needs to happen frequently, you should consider a more scalable approach, perhaps one that does not promise transactional storage but is more scalable instead. Anything from a fast relational database to simple files on the filesystem might be an option here.

Session data containers

Zope's session framework abstracts data storage into session data containers. These are utilities providing `ISessionDataContainer` from the `zope.`

`app.session` package. The utilities are usually local so that the storage policy can be changed within each site. Furthermore, if the session data container stores the data persistently in the ZODB, it needs to be a local persistent utility anyway.

Zope comes with two implementations of the session data container. One of them, *Persistent Session Data Container*, stores the data persistently in the ZODB. The other one, *RAM Session Data Container* uses a memory-based ZODB storage to store session data in RAM. While the latter may certainly be faster for frequent access, be aware of the fact that it also introduces other scalability problems. For example, it pretty much rules out the usage of load balancers, unless server affinity is used.

Let us use the persistent session data container in our example application, being well aware of the risks it poses. In the next section where we will implement components that make use of sessions we will have to make sure that we do not use the session storage in an inefficient way.

Configuring the persistent session data container

Session data containers have at least two configurable settings. The *timeout* specifies the number of seconds after which session data is declared stale and scheduled for removal. The *resolution* defines a time period in seconds that the storage will wait until it does the next write action (which also includes deleting stale session data). Session data will live at least as long as the resolution period, though the actual timeout should always be set higher than the resolution. The default settings are 3600 seconds for the timeout and 300 seconds for the resolution period.

To ensure that *WorldCookery* sites are always equipped with client ID managers and session data containers, we add a new subscriber to `INewWorldCookerySiteEvent` that adds them to all new sites. The code is shown in Example 20.2.1. The registration of the subscriber happens with a standard `subscriber` directive, just like any of the subscribers we have written before.

We should also make sure that older sites are properly evolved by bumping the current database generation to 2 in the definition of `WorldCookerySchemaManager` and adding an evolution script for the generation. That evolution script is shown in Example 20.2.2.

Summary

- Session data can be stored in various ways with varying consequences regarding scalability.
- Using the ZODB to store session data allows you to store just about anything in sessions. However, it introduces scalability issues. Like

Example 20.2.1 Creating client ID manager and session data containers programmatically (session.py)

```
1  from zope.component import adapter
2  from zope.app.session.http import ICookieClientIdManager
3  from zope.app.session.http import CookieClientIdManager
4  from zope.app.session.interfaces import ISessionDataContainer
5  from zope.app.session.session import PersistentSessionDataContainer
6  from worldcookery.interfaces import INewWorldCookerySiteEvent
7
8  @adapter(INewWorldCookerySiteEvent)
9  def setUpClientIdAndSessionDataContainer(event):
10     sm = event.object.getSiteManager()
11
12     clientids = CookieClientIdManager()
13     clientids.namespace = u'worldcookery'
14     clientids.cookieLifetime = 3600
15     sm['clientids'] = clientids
16     sm.registerUtility(sm['clientids'], ICookieClientIdManager)
17
18     session_data = PersistentSessionDataContainer()
19     session_data.timeout = 3600
20     session_data.resolution = 5
21     sm['session_data'] = session_data
22     sm.registerUtility(sm['session_data'], ISessionDataContainer)
```

13–14 and 19–20. We have programmatically instantiated and registered local utilities before, this time it is not much different. In these lines, we only provide some default settings for the client ID manager and the session data container.

Example 20.2.2 Evolution script for generation 2 (generations/evolve2.py)

```
1  from zope.component.interfaces import ObjectEvent
2  from zope.app.zopeappgenerations import getRootFolder
3  from zope.app.generations.utility import findObjectsProviding
4  from worldcookery.interfaces import IWorldCookerySite
5  from worldcookery.session import setUpClientIdAndSessionDataContainer
6
7  def evolve(context):
8      """Setup client ID manager and session data container."""
9      root = getRootFolder(context)
10     for site in findObjectsProviding(root, IWorldCookerySite):
11         sm = site.getSiteManager()
12         if u'session_data' not in sm:
13             setUpClientIdAndSessionDataContainer(ObjectEvent(site))
```

most transactional databases, the ZODB does not handle frequent write transactions very well.

- Zope's session machinery stores session data in session data containers.
- There are two default implementations of session data containers, one that stores data in a transactional RAM storage, and one that stores data in the regular ZODB storage.

Flashback

Zope 2 users may find that Zope 3's session terminology sounds familiar. In Zope 2, a *browser ID manager* identifies clients and a *session data manager* provides access to the storage. However, the session data manager is not the storage itself. It only looks up the storage by traversing a given path in the object database. By default this path points to a *transient object container* placed in a *temporary folder*. Temporary folders store their data in a RAM-based ZODB storage while transient object containers handle data that is to be expired after a user-specified amount of time. It is possible to point the data manager to a folder inside the persistent object tree to avoid storing session data in memory.

20.3 Using sessions

We have talked about the two requisites for dealing with sessions, identifying clients and storing session data. We discussed different approaches and their advantages and disadvantages. Let us put sessions into use now.

Accessing session data

Components using sessions rarely have to operate with the `IClientId` adapter and the `ISessionDataContainer` utility directly. Instead they can simply adapt the request to `ISession`. This adapter takes care of identifying the client and storing data in the session data container. `ISession` objects fulfil the Python mapping API. In other words, they behave like dictionaries.

Applications that want to store session data are supposed to store their data under an application-specific key, much like with annotations. This is demonstrated by continuing the interpreter example session from Section 20.2. First we register a session data container:

```
>>> from zope.app.session.session import \
...     PersistentSessionDataContainer
>>> from zope.app.session.interfaces import ISessionDataContainer
>>> from zope.component import provideUtility
>>> provideUtility(PersistentSessionDataContainer(),
...                  ISessionDataContainer)                          ▼
```

Now we have to register the ISession adapter:

```
>>> from zope.app.session.session import Session
>>> from zope.component import provideAdapter
>>> provideAdapter(Session)                                          ▼
```

Finally, we can associate some data with a particular request. Note that we do not store the data directly on the ISession object but in the worldcookery subitem to prevent clashes with other applications:

```
>>> session = ISession(request1)['worldcookery']
>>> session['message'] = u"Remember me!"                             ▼
```

We can access the data again via the ISession adapter during subsequent requests with the same client ID. Other clients will not see the data:

```
>>> request3 = TestRequest(environ={'REMOTE_ADDR': '192.168.1.10'})
>>> ISession(request3)['worldcookery']['message']
u'Remember me!'
>>> ISession(request2)['worldcookery']['message']
Traceback (most recent call last):
  ...
KeyError: 'message'
```

Common example for sessions

A typical application of sessions is to remember objects as the visitor browses through the site. In an online shop, for example, this would be the virtual shopping cart. The visitor can add and remove items from the list and do something with it later, e.g. place an order of the products in the shopping cart. Logging in is not necessarily required for any of these actions.

Let us extend the demo application so that visitors can "remember" and go back to recipes they like. The *World Cookery* application will remember the recipes for them in a session. If the recipes were products and the *World Cookery* application were an online shop, this would be very much like a shopping cart implementation. Note that this usage of sessions meets the requirements of any ZODB-based storage: Writes are infrequent because they only happen when the user specifically wants to remember a recipe.

To reference the objects that are to be "remembered", we will avoid direct object references. That way, the life time of remembered objects is not affected by the fact that they are referenced by a session. Avoiding direct object references also allows us to reference arbitrary objects that do not necessarily live in the ZODB. As we have learned in the previous chapter, integer IDs are perfect for such kinds of references.

The component that provides the user interface and talks to the session machinery is once again a viewlet. Like the ratings viewlet in Chapter 14, it is a complex viewlet that not only renders part of the application's UI but also acts upon a request when the user chooses to remember or forget an item. The implementation of the viewlet is shown in Example 20.3.1. The Page Template that renders the viewlet is shown in Example 20.3.2.

Fig. 20.1. Remembering recipes in a session.

Summary

- Session data can be stored by adapting the request to ISession. Using the client ID manager and the session data container directly is not necessary.
- In Page Templates, session data can be accessed through the session TALES namespace adapter.
- In order to prevent clashes with other applications, session data must be stored under an application-specific key.

Example 20.3.1 Viewlet that allows users to "remember" objects on the
web site (`skin/remember.py`)

```python
1   from persistent.list import PersistentList
2   from zope.component import getUtility
3   from zope.viewlet.viewlet import ViewletBase
4   from zope.exceptions import UserError
5   from zope.i18nmessageid import MessageFactory
6   _ = MessageFactory('worldcookery')
7
8   from zope.app.pagetemplate import ViewPageTemplateFile
9   from zope.app.session.interfaces import ISession
10  from zope.app.intid.interfaces import IIntIds
11
12  KEY = 'worldcookery'
13
14  class RememberViewlet(ViewletBase):
15
16      def update(self):
17          remember = self.request.form.get('worldcookery.remember')
18          if remember is not None:
19              intid = getUtility(IIntIds).queryId(self.context)
20              if intid is None:
21                  raise UserError(_(u"This object cannot be remembered."))
22              session = ISession(self.request)[KEY]
23              remembered = session.setdefault('remembered', PersistentList
                    ())
24              if intid in remembered:
25                  raise UserError(_(u"This object is already remembered."))
26              remembered.append(intid)
27
28          forget = self.request.form.get('worldcookery.forget')
29          if forget is not None:
30              forget = int(forget)
31              session = ISession(self.request)[KEY]
32              remembered = session.get('remembered', [])
33              if forget not in remembered:
34                  raise UserError(_(u"Cannot forget an object that was "
35                                    u"not remembered."))
36              remembered.remove(forget)
37
38      render = ViewPageTemplateFile('remember.pt')
39
40      def getRememberedItems(self):
41          intids = getUtility(IIntIds)
42          session = ISession(self.request)[KEY]
43          remembered = session.get('remembered', [])
44          return ({'id': intid, 'object': intids.queryObject(intid)}
45                      for intid in remembered)
```

12 and 22.   Session data should be stored in an application-specific subitem of the
ISession adapter. The dotted package name of the application can serve as
the key. As with annotations, it is always a good idea to define this as a de
facto string constant.

Example 20.3.1 (continued)

1 and 23. We store the integer IDs of the remembered objects in a persistent list so that changes to the list are automatically stored. Since we do not expect to remember more than a couple of objects at a time, it is not necessary to use a BTree set here.

40–45. This helper will be used by the Page Template to render a list of already remembered objects.

Example 20.3.2 Template rendering the "remember" viewlet (skin/remember.pt)

```
1   <div id="ratings" class="box" i18n:domain="worldcookery">
2     <h1 i18n:translate="heading-remember">Remember</h1>
3
4     <form action="" tal:attributes="action request/getURL" method="post">
5       <input type="submit" name="worldcookery.remember"
6              value="Remember this item"
7              i18n:attributes="value remember-button"
8              />
9
10      <p tal:condition="request/session:worldcookery/remembered | nothing">
11        <strong i18n:translate="heading-remembered-items">
12          Remembered items:
13        </strong>
14      </p>
15
16      <ul>
17        <li tal:repeat="item view/getRememberedItems">
18          <a href="" tal:attributes="href item/object/@@absolute_url"
19             tal:content="item/object/zope:title">object title</a>
20          (<a href="" tal:attributes="href string:${request/getURL}?
                 worldcookery.forget=${item/id}">x</a>)
21        </li>
22      </ul>
23    </form>
24
25  </div>
```

10. Session data can also be accessed from Page Templates using the session TALES namespace adapter which is the ZPT equivalent to the ISession adapter. Here we use the adapter to check whether any objects have been remembered.

17. To present a list of already remembered objects we use the helper method from the viewlet class instead of using the TALES namespace adapter. The reason is that the session only stores integer IDs of the objects which we need to convert back to objects. This is better done in Python code.

21

Security

This chapter gives you a look at Zope's security architecture. Security is crucial to most web applications, especially when they are exposed to the Internet. This discussion has been postponed until now for two reasons. Firstly, we wanted to get started on the example application without having to worry too much about security initially. Secondly, understanding the security system requires an understanding of how Zope itself works. For example, understanding the concept of a trusted adapter requires an understanding of the fundamental concept of an adapter.

21.1 Overview

Zope allows us to separate security concerns from functionality. That way components implementing application functionality usually do not have to deal with security directly. Zope makes its security machinery flexible by breaking it into several high-level and low-level components that interact with each other. This allows us to customize certain security components and alter the behaviour of the overall security machinery.

In this section we will introduce the different types of security components before we dive into hands-on examples on the interpreter shell. The purpose of this is not to improve the security of our example application. Rather, it should make us understand how security components interact, which is the key to providing custom security implementations and ensuring applications are secure overall.

High-level components

Zope's security system relies on several high-level components which influence the way security checking is performed. They are also projections of Zope's fundamental security concepts. Some of these components are likely to be customized in applications with specific requirements regarding security, unlike low-level components which do not determine security behaviour as much. The following list gives detailed definitions and explanations for each security component. If not specified otherwise, the described machinery is defined in the `zope.security` package.

Permission Permissions protect component functionality. Usually they describe a certain action and the kind of access that is required to carry it out. Components and component look-up can be protected by permissions.

Principal Any entity that interacts with the application is called a principal. This can be an unauthenticated browser client, a user who logged in using some form of credentials, or some other entity. Principals take place in participations. They are described by the `IPrincipal` interface.

Group A group is a special type of principal. Groups contain principals, and since groups are principals themselves, groups can also contain other groups. Unlike other principals, groups usually do not authenticate with the system. Whether or not a principal inherits the grants of its groups is up to the security policy. Groups are described by the `IGroup` interface.

Participation Participations are the means by which a single principal interacts with the system in terms of security. A Zope request, for example, is a participation. Participations are described by the `IParticipation` interface.

Interaction An interaction aggregates all current participations. Most importantly, interactions are the actual components that check whether principals have a certain permission on an object. Usually, interactions begin with an incoming request and end when the response has been sent out to the client. In a way they are to security what transactions are to storages. Interactions provide `IInteraction`.

Security policy Security policies are simple callables that return an interaction. By registering a custom security policy one can influence which interaction implementation is being used, thus the way security checking is performed. Usually, a security policy is a class *providing* `ISecurityPolicy` and *implementing* `IInteraction` (classes are callables which return an instance of themselves). Simple security policies reside in `zope.security.simplepolicies`. The default one for the Zope application server can be found under `zope.app.securitypolicy`.

Low-level components

The following components operate on a low level. They do much of the work in Zope's security system and thus make it possible to abstract security issues into more high-level components. They also allow us to work with objects in security contexts transparently. These components are generally not customized because the high-level security components depend on them.

Security proxy Any object that is exposed to security-sensitive components such as views is wrapped in a security proxy. These proxies protect the object against unauthorized access and modification. The checking whether an object access is authorized or not is delegated to checkers. Objects have to be wrapped in security proxies explicitly. The publication object takes care of this during traversal when an object is published to the web. Once an object is wrapped, all objects retrieved from it through attribute access or method calls are proxied as well. Immutable objects such as strings and tuples are not wrapped since they cannot be changed anyway. Security proxies may not be persisted.

Checker Checkers perform the security checking for security proxies. A security proxy asks the checker whether a certain action is allowed on an object. The checker can decide whether the access is authorized based on many criteria. The most common checker is the permission-based one that looks up a permission that is required for the action in question and then asks the interaction whether the current participants have that permission on the object.

Checkers and security proxies

To give you an idea how these components work together, let us have them interact on the interactive interpreter shell. We start out with defining a checker for our `Recipe` class. We would normally do that with security declarations in ZCML using the `require` directive. For this example we simply protect one attribute, for example `name`, with an arbitrary permission that is not `zope.Public`:

```
$ python
>>> from worldcookery.recipe import Recipe
>>> from zope.security.checker import NamesChecker, defineChecker
>>> defineChecker(Recipe, NamesChecker(('name',),
...                                    'some.permission'))          ▼
```

Now we slip into the role of the publication object and "find" a recipe object. We do what we must do to protect it towards user-invoked code: We wrap it in a security proxy. That is done using `ProxyFactory`. Note that we do not provide any information about *how* the object will be protected. That is a different concern and it is handled by the checker we just defined.

```
>>> pudding = Recipe()
>>> pudding.name = u'Pudding'
>>> from zope.security.proxy import ProxyFactory
>>> wrapped_pudding = ProxyFactory(pudding)                          ▼
```

You might remember contained proxies from Chapter 15. Security proxies are a different flavour of proxy but essentially behave very much like security proxies. To the outside, a wrapped object looks just like the original. Only the object's type tells the real story:

```
>>> wrapped_pudding
<worldcookery.recipe.Recipe object at 0x35cd70>
>>> type(wrapped_pudding)
<type 'zope.security._proxy._Proxy'>                                 ▼
```

Note that at this point any attribute that was not protected with a permission cannot be accessed anymore. Any attempt will result in a ForbiddenAttribute error:

```
>>> wrapped_pudding.ingredients
Traceback (most recent call last):
...
zope.security.interfaces.ForbiddenAttribute:
('ingredients', <worldcookery.recipe.Recipe object at 0x35cd70>)    ▼
```

Starting and ending interactions

When we now slip into the role of user-invoked code that has to operate on the wrapped object, for example a browser view, we realize very quickly that we forgot to start an interaction:

```
>>> wrapped_pudding.name
Traceback (most recent call last):
...
AttributeError: 'zope.thread.local' object has no attribute
'interaction'                                                       ▼
```

As this example demonstrates, all components that have to deal with security-proxied objects need to be executed during an interaction. A new interaction is started using the newInteraction function. This function executes the security policy callable which is ParanoidSecurityPolicy by default. This particular security policy implementation only ever allows participations involving the system user, a special principal for carrying out system activities. Note that when the Zope application server starts up, it configures a different security policy by default, found in zope.app.securitypolicy, which is more sensible for real applications. The

`ParanoidSecurityPolicy` is only the default in the absence of any such configuration being loaded.

In order to simulate what happens when a participant does not have the authorization to access an attribute, we start an interaction with a participation that does not have any principal. For `ParanoidSecurityPolicy`, such a participation should definitely not suffice for access:

```
>>> class InterpreterParticipation(object):
...         interaction = principal = None
...
>>> from zope.security.management import newInteraction
>>> newInteraction(InterpreterParticipation())           ▼
```

As expected, we are not allowed to access the name attribute. We are also not allowed to set it:

```
>>> from zope.security import canAccess, canWrite
>>> canAccess(wrapped_pudding, 'name')
False
>>> canWrite(wrapped_pudding, 'name')
False                                                    ▼
```

Notice that we use `canAccess` and `canWrite` in this example. These two functions are reliable ways to determine if the current interaction can access a given method or attribute value, or can write a given attribute value. Notice that even if a method changes an object (e.g. a container's `__setitem__`), from the perspective of this API, you ask whether the current interaction can access the method, not write the method.

If we now try to access the attribute even though we are not allowed to, we will get an `Unauthorized` error:

```
>>> wrapped_pudding.name
Traceback (most recent call last):
...
zope.security.interfaces.Unauthorized: ('name', 'some.permission')  ▼
```

Note that there is a vast difference between `Unauthorized` and `ForbiddenAttribute`! The latter indicates that code is trying to access an attribute that has no security declarations. That means either the code is accessing something it is not supposed to access, or the application is missing some important security declarations. `Unauthorized`, on the other hand, indicates that the privileges of the current interaction's participations are not sufficient to access a properly protected attribute with security declarations.

If we wanted to be authorized to access the attribute we would have to satisfy `ParanoidSecurityPolicy`. The way to do that is to either add a system user participation to the current interaction or to create a new interaction with that participation. If we wanted to do the latter, we are told that we first need to end the existing interaction.

```
>>> from zope.app.appsetup.appsetup import \
...     SystemConfigurationParticipation
>>> newInteraction(SystemConfigurationParticipation())
Traceback (most recent call last):
...
AssertionError: newInteraction called while another interaction is
active:
...                                                             ▼
```

As with transactions in a database system, there can only ever be one current interaction. In the case of interactions, this is a rule that applies per thread. An interaction is ended with the endInteraction function. After having called this function we can create an interaction in which the system user participates:

```
>>> from zope.security.management import endInteraction
>>> endInteraction()
>>> newInteraction(SystemConfigurationParticipation())          ▼
```

We are authorized for accessing the attribute now. Modifying it is still not allowed because we only protected it for access, not for writing.

```
>>> canAccess(wrapped_pudding, 'name')
True
>>> wrapped_pudding.name
u'Pudding'
>>> canWrite(wrapped_pudding, 'name')
False                                                           ■
```

When does Zope proxy objects?

In general, Zope creates proxies to protect objects when they are exposed to security-sensitive environments. You can think of security proxies as space suits in which objects are wrapped before they are sent into outer space. There are a few basic types that are not proxied because they are immutable by design. Among these are all number and string types (including Booleans and i18n messages). Zope developers sometimes jokingly refer to these objects as "rocks" because they do not need space suits.

In practice, the security proxying happens in Zope's publication machinery. It wraps all objects found during traversal, which includes both content objects and views. That way, the publisher will only be able to publish a view if the current principal has the permissions to access the (proxied) view object. Similarly, the view will only be able to perform actions on its (proxied) context if the principal has permissions for this. It may very well be that the principal has sufficient privileges to access a view, but not the underlying content object. The security machinery will ensure that access is still denied by raising an Unauthorized exception.

Summary

- Zope's security system relies on low-level and high-level components. The former are seldom customized, the latter are intended to be customized for complex security requirements.
- Principals (users) participate in interactions, for example through a request.
- Components that are found during traversal (content objects, views) are wrapped in security proxies to protect them from unauthorized access.
- Security proxies delegate the security checking to checkers which can decide authorization based on different circumstances, usually the privileges of the participants in an interaction.
- Interactions, which decide whether a participant in an interaction (a principal) is authorized for a certain permission, are pluggable through different security policies.

Flashback

Many security concepts found in Zope 3 today have evolved from their Zope 2 predecessors. For example, some high-level security components have been inspired by the following components in Zope 2:

Permissions In both Zope 2 and Zope 3, attributes and methods of a class can be protected with permissions that can then be granted or denied to users.

Security manager Being instantiated on a per-thread basis, the security manager is very similar to an interaction in Zope 3. It builds the bridge between the security context and the security policy.

Security context The security context represents the user and is in that sense similar to a participation in Zope 3.

Security policy The policy does the actual security checks and decides whether an action is authorized or not, much like the security policy in Zope 3. Like the default security policy in Zope 3, it uses roles to determine a user's privileges.

In contrast to the high-level components, Zope 2 is very different from Zope 3 at the low level. Security-sensitive objects are not proxied. Rather, code that deals with such objects has to perform the checks manually (such as using `guarded_getattr` from `AccessControl` instead of plain `getattr`). Untrusted code (code that is entered through the management interface) is recompiled to use the guarded versions of Python built-ins everywhere.

Rocky says...

J2EE developers should be prepared to venture into new and powerful
territory with the Zope security model. Note that restricting security on
per-attribute basis will seem somewhat familiar to restricting access on
a per-role basis to EJB methods. But Zope's security model is far more
fine-grained (by introducing permissions). It should also be observed that
while JAAS (Java Authentication and Authorization Service) has some
similar concepts, Zope's security model is quite different.

21.2 Permissions

Permissions protect certain actions that a user might perform, such as viewing a page, editing a piece of content, managing a set of components, etc.
Principals can be granted or denied permissions, in which case they will or
will not be allowed to perform the associated actions.

Permission are identified by IDs (dotted names). For example, `zope.
View` denotes the typical view permission in Zope. The *public permis-
sion* is always available to everybody. In ZCML, it is available under the
`zope.Public` name, in Python it is identified by the `zope.security.
checker.CheckerPublic` global variable. A component that is protected
with this is practically accessible by anyone.

Fine-grained permissions

So far we have mainly used only two permissions, `zope.View` for actions
related to viewing and `zope.ManageContent` for actions related to editing.
That means adding and editing kitchen tools currently requires the same
permissions as adding and editing recipes. Viewing a recipe and rating is
also protected by the same permission. Anyone who can view a recipe can
also rate it. In some setups, this *might* not make a difference, but often you
would like to be flexible about who are allowed to do what. In other words,
fine-grained permissions should be used as much as possible.

Let us now define fine-grained permissions with which we will protect
the individual components of the *World Cookery* application. These permissions will be very specific to our application. Therefore, we will use the
`worldcookery` prefix in their dotted name. Example 21.2.1 lists the permission definitions.

Now that we have defined our own permissions, we can change the configuration of other *World Cookery* components so that they are protected
appropriately. Since the change involves no more than a simple search and

Table 21.1. Zope's default permissions (excerpt)

ID	Title	Description
zope.Public	Public	No security checking, available to everyone.
zope.Security	Change security settings	Grant/revoke permissions and assign roles.
zope.SendMail	Send out mail with arbitrary from and to addresses	Be able to send emails in the course of a request.
zope.UndoAllTransactions	Undo all transactions	Be able to undo all transactions, regardless of who initiated them.
zope.UndoOwnTransactions	Undo one's one transactions	Be able to undo one's own transactions.
zope.View	View	Necessary to view objects.
zope.ManageContent	Manage Content	Add, edit and delete Zope's default content objects.
zope.ManageCode	Manage Code	Manage executable code, including Python, SQL, ZPT, etc.
zope.ManageServices	Manage Services	Add and configure local components and site managers.
zope.ManageApplication	Manage Application	Manage the Zope Application, such as Restart/Shutdown or packing the ZODB.
zope.app.apidoc.UseAPIDoc	Access Online API documentation	Access the online APIDoc tool that provides ad-hoc information on registered components.
zope.app.dublincore.view	View Dublin Core Meta Data	Access an object's Dublin Core metadata.
zope.app.dublincore.change	Change Dublin Core Meta Data	Edit an object's Dublin Core metadata.

Example 21.2.1 Defining fine-grained permissions for the World Cookery application (`permissions.zcml`)

```
 1  <configure xmlns="http://namespaces.zope.org/zope">
 2
 3    <permission
 4        id="worldcookery.ViewRecipes"
 5        title="View recipes"
 6        />
 7
 8    <permission
 9        id="worldcookery.EditRecipes"
10        title="Edit recipes"
11        />
12
13    <permission
14        id="worldcookery.ViewRecipeFolders"
15        title="View recipe folders"
16        />
17
18    <permission
19        id="worldcookery.EditRecipeFolders"
20        title="Edit recipe folders"
21        />
22
23    <permission
24        id="worldcookery.EditKitchenTools"
25        title="Edit kitchen tools"
26        />
27
28    <permission
29        id="worldcookery.Rate"
30        title="Rate objects"
31        />
32
33    <permission
34        id="worldcookery.ViewPDF"
35        title="View PDF rendering of objects"
36        />
37
38    <permission
39        id="worldcookery.Subscribe"
40        title="Subscribe to objects via email"
41        />
42
43  </configure>
```

replace, file listings are not provided again for brevity. Note that since we defined the permissions in a separate ZCML file, it has to be included explicitly with the following statement at the top of `configure.zcml`:

```
<include file="permissions.zcml" />
```

Mapping permissions

By protecting World Cookery components with custom permissions, we have made the application temporarily unusable because none of the permissions have yet been yet granted to a principal. We could either grant all the individual permission to the principals, or we could group the permission somehow (e.g. all view related ones and all edit related ones). This is especially useful when applications need to be flexible in terms of security, but should provide sensible defaults.

One way to do with this is to map all the fine-grained permissions back to a common permission with the `meta:redefinePermission` ZCML directive, for example:

```
<meta:redefinePermission
    from="worldcookery.ViewRecipes"
    to="zope.View"
    />
```

This directive should occur after the `worldcookery.ViewRecipes` permission has been defined. The effect is that all subsequent ZCML directives using `worldcookery.ViewRecipes` will actually use `zope.View` to protect a component.

At first sight, mapping fine-grained permissions back to more general ones seems counter-productive after having introduced the fine-grained ones in the first place. However, you could at any time remove the `meta:redefinePermission` directives and regain the flexibility by grant the permissions individually.

Another way to group permissions in order to make granting and revoking privileges easier is to use *roles* which specific to Zope's default security policy. They are covered in the next section.

Summary

- Permissions protect actions that can be performed by a user.
- Fine-grained permissions allow flexible management of security privileges.
- A permission can be mapped to another one in ZCML when it is considered equivalent in a particular application or deployment.

Using Zope 2

The concepts of permissions should sound very familiar to the Zope 2 developer. Only a few things have changed. Zope 3 permissions are identified by IDs, and can optionally have a title and description. Permissions need to be explicitly defined through ZCML before they can be used in security declarations. That way, typos in security declarations do not create new permissions, like they do in Zope 2.

All of the traditional ways of making security declarations about classes in Zope 2 involves code within the class body, which makes it impossible to change security declarations without modifying a class's code. Fortunately, Zope 2 has supported defining and declaring permissions through ZCML for a few versions now. This works exactly like in Zope 3 with the `permission` and `class` directives. The following list gives an overview of how the old in-line security declarations map to ZCML:

`declareProtected` protects an attribute with a certain permission. In ZCML, this is done via the `require` subdirective of the `class` directive. Zope 2 makes all of its standard permissions available under dotted names (e.g. the *View* permission can be referred to as `zope2.View`, the CMF's *Modify Portal Content* as `cmf.ModifyPortalContent`).

`declarePrivate` makes an attribute inaccessible from untrusted code. This corresponds conceptually to not having security declarations in Zope 3. The behaviour can still be expressed in Zope 2 by protecting the attribute with the `zope2.Private` permission.

`declarePublic` makes an attribute publicly accessible. In ZCML you would either protect it with the `zope.Public` permission or use the `allow` ZCML subdirective instead of `require`.

21.3 Roles

Zope's default security policy, provided by the `zope.app.securitypolicy` package, introduces a useful concept to the security machinery: *roles*. When people join in collaborative processes to do a certain job, they divide up their responsibilities among themselves. Who is responsible for what is often given by a certain hierarchy within the group or the different abilities of the participants. Sometimes people are responsible for two or more separate things. That responsibility is a *role*.

You can think of roles as different hats. A person might possess several hats but can really only wear one at a time (anything else would look very silly). It is the same with roles. A principal in an application might have several roles assigned, but can carry out only one at a time. A good example are the roles *Editor* and *Publisher* in a simple content management or publishing system. A person might actually have both, but before publishing something, it has to be written first! Thus the person will first wear the "editor hat" and then the "publisher hat," maybe even the "reviewer hat"while proofreading in between.

In terms of security assertions, a role is a logical grouping of permissions. Instead of granting or denying each individual permission to a principal, you assign a role that combines all of the permission relevant to the responsibilities of the role. The responsibility-driven approach can be seen as orthogonal to groups. Groups are logical aggregations of principals (not permissions) and can for instance be used to express department hierarchies.

Note that roles are *not* fundamental security components in Zope. They are a concept specific to Zope's default security policy. Other security policies might determine principal privileges in a different way. Security policies are replaceable and can be customized according to an application's needs.

Defining and granting roles

To make the World Cookery application usable again we define roles according to the typical activities of users in the application. A sensible approach would be to divide responsibilities into those who write recipes (editors) and those who read them (visitors). Example 21.3.1 defines the two roles and grants the permissions we defined earlier to them accordingly. As with `permissions.zcml`, this file also has to be included at the top of `configure.zcml`, below `permissions.zcml`.

We still have not made the application usable again, but we are a step closer. Principals that have the `zope.Manager` role (such as the user that is created when creating a Zope instance) always have full access, so we do not need to take care of them. It is the anonymous principal that currently lacks the proper privileges. Before, anonymous was able to view recipes because it is granted the `zope.View` permission by default. If we wanted to restore that situation, we would have to grant it the `worldcookery.Visitor` role. That is best done in an instance's `etc/principals.zcml` file where the unauthenticated principal is defined. Simply add the following directive to the bottom of the file:

```
<grant
    role="worldcookery.Visitor"
    principal="zope.anybody"
    />
```

As you can see, the `grant` directive can also be used to grant a role to a principal.

With the anonymous users granted the `worldcookery.Visitor` role, we should now be able to view recipes again without authenticating. As for editing recipes, it seems obvious that editors should not be granted manager privileges. The `zope.Manager` principal really is just a development

Example 21.3.1 Defining roles in the World Cookery application
(`roles.zcml`)

```
1  <configure xmlns="http://namespaces.zope.org/zope">
2
3    <role
4        id="worldcookery.Visitor"
5        title="Visitor of the WorldCookery website"
6        />
7
8    <role
9        id="worldcookery.Editor"
10       title="An editor in the WorldCookery website"
11       />
12
13   <grant
14       permission="worldcookery.ViewRecipes"
15       role="worldcookery.Visitor"
16       />
17
18   <grant
19       permission="worldcookery.EditRecipes"
20       role="worldcookery.Editor"
21       />
22
23   <grant
24       permission="worldcookery.ViewRecipeFolders"
25       role="worldcookery.Visitor"
26       />
27
28   <grant
29       permission="worldcookery.EditRecipeFolders"
30       role="worldcookery.Editor"
31       />
32
33   <grant
34       permission="worldcookery.EditKitchenTools"
35       role="worldcookery.Editor"
36       />
37
38   <grant
39       permission="worldcookery.Rate"
40       role="worldcookery.Visitor"
41       />
42
43   <grant
44       permission="worldcookery.ViewPDF"
45       role="worldcookery.Visitor"
46       />
47
48   <grant
49       permission="worldcookery.Subscribe"
50       role="worldcookery.Visitor"
51       />
52
53  </configure>
```

Example 21.3.1 (continued)

3–11.   Roles are defined using the `role` directive. Like permissions, they are identified by a dotted name and should have an explanatory title.

13–51.   The `grant` directive can be used to grant permissions to roles.

---

or emergency user that should be disabled for production systems (as should any non-anonymous principal that is defined through ZCML because the password appears in plain text). In the next chapter we will learn how to manage principals and their grants properly.

Local roles and grants

As mentioned briefly in Chapter 2, roles are named utilities. The utility name is the role identifier (the dotted name) and they provide `IRole` from the `zope.app.securitypolicy` package. As we know from Chapter 18, utilities can be created and registered locally. That means we can also define roles locally.

It is also possible to make local grants, meaning that a certain principal only has certain roles or that a certain role only has certain permissions in a particular area. These grants, managed by the security policy, are stored in an object's annotations; that way, any annotatable object can be the location of local grants. If the object is located in a location hierarchy, grants from parent objects are acquired. Local grants can override (and revoke) global grants and grants from parents.

Local grants can be managed in the ZMI. Go to the location in which you would like to make the local grant and select *Grant* from the actions menu. You can then decide whether you would like to grant permissions to roles or roles to principals.

Summary

- Roles group together permissions necessary for a set of related actions, thus provide a way to spell out security in a responsibility-driven manner.
- Roles are a feature of Zope's default security policy and are specific to it.
- Roles are named utilities providing `IRole`. Global roles are defined using the `role` ZCML directive.
- Roles are granted to principals much like single permissions are. Global grants are made through the `grant` ZCML directive.

Grants for the selected principal

Change

Roles	Allow	Unset	Deny		Permissions	Allow	Unset	Deny
An editor in the WorldCookery website	○	⊙	○		Edit kitchen tools	○	⊙	○
Everybody	○	⊙	○		Edit recipe folders	○	⊙	○
Site Manager	○	⊙	○		Edit recipes	○	⊙	○
Site Member	○	⊙	○		Rate objects	○	⊙	○
Visitor of the WorldCookery website	○	⊙	○		Subscribe to objects via email	○	⊙	○
^ top					View PDF rendering of objects	○	⊙	○
					View recipe folders	○	⊙	○
					View recipes	○	⊙	○
					Add Images	○	⊙	○
					Add SQL Scripts	○	⊙	○
					Change security settings	○	⊙	○
					Manage Application	○	⊙	○
					Manage Code	○	⊙	○
					Manage Content	○	⊙	○
					Manage Principals	○	⊙	○
					Manage Service Bindings	○	⊙	○
					Manage Services	○	⊙	○
					Manage Site	○	⊙	○
					Send out mail with arbitrary from and to addresses	○	⊙	○
					Undo all transactions	○	⊙	○
					Undo one's one transactions	○	⊙	○
					View	○	⊙	○
					Change Dublin-Core Meta Data	○	⊙	○
					View Dublin-Core Meta Data	○	⊙	○
					Introspect Object Classes and Interfaces	○	⊙	○
					Use Database Connections	○	⊙	○
					^ top			

Fig. 21.1. Making local grants through the ZMI.

- Roles and grants can be defined locally. Local roles are simply local utilities. Local grants can be stored on any annotatable object (through annotations).

Flashback

Like permissions, roles are borrowed from Zope 2. In Zope 3's predecessor, roles are a fundamental concept of the security system and can not be steered around. In fact, the Zope 2 security system is much more monolithic and a lot less flexible than the one in Zope 3. This, for instance, makes Zope 3's security machinery easier to audit, which is an important aspect when building applications that might need to be security-certified. The Component Architecture allows different components to focus on different jobs. This eases security customization, and also makes it easier to identify and audit custom security features. In fact, Zope 3 is undergoing Common Criteria Certification, which is being made easier by these aspects of its security implementation.

22

Authentication and User Management

In the last chapter we discussed how users (known as principals) interact with Zope's security system. In this chapter we look at how users are authenticated.

22.1 The Pluggable Authentication Utility

In Zope, users are authenticated by authentication utilities. These utilities provide IAuthentication from the zope.app.security package. Zope has two implementations of this interface. One is the principal registry which is registered as a global utility and lets you define principals in ZCML (usually done in etc/principals.zcml). This global utility is the fallback if no local authentication utility is defined. It is what we have been using so far.

A local, persistent implementation of IAuthentication is the *pluggable authentication utility* (PAU) from the zope.app.authentication package. It is called "pluggable" because it defers all its work to plug-ins. When customizing Zope's authentication system, you will therefore only have to implement custom plug-ins to the PAU rather than implementing a whole custom authentication utility.

The PAU divides its work into two categories:

Extracting credentials. Plug-ins providing ICredentialPlugin extract the user's credentials from the request and return them. Given a request, the PAU will loop through all available credential plug-ins and try to obtain credentials from them one by one. Credential plug-ins are also responsible for challenging the user to provide credentials (e.g. displaying a login form) and logout. Zope comes with several challenge plug-ins out of the box, such as one for HTTP Basic Authentication and one that keeps credentials in a session.

Authenticating credentials. Plug-ins providing IAuthenticatorPlugin authenticate credentials against an authentication system such as a user database or a directory service. For every successfully extracted set of credentials, the PAU iterates over the authenticator plug-ins in order to authenticate with these credentials. If none of the authenticator plug-ins can authenticate the credentials, the next credential plug-in will be used.

Configuring the PAU

The PAU is a local, persistent utility. It can be added by choosing *Pluggable Authentication Utility* from the *Add* menu, preferably inside a site manager.

In the add form we will be asked to set a prefix for the utility. This is used as a prefix for all principal IDs coming from this utility and ensures the uniqueness of principal IDs throughout the whole Zope instance (which is a requirement of Zope's security system). Note that in future Zope versions, PAUs will probably not have prefixes anymore. Instead, their authenticator plug-ins will be required to generate instance-wide unique principal IDs. Currently they are only required to generate IDs that are unique within their PAU. Anticipating this change, we can leave the PAU's prefix empty.

After having added the PAU, we can configure its active plug-ins. Plug-ins are found in two ways:

Contained objects. The PAU is not only a persistent utility, it is also a container at the same time. It can contain any ICredentialsPlugin or IAuthenticatorPlugin object. Plug-ins are added to a PAU via the standard *Add* menu in the *Plugins* view.

Named utilities. Plug-ins that do not need to be persistent or do not need to provide through-the-web configuration can be registered as global named utilities. You can also register persistent plug-ins as local utilities if they are not located inside a PAU for any reason.

Available plug-ins need to be explicitly activated before the PAU will use them. This can be done in the *Configure* management tab. The PAU will iterate over the plug-ins in the order they are defined.

Summary

- Zope authenticates users with an IAuthentication utility.
- The principal registry is the default, global IAuthentication utility. It allows defining principals through ZCML.
- Custom authentication is done with the Pluggable Authentication Utility (PAU). It defers all its work to plug-ins.
- Credential plug-ins challenge the user to provide credentials and extract those from the request.
- Authenticator plug-ins verify the credentials in a user database or directory service.

Using Zope 2

The PAU in Zope 3 has been inspired by the PluggableAuthService (PAS), a highly customizable replacement for Zope 2's standard user folder. If you are using Zope 2, it is recommended to use PAS because it is much more flexible than the standard user folder and also because it is conceptually close to the PAU. PAS is not a standard part of Zope 2, but it can be downloaded from the Zope community website.[1]

Rocky says...

Conceptually PAU style authentication development will be on par with Java's JAAS. Java developers will find the separation of authentication and security concerns in PAU very similar. Just watch out for the radically different APIs and manner in which to register new plug-ins.

22.2 Login and logout with credential plug-ins

Whenever a user has insufficient privileges, the security machinery will raise an `Unauthorized` exception. When that happens, the PAU uses its credential plug-ins to challenge the user to log in. After the user has logged in, the credential plug-in also extracts the login credentials provided by the user. If possible, credential plug-ins will also allow the user to log out. In case none of the credential plug-ins can or want to challenge the user (possibly because he or she is already logged in), a view for the `Unauthorized` exception is displayed.

The PAU comes with several credential plug-ins included:

HTTP Basic-Auth challenges the client via HTTP Basic Authentication by sending a `401 Unauthorized` response with a *WWW-Authenticate* header. The authorization realm is configurable, the global utility that is registered by default uses the *Zope* realm. Basic Authentication is considered not to be very user-friendly because most browser clients open a pop-up window when login credentials are requested. It is also difficult to provide logout functionality because once challenged, clients will typically continue to send credentials with all subsequent requests. HTTP Basic Authentication is the safest way to ensure compatibility with non-browser HTTP clients, though.

---

[1] PluggableAuthService downloads `<http://www.zope.org/Products/PluggableAuthService>`

Session Credentials challenges the user by redirecting to a login form. The
login form is a separate, configurable view that can therefore be easily
customized. Once the user has supplied the credentials through the login
form, this plug-in will store them in a session. That way, the client will
be logged in for all subsequent requests (if the credentials were correct)
until the user logs out. At that point session data will we wiped. Storing
credentials in a session is similar to storing them in a browser cookie,
except that no potentially security-critical information has to be stored
on the client. On the other hand, the session credentials plug-in requires
the session machinery which may not always be desirable to use.

FTP Credentials extracts credentials from an FTP request. Since FTP has
a built-in authentication protocol, it is not necessary to configure or customize this plug-in.

No challenge if authenticated does not actually extract credentials from the
request. However, if configured with a higher priority than another credential plug-in, it will prevent challenging already authenticated users
when their privileges are insufficient for a certain action. Otherwise they
would challenged again in this case and be given the opportunity to re-
authenticate using a different set of credentials.

Storing credentials in a browser cookie

In most cases, the session credential plug-in is the best choice for a user-
friendly login/logout system. If you absolutely do not want to use sessions,
you could store the credentials in a browser cookie. Bear in mind though that
this will store potentially security-critical information on the client.

To implement a *cookie credentials plug-in*, we only have to implement a
utility that provides `ICredentialsPlugin`. Since the cookie-based plug-
in should also challenge the user via a login form, we can simply base the
implementation on the existing session credentials plug-in. We only have to
override the methods that take care of extracting the credentials and deleting
them for logout. Example 22.2.1 shows the implementation.

We can register the cookie credentials plug-in as a global utility (example listing omitted). This will make it immediately available within all PAU
instances. It is also sensible to provide an entry for the *Add* menu and an
edit form, so that the plug-in can be added to a particular PAU instance and
configured there. Example 22.2.2 shows the edit form that lets you do that
(configuration omitted).

Since we have not yet added authenticator plug-ins to our PAU instance,
we will have to defer the testing of the cookie credentials plug-in to the next
section. It will also show how to customize the login form.

Example 22.2.1 Cookie credentials plug-in for the PAU
(`cookiecredentials.py`)

```
1   import base64, urllib
2   from zope.interface import Interface, implements
3   from zope.schema import ASCIILine
4   from zope.publisher.interfaces.http import IHTTPRequest
5   from zope.i18nmessageid import MessageFactory
6   _ = MessageFactory('worldcookery')
7   from zope.app.authentication.session import SessionCredentialsPlugin
8
9   class ICookieCredentials(Interface):
10
11      cookie_name = ASCIILine(
12          title=_(u'Cookie name'),
13          description=_(u'Name of the cookie for storing credentials.'),
14          required=True
15          )
16
17  class CookieCredentialsPlugin(SessionCredentialsPlugin):
18      implements(ICookieCredentials)
19      cookie_name = 'worldcookery.auth'
20
21      def extractCredentials(self, request):
22          if not IHTTPRequest.providedBy(request):
23              return
24
25          login = request.get(self.loginfield, None)
26          password = request.get(self.passwordfield, None)
27          cookie = request.get(self.cookie_name, None)
28
29          if login and password:
30              val = base64.encodestring('%s:%s' % (login, password))
31              request.response.setCookie(self.cookie_name,
32                                         urllib.quote(val),
33                                         path='/')
34          elif cookie:
35              val = base64.decodestring(urllib.unquote(cookie))
36              login, password = val.split(':')
37          else:
38              return
39
40          return {'login': login, 'password': password}
41
42      def logout(self, request):
43          if not IHTTPRequest.providedBy(request):
44              return
45          request.response.expireCookie(self.cookie_name, path='/')
```

9–15. This interface specifies a configuration option of the cookie credentials plug-in: The name of the cookie that will be used is configurable. That way, different installations on the same server could use different cookie names, for instance.

Example 22.2.1 (continued)

7 and 17.   By subclassing from the session credentials plug-in, we inherit the
`challenge` method which challenges users by redirecting to a login form. We
also inherit the implementation of `IBrowserFormChallenger` which specifies a few fields for configuring which login view to redirect to and which fields
the login name and password will be stored in. The base class also provides
some sensible default values for that.

30, 32, and 35.   Instead of storing the login name and password as plain text in
the cookie, we encode it in base 64 (and ensure the output is properly quoted
for cookie values). This is far from being secure, though it is not any better
than HTTP Basic-Auth (which also sends base 64 encoded strings).

Example 22.2.2 Edit form for the cookie credentials plug-in
(`browser/cookiecredentials.py`)

```
1   from zope.formlib.form import EditForm, Fields
2   from zope.formlib.namedtemplate import NamedTemplate
3   from zope.i18nmessageid import MessageFactory
4   _ = MessageFactory('worldcookery')
5   from zope.app.authentication.session import IBrowserFormChallenger
6
7   from worldcookery.cookiecredentials import ICookieCredentials
8
9   class CookieCredentialsEditForm(EditForm):
10      form_fields = Fields(ICookieCredentials) + Fields(
            IBrowserFormChallenger)
11      label = _(u"Configure cookie credentials plugin")
12      template = NamedTemplate('worldcookery.form')
```

5.   The `IBrowserFormChallenger` schema describes configuration options of the
session credentials plug-in, such as the name of the login form and the form
fields for login name and password.

10.   As you can see, a set of form fields can be added to another one. The rendered
form will contain fields from both schemas.

Enabling logout

Our credentials plug-in properly implements the `logout` method. However
the `login_logout` view we used in the toolbar viewlet does not know that.
For all it knows, the active credentials plug-in might not support logout
(like the HTTP Basic-Auth plug-in, for instance). We will therefore have to
explicitly tell it to enable the *Logout* view by registering the following adapter:

```
<adapter factory="zope.app.security.LogoutSupported" />
```

Summary

- When an Unauthorized exception occurs, the PAU will let its credentials plug-ins challenge the user to provide login credentials.
- The PAU comes with two HTTP credentials plug-ins included. One challenges and extracts credentials via HTTP Basic-Auth. The other one stores credentials in a session.
- Credential plug-ins will always challenge upon an Unauthorized exception, even if the user is already authenticated. The *No challenge if authenticated* plug-in prevents that.
- While credential plug-ins have to implement a logout method, they may not support logout. To enable logout functionality, a special adapter has to be registered.

22.3 Managing principals with authenticator plug-ins

Authenticator plug-ins represent the actual authentication system within the Zope application. They verify a given set of credentials according to a user database or a directory service. The PAU comes with a simple authenticator plug-in that acts as a persistent user storage. It will authenticate credentials against the principals defined inside itself. Other authenticators that authenticate credentials against directory services such as LDAP or Active Directory are also possible.

Principal Folder and Group Folder

The PAU comes with two authenticator plug-ins, a *Principal Folder* and a *Group Folder*. Both store their principal information persistently in the ZODB. In fact, they are regular containers for the principals and let you define new principals or groups, respectively, through the *Add* menu, as shown in Figure 22.1.

When editing a group, you may also search for principals and assign that group to them. Principals can be in multiple groups. With Zope's default security policy, principals will inherit the grants of their groups. Granting privileges to groups works like granting privileges to any other principal. After all, groups are just principals.

After having created a principal you can log out and log in again using the newly created account. Note, though, that the principal is only available at the site level at which you created it. Thus, if you try to log in to access an object higher in the hierarchy than the worldcookery_site folder, our PAU instance will not be found and your credentials cannot be

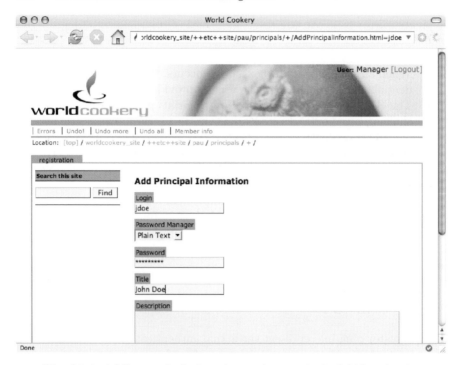

Fig. 22.1. Adding a principal to the persistent principal folder plug-in.

authenticated. Also be aware that you will need to grant your newly created principals the worldcookery.Visitor role, just like we had to grant it to the anonymous principal in etc/principals.zcml at the end of the previous chapter. Otherwise, the new account will not be usable in the *World Cookery* application.

A simplistic authenticator plug-in

In many cases, web applications need to authenticate against existing user databases. Unless a commonly used user database like LDAP is used, you may have to implement a custom authenticator plug-in for the PAU. A typical example is storing logins and passwords in a relational database. Fortunately, implementing an authenticator plug-in is as straight-forward as implementing a credentials plug-in. You only have to fulfil the IAuthenticatorPlugin API which requires the plug-in to do two things: authenticate a given set of credentials and retrieve information about a principal for a given principal ID.

For demonstration purposes, let us implement a very simple authenticator plug-in that authenticates users against a passwd-like file. This is a plain text file in which each line contains a user's login and password information, separated by a colon. We will also add a third column for the principal's real name, e.g.:

```
philipp:secret:Philipp von Weitershausen
john:verysecret:John Doe
```

Example 22.3.1 shows the implementation of an authenticator plug-in that reads a file of this format for authentication. We also provide add and edit forms for the plug-in, but those example listings are omitted here as they show nothing we have not already covered regarding automated forms.

Example 22.3.1 Authenticator plug-in for `passwd`-like files (`passwdauth.py`)

```
1  from persistent import Persistent
2  from zope.interface import Interface, implements
3  from zope.schema import TextLine
4  from zope.location.interfaces import ILocation
5  from zope.i18nmessageid import MessageFactory
6  _ = MessageFactory('worldcookery')
7  from zope.app.authentication.interfaces import IAuthenticatorPlugin
8  from zope.app.authentication.principalfolder import PrincipalInfo
9
10 class IPasswd(Interface):
11
12     prefix = TextLine(
13         title=_(u"Prefix"),
14         description=_(u"Prefix to be added to all principal IDs"),
15         missing_value=u'',
16         default=u'',
17         readonly=True
18         )
19
20     filename = TextLine(
21         title=_(u"File name"),
22         description=_(u"Absolute path to the data file"),
23         required=True
24         )
25
26 class PasswdAuthenticator(Persistent):
27     implements(IPasswd, IAuthenticatorPlugin, ILocation)
28     __parent__ = __name__ = None
29
30     def __init__(self, prefix=u'', filename=None):
31         self.prefix = prefix
32         self.filename = filename
33
34     def _filedata(self):
35         if self.filename is None:
36             raise StopIteration
37         for line in file(self.filename):
38             yield line.strip().split(':', 3)
```

Example 22.3.1 (continued)

```
39    def authenticateCredentials(self, credentials):
40        if not (credentials and 'login' in credentials and
41                'password' in credentials):
42            return
43        login, password = credentials['login'], credentials['password']
44        for username, passwd, title in self._filedata():
45            if (login, password) == (username, passwd):
46                return PrincipalInfo(self.prefix+login, login,
47                                      title, title)
48
49    def principalInfo(self, id):
50        if id.startswith(self.prefix):
51            login = id[len(self.prefix):]
52            for username, passwd, title in self._filedata():
53                if login == username:
54                    return PrincipalInfo(id, login, title, title)
```

12–18.   Principal IDs must be unique within a Zope instance. The simplest way to ensure that is to give your authenticator plug-ins prefixes that they apply to their principals. That way, their IDs will not collide with IDs of principals from other authenticator plug-ins.

40–48.   This method authenticates the given credentials. For the `passwd` authenticationwe only have to look inside the file and compare user name and password. If successful, an object providing `IPrincipalInfo` from the `zope.app.authentication` package is supposed to be returned. We simply use an already existing implementation of that interface. Just note that we are adding our prefix to the the login name so that principal IDs are unique.

50–55.   This method allows the authentication system to retrieve an `IPrincipalInfo` object for an arbitrary principal that is part of this authenticator plug-in.

A custom authenticator plug-in for sign-up

Many Internet applications, especially portals and community websites, allow visitors to sign up for a user account. That way users create their own accounts and site administrators merely have to control their privileges. As we are building a community-oriented application in this book, this feature should definitely be included. Therefore, let us dive a bit deeper into the authentication system and see how to effectively manage principals and their grants programmatically.

To support member sign-up we will provide a custom authenticator plug-in based on the Principal Folder implementation, mostly because it stores principals persistently in the ZODB, which makes it very easy to manage them programmatically. Our custom plug-in extends the functionality of its base class with two important methods, one for signing up as a new user and one for changing a principal's title and its password. Example 22.3.2 shows the interface that describes those methods and the implementation using `PrincipalFolder` as a base class. The usual security configuration is omitted once again.

Example 22.3.2 Persistent authenticator plug-in with sign-up functionality (`signup.py`)

```python
1   from zope.interface import Interface, implements
2   from zope.schema import List, Choice
3   from zope.i18nmessageid import MessageFactory
4   _ = MessageFactory('worldcookery')
5   from zope.app.authentication.principalfolder import PrincipalFolder
6   from zope.app.authentication.principalfolder import InternalPrincipal
7
8   class ISignup(Interface):
9
10      signup_roles = List(
11          title=_(u"Roles for new principals"),
12          description=_(u"These roles will assigned to new principals."),
13          value_type=Choice(vocabulary="Role Ids"),
14          unique=True
15          )
16
17      def signUp(login, password, title):
18          """Add a principal for yourself.  Returns the new principal's ID
19          """
20
21      def changePasswordTitle(login, password, title):
22          """Change the principal's password and/or title.
23          """
24
25  class SignupPrincipalFolder(PrincipalFolder):
26      """Principal folder that allows users to sign up.
27      """
28      implements(ISignup)
29
30      signup_roles = []
31
32      def signUp(self, login, password, title):
33          self[login] = InternalPrincipal(login, password, title)
34          return self.__parent__.prefix + self.prefix + login
35
36      def changePasswordTitle(self, login, password, title):
37          if login not in self:
38              raise ValueError("Principal is not managed by this "
39                               "principal source.")
40          principal = self[login]
41          principal.password = password and password or principal.password
42          principal.title = title and title or principal.title
```

Example 22.3.2 (continued)

5 and 25.   We base our custom authenticator plug-in on `PrincipalFolder`. That way we do not have to worry about any of the actual plug-in functionality, we inherit all that from the base class and can focus on sign-up.

6 and 33.   Principal folders do not manage actual principals but "internal principals" which are persistent and contained objects. The authenticator plug-in will create `IPrincipal` objects from these when needed.

For the sign-up functionality, we define three new permissions as shown in Example 22.3.3: `worldcookery.SignUp`, `worldcookery.ManageSignUp`, `worldcookery.ChangePassword`. The sign-up related methods of our custom authenticator plug-in have been protected with these. Then we only need to grant them to roles, as shown in Example 22.3.4. We also define a new role in that example, `worldcookery.Member`. It can be granted to principals that are signing up. By granting individual permissions to that role, you can then give signed up users more privileges than mere visitors.

Example 22.3.3 Sign-up related permissions (`permissions.zcml`)

```
1   <configure xmlns="http://namespaces.zope.org/zope">
2
3       ...
4
5       <permission
6           id="worldcookery.SignUp"
7           title="Sign up as a user to the site"
8           />
9
10      <permission
11          id="worldcookery.ManageSignUp"
12          title="Manage user sign up"
13          />
14
15      <permission
16          id="worldcookery.ChangePassword"
17          title="Change a principal's password"
18          />
19
20  </configure>
```

Example 22.3.4 Granting sign up-related permissions to roles (`roles.zcml`)

```
1  <configure xmlns="http://namespaces.zope.org/zope">
2
3    <role
4        id="worldcookery.Visitor"
5        title="Visitor of the WorldCookery website"
6        />
7
8    <role
9        id="worldcookery.Editor"
10       title="An editor in the WorldCookery website"
11       />
12
13   <role
14       id="worldcookery.Member"
15       title="A member of the WorldCookery website"
16       />
17
18   ...
19
20   <grant
21       permission="worldcookery.SignUp"
22       role="worldcookery.Visitor"
23       />
24
25   <grant
26       permission="worldcookery.ChangePassword"
27       role="worldcookery.Member"
28       />
29
30  </configure>
```

Browser views for sign-up

Now that we have an authenticator plug-in that provides sign-up functionality, we should make a few browser pages that actually let users enter and change their user information. Example 22.3.5 shows the HTML form through which users can sign up. The form for changing their information (full name and password) works similarly which is why it is not shown here. Example 22.3.6 shows the form handler view that takes care of the actual sign-up. We are omitting the view that is responsible for changing a principal's title and password.

Custom login form

Our application is now almost ready for people who would like to participate as members of the website. We only need to point visitors to the sign-up

Example 22.3.5 Sign-up form (`browser/signup.pt`)

```
1   <html xmlns="http://www.w3.org/1999/xhtml"
2         xmlns:metal="http://xml.zope.org/namespaces/metal"
3         xmlns:i18n="http://xml.zope.org/namespaces/i18n"
4         metal:use-macro="context/@@standard_macros/dialog"
5         i18n:domain="worldcookery">
6   <head>
7     <title metal:fill-slot="title" i18n:translate="">Sign up</title>
8   </head>
9   <body>
10  <div metal:fill-slot="body">
11
12    <h1 i18n:translate="">Sign up</h1>
13
14    <form action="@@signup" method="post">
15      <div class="row">
16        <div class="label">
17          <label for="login" i18n:translate="">Login name:</label>
18        </div>
19        <div class="field">
20          <input type="text" name="login" id="login" />
21        </div>
22      </div>
23      <div class="row">
24        <div class="label">
25          <label for="title" i18n:translate="">Full name:</label>
26        </div>
27        <div class="field">
28          <input type="text" name="title" id="title" />
29        </div>
30      </div>
31      <div class="row">
32        <div class="label">
33          <label for="password" i18n:translate="">Password:</label>
34        </div>
35        <div class="field">
36          <input type="password" name="password" id="password" />
37        </div>
38      </div>
39      <div class="row">
40        <div class="label">
41          <label for="confimration" i18n:translate="">Confirm password:</
                label>
42        </div>
43        <div class="field">
44          <input type="password" name="confirmation" id="confirmation" />
45        </div>
46      </div>
47
48      <div class="row">
49        <input type="submit" name="worldcookery.SignUp" value="Sign up"
50               i18n:attributes="value button-signup" />
51      </div>
52    </form>
53
54  </div>
55  </body>
56  </html>
```

Example 22.3.6 Sign-up browser view (`browser/signup.py`)

```
1   from zope.i18nmessageid import MessageFactory
2   _ = MessageFactory('worldcookery')
3   from zope.component import getUtility
4   from zope.publisher.browser import BrowserView
5   from zope.exceptions.interfaces import UserError
6   from zope.security.proxy import removeSecurityProxy
7
8   from zope.app.pagetemplate import ViewPageTemplateFile
9   from zope.app.security.interfaces import IAuthentication
10  from zope.app.authentication.interfaces import IPluggableAuthentication
11  from zope.app.securitypolicy.interfaces import IPrincipalRoleManager
12
13  from worldcookery.signup import ISignup
14
15  class BaseSignUpView(BrowserView):
16
17      def _signupfolder(self):
18          pau = getUtility(IAuthentication)
19          if not IPluggableAuthentication.providedBy(pau):
20              raise LookupError("Signup requires a PAU instance.")
21
22          for name, plugin in pau.getAuthenticatorPlugins():
23              if ISignup.providedBy(plugin):
24                  return plugin
25
26          raise TypeError("Signup requires a sign-up capable athenticator "
27                          "plugin.")
28
29  class SignUpView(BaseSignUpView):
30
31      signUpForm = ViewPageTemplateFile('signup.pt')
32
33      def signUp(self, login, title, password, confirmation):
34          if confirmation != password:
35              raise UserError(_(u"Password and confirmation didn't match"))
36          folder = self._signupfolder()
37          if login in folder:
38              raise UserError(_(u"This login has already been chosen."))
39          principal_id = folder.signUp(login, password, title)
40
41          role_manager = IPrincipalRoleManager(self.context)
42          role_manager = removeSecurityProxy(role_manager)
43          for role in folder.signup_roles:
44              role_manager.assignRoleToPrincipal(role, principal_id)
45          self.request.response.redirect("@@welcome.html")
46
47  ...
```

5, 35, and 38.   Wherever the sign-up action has to be aborted because of an error, we raise `UserError` because only this exception type (and derived ones) will be shown to the user (as opposed to any other exception which simply generates a *System error* message). `UserError` also allows us to pass an i18n message as the error message so that it will be translated.

Example 22.3.6 (continued)

17–27.   The sign-up view is meant to be a view for regular content-space components (it probably makes most sense to register it for ISite). That means we
have to acquire the sign-up authenticator plug-in so we can add the principal
to it. We do that by first acquiring an authentication utility, making sure that
we really got a PAU instance. Then we iterate over the available authenticator
plug-ins in the PAU and use the first sign-up capable one that we find.

41–45.   Here we grant the requested roles to newly created principals. We do
that by adapting the context (the place where users are signing up) to
IPrincipalRoleManager. This adapter manages local grants of roles to
principals. Since it is a trusted adapter, it itself will be security-proxied. The
principal currently participating in the interaction is most probably the unauthenticated user (after all, why would anyone else sign up for an account?)
which does not have any role-granting privileges. Therefore, we have to ignore
all security checking at this point and remove the security proxies manually using the removeSecurityProxy function. Note that you should only do this
if you really know what you are doing!

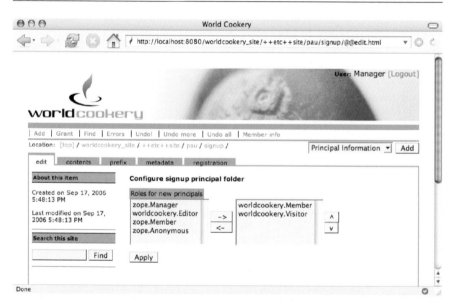

Fig. 22.2. The roles that are granted to principals upon sign-up can be selected

forms. This is probably best done in a custom login form. Example 22.3.7
has a listing of the login view class that displays the login form template
(shown in Example 22.3.8) unless the user has provided credentials and has
successfully authenticated. In that case, we redirect to the page that the user
was originally viewing.

To enable the custom login form, we register it as a browser page called
wclogin.html and for * so it is available everywhere. Then we only
have to configure our session or cookie credentials plug-in, or any other
IBrowserFormChallenger plug-in to redirect to wclogin.html instead
of Zope's standard form.

Example 22.3.7 Login view that displays a login form or redirects to the
user's origin (browser/login.py)

```
1  from zope.publisher.browser import BrowserPage
2  from zope.app.pagetemplate import ViewPageTemplateFile
3  from zope.app.security.interfaces import IUnauthenticatedPrincipal
4
5  class LoginPage(BrowserPage):
6
7      template = ViewPageTemplateFile('login.pt')
8
9      def __call__(self):
10         request = self.request
11         if (not IUnauthenticatedPrincipal.providedBy(request.principal)
12             and 'worldcookery.Login' in request):
13             camefrom = request.get('camefrom', '.')
14             request.response.redirect(camefrom)
15         else:
16             return self.template()
```

A browser test demonstrating the sign-up functionality along with the
cookie credentials plug-in from the previous section was recorded using the
browser test recorder. It is available for reference at browser/signup.txt.

Conclusion

It should be mentioned that the sign-up authenticator plug-in implementation
from above cheats in several ways, mostly to keep the example listings short.
The most blatant cheat is that it mixes an authentication component (the
authenticator plug-in) with roles, a concept of a certain security policy. That
makes the sign-up plug-in rather useless without Zope's default policy. If we
were aiming at more pluggability, we should refactor the sign-up functionality
so that it made use of events, for example.

Example 22.3.8 Login form for cookie-based authentication
(`browser/login.pt`)

```
1   <html xmlns="http://www.w3.org/1999/xhtml"
2         xmlns:tal="http://xml.zope.org/namespaces/tal"
3         xmlns:metal="http://xml.zope.org/namespaces/metal"
4         xmlns:i18n="http://xml.zope.org/namespaces/i18n"
5         metal:use-macro="context/@@standard_macros/dialog"
6         i18n:domain="worldcookery">
7   <head>
8     <title metal:fill-slot="title" i18n:translate="">Please log in</title>
9   </head>
10  <body>
11  <div metal:fill-slot="body">
12
13    <h1 i18n:translate="">Please log in.</h1>
14
15    <form action="" method="post">
16      <div class="row">
17        <div class="label">
18          <label for="login" i18n:translate="">Login name:</label>
19        </div>
20        <div class="field">
21          <input type="text" name="login" id="login" />
22        </div>
23      </div>
24      <div class="row">
25        <div class="label">
26          <label for="password" i18n:translate="">Password:</label>
27        </div>
28        <div class="field">
29          <input type="password" name="password" id="password" />
30        </div>
31      </div>
32
33      <div class="row">
34        <input type="hidden" name="camefrom" value=""
35               tal:attributes="value request/camefrom | nothing">
36        <input type="submit" name="worldcookery.Login" value="Log in"
37               i18n:attributes="login button-login" />
38      </div>
39    </form>
40
41    <p>
42      <span i18n:translate="">Not a member yet?</span>
43      <a href="@@signup.html" i18n:translate="">Sign up for a user
44      account now!</a>
45    </p>
46
47  </div>
48  </body>
49  </html>
```

Fig. 22.3. User signing up as a member of the *World Cookery* website.

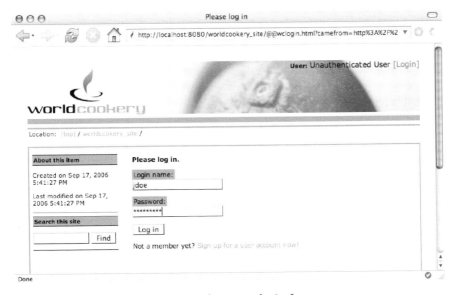

Fig. 22.4. A custom login form.

Summary

- The PAU uses authenticator plug-ins to verify login credentials.
- In order to guarantee the uniqueness of principal IDs within a PAU instance, authenticator plug-ins typically use a (configurable) prefix for all of their principals.
- The PAU comes with two authenticator plug-ins out of the box. They manage principals or groups, respectively, persistently in the ZODB.
- Custom authenticator plug-ins that authenticate against an existing user database or directory service only have to be able to authenticate a set of credentials and return information about a principal of a given ID.
- Custom login forms can easily be implemented and configured in IBrowserFormChallenger-capable credential plug-ins.

Flashback

In Zope 2, users are managed by *user folders*. These are containers that live inside regular content space folders and always have to be named acl_users. Zope 2 comes with a standard user folder implementation which stores users in the ZODB. There are also a plethora of third-party user folders that either target specific types of user databases (e.g. LDAP) or extensibility.

22.4 Principal metadata

As a final topic in this chapter we will look at associating additional data with principals. It is often required to know more about a principal than just its login name and title. Most principals represent real people with names, phone numbers, email addresses, etc. In short, there are many cases for associating metadata with principals.

The principal annotation utility

When we hear *metadata* we should obviously immediately think of annotations. The problem with principals is that they are not necessarily stored in the ZODB. They can be globally defined in ZCML or come from a PAU authenticator plug-in or any other authentication utility implementation. Since not all external user database systems support additional user metadata, especially arbitrary metadata, we often want to store principal metadata in the

ZODB, even though the principal itself might not be a persistent object at all. This functionality is provided by the *principal annotation utility*.

The principal annotation utility is a local, persistent utility that functions as storage for annotations objects (objects providing IAnnotations). The utility has to be local so that it can store the annotation data persistently. By default, an empty ZODB instance created by Zope 3 already contains an instance of the principal annotation utility in the site manager of the root folder. For most setups that instance should be sufficient. After all, principal IDs (which are used to identify principals for annotations) are unique throughout the whole system.

A short example of user metadata

As a short example of principal annotations, consider some very basic member information as described by IMemberinfo in Example 22.4.1. This interface

---

Example 22.4.1 Interface describing a simple user information (interfaces.py)

```
1   ...
2
3   import re
4   from zope.schema import ValidationError
5
6   class NotAnEmailAddress(ValidationError):
7       __doc__ = _(u"This is not a valid email address")
8
9   regex = r"[a-zA-Z0-9._%-]+@([a-zA-Z0-9-]+\.)*[a-zA-Z]{2,4}"
10  check_email = re.compile(regex).match
11  def validate_email(value):
12      if not check_email(value):
13          raise NotAnEmailAddress(value)
14      return True
15
16  class IMemberInfo(Interface):
17
18      first = TextLine(
19          title=_(u"First name"),
20          required=True
21          )
22
23      last = TextLine(
24          title=_(u"Last name"),
25          required=True
26          )
27
28      email = TextLine(
29          title=_(u"Email address"),
30          required=False,
31          constraint=validate_email
32          )
```

contains three fields: first name, last name, and email address. For the latter field, an additional constraint in form of a regular expression is given so that values entered for the email address actually have to be in the form of an email address. This saves us from having to write a special email field.

Now we write an adapter for principals that provides our IMemberinfo. This adapter works pretty much like any other annotation-based adapter we have written so far. Example 22.4.2 shows the adapter implementation.

Example 22.4.2 Member information adapter for principal objects (`memberinfo.py`)

```
1   from persistent.dict import PersistentDict
2   from zope.interface import implements
3   from zope.component import adapts
4   from zope.security.interfaces import IPrincipal
5   from zope.annotation.interfaces import IAnnotations
6   from worldcookery.interfaces import IMemberInfo
7
8   KEY = "worldcookery.memberinfo"
9
10  class MappingProperty(object):
11
12      def __init__(self, name):
13          self.name = name
14
15      def __get__(self, inst, class_=None):
16          return inst.mapping[self.name]
17
18      def __set__(self, inst, value):
19          inst.mapping[self.name] = value
20
21  class MemberInfo(object):
22      implements(IMemberInfo)
23      adapts(IPrincipal)
24
25      def __init__(self, context):
26          annotations = IAnnotations(context)
27          mapping = annotations.get(KEY)
28          if mapping is None:
29              blank = {'first': u'', 'last': u'', 'email': u''}
30              mapping = annotations[KEY] = PersistentDict(blank)
31          self.mapping = mapping
32
33      first = MappingProperty('first')
34      last = MappingProperty('last')
35      email = MappingProperty('email')
```

Testing

As usual we can give the adapter a quick test drive on the interactive interpreter shell. Before we can start, though, we need to set up the principal annotation utility and the IAnnotations adapter for principals:

```
$ python
>>> from zope.component import provideUtility
>>> from zope.app.principalannotation import \
...     PrincipalAnnotationUtility
>>> from zope.app.principalannotation.interfaces import \
...     IPrincipalAnnotationUtility
>>> utility = PrincipalAnnotationUtility()
>>> provideUtility(utility, IPrincipalAnnotationUtility)
>>>
>>> from zope.component import provideAdapter
>>> from zope.app.principalannotation import annotations
>>> provideAdapter(annotations)                                    ▼
```

Now we can start. As a principal object, we simply use a dummy implementation. All it really needs is an ID so that the utility can identify it:

```
>>> from zope.security.interfaces import IPrincipal
>>> from zope.interface import implements
>>> class DummyPrincipal(object):
...     implements(IPrincipal)
...     id = "sloopy_joe"
>>> sloppy_joe = DummyPrincipal()                                  ▼
```

With this principal object we invoke the IMemberinfo adapter and store some user metadata on it:

```
>>> from worldcookery.memberinfo import Memberinfo
>>> info = MemberInfo(sloppy_joe)
>>> info.first = u"Sloppy"
>>> info.last = u"Joe"
>>> info.email = u"sloppyjoe@usafood.com"                          ▼
```

Not surprisingly, retrieving the information works just as well:

```
>>> info.first, info.last, info.email
(u'Sloppy', u'Joe', u'sloppyjoe@usafood.com')                      ▼
```

The utility instance has stored our data in the IAnnotations object:

```
>>> utility.hasAnnotations(sloppy_joe)
True
>>> annotations = utility.getAnnotations(sloppy_joe)
>>> items = list(annotations['worldcookery.memberinfo'].items())
>>> items.sort()
>>> tuple(items)
(('email', u'sloppyjoe@usafood.com'), ('first', u'Sloppy'),
 ('last', u'Joe'))                                                 ■
```

Like many other interpreter sessions, this one was also added as a doctest and can be found at `memberinfo.txt` for reference.

Now we only need to register the `IMemberInfo` adapter. This is done with the regular `adapter` directive. It is not necessary to make this adapter a trusted adapter like the other annotations-based ones, because the principal object is typically not security-proxied.

Browser form for editing member information

Now we would like to give principals the ability to edit their own member information. This is a classic use case for automated edit forms, especially since we already have an `IMemberInfo` schema. This form is different from the add and edit forms we have written so far in various ways:

- The "context" of the browser page is not the object that is edited in the form. The form context is the current principal whereas the browser page context could be any object.
- The object that we are editing (the principal) does not provide the schema (`IMemberInfo`) that we use as a base for the automated form.

The second issue is not a problem because the form machinery in `zope. formlib` automatically adapts the object that is to be edited to the form fields' schema. That means our `IMemberInfo` adapter will be used to store the form data, which is exactly what we want. The first issue, however, makes it impossible to use the convenient `EditForm` base class because `EditForm` assumes that the browser page context and form context are the same object. Therefore we have to use the more generic `FormBase` base class and customize some of the form API that is described in `zope.formlib`'s `IFormBaseCustomization` interface. Example 22.4.3 shows how to do that.

Doing more with user metadata

The example presented in this chapter is a short introduction to managing user metadata. We have not looked at other possible use cases for storing user metadata. For example, we could make a lot of use of a principal's email address, such as sending an email when the password has been forgotten. In Chapter 16, we wrote a small email notification framework with subscription capabilities. This framework could be modified so that authenticated principals do not have to enter their email address, it would be taken from their member information instead. Finally, the sign up forms that were developed in this chapter could be extended with the fields from `IMemberInfo` so that users signing up provide their metadata along with the login information.

Example 22.4.3 Form for editing a principal's member information
(`browser/memberinfo.py`)

```
1  from zope.formlib.form import FormBase, Fields, haveInputWidgets
2  from zope.formlib.form import action, applyChanges, setUpEditWidgets
3  from zope.formlib.namedtemplate import NamedTemplate
4  from zope.i18nmessageid import MessageFactory
5  _ = MessageFactory('worldcookery')
6  from worldcookery.interfaces import IMemberInfo
7
8  class MemberInfoForm(FormBase):
9      form_fields = Fields(IMemberInfo)
10     label = _(u"Edit your member info")
11     template = NamedTemplate('worldcookery.form')
12
13     def setUpWidgets(self, ignore_request=False):
14         self.adapters = {}
15         self.widgets = setUpEditWidgets(
16             self.form_fields, self.prefix, self.request.principal,
17             self.request, adapters=self.adapters,
18             ignore_request=ignore_request
19             )
20
21     @action(_(u"Save"), condition=haveInputWidgets)
22     def handleSaveButton(self, action, data):
23         principal = self.request.principal
24         if applyChanges(principal, self.form_fields, data, self.adapters)
               :
25             self.status = _(u"Changes saved.")
26         else:
27             self.status = _(u"No changes.")
```

13–19. The `setUpWidgets` method is responsible for initializing the widgets for
a form. We do this almost exactly like edit forms, except that we use the
principal object as a basis for initial widget data. The `setUpEditWidgets`
helper function that we use here is documented in the `IFormAPI` interface
which is provided by the `zope.formlib.form` module.

21–27. The form machinery allows us to specify what should happen when a form
has been submitted and validated either successfully or unsuccessfully. Actions are objects providing `IAction` and have methods such as `success` and
`failure` to express that. The `action` decorator provides an easy way of turning a class method into an action. The method becomes the action's success
handler. In addition to that we can specify a label that will be used when
rendering an action as a submit button.
Here we define an action very similar to the one edit forms define, except that
we apply the form data to the principal object and not the form's context.

Fig. 22.5. Editing member information

Summary

- It is often desirable to associate additional (meta)data with principals.
- Principal objects do not have to be persistent since they can come from any sort of user database.
- The principal annotation utility allows storing principal metadata as annotations in the ZODB, even though the principal object itself might not be a ZODB-persistent object.
- The form machinery automatically adapts the edited object to the form fields' schema if the schema is not provided by the object.
- Actions are components associated with forms that implement the form business logic upon valid or invalid form data. Actions are typically rendered as submit buttons in forms.

23

Debugging Zope

No software is bug-free. In fact, a great part of a software developer's time is spent finding and fixing bugs. The more complicated a system gets, the more complicated it usually is to find and fix bugs. Fortunately, Zope provides tools to help you debug Zope-based applications. They are introduced in this chapter.

23.1 Self-documenting code with APIDoc

Python code is can document itself in various ways, for example through docstrings and Python's ability to introspect pretty much all objects, including their classes, methods, and attributes. There are a number of tools that make this information available for a human-readable reference. Python's built-in `help` function and its equivalent `pydoc` command line program for instance display information about arbitrary objects (incl. modules, classes, functions, etc.) in a way similar to `man` pages on Unix. Third-party programs like epydoc[1] generate HTML files with similar information, but with the ability to browse through a project's code using hyperlinks.

While these tools work with Zope, they do not know anything about Zope's Component Architecture and do not display useful information such as the interfaces a component provides or even component registrations. For this reason, Zope comes with its own documentation tool called *APIDoc*. It is a tool that runs within Zope and therefore requires a running Zope instance. That also allows APIDoc to inspect the global component registries.

Developer mode

By default, Zope's debugging and development features such as APIDoc are disabled and need to be explicitly enabled. This is done in your instance's `etc/zope.conf` file by adding the following line:

---

[1] epydoc homepage <http://epydoc.sourceforge.net>

```
devmode on
```

This will enable a ZCML feature called `devmode`. Zope's debugging and development tools will only be registered when this ZCML feature is present. They typically have an appropriate `zcml:condition` attribute in their configuration directives, e.g.:

```
<configure
    xmlns="http://namespaces.zope.org/zope"
    xmlns:zcml="http://namespaces.zope.org/zcml"
    zcml:condition="have devmode">
  ...
</configure>
```

For more information on ZCML features, browse back to the first section of Chapter 13 or refer to Appendix B.

Note that developer mode should only be enabled on development instances, not in production systems! Leaving developer mode enabled is a security risk because visitors may easily find out about the internals of your application.

Using APIDoc and the introspector

After enabling developer mode and restarting Zope, you will notice that objects have a new management tab, *Introspector*. In this tab you can see the interfaces that the object provides, its class and base classes, its methods and attributes as well as its annotations (if it is annotatable). You can also click on any of the interfaces or classes to see more information about them. These links will directly take you to the APIDoc tool.

You can visit the APIDoc tool yourself at `http://localhost:8080/++apidoc++`. If you already know epydoc, you will see that the APIDoc interface is similar. APIDoc has five categories:

Book compiles developer documentation such as doctests and other text files within Python packages. Most of Zope's own doctests are already registered there.

Code Browser lets you search for classes and view their methods and attributes as well as base classes. You can also browse through Zope's own sources.

Interfaces, Interface Types lets you find interfaces and view their basic information such as attributes, schema fields, and method definitions. For each interface you can also get a list of adapters registered for this interface, as well as a list of views for the various protocols.

Utilities provides a way to look at utilities defined in the global utility registry.

ZCML Reference gives an overview of all known ZCML directives in the various namespaces, as well as their parameters.

APIDoc's ability to look at the global adapter and utility registries are especially useful when debugging complex applications. They allow you to check whether your registrations are active and whether they apply as intended.

Registering your own documentation with APIDoc

In Chapter 5 we made the `IRecipe` interface an `IContentType` with the `interface` ZCML directive. This directive also registers the interface as a utility, making it available to APIDoc that way. It is therefore a good idea to register interfaces through ZCML.

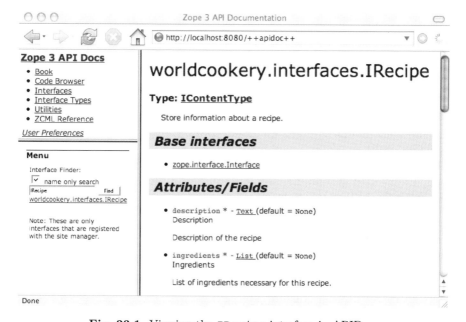

Fig. 23.1. Viewing the `IRecipe` interface in APIDoc.

We can also make our doctests available in an APIDoc book chapter. This can be done easily in ZCML using the `apidoc:bookchapter` directive. In addition to that we can register the `worldcookery` package as a browseable module for APIDoc's code browser module. Example 23.1.1 shows an excerpt from `configure.zcml` that does all this.

Example 23.1.1 Registering doctests as APIDoc book chapters
(`configure.zcml`)

```
1    ...
2    <configure xmlns:apidoc="http://namespaces.zope.org/apidoc"
3              xmlns:zcml="http://namespaces.zope.org/zcml"
4              zcml:condition="have apidoc">
5
6      <apidoc:rootModule module="worldcookery" />
7
8      <apidoc:bookchapter
9          id="worldcookery"
10         title="World Cookery"
11         />
12
13     <apidoc:bookchapter
14         id="filerepresentation"
15         title="File representation"
16         doc_path="filerepresentation.txt"
17         parent="worldcookery"
18         />
19
20     <apidoc:bookchapter
21         id="folder"
22         title="Recipe folder"
23         doc_path="folder.txt"
24         parent="worldcookery"
25         />
26
27     ...
28
29   </configure>
30   ...
```

4. When the APIDoc tool is enabled, it registers a ZCML feature called `apidoc`. By using this feature in a ZCML condition, we ensure that the following directives are only executed when the APIDoc tool is actually available.

8–11. This directive makes the `worldcookery` package available to APIDoc's code browser.

8–11. Here we define a "chapter" for APIDoc. This chapter does not have any contents itself, we just use it to add sub-chapters below.

13–18 and 20–25. These directives register two of our doctests as chapters below the *World Cookery* entry.

Summary

- Standard Python documentation tools do not make use of Zope's interface declarations and cannot display component registrations.
- Zope comes with an online documentation tool called APIDoc that allows browsing through code, interface declarations, component registrations and ZCML directives.
- APIDoc also provides a compilation of developer documents and doctests. It is possible to register your own text files as chapters.
- Development tools like APIDoc are only loaded when developer mode has been switched on in `zope.conf`.

Flashback

Zope 2 has something similar to developer mode called *debug mode*. The difference is that enabling debug mode typically just changes the behaviour of already available components while developer mode in Zope 3 is a switch to explicitly enable certain components that are useful during development. Neither should be enabled on production systems.

Rocky says...

Java developers should think of APIDoc as a dynamically updated (live) version of JavaDocs. The nice thing here is that all code that is inserted into the system like third-party libraries will automatically have their APIs made available without having to dig through release files.

23.2 Online debugging tools

In this section we look at some online Zope debugging tools that can help you track down errors in your code.

The error reporting utility

When an exception occurs within Zope, it is logged via the standard Python logging API to the event log that is configured in `zope.conf`. Exceptions are also logged with the *error reporting utility* which can record exceptions and their tracebacks and make them available for debugging later on. This is useful when it is difficult to access the event log or when the exceptions do not appear in the event log. The fact that the utility records a given number of exceptions also makes it easier to review errors that occurred in the past, for example when examining a production instance.

The default implementation of the error reporting utility is a local, persistent one. In a standard Zope instance, the root folder's site manager already contains a configured instance of the error reporting utility. Of course you can register your own instances in other locations if you would like to catch errors that only occur in a specific location. The nearest error reporting utility will be logging the error.

The error reporting utility can be configured to ignore certain exceptions. In a production instance, for example, it makes sense to ignore Unauthorized and NotFound exceptions as well as UserError, because these errors can easily be provoked by users. During development, however, it often makes sense to enable the their logging.

Debugging Page Templates

Zope allows us to manage complex user interfaces quite well, thanks to Page Template macros and content providers. But that complexity has a price. It makes it more difficult to understand why a page renders the way it does and where its elements come from. Fortunately, Page Templates support two mechanisms to annotate their output with debug information which alleviate these problems.

Usually Page Templates remove the TAL, METAL and i18n instructions from the template when it is rendered. This can be disabled by setting an appropriate debug flag on the request, which is best done by inserting ++debug++tal as an additional path element into the URL. All Page Templates will continue to render normally except that they will not remove any Page Template specific instructions from the result.

Another flag, ++debug++source, will cause Page Template to annotate the rendered result with information about the Page Template's source file. The file name and line number of each Page Template file involved will be written into XML comments.

Note that you can combine debug namespace features using URL elements either like ++debug++tal/++debug++source or merely ++debug++tal, source. Keep in mind that the ++debug++ traversal namespace is only available when developer mode has been enabled.

Debug skin

By default, Zope only renders proper pages for exceptions like NotFound, Unauthorized and UserError. Other, more low-level exceptions do not cause a page with a problem description to be rendered. This is so that sensitive information about the application, such as a potential security hole,

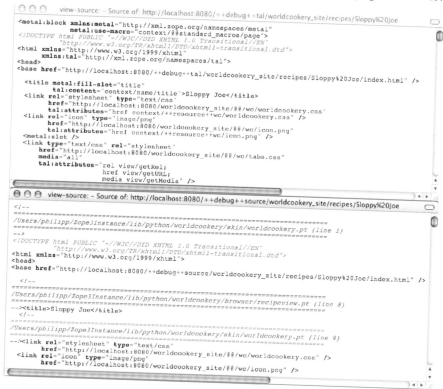

Fig. 23.2. Debugging Page Template output.

is not revealed to the user. For the same reason, exception tracebacks are not shown by default.

For debugging purposes, it is often very useful to see the exact error description including a traceback. With the right exception views, it would even be possible to see a traceback every time an exception occurs, without having to go to the event log or the error reporting utility first. Fortunately, Zope already provides such views as part of a debug skin. You have several choices regarding the way to enable them:

- You can use the *Debug* skin, for example via the `++skin++Debug` path element in a URL. This is a skin based on Zope's default skin, *Rotterdam* and has the debug-enabled exception views.
- You can insert the `++debug++errors` path element into a URL. This will cause the *Debug* skin to be applied to the request as well, though only in addition and not instead of an already active skin.
- You can derive a custom skin from `IDebugLayer`, made available by the `zope.app.debugskin` package. This will cause your custom skin

to inherit the debug-enabled exception views. No extra path elements and no developer mode are needed in the URL in this case.

Summary

- Zope logs exceptions to the event log as well as to the error reporting utility which can record a given number of exceptions and their traceback for future examination.
- Page Templates can annotate their rendered output with debug information, such as the original template instructions and names of the source files.
- The *Debug* skin provides alternate views for exceptions that display useful debugging information such as the traceback.

Using Zope 2

The error reporting utility has been inspired by the `error_log` object of Zope 2. Its functionality is pretty much identical. The only difference between the two is the way they are looked up. In Zope 3, we do a utility look-up whereas in Zope 2, the `error_log` is acquired via inherited attributes.

23.3 Using the Python debugger

Sometimes passive debugging tools like the ones describe above are not powerful enough to track down difficult problems. In these cases it is helpful to use interactive tools. We have already used Zope's debug shell (`debugzope`). It lets you work with a configured Zope instance and gives you access to the ZODB root object on the Python interpreter prompt.

Another useful tool like this is Python's debugger, pdb. It is part of Python's standard library and therefore documented as part of the standard library reference.[2] A common way to use pdb is to manually set a break point somewhere in the code by adding the following line:

```
import pdb; pdb.set_trace()
```

After restarting Zope using the `runzope` script or `zopectl fg`, you only have to load a page in your browser that provokes the code with the break point to be executed. Zope will then drop into them pdb prompt where you can interactively debug the code on the pdb command line.

---

[2] pdb documentation in Python's standard library reference <http://docs. python.org/lib/module-pdb.html>

Post-mortem debugging HTTP server

Zope makes debugging with pdb even easier when you want to debug exceptions occurring in your application. When using the `PostmortemDebuggingHTTP` server, which is a variant of the regular HTTP server, Zope will automatically drop into pdb whenever it encounters an exception. Thanks to pdb's post-mortem mode, the debugging session will start where the exception is raised. That way you examine the circumstances that lead to the exception.

To enable the post-mortem debugging HTTP server, add the following entry to your instance's `etc/zope.conf` file:

```
<server>
  type PostmortemDebuggingHTTP
  address 9080
</server>
```

Of course, the port can be different on your machine. In any case it is a good idea to configure this server instance *in addition* to a standard HTTP server. The usual port 8080 is therefore not available. Also note that the debugging HTTP server only works when using a Twisted-based instance.

When using the post-mortem debugging HTTP server, you should be careful about not generating unnecessary exceptions. Actions that would normally not show problems, such as an unresolvable path (`NotFound`) or insufficient privileges (`Unauthorized`) will cause a pdb prompt with this server. It is therefore a good idea to manually log in before provoking the exception that is to be debugged.

It can also happen that by the time you get to the pdb prompt, the ZODB connection has been closed already. If this is a problem for your debugging, you may need to use a manual break point using `pdb.set_trace()` as described above.

Summary

- Zope's debug shell starts an interpreter prompt with a fully configured Zope instance and access to the ZODB root object.
- Python's debugger lets you set break points and interactively step through any Python code.
- Zope provides a post-mortem debugging HTTP server that drops into pdb's post-mortem mode whenever an exception occurs in the application.

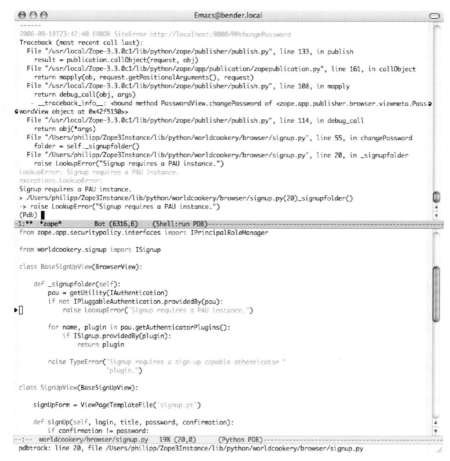

Fig. 23.3. The post-mortem debugging HTTP server drops into pdb when an exception occurs.

Rocky says...

Pdb will be the obvious counterpart to jdb for java developers. While the commands may not be exactly the same, the functionality is pretty similar.

Packaging and Deployment

Our global community web application for hobbyist cooks is now complete. In earlier chapters we built a website for sharing and storing recipes. The web application also now supports several Internet protocols, data formats and authentication schemes. This chapter looks at packaging the application and deploying it on a production server.

24.1 Packaging an application

So far we have simply copied the worldcookery package to the Zope instance directory in order to install it. While this is an acceptable approach while developing a package, it is a complex solution for people who simply want to install *World Cookery* themselves. To make things simpler we will create a distribution of the worldcookery package along with easy-to-use installation routines.

Creating a distribution

While general package information (README.txt files, installation guides, etc.) and installation routines can be placed inside the Python package, it is often preferable to place them in a top-level directory of the distribution and put the Python sources in a src directory. Figure 24.1 shows how this directory structure is used to create a distribution of the worldcookery package.

Python comes with a packaging and distribution system called *distutils* [3]. It allows us to easily create installation and packaging routines for our package. All we have to do is write a simple Python script that is by convention called setup.py and place it in the root of the distribution. This script can be used to install the worldcookery application and to create distributable packages in "tarball" format.

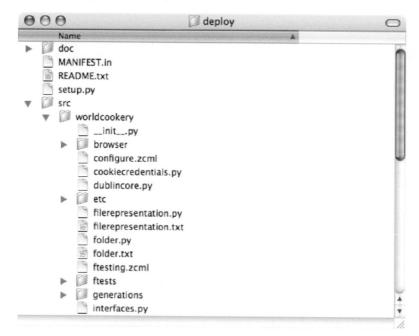

Fig. 24.1. Typical directory structure for distributions.

However distutils traditionally has a problem. It does not handle nicely the extra data files (ZCML, doctests, Page Templates, message catalogs, etc.) that Zope packages typically include. An extension to distutils, *setuptools* [23], makes this a lot easier. Setuptools also provides a packaging format to distribute and install Python packages more easily. It is called *eggs* [14] and has the following features:

- Eggs include metadata, such as dependency information. Setuptools can make use of this information to automatically resolve dependencies of an egg.
- Eggs can be conveniently distributed as ZIP files. Since Python can import modules directly from ZIP files, eggs can easily be installed by being included on the PYTHONPATH.
- Eggs allow application plug-ins to register themselves using *entry points*. Several Python applications use those as their plug-in mechanism.

Setuptools can be installed using the ez_setup.py script from the setuptools homepage.[1]

To make an egg of the worldcookery package, we just have to provide the setup.py script. This script invokes setuptools and provides it with

---

[1] Setuptools homepage <http://peak.telecommunity.com/DevCenter/setuptools>

information about the egg that is to be created. See Example 24.1.1. We also
need to tell setuptools what kind of data files it should include in the egg.
This is done in a MANIFEST.in file which contains only the following line:

```
recursive-include src *.txt *.zcml *.pt *.css *.js *.png *.dat *.pot
                   *.po *.mo
```

Example 24.1.1 Setup script for the worldcookery package (setup.py)

```
1   from setuptools import setup, find_packages
2
3   setup(name='worldcookery',
4         version='2.0',
5         url='http://worldcookery.com/Downloads',
6         description='World Cookery',
7         author='Philipp von Weitershausen',
8         author_email='philipp@weitershausen.de',
9         long_description=file('README.txt').read(),
10        classifiers=['Development Status :: 5 - Production/Stable',
11                     'Framework :: Zope3',
12                     'Intended Audience :: Developers'],
13        packages=find_packages('src'),
14        package_dir={'': 'src'},
15        include_package_data=True,
16        zip_safe=False,
17        )
```

4–12. Apart from data relevant to packaging, we can also provide some metadata
about the package. Setuptools uses the version information, for example, to
distinguish different versions of a package in order to satisfy dependencies on
specific versions. The other metadata is used when the package is uploaded to
the Python Cheese Shop.

13. We need to explicitly tell the setup routine which packages should be included
in the distribution. The find_packages function we use here finds all packages
and subpackages in a given directory.

14. Here we define the src directory as the default location for packages. When
creating the distribution, setuptools will look there for the package source code.

15. With this flag we enable the inclusion of data files within packages. The files
to be considered data files are specified in the MANIFEST.in file.

16. Eggs can be installed in ZIP form, rather than directories. Since Zope needs
to access data files inside packages and currently does not support accessing
them from ZIP files, we need to declare Zope-related eggs as *not* ZIP-safe.

We can now invoke the `setup.py` script to create an egg, using the following command line:

```
python setup.py bdist_egg
```

This will place a ZIP file called `worldcookery-2.0-py2.4.egg` into a newly created `dist` directory. That file is the egg for `worldcookery` which we can now distribute to everyone who wants to install the *World Cookery* application. For example, if we want to make it available to a broader audience, we can easily register it with the Python Cheese Shop and upload the egg using the following commands:

```
python setup.py register
python setup.py bdist_egg upload
```

Note that this requires an account at the Cheese Shop.

Installing a distribution

Now that we can distribute the `worldcookery` package in a handy format, you may be wondering how to install it into a Zope instance. Generally we have two choices for installing Python packages. We can install them either into the global `site-packages` directory that Python provides for add-on packages, or directly into the Zope instance. The latter has several advantages. Firstly, you may not have privileges to write to the global `site-packages` directory. Secondly, when installing packages directly into the instance, different instances can have different versions of the same package. They are also independent of any changes to the global setup. An installation local to the instance gives you more control.

Eggs are installed using the `easy_install` command that is part of setuptools. It can be used in several ways:

`easy_install` *filename* installs the given egg directly.

`easy_install` *url* downloads an egg from the given location and installs it.

`easy_install` *package_name* looks for the package on the Python Cheese Shop and tries to find a downloadable format, e.g. an egg or a regular source distribution. If it is successful, it will download the package and install it as an egg.

Unless specified otherwise, `easy_install` will install the package into the global `site-packages` directory. We could install packages directly into our Zope instance by telling `easy_install` to put the eggs in the instance's `lib/python` directory. However, that will not make them available on Python's package search path, because the `lib/python` directory is not registered with Python's `site.py` module to contain eggs.

A simple way to enable eggs in the `lib/python` directory is to use the `workingenv.py` script which is available from the Cheese Shop.[2] It can turn our Zope instance into a *working environment*. That is a place where additional packages are installed locally and without any interference from the global package setup (e.g. `site-packages`). To turn our existing Zope instance into a working environment, we issue the following command:

```
~$ python workingenv.py --home Zope3Instance
```

Here `Zope3Instance` denotes the instance directory.

You will notice that while converting our Zope instance into a working environment, `workingenv.py` has installed separate copies of setuptools and `easy_install` there. This means that the instance is now self-contained in terms of any package installation. To decouple ourselves from the global environment, we execute the following line inside the instance:

```
~/Zope3Instance$ source bin/activate
```

On Windows, simply execute the `bin\activate.bat` file. We can now use the `easy_install` script from our working environment to install packages that are specific to that instance. They will end up in the instance's `lib/python` directory as usual. For example, the following line will install the `worldcookery` egg we created previously:

```
~/Zope3Instance$ bin/easy_install path/to/worldcookery-2.0-py2.4.egg
```

Note that this only installs the `worldcookery` package in egg form, it does not automatically install the ZCML configuration files necessary in the instance's `etc/package-includes` directory.

Summary

- Distutils and setuptools provide a way to easily package Python software for distribution.
- Python eggs are a packaging format that support package metadata (such as dependency information) and easy distribution as ZIP files.
- Python tools comes with the `easy_install` package manager that can install eggs including their dependencies globally or in a working environment.
- By turning a Zope instance into a working environment it becomes independent from global package installation. Eggs can easily be installed into working environments.

---

[2] Cheese Shop page for `workingenv.py` <http://cheeseshop.python.org/pypi/workingenv.py>

> **Rocky says...**
>
> Eggs and Java jars are pretty synonymous. The difference here is that
> Python doesn't have a web-specific version of an egg which means eggs
> will take the place of jars, wars, and ears. In addition, eggs support a more
> involved dependency configuration in their metadata which can dictate
> which versions of an external library are required. While this makes it
> easier for Python to automatically fetch required libraries, some argue
> this is the responsibility of the OS in use.

24.2 Preparing a production instance

After installing all the necessary packages inside an instance, our Zope instance is now almost ready for production. There are just a few things you
should be aware of before going online.

Controlling an instance on Windows

As mentioned in Chapter 3, you can control Zope instances on Unix with the
bin/zopectl script. It allows you to start, stop, restart instances and the
like, but due to its design it does not work on Windows. Fortunately, Windows
has its own built-in mechanism for controlling long running processes called
services. Services are similar to Unix daemons. They are started when the
system boots and do not require a window (such as the shell that Zope would
otherwise be running) to remain open. Applications like Zope should always
be run as services when in production mode.

To register a Zope instance as a service, you first need to make sure that
you have the Python Win32 extensions[3] installed. Then you can register the
instance with the following command on the Windows command line inside
your instance directory:

```
C:\Zope3Instance> python bin\zopeservice.py --startup auto install
Registering the Python Service Manager...
Installing service Zope_-2124328379
Service installed
```

After the service has been registered, it will be available in the *Services* section
of Windows' *Control Panel* from where you can start and stop it as well as
control its behaviour. See Figure 24.2. Before removing a Zope instance, you
should also use the zopeservice.py script to unregister the service. This
cannot be done later in the Control Panel. To unregister, make sure the
service is stopped and issue the following command:

---

[3] Python Win32 extensions homepage <http://starship.python.net/
crew/skippy/win32/Downloads.html>

```
C:\Zope3Instance> python bin\zopeservice.py remove
Registering the Python Service Manager...
Removing service Zope_-2124328379
Service removed
```

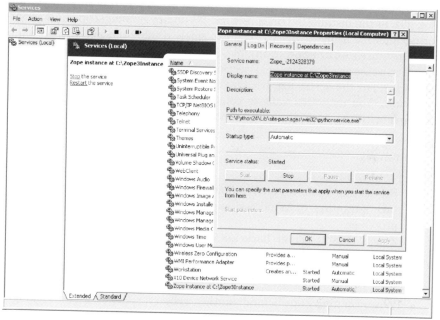

Fig. 24.2. Controlling a Zope instance as a Windows service.

Configuring servers

In general, Zope supports any WSGI-capable server backend, though only `twisted.web2` and Zope's own `zope.server` are supported out of the box. By default, the `mkzopeinstance` script chooses the Twisted backend. You can tell it to create an instance with the `zope.server` backend by providing the `--zserver` switch.

Note that the Twisted backend is the intended replacement for Zope's own server in the long term, even though it is known to be slower than the older `zope.server` backend. Exact numbers will vary from application to application. It is therefore a good idea to conduct benchmarks with the two backends to see whether the impact on your application's performance is noticeable.

For deployment, it is also a good idea to disable any additional server instances that were enabled during development (e.g. the FTP server or the post-mortem debugging HTTP server), unless your application depends on them, of course.

Configuring logging

By default, Zope writes an access log and an event log to both `stdout` and log files in the instance's `log` directory. If you are running Zope as a service or daemonized using `zopectl`, you can safely disable the `stdout` option in your instance's `etc/zope.conf` file. Moreover, if you are using Zope behind another webserver (see the next section), you may only be interested in the event log, not the access log, because the server in front of Zope already logs page hits. You may also want to consider rotating your logs frequently, for example with the `logrotate` program.

Summary

- Production instances on Windows should be registered as services to take advantage of Windows' support for long running daemon-like processes.
- Zope's default server backend is `twisted.web2`, even though is known to be slower than Zope's older `zope.server`.
- Benchmarks can help choosing which server backend is appropriate for a particular application.
- When running Zope behind another webserver, Zope's access logging can usually be disabled in favour of the main webserver's access log.

Using Zope 2

For production environments, Zope 2 is generally better supported on the Windows platform than Zope 3. The Windows distribution for Zope 2 comes with its own Python and already includes the Win32 extensions. The automatic installer also creates an instance for you which it will register as a Windows service by default.

24.3 Virtual hosting

As we know from Chapter 18, Zope's site machinery makes it possible to serve different websites from the same Zope instance. These can even be made available under different host names, even though there is only one Zope instance on one server. This technique is called *virtual hosting*.

Virtual hosting is often done with just one IP address. Web servers can figure out which website the incoming request is supposed to go to because most HTTP clients send the desired hostname in the `Host` HTTP header. Zope by itself does not interpret this header, though it would be possible to provide a custom traverser or a WSGI middleware that does. Most of the time, however, third-party webserver software is placed in front of Zope. The most common set-up is:

- The Zope HTTP server is configured to only listen on `localhost` on a high port such as 8080. That means it can be run under a non-privileged user account which increases the security of the Zope sandbox. Only binding it to `localhost` ensures that no one from the outside gains access to Zope directly.

- A third-party webserver such as Apache,[4] listens to port 80 (the standard port for HTTP) and delegates incoming requests to the Zope server on port 8080. Optionally, the URL can be rewritten to gain or lose path segments. That way, the root of the Zope hierarchy does not necessarily have to match the root of the served pages' hierarchy.

This system is very flexible, and has some advantages even if you are only hosting a single application:

- You can designate certain areas of a website to be served by the main webserver instead of Zope, for example as a download area for large files that you want to keep outside the ZODB.

- If the webserver in front of Zope supports SSL, you can easily serve a Zope application over encrypted connections, even though ZServer does not support SSL.

- When delegating pages to Zope, you can set up caching in between the webserver and Zope, for example using Squid or Apache's *mod_cache*. This can lead to great performance increases (see the next section).

These points also apply to applications that do not require virtual hosting because they need to be served under several host names. Experience has shown that it is usually recommended to use the virtual hosting approach for production systems, even if only one host name is involved. While development setups are often better off with a bare Zope, you may want to develop with a third-party server in front of Zope if the application heavily depends on the main webserver's behaviour (e.g. when doing caching).

Rewriting URLs

Zope generates URLs from object paths. The most convenient way to do that is the `absolute_url` view which we have used several times already. The problem is that when Zope is hidden behind a dedicated webserver that manages virtual hosting, Zope only ever receives requests on

---

[4] Apache webserver homepage <http://httpd.apache.org>

`http://localhost:8080`. It thinks that somebody is always accessing it from a web browser on the local machine, whilst in reality the webserver software is just proxying requests for remote clients.

Even though it does not support virtual hosting per se, Zope allows URL rewriting so that the URLs it generates match the URLs that a Zope website is accessed under from the outside. For example, imagine that the *World Cookery* website lives in the `worldcookery_site` folder. That means it can be accessed through the bare Zope server as `http://localhost:8080/worldcookery_site`. Of course, we would like it to appear under `http://worldcookery.com`. Therefore we need to tell Zope to strip of the `http://localhost:8080/worldcookery_site` part and prepend `http://worldcookery.com` instead when generating URLs.

Rewriting URLs is achieved through a traversal adapter. We already know `++view++`, `++skin++` and `++debug++`. The one for URL rewriting is called `++vh++`. It is used in the following way:

```
http://host:port/path/to/site/++vh++virtual_protocol:
     virtual_host:virtual_port/virtual_path/++/
```

In our case, it would be:

```
http://localhost:8080/worldcookery_site/
     ++vh++http:worldcookery.com:80/++/
```

This tells Zope to rewrite URLs so that they use the HTTP protocol (an alternative would be HTTPS, for example), `worldcookery.com` for the host name of the virtual host and port 80 for the virtual port. It is important to always specify the port even if it is the standard HTTP port 80. If you try the above URL in a web browser, you will see that all URLs generated by Zope now will start with `http://worldcookery.com`. This causes pages to be rendered without any custom styles because the stylesheet references point to non-existing files at `http://worlcookery.com`.

Apache in front of Zope

The most successful webserver on the Internet is the Apache HTTP server. Its advantage is that it runs on both Unix-based and Windows operating systems which is why we will describe setting up our example application in a virtual hosting environment using this software. Other webservers or web proxies have similar functionality, so any lesson learned here should be adaptable to other systems.

In the following we assume that you have a running installation of the Apache 2 webserver. In addition, the following Apache shared modules are required:

mod_proxy and *mod_proxy_http* These modules allow the Apache webserver to act as a proxy between the user client and Zope.

mod_rewrite (optional) This module allows rewriting URLs from within Apache. This is useful when serving local pages and pages from Zope in the same virtual host.

The example listings configure the virtual host settings for the fictitious worldcookery.com website.

Apache allows us to configure virtual hosts by using the <VirtualHost> environments in its configuration file. Virtual hosts based on the Host HTTP header have to be enabled with the following directive:

```
NameVirtualHost *
```

Make sure it is in the main Apache configuration file.

We now have two options for configuring the proxying to Zope. The easiest way is to use the simple ProxyPass and ProxyPassReverse directives. Example 24.3.1 shows the configuration of a virtual hosting using these directives. The disadvantage here is that every request that is identified to be handled by this virtual host goes to Zope. There is no way to declare an exception, for example to serve certain files statically.

Example 24.3.1 Simple Apache 2 virtual host configuration (doc/apache2-proxypass.conf)

```
1   <VirtualHost *>
2       ServerName worldcookery.com
3       ServerAlias worldcookery.com *.worldcookery.com
4       ServerAdmin webmaster@worldcookery.com
5       DocumentRoot "/var/www/worldcookery"
6
7       CustomLog "logs/worldcookery-access.log" combined
8       ErrorLog "logs/worldcookery-error.log"
9       LogLevel warn
10      ServerSignature On
11
12      ProxyPass / http://localhost:8080/worldcookery_site/++vh++http:
            worldcookery.com:80/++
13      ProxyPassReverse / http://localhost:8080/worldcookery_site/++vh++http
            :worldcookery.com:80/++
14  </VirtualHost>
```

12–13. ProxyPass and ProxyPassReverse tell Apache to forward incoming requests to the following URL and to send the response that came out of that URL back to the original client. As a URL we use the one that rewrites URLs according to the virtual host used. It is the same one that we tested in a web browser earlier.

The other possibility is to use the advanced mod_rewrite module. It allows URL rewriting within Apache based on regular expression matches. This lets us serve certain URLs from the file system, for example, while the rest is patched through to Zope. It would also allow us to combine several Zope instances under one virtual host. An example configuration file using the rewrite functionality is shown in Example 24.3.2.

Example 24.3.2 Advanced Apache 2 virtual host configuration (doc/apache2-rewrite.conf)

```
1   <VirtualHost *>
2       ServerName worldcookery.com
3       ServerAlias worldcookery.com *.worldcookery.com
4       ServerAdmin webmaster@worldcookery.com
5       DocumentRoot "/var/www/worldcookery"
6
7       CustomLog "logs/worldcookery-access.log" combined
8       ErrorLog "logs/worldcookery-error.log"
9       LogLevel warn
10      ServerSignature On
11
12      RewriteEngine On
13      RewriteRule ^/files/(.*) - [L]
14      RewriteRule ^/(.*) \
15          http://localhost:8080/worldcookery_site/++vh++http:%{SERVER_NAME
                }:80/++/$1 [P,L]
16  </VirtualHost>
```

13. This rewrite rule tells Zope to serve all URLs that begin with /files/ to serve locally from the file system. This could be useful for a download area where large files can be downloaded from that would bloat the ZODB instance otherwise.

14–15. This rewrite rule enables the proxy function for all other URLs so that content is pulled from the Zope instance. Again we specify the URL that takes care of rewriting.

To enable these settings in Apache, you can either copy and paste them into the web server's configuration file, usually httpd.conf or apache2.conf, or you can copy one of the files to the Apache configuration directory and use the following statement to have it included:

```
Include "/etc/apache2/apache2-proxypass.conf"
```

Or, if you prefer using the mod_rewrite approach:

```
Include "/etc/apache2/apache2-rewrite.conf"
```

Testing

To test whether the virtual host setup works, make sure your Zope instance is running under the port specified (usually 8080) and the Apache 2 server is also running. Now you need to make the operating system think that your local machine is actually `worldcookery.com`. This can be done most easily in the `hosts` file. On Unix-like operating systems, this file resides in the `/etc` directory. On recent Windows versions, it can be found under `C:\Windows\system32\drivers\etc`. Add the following line to the file using a simple text editor:

```
127.0.0.1   worldcookery.com
```

Now you should be able to open the URL `http://worldcookery.com` in a normal web browser and see your Zope instance served via Apache.

Summary

- Virtual hosting allows one server to be responsible for different host names.
- Zope itself does not support virtual hosting out-of-the box but it supports URL rewriting so that it can be used behind third-party webservers.
- The popular Apache webserver is installed on many systems. It provides virtual hosting capabilities and is the recommended webserver to be used in front of Zope.

Using Zope 2

Zope 2 provides simple built-in virtual hosting functionality through *Virtual Host Monster* (VHM) objects. Once added to a folder, it hooks itself into object traversal and can dispatch requests to different folders based on the `Host` HTTP header. Using the VHM in this direct way is very uncommon for production systems, though. For performance as well as security reasons, most setups only use the VHM for URL rewriting and handle incoming requests with a third-party webserver like Apache in front of Zope, as described for Zope 3 above. Like in Zope 3, URL rewriting is done by inserting special identifiers into the URL:

```
http://host:port/path/to/site/VirtualHostBase/virtual_protocol/
    virtual_host:virtual_port/_vh_virtual_path/VirtualHostRoot/
```

For example:

```
http://localhost:8080/worldcookery_site/VirtualHostBase/http/
    www.worldcookery.com:80/VirtualHostRoot/
```

24.4 Improving scalability

Except for resources which are usually static content, most pages served by Zope are dynamic. Serving a page in Zope means traversing through the object hierarchy, authenticating, reading data from the database, rendering templates, etc. All that takes a certain time. If your site is hit with a lot of requests within a short period of time, it may be possible that your single Zope instance is overwhelmed and cannot return the response to its clients in an appropriate time span. In this case your site has a scalability problem which needs to be addressed.

Before deploying an instance to a production server, it is a good idea to see how well it performs. There are numerous choices for HTTP benchmarking software. The Apache webserver, for example, comes with a useful tool called ab that lets you perform benchmarks on HTTP servers and is especially good for measuring how many requests per second the server is able to handle. This number can serve as a good indicator as to whether any actions on improving scalability of the applications, such as the ones discussed below, are fruitful.

Client-side caching

If you find your site performs poorly under the anticipated or experienced load, you should consider caching Zope's responses. Clients that support HTTP 1.1 may be told to cache content using the Cache-Control HTTP header. Even when using HTTP 1.0, most browsers will try to cache retrieved pages based on the Expires and Last-Modified headers.

It is therefore a good idea to set these headers for pages that can be cached on the client without problems. Zope already sets the HTTP 1.0 headers for browser resources based on the resource files' modification dates. Management pages like edit forms should probably not be cached, but they are typically not invoked that frequently, either.

Server-side caching

Having only the client cache pages has some disadvantages. For example, clients can choose to simply ignore the relevant HTTP headers and start a new request for every page reload. Furthermore, to be able to cache a page in the first place, clients have to get it from the application at least once. If most of the page hits you get on your site are due to first-time views, client-side caching will not help much to reduce the load on your application. In this case you may want to cache on the server.

As demonstrated in the previous section, you typically run third-party server software like Apache in front of Zope to serve static files on the same host and to get virtual hosting support, including support for SSL. This server in front of Zope is also a good place to do server-side caching.

The Apache HTTP server, for example, comes with caching support in the *mod_cache* module. It is a good choice for setting up server-side caching without involving too much additional machinery, provided you are already using Apache in front of Zope for virtual hosting. Highly frequented sites usually use a dedicated proxy software for caching, such as Squid.[5] The configuration of such a setup is very specific to the application and the deployment environment and can therefore not be covered here.

Balancing the load with ZEO

While caching works for sites with content that does not change too often, it is difficult to do for applications with very dynamic pages. Personalized applications like *World Cookery* that allow you to log in or remember things in a session will not benefit much from caching because personalized pages cannot be cached. In this case, spreading the work over several machines in a *cluster* is the obvious solution to improve scalability. A *load-balanced cluster* will also be more tolerant towards failures on one server because there would be others to take over the work. Load balancers typically used with Zope are *Pound*[6] and *balance*.[7]

Load balancing a Zope-based application essentially means setting up identical Zope instances on each of the servers. The only problem is that if these applications use the ZODB, they probably want to have access to the same ZODB instance. Fortunately, the ZODB allows multiple Zope instances to access the same database instance through *Zope Enterprise Objects* (ZEO).

Instead of using the ZODB's default storage that writes data into a file on the local file system (*FileStorage*), Zope instances use *ClientStorage* which connects to a storage server and fetches the data from there. This storage server is usually called the *ZEO server*, while the Zope instances that connect to the storage server are called *ZEO clients* (even though they typically are HTTP servers themselves).

Note that a ZEO setup does not necessarily have to involve multiple machines. It is often useful to use ZEO during development, for example when debugging while a running Zope application is running. Moreover, if you are using just one production server, but with multiple processors, it also makes sense to use ZEO with multiple ZEO clients so that the work is spread equally over the processors.

Setting up a ZEO environment

Setting up a ZEO server instance is as straight-forward as setting up a Zope instance. Simply execute the `mkzeoinstance` script from your Zope in-

---

[5] Squid homepage <http://www.squid-cache.org>

[6] Pound homepage <http://www.apsis.ch/pound/>

[7] balance homepage <http://www.inlab.de/balance.html>

stallation, providing the path for the instance that is to be created as an argument:

```
~$ /usr/local/Zope-3.x.y/bin/mkzeoinstance ZEOInstance
```

On Windows you would issue something like the following command:

```
C:\> python \Python24\Scripts\mkzeoinstance ZEOInstance
```

A ZEO instance is very similar to a Zope instance. The `bin` directory contains the `runzeo` start script (the equivalent of `runzope`) as well as a `zeoctl` (the equivalent of `zopectl`). Like its Zope counterpart, `zeoctl` only works on Unix systems. Windows support is rather poor for ZEO, unfortunately. ZEO instances lack a `runzeo.bat` file and cannot be registered Windows services as of this writing, either. You can still run a ZEO server on Windows by providing your own `runzeo.bat` as shown in Example 24.4.1, but it is not recommended to do so in a production environment.

Example 24.4.1 ZEO start script for Windows (doc/`runzeo.bat`)

```
1  @echo off
2  set PYTHON=C:\Python24\python.exe
3  set ZODB3_HOME=C:\Python24\Lib\site-packages
4  set INSTANCE_HOME=C:\ZEOInstance
5
6  set RUNZEO=%ZODB3_HOME%\ZEO\runzeo.py
7  set CONFIG_FILE=%INSTANCE_HOME%\etc\zeo.conf
8  "%PYTHON%" "%RUNZEO%" -C "%CONFIG_FILE%" %1 %2 %3 %4 %5 %6 %7
```

2–4. Customize these values according to your installation.

The `etc` directory of a ZEO instance contains the configuration of the ZEO server, `zeo.conf`, which reads very much like `zope.conf`. There you can configure the database that the ZEO server will use. As for stand-alone Zope instances, ZEO servers by default use a *FileStorage* database at `var/Data.fs`. If you are switching from a stand-alone setup to a ZEO setup, you can simply copy Zope's `Data.fs` file to the ZEO instance.

The `zeo.conf` file also lets you configure the port on which the ZEO server accepts connections from its ZEO clients, the Zope instances. Their configuration needs to be changed from the default *FileStorage* to *ClientStorage*. To do that, remove the `<filestorage>` subsection of the `<zodb>` section and add something like the following lines instead:

```
<zodb>
  <zeoclient>
    server zeoserver:8100
    storage 1
    cache-size 128MB
  </zeoclient>
</zodb>
```

With this configuration in place, the Zope instance will connect to the ZEO server at `zeoserver`. Since ZEO servers can serve multiple database at once, we have to select which one to use. We can also set a size for a local object cache that the ZEO client maintains so that it does not have to fetch objects from the ZEO server all the time. Giving the ZEO a decent client cache size is highly recommended.

Summary

- A single Zope instance serving a highly frequented site by itself can easily run into scalability problems.
- Enabling both client-side and server-side caching can be used to reduce the load on the Zope instance. For the client-side caching, HTTP proxies such as Apache's *mod_cache* or Squid are typically used in front of Zope.
- For sites with very dynamic pages, caching may not be an applicable technique to improve scalability.
- Zope instances can be clustered to spread the work over multiple machines. They can share a single ZODB instance by connecting to a ZEO server.
- The ZEO server runs a ZEO instance which is created and configured much like a Zope instance.

Using Zope 2

Everything discussed in this section also applies to a Zope 2 setup, except for the ZODB section in a ZEO client's `zope.conf`. When using Zope 2, it must read:

```
<zodb_db main>
  mount-point /
  <zeoclient>
    server zeoserver:8100
    storage 1
    cache-size 128MB
  </zeoclient>
</zodb_db>
```

Part IV

Appendices

A

API Reference

As a large framework, Zope has a lot of APIs. Fortunately, all of them are documented in interfaces, and most of them in doctests. You should therefore always consult the interfaces (and doctests when available) whenever you have an unanswered question about one of Zope's APIs. The APIDoc tool makes these interfaces and documents available for reading in a comfortable way.

This appendix focuses on Zope's convenience APIs, the ones that are used the most. Most of the functions covered here come from one of the following packages:

- `zope.interface`
- `zope.component`
- `zope.traversing`
- `zope.security`

Conventions

Many `zope.component` functions follow certain conventions. You will find them easier to use when you know these idioms. The following list gives an overview:

- Functions that acquire a certain type of component are usually named `getComponent`. When look up fails, they will raise `ComponentLookupError`. The majority of those functions has a `queryComponent` equivalent that performs the same task but accepts a *default* parameter (which defaults to `None`). When the look-up fails, this function will not raise an error but return the default value.
- Most look-up functions from `zope.component` accept a *context* parameter. It allows the caller to influence in which context the component look-up shall be carried out. When provided, the *context* value will be adapted to `IComponentLookup` and the resulting component registry will be used to perform the look-up. This method of context-based

look-up is rarely used within the Zope application server, as the active component registry is set during traversal there.

- Utilities, adapters and multi-adapters can occur in named flavours. Their unnamed flavours are always registered with an *empty string* for their name, not (as you may think) with None. Therefore, the *name* argument on the corresponding look-up methods defaults to u'', meaning it will by default acquire unnamed components.

absoluteURL

Computes an absolute URL of an object.

Synopsis

absoluteURL (*object*, *request*)

Origin

zope.traversing.browser

Description

absoluteURL computes an absolute URL of the given *object* for a certain *request*. A TypeError is raised if the URL cannot be computed, for example because of insufficient location information.

Examples

A call to absoluteURL,

```
>>> from zope.traversing.browser import absoluteURL
>>> absoluteURL(obj, request)
```

is equivalent to the following view look-up:

```
>>> from zope.component import getMultiAdapter
>>> from zope.traversing.browser.interfaces import IAbsoluteURL
>>> getMultiAdapter((ob, request), IAbsoluteURL)()
```

See also

getPath

adapts, adapter

Declares which interfaces an adapter factory adapts.

Synopsis

```
adapts ( *interfaces )
@adapter ( *interfaces )
```

Origin

```
zope.component (IComponentArchitecture)
```

Description

`adapts` and `adapter` allow you to declare which interfaces an adapter factory adapts. For single adapters, only one interface should be specified. For multi-adapters, you need to specify as many interfaces as objects are adapted by the factory. Including this information at definition time allows you to omit it when registering the factory with `provideAdapter` or the `zope:adapter` ZCML directive.

The `adapts` function is used inside a class body, whereas the `adapter` decorator is used when implementing an adapter factory as a function or method.

Examples

Views are multi-adapters for the object they present and the request, like this browser page:

```
>>> from zope.component import adapts
>>> from zope.publisher.browser import BrowserPage
>>> from zope.publisher.interfaces.browser import IBrowserRequest
>>> from worldcookery.interfaces import IRecipe
>>>
>>> class ViewRecipe(BrowserPage):
...     adapts(IRecipe, IBrowserRequest)
...     def __call__(self):
...         response = self.request.response
...         response.setHeader('Content-Type', 'text/plain')
...         return self.context.name
...
```

The Component Architecture also allows us to implement event subscribers as a type of adapter (handler). The adapted object is the event whose type we can specify with the `adapter` decorator:

```
>>> from zope.component import adapter
>>> @adapter(IDinnerIsDone)
... def tellFamily(event):
...     print "Dinner is ready! We're having a " \
...            "delicious %s!" % event.recipe.name
...
```

See also

provideAdapter; zope:adapter, zope:subscriber ZCML directives

alsoProvides

Declares additional interfaces on an object.

Synopsis

alsoProvides (*object*, **interfaces*)

Origin

zope.interface (IInterfaceDeclaration)

Description

alsoProvides adds *interfaces* to the list of interfaces that *object* provides directly.

Examples

A call to alsoProvides, e.g.:

```
>>> from zope.interface import alsoProvides
>>> from worldcookery.skin.interfaces import IWorldCookerySkin
>>> alsoProvides(request, IWorldCookerySkin)
```

is equivalent to a call to directlyProvides when including all already provided interfaces:

```
>>> from zope.interface import directlyProvides, directlyProvidedBy
>>> directlyProvides(request, directlyProvidedBy(request),
...                  IWorldCookerySkin)
```

See also

directlyProvides, noLongerProvides

canAccess, canWrite

Checks whether an object's attribute can be read or written.

Synopsis

```
canAccess ( object, name )
canWrite ( object, name )
```

Origin

zope.security

Description

canAccess determines whether the participants of the current interaction are allowed to access the *name* attribute of *object*. canWrite checks whether they can set the attribute's value. *object* is a security-proxied object.

Examples

Let us pretend that canAccess reports that an attribute of a security-proxied object cannot be accessed:

```
>>> from zope.security.proxy import ProxyFactory
>>> wrapped_pudding = ProxyFactory(pudding)
>>> from zope.security import canAccess
>>> canAccess(wrapped_pudding, 'name')
False
```

In this case you will get an Unauthorized exception if you try to access it anyway:

```
>>> wrapped_pudding.name
Traceback (most recent call last):
...
zope.security.interfaces.Unauthorized: ('name', 'some.permission')
```

See also

checkPermission; zope:class ZCML directive

canonicalPath

Returns a canonical absolute path for a given path or object.

Synopsis

canonicalPath (*path_or_object*)

Origin

zope.traversing.api (ITraversalAPI)

Description

If passed an object, canonicalPath will return its absolute physical path, exactly like getPath. If passed a string or Unicode object, it will treat it as an object path with / separators and return a normalized version, meaning it will resolve . and .. segments.

Examples

When passed an object, canonicalPath works just like getPath (see getPath example):

```
>>> from zope.traversing.api import canonicalPath
>>> canonicalPath(son)
u'/father/son'
```

When passed a string or Unicode object, it normalizes the path:

```
>>> canonicalPath('/foo/.././bar')
u'/bar'
```

See also

getPath, joinPath

classImplements, classImplementsOnly

Declares interfaces implemented by a class.

Synopsis

classImplements (*class*, *interfaces*)

Origin

zope.interface (IInterfaceDeclaration)

Description

classImplements adds the interfaces specified in *interfaces* to the list of interfaces that *class* implements, either directly or via base classes.

classImplementsOnly sets the interfaces that *class* implements disregarding of *class*'s base classes or interfaces that *class* already implements.

Examples

A class can declare that it implements an interface inside its class definition, e.g.:

```
>>> from zope.interface import implements
>>> from worldcookery.interfaces import IRecipe
>>> class Recipe(object):
...     implements(IRecipe)
...
```

Alternatively, we can use classImplements from outside the class definition:

```
>>> from zope.interface import classImplements
>>> class Recipe(object):
...     pass
>>> classProvides(Recipe, IRecipe)
```

Likewise, implementsOnly is the equivalent of classImplementsOnly for declarations inside the class definition.

See also

implements, implementsOnly; zope:class ZCML directive.

classProvides

Declares interfaces provided by a class inside the class definition.

Synopsis

classProvides (*interfaces*)

Origin

`zope.interface (IInterfaceDeclaration)`

Description

`classProvides` sets interfaces that a class provides from inside the class definition. Classes rarely *provide* an interface, usually they *implement* them. Notable exceptions are classes that are used as vocabulary factories. They provide `IVocabularyFactory`.

`classProvides` can only be used once in a class definition.

Examples

A call to `classProvides` inside a class definition, e.g.:

```
>>> from zope.interface import classProvides
>>> from zope.interface.interfaces import IInterface
>>> from zope.schema.interfaces import IVocabularyFactory
>>> from zope.app.component.vocabulary import UtilityVocabulary
>>> class InterfacesVocabulary(UtilityVocabulary):
...     classProvides(IVocabularyFactory)
...     interface = IInterface
...
```

is equivalent to using `alsoProvides` or `directlyProvides` later on:

```
>>> from zope.interface import alsoProvides
>>> class InterfacesVocabulary(UtilityVocabulary):
...     interface = IInterface
...
>>> alsoProvides(InterfacesVocabulary, IVocabularyFactory)
```

See also

`alsoProvides`, `directlyProvides`,

createObject

Creates an object using a factory.

Synopsis

`createObject ( name, *args, **kw )`

Origin

`zope.component` (`IComponentArchitecture`)

Description

`createObject` invokes a factory named *name* to create a new object. It passes **args* and ***kw* to the factory.

Examples

A call to `createObject`,

```
>>> from zope.component import createObject
>>> createObject(u'worldcookery.Recipe')
```

can always be written as an explicit factory look-up:

```
>>> from zope.component import getUtility
>>> from zope.component.interfaces import IFactory
>>> getUtility(IFactory, u'worldcookery.Recipe')()
```

See also

`getFactoriesFor`, `getUtility`

directlyProvidedBy

Returns an object's directly provided interfaces

Synopsis

`directlyProvidedBy ( object )`

Origin

`zope.interface` (`IInterfaceDeclaration`)

Description

`directlyProvidedBy` returns the interfaces that are directly provided by *object*. The return value is an `IDeclaration` object.

In contrast to `providedBy`, `directlyProvidedBy` only returns the interfaces that the object provides *directly*. It does not return the interfaces that the object provides due to the interfaces that the class implements.

Examples

If you have an object that provides an interface because its class implements it, the interface will not be in the object's directly provided interfaces:

```
>>> IRecipe.providedBy(IRecipe)
True
>>> from worldcookery.interfaces import IRecipe
>>> IRecipe in directlyProvidedBy(recipe)
False
```

If you, however, add an interface to the object's directly provided ones, directlyProvidedBy will include it:

```
>>> from zope.interface import alsoProvides
>>> from zope.annotation.interfaces import IAttributeAnnotatable
>>> alsoProvides(recipe, IAttributeAnnotatable)
>>> IAttributeAnnotatable in directlyProvidedBy(recipe)
True
```

See also

directlyProvides, noLongerProvides

directlyProvides

Declares an object's directly provided interfaces.

Synopsis

directlyProvides (*object*, **interfaces*)

Origin

zope.interface (IInterfaceDeclaration)

Description

directlyProvides sets the interfaces that *object* provides directly. Any interfaces that *object* already provides directly will be overwritten. In most cases, it is therefore better to use alsoProvides, unless you really want to change the directly provided interfaces.

Examples

The reference page for alsoProvides shows an example of directlyProvides.

See also

alsoProvides, noLongerProvides

getAdapter, queryAdapter

Acquires a named adapter for a given object.

Synopsis

```
getAdapter ( object, interface, name, context=None )
queryAdapter ( object, interface, name, default=None,
               context=None )
```

Origin

zope.component (IComponentArchitecture)

Description

getAdapter looks up a named adapter for *object* providing *interface*. Note that regular (unnamed) adapters should be acquired by calling the interface directly.

context can be used to make the underlying component registry look-up context-dependent.

If the adapter is not found, ComponentLookupError is raised. queryAdapter works like getAdapter except that it accepts a *default* parameter whose value is returned when the adapter look-up fails. This defaults to None.

Examples

Zope uses named adapters that are not multi-adapters for file factories, among others. In the following example we retrieve a file factory that is responsible for the .recipe file extension:

```
>>> from zope.component import getAdapter
>>> from zope.filerepresentation.interfaces import IFileFactory
>>> getAdapter(folder, IFileFactory, '.recipe')
```

See also

getMultiAdapter, provideAdapter; zope:adapter ZCML directive

getAllUtilitiesRegisteredFor

Returns all utilities registered for an interface.

Synopsis

getAllUtilitiesRegisteredFor (*interface*, *context=None*)

Origin

zope.component (IComponentArchitecture)

Description

getAllUtilitiesRegisteredFor finds and returns *all* utilities that are registered for *interface*. This includes utilities that are registered for more specific interfaces than *interface* and named utilities that override other named utilities. In short, getAllUtilitiesRegisteredFor returns all utilities, whether they have been overridden or not. The returned value is an iterable.

Examples

getAllUtilitiesRegisteredFor is used by the integer ID and catalog machineries to notify all integer ID utilities and all catalogs, not just the currently active ones, upon object events, e.g.:

```
>>> from zope.component import getAllUtilitiesRegisteredFor
>>> from zope.app.catalog.interfaces import ICatalog
>>> for catlog in getAllUtilitiesRegisteredFor(ICatalog):
...      catalog.index_doc(int_id, obj)
...
```

See also

getUtilitiesFor, getUtility, provideUtility; zope:utility ZCML directive.

getDefaultViewName, queryDefaultViewName

Returns the name of the default view for a given object.

Synopsis

getDefaultViewName (*object, request, context=None*)
queryDefaultViewName (*object, request, default=None,*
                         context=None)

Origin

zope.app.publisher.browser

Description

getDefaultViewName returns the name of the default view for *object*
and the request type of *request*. Within the Zope application server, this is
usually index.html for browser requests but can be changed individually
for different interfaces through ZCML.

context can be used to make the underlying component registry look-up
context-dependent.

If a default view name cannot be found, ComponentLookupError is
raised. queryDefaultViewName works like getDefaultViewName except that it accepts a *default* parameter whose value is returned when the
look-up fails. This defaults to None.

Examples

The default view name for objects in the context of a browser request usually
is index.html:

```
>>> from zope.app.publisher.browser
>>> getDefaultViewName(obj, request)
u'index.html'
```

See also

browser:defaultView ZCML directive

getFactoriesFor

Returns factories that can create objects providing a certain interface.

Synopsis

getFactoriesFor (*interface, context=None*)

Origin

`zope.component (IComponentArchitecture)`

Description

`getFactoriesFor` returns all factories that instantiate objects of a certain kind. In other words, objects created with these factories will always provide *interface*. The returned value is an iterable wherein each item is a (name, factory) tuple.

context can be used to make the underlying component registry look-up context-dependent.

Examples

You might remember from Chapter 13 that Zope has a small framework for rendering formatted text as HTML. Renderers are implemented as views for certain source types which can be created using appropriate factories. All source types have the base interface `ISource`. The following example retrieves all factories that create `ISource` objects:

```
>>> from zope.component import getFactoriesFor
>>> from zope.app.renderer import ISource
>>> from pprint import pprint
>>> pprint(list(getFactoriesFor(ISource)))
[(u'zope.source.rest',
  <zope.app.renderer.SourceFactory object at 0x2cf6250>),
 (u'zope.source.plaintext',
  <zope.app.renderer.SourceFactory object at 0x2ca8e50>),
 (u'zope.source.stx',
  <zope.app.renderer.SourceFactory object at 0x2cb3710>)]
```

See also

`createObject`

getGlobalSiteManager

Returns the global component registry.

Synopsis

`getGlobalSiteManager()`

Origin

`zope.component` (`IComponentArchitecture`)

Description

`getGlobalSiteManager` returns the global component registry (also known as site manager), regardless of which local site manager might be active due to traversal.

Examples

`getGlobalSiteManager` can be used whenever you want to explicitly look up or register global components. This is used during ZCML processing, for example, where all components are to be registered as global components. The convenience registration API in `zope.component` also looks up the global component registry. For example, writing

```
>>> from zope.component import provideUtility
>>> from worldcookery.kitchentools import KitchenToolsFromFile
>>> provideUtility(KitchenToolsFromFile())
```

is equivalent to

```
>>> from zope.component import getGlobalSiteManager
>>> getGlobalSiteManager().registerUtility(KitchenToolsFromFile())
```

See also

`getSiteManager`

getMultiAdapter, queryMultiAdapter

Acquires a multi-adapter for given combination of objects.

Synopsis

```
getMultiAdapter ( objects, interface, name=u'',
                  context=None )
queryMultiAdapter ( objects, interface, name=u'',
                    default=None, context=None )
```

Origin

`zope.component` (`IComponentArchitecture`)

Description

getMultiAdapter adapts a combination of objects given in the *object* tuple to *interface*. An optional *name* can be given to look up a named multi-adapter. Unnamed adapters have an empty name.

context can be used to make the underlying component registry look-up context-dependent.

If no adapter is found, ComponentLookupError is raised. queryMultiAdapter works like getMultiAdapter except that it accepts a *default* parameter whose value is returned when the adapter look-up fails. This defaults to None.

Examples

Views are named multi-adapters since they adapt both an object and a request to some presentation interface, e.g. IBrowserPublisher or IInputWidget (widgets are views for schema fields):

```
>>> from zope.component import getMultiAdapter
>>> from zope.publisher.interfaces.browser import IBrowserPublisher
>>> getMultiAdapter((obj, request), IBrowserPublisher,
...                     name=u'index.html')
```

Content providers are also looked up as named multi-adapters for an object, a request and the view that the content provider is a part of:

```
>>> from zope.contentprovider.interfaces import IContentProvider
>>> getMultiAdapter((obj, request, view), IContentProvider,
...                     name=u"worldcoookery.Logo")
```

See also

getAdapter, provideAdapter; zope:adapter ZCML directive

getName

Returns the name of an object.

Synopsis

getName (*object*)

Origin

zope.traversing.api (ITraversalAPI)

Description

getName returns the name of an object. It does so by adapting the object to IPhysicallyLocatable. This adaption works out-of-the-box with objects providing ILocation or objects that are location proxied. If no adapter can be found, TypeError is raised.

Examples

getName can only retrieve the name of objects that can be adapted to IPhysicallyLocatable:

```
>>> from zope.location import Location
>>> obj = Location()
>>> obj.__name__ = u"location"
>>> from zope.traversing.api import getName
>>> getName(obj)
u'location'
```

The failing adaption raises a TypeError otherwise:

```
>>> obj = object()
>>> getName(obj)
Traceback (most recent call last):
...
TypeError: ('Could not adapt', <object object at 0x3544a0>,
<InterfaceClass zope.traversing.interfaces.IPhysicallyLocatable>)
```

See also

getPath

getParent

Returns an object's parent.

Synopsis

getParent (*object*)

Origin

zope.traversing.api (ITraversalAPI)

Description

getParent returns the parent of *object* that is located in an object hierarchy, in other words, it can be adapted to IPhysicallyLocatable. In case *object* is the root object of the hierarchy, None is returned. If *object* cannot be adapted to IPhysicallyLocatable, TypeError is raised.

For objects using Zope's location machinery (providing ILocation or IContained, either themselves or by proxy), getParent will simply return the __parent__ attribute.

Examples

For locatable objects in regular Zope web applications, a call to getParent,

```
>>> from zope.traversing.api import getParent
>>> getParent(obj)
```

is equivalent to simply working with the __parent__ attribute:

```
>>> obj.__parent__
```

See also

getParents, getRoot

getParents

Returns an object's parents.

Synopsis

getParents (*object*)

Origin

zope.traversing.api (ITraversalAPI)

Description

getParents returns a list of an *object*'s parent objects. *object* needs to be located in an object hierarchy, in other words, it must be adapted to IPhysicallyLocatable. In case *object* is the root object of the hierarchy, an empty list is returned. If *object* cannot be adapted to IPhysicallyLocatable or if the location hierarchy does not go all the way up to the root object (an object providing IContainmentRoot), TypeError is raised.

Examples

Imagine three objects in a location hierarchy with grandfather mimicking the root object:

```
>>> from zope.location import Location, locate
>>> from zope.traversing.interfaces import IContainmentRoot
>>> son = Location()
>>> father = Location()
>>> grandfather = Location()
>>>
>>> locate(son, father, name=u"son")
>>> locate(father, grandfather, name=u"father")
>>> from zope.interface import alsoProvides
>>> alsoProvides(grandfather, IContainmentRoot)
>>>
>>> from zope.traversing.api import getParents
>>> getParents(son) == [father, grandfather]
True
```

See also

getParent, getRoot

getPath

Returns the physical path of an object.

Synopsis

getPath (object)

Origin

zope.traversing.api (ITraversalAPI)

Description

getPath returns the physical path of an object. It does so by adapting the object to IPhysicallyLocatable. This adaption works out-of-the-box with objects providing ILocation or objects that are location proxied. If no adapter can be found or the location hierarchy does not go all the way up to the root object (an object providing IContainmentRoot), TypeError is raised.

Examples

Imagine three objects in a location hierarchy with grandfather mimicking the root object:

```
>>> from zope.location import Location, locate
>>> from zope.traversing.interfaces import IContainmentRoot
>>> son = Location()
>>> father = Location()
>>> grandfather = Location()
>>>
>>> locate(son, father, name=u"son")
>>> locate(father, grandfather, name=u"father")
>>> from zope.interface import alsoProvides
>>> alsoProvides(grandfather, IContainmentRoot)
>>>
>>> from zope.traversing.api import getPath
>>> getPath(son)
u'/father/son'
```

See also

absoluteURL, canonicalPath, joinPath, getName

getRoot

Returns the root object in a location hierarchy.

Synopsis

getRoot (*object*)

Origin

zope.traversing.api (ITraversalAPI)

Description

When an object is located in an object hierarchy, in other words, when it can be adapted to IPhysicallyLocatable, getRoot traverses back to the parent of the hierarchy (the object providing IContainmentRoot and returns this object. If the object cannot be adapted or the location hierarchy does not go all the way up to the root object, TypeError is raised.

For objects contained in Zope containers within regular Zope web applications, getRoot will return the root folder of the ZODB instance the objects are stored in.

Examples

Imagine three objects in a location hierarchy with grandfather mimicking the root object:

```
>>> from zope.location import Location, locate
>>> from zope.traversing.interfaces import IContainmentRoot
>>> son = Location()
>>> father = Location()
>>> grandfather = Location()
>>>
>>> locate(son, father, name=u"son")
>>> locate(father, grandfather, name=u"father")
>>> from zope.interface import alsoProvides
>>> alsoProvides(grandfather, IContainmentRoot)
>>>
>>> from zope.traversing.api import getRoot
>>> getRoot(son) is grandfather
True
```

See also

getParents

getSiteManager

Returns the currently active component registry.

Synopsis

getSiteManager (*context=None*)

Origin

zope.component (IComponentArchitecture)

Description

getSiteManager returns the currently active component registry, also known as site manager. An application-specific policy defines which component registry that is. In Zope 3, traversing over a site will make its site manager the currently active one. Fallback is the global service manager.

To manually influence which service manager should be returned, one can pass a value for the optional *context* parameter. This will then be adapted to IComponentLookup and the adapter will be returned.

Examples

Most functions in the Component Architecture API are convenience functions. For example, looking up a utility can be done using the convenience API,

```
>>> from zope.component import getUtility
>>> from worldcookery.interfaces import IKitchenTools
>>> getUtility(IKitchenTools)
```

or by first looking up the active site manager and performing the look-up there:

```
>>> from zope.component import getSiteManager
>>> getSiteManager().getUtility(IKitchenTools)
```

See also

getGlobalSiteManager

getUtilitiesFor

Returns named utilities for a given interface.

Synopsis

getUtilitiesFor (*interface*, *context=None*)

Origin

zope.component (IComponentArchitecture)

Description

getUtilitiesFor returns an iterable of named utilities registered for a certain *interface*. Elements in the iteration are (name, utility) pairs.

getUtilitiesFor differs from getAllUtilitiesRegisteredFor in that it does not return overridden utilities. It returns one utility per name and interface. Moreover, getAllUtilitiesRegisteredFor only returns utility instances, no names, since it is only interested in their subscription status, not by which name they were registered.

Examples

getUtilitiesFor obviously only makes sense for named utilities, not for singletons. Common named utilities are roles as defined by the default Zope security policy:

```
>>> from zope.component import getUtilitiesFor
>>> from zope.app.securitypolicy.interfaces import IRole
>>> from pprint import pprint
>>> pprint(list(getUtilitiesFor(IRole)))
[(u'zope.Manager',
  <zope.app.securitypolicy.role.Role object at 0x30ffc50>),
 (u'zope.Member',
  <zope.app.securitypolicy.role.Role object at 0x30ffe90>),
 (u'zope.Anonymous',
  <zope.app.securitypolicy.role.Role object at 0x30f9190>)]
```

See also

getAllUtilitiesRegisteredFor, getUtility, provideUtility; zope:utility ZCML directive

getUtility, queryUtility

Looks up a utility.

Synopsis

getUtility (*interface, name='', context=None*)
queryUtility (*interface, name='', default=None*
                    context=None)

Origin

zope.component (IComponentArchitecture)

Description

getUtility acquires a utility providing *interface*. An optional *name* can be given when a named utility should be looked up. *context* can be used to make the underlying component registry look-up context-dependent.

If a utility cannot be found, ComponentLookupError is raised. queryUtility works like getUtility except that it accepts a *default* parameter whose value is returned when the view look-up fails. This defaults to None.

Examples

Look up a regular (singleton) utility:

```
>>> from zope.component import getUtility
>>> from worldcookery.interfaces import IKitchenTools
>>> getUtility(IKitchenTools)
```

Look up a named utility:

```
>>> from zope.security.interfaces import IPermission
>>> getUtility(IPermission, name=u'worldcookery.EditRecipes')
```

See also

getAllUtilitiesRegisteredFor, getUtilitiesFor,
provideUtility; zope:utility ZCML directive

handle

Invokes all handlers for the given objects

Synopsis

handle (*objects)

Origin

zope.component (IComponentArchitecture)

Description

handle looks up all handlers for the given set of objects and invokes them.
Handlers are commonly used to implement event subscribers. They are a
special kind of subscription adapter as their "factories" are not expected to
return anything. In other words, they can return None. Conventional adapter
factories (including subscription adapter factories) can return None to indicate that the adapter look-up has failed.

Examples

Invoking all handlers for an object, e.g.:

```
>>> from zope.component import handle
>>> from zope.lifecycleevent import ObjectCreatedEvent
>>> handle(ObjectCreatedEvent(recipe))
```

is equivalent to looking up the subscribers that provide None:

```
>>> from zope.component import subscribers
>>> for ignored in subscribers((ObjectCreatedEvent(recipe),), None):
>>>     pass
```

See also

subscribers, provideHandler; zope:subscriber ZCML directive

implementedBy

Returns the interfaces a callable implements

Synopsis

implementedBy (*callable*)

Origin

zope.interface (IInterfaceDeclaration)

Description

implementedBy returns the interfaces that are implemented by *callable*.
callable can be a class or a function. The return value is an IDeclaration
object.

Examples

The implementedBy function works on classes:

```
>>> from zope.interface import implementedBy
>>> from worldcookery.interfaces import IRecipe
>>> from worldcookery.recipe import Recipe
>>> IRecipe in implementedBy(Recipe)
True
```

as well as functions:

```
>>> from zope.interface import implementer
>>> @implementer(IRecipe)
... def createRecipe()
...     return Recipe()
...
>>> IRecipe in implementedBy(createRecipe)
True
```

Note that to express the above, you would usually use an interface's *implementedBy* method:

```
>>> IRecipe.implementedBy(Recipe)
True
>>> IRecipe.implementedBy(createRecipe)
True
```

See also

classImplements, implements, implementer

implements, implementsOnly, implementer

Declares which interfaces a class or function implements.

Synopsis

```
implements ( *interfaces )
implementsOnly ( *interfaces )
@implementer ( *interfaces )
```

Origin

zope.component (IComponentArchitecture)

Description

implements, implementsOnly and implementer allow you to declare which interfaces a class or function provides.

implements and implementsOnly are meant to be used inside a class definition, though only either one is allowed at the same time and only once. Like classImplementsOnly, implementOnly disregards any interfaces from the base classes.

implementer is used as a decorator for functions.

Examples

The reference page for `implementedBy` shows examples of `implements` and `implementer`.

See also

`classImplements`, `classImplementsOnly`; `zope:class` ZCML directive.

isinstance

Checks whether an object object is an instance of a class.

Synopsis

`isinstance ( object, class )`

Origin

`zope.security.proxy`

Description

Like the `isinstance` function that is built into Python, `zope.security.proxy.isinstance` checks whether *object* is an instance of a class *class* and returns either `True` or `False`. The difference to the built-in version is that this also works when *object* is security proxied.

Examples

`isinstance` works like the built-in equivalent when dealing with regular objects, e.g. an integer:

```
>>> from zope.security.proxy import isinstance
>>> isinstance(2, int)
True
```

In case an object is security proxied, the built-in `isinstance` function fails. `zope.security.proxy.isinstance` returns the expected value:

```
>>> from worldcookery.recipe import Recipe
>>> pudding = Recipe()
>>> from zope.security.proxy import ProxyFactory
>>> wrapped_pudding = ProxyFactory(pudding)
```

```
>>> wrapped_pudding
<worldcookery.recipe.Recipe object at 0x35cd70>
>>> type(wrapped_pudding)
<type 'zope.security._proxy._Proxy'>
>>> __builtins__.isinstance(wrapped_pudding, Recipe)
False
>>> from zope.security.proxy import isinstance
>>> isinstance(wrapped_pudding, Recipe)
True
```

See also

__builtins__.isinstance

joinPath

Joins path segments or parts of paths.

Synopsis

joinPath (*path*, *args*)

Origin

zope.traversing.api (ITraversalAPI)

Description

Join two or more path segments or parts of paths together to one path. *path* should not end in / (unless it is the root element itself). Path segments that are to be added should not start or end with / either. They may, however, contain . and .. to indicate the current or parent location relative to the previous segment. Overall, its behaviour is very similar to the one of os.path.join from the Python standard library.

Examples

Join multiple path segments:

```
>>> from zope.traversing.api import joinPath
>>> joinPath('/foo', '..', './bar')
u'/bar'
```

See also

canonicalPath, getPath

moduleProvides

Declares the interfaces that the current module provides

Synopsis

moduleProvides (*interfaces*)

Origin

zope.interface (IInterfaceDeclaration)

Description

moduleProvides sets the interfaces that the current module provides. This can be used to declare that the module conforms to APIs expressed in these interfaces. It can also be used to set Python's __all__ variable that controls which symbols are exported from the module.

moduleProvides used, for example, in the zope.interface module itself because it provides IInterfaceDeclaration. Many other modules that provide an API, such as zope.component and zope.traversing.api contain similar lines.

Examples

The zope.component module contains the following lines:

```
moduleProvides(IComponentArchitecture,
               IComponentRegistrationConvenience)
__all__ = tuple(IComponentArchitecture)
```

This is equivalent to setting the interface from the outside:

```
>>> from zope.interface import alsoProvides
>>> import zope.component
>>> alsoProvides(zope.component, IComponentArchitecture,
...              IComponentRegistrationConvenience)
```

See also

alsoProvides, directlyProvides

noLongerProvides

Remove a directly provided interface from an object

Synopsis

noLongerProvides (*object*, *interface*)

Origin

zope.interface (IInterfaceDeclaration)

Description

noLongerProvides removes *interface* from the list of *object*'s directly provided interfaces. It leaves *object* unchanged if it does not provide *interface* and raises ValueError if *object* provides *interface* because its class implements it.

Examples

If an object does not provide the interface to be removed, it is left unchanged:

```
>>> from zope.interface import noLongerProvides
>>> from zope.annotation.interfaces import IAttributeAnnotatable
>>> IAttributeAnnotatable.providedBy(recipe)
False
>>> noLongerProvides(recipe, IAttributeAnnotatable)
```

If you are trying to remove an interface that an object provides through its class, ValueError will be raised:

```
>>> from worldcookery.interfaces import IRecipe
>>> noLongerProvides(recipe, IRecipe)
Traceback (most recent call last):
  ...
ValueError: Can only remove directly provided interfaces.
```

Only *directly* provided interfaces can be removed:

```
>>> from zope.interface import alsoProvides
>>> alsoProvides(recipe, IAttributeAnnotatable)
>>> IAttributeAnnotatable.providedBy(recipe)
True
>>> noLongerProvides(recipe, IAttributeAnnotatable)
>>> IAttributeAnnotatable.providedBy(recipe)
False
```

A call to noLongerProvides is equivalent to calling directlyProvides and "subtracting" the interface that is to be removed:

```
>>> from zope.interface import directlyProvides, directlyProvidedBy
>>> directlyProvides(
...     recipe,
...     directlyProvidedBy(recipe)-AttributeAnnotatable
... )
```

See also

alsoProvides, directlyProvides

provideAdapter

Registers an adapter factory with the global component registry.

Synopsis

provideAdapter (*factory, adapts=None, provides=None, name=u''*)

Origin

zope.component (IComponentRegistrationConvenience)

Description

provideAdapter registers an adapter factory with the global component registry. The adapter factory adapts a given number of objects (specified by *adapts*) to provide an interface (specified by *provides*). If *name* is a non-empty string, a named adapter is registered.

If *factory* has an adapts or adapter declaration of the adapted interfaces, the *adapts* parameter is optional. In case it is still specified, it overrides the factory's declaration. If *factory* implements only one interface, the *provides* parameter can be omitted as well.

Note that component registration is a configuration activity. provideAdapter should therefore only be used from tests or application setup routines, like the other functions of the IComponentRegistrationConvenience API.

Examples

After registering an adapter factory with the global component registry,

```
>>> from zope.component import provideAdapter
>>> from worldcookery.size import RecipeSize
>>> provideAdapter(RecipeSize)
```

it is available for adapter look-up:

```
>>> from zope.size.interfaces import ISized
>>> size = ISized(falafel)
>>> isinstance(size, RecipeSize)
True
```

See also

adapts, getAdapter, getMultiAdapter; zope:adapter ZCML directive

provideHandler

Registers a handler with the global component registry.

Synopsis

provideHandler (*handler, adapts=None*)

Origin

zope.component (IComponentRegistrationConvenience)

Description

provideHandler registers a handler with the global component registry. A handler is executed for a given number of objects (specified by *adapts*). If *handler* has an adapts or adapter declaration of the adapted interfaces, the *adapts* parameter is optional. In case it is still specified, it overrides the handler's declaration.

Note that component registration is a configuration activity. provideHandler should therefore only be used from tests or application setup routines, like the other functions of the IComponentRegistrationConvenience API.

Examples

When the handler has an `adapts` or `adapter` declaration, e.g.:

```
>>> from zope.component import adapter
>>> @adapter(IDinnerIsDone)
... def tellFamily(event):
...     print "Dinner is ready! We're having a " \
...           "delicious %s!" % event.recipe.name
...
```

its registration is a simple call to `provideHandler`:

```
>>> from zope.component import provideHandler
>>> provideHandler(tellFamily)
```

See also

adapts, zope:subscriber ZCML directive

provideSubscriptionAdapter

Registers a subscription adapter factory with the global component registry.

Synopsis

provideSubscriptionAdapter (*factory, adapts=None,*
                              provides=None)

Origin

zope.component (IComponentRegistrationConvenience)

Description

provideSubscriptionAdapter registers a subscription adapter factory with the global component registry. The factory adapts a given number of objects (specified by *adapts*) to provide an interface (specified by *provides*). Subscription adapters differ from regular adapters in that a look up returns *all* applicable adapters for an object, not just one.

If *factory* has an adapts or adapter declaration of the adapted interfaces, the *adapts* parameter is optional. In case it is still specified, it overrides the factory's declaration. If *factory* implements only one interface, the *provides* parameter can be omitted as well.

Note that component registration is a configuration activity. provideSubscriptionAdapter should therefore only be used from tests or application setup routines, like the other functions of the IComponentRegistrationConvenience API.

Examples

Subscription adapter factories are registered almost like regular adapter factories (see `provideAdapter`). Subscription adapters are looked up with the `subscribers` function.

See also

`adapts`, `subscribers`; `zope:subscriber` ZCML directive

provideUtility

Registers a utility with the global component registry.

Synopsis

`provideUtility ( component, provides=None, name=u'' )`

Origin

`zope.component (IComponentRegistrationConvenience)`

Description

`provideUtility` registers a utility with the global component registry. The utility provides a certain interface as specified by *provides*. This parameter can be omitted if *component* only implements one interface. If *name* is a non-empty string, a named utility is registered.

Note that component registration is a configuration activity. `provideUtility` should therefore only be used from tests or application setup routines, like the other functions of the `IComponentRegistrationConvenience` API.

Examples

When the object provides only one interface, it is registered as a utility with a simple call to `provideUtility`:

```
>>> from zope.component import provideUtility
>>> from worldcookery.kitchentools import KitchenToolsFromFile
>>> provideUtility(KitchenToolsFromFile())
```

See also

`getUtility`; `zope:utility` ZCML directive

providedBy

Returns the interfaces the object provides

Synopsis

```
providedBy ( object )
```

Origin

`zope.interface` (`IInterfaceDeclaration`)

Description

`providedBy` returns the interfaces that are provided by *objects*, both directly provided interfaces as well as those that are provided through *object*'s class. The return value is an `IDeclaration` object.

Examples

`providedBy` includes interfaces directly from the object as well as interfaces from its class:

```
>>> from zope.interface import alsoProvides, providedBy
>>> from zope.annotation.interfaces import IAttributeAnnotatable
>>> alsoProvides(recipe, IAttributeAnnotatable)
>>> list(providedBy(recipe))
[<InterfaceClass zope.annotation.interfaces.IAttributeAnnotatable>,
<InterfaceClass worldcookery.interfaces.IRecipe>]
```

See also

`alsoProvides, directlyProvidedBy directlyProvides`

queryType

Returns the nearest type interface for an object.

Synopsis

```
queryType ( object, interface )
```

Origin

`zope.app.interface`

Description

Often, interfaces are used to express types. Then these interfaces provide an additional type interface. For example, content type interfaces provide `IContentType`. For a given object *object*, queryType returns the nearest provided interface of a certain type. None is returned if the object does not provide an interface of the given type.

Examples

The most prominent example of interface types are content types. Without a designated content type interface, recipes object do not have a content type:

```
>>> from zope.app.content.interfaces import IContentType
>>> from worldcookery.interfaces import IRecipe
>>> from worldcookery.recipe import Recipe
>>> from zope.app.interface import queryType
>>> queryType(Recipe(), IContentType)
```

If we turn `IRecipe` into a content type (meaning, `IRecipe` will now provide `IContentType`), a recipe's content type will now be `IRecipe`:

```
>>> from zope.interface import alsoProvides
>>> alsoProvides(IRecipe, IContentType)
>>> queryType(Recipe(), IContentType)
<InterfaceClass worldcookery.interfaces.IRecipe>
```

See also

Chapter 5

subscribers

Retrieves subscribers for a given set of objects.

Synopsis

subscribers (*required*, *provided*, *context=None*)

Origin

`zope.component (IComponentArchitecture)`

Description

`subscribers` retrieves all subscription adapters that provide the interface specified as *provided* for a given set of *objects*. Subscription adapters are different from regular adapters in that the result of an adapter look-up can be many objects instead of just one (or none).

context can be used to make the underlying component registry look-up context-dependent.

Examples

A common variant of subscription adapter, handlers, are used in Zope's event system. See `handle` for more information.

See also

`handle`, `provideHandler`, `provideSubscriptionAdapter`; `zope:subscriber` ZCML directive

traverse

Traverses path relative to an object.

Synopsis

`traverse ( object, path, default=None, request=None )`

Origin

`zope.traversing.api` (`ITraversalAPI`)

Description

`traverse` resolves an object path relative to *object*. *path* is a string or Unicode object wherein the path segments are separated by /. *request* should be passed when invoking from presentation code. `traverse` will then also take traversal *views* into account instead of just traversal *adapters*. If a *default* value is given, it will be returned when the path cannot be traversed. Otherwise, `TraversalError` will be raised.

Examples

Resolving a regular object path:

```
>>> from zope.traversing.api import traverse
>>> traverse(folder, u'recipes/italian/tiramisu')
```

Resolve an object path and take presentation-specific traversal adapters into account, such as ++skin++, @@, etc.:

```
>>> from zope.traversing.api import traverse
>>> traverse(site, u'++skin++WorldCookery/@@index.html', request)
```

See also

traverseName

traverseName

Traverses a single step relative to an object.

Synopsis

traverseName (*object*, *name*, *default=None*,
                  traversable=None, *request=None*)

Origin

zope.traversing.api (ITraversalAPI)

Description

traverseName resolves a single path segment relative to the object *object*. *name* is a string or Unicode object containing path segment to be resolved. You can optionally pass an object providing ITraversable for the *traversable* parameter which will be used to carry out the actual path resolution. Otherwise the object will be adapted to ITraversable.

request should be passed when invoking from presentation code. traverseName will then also take traversal *views* into account instead of just traversal *adapters*. If a *default* value is given, it will be returned when the path cannot be traversed. Otherwise, TraversalError will be raised.

Examples

Resolving a regular path segment:

```
>>> from zope.traversing.api import traverseName
>>> traverseName(folder, u'subfolder')
```

Resolve a path segment and take presentation-specific traversal adapters into account, such as ++skin++, @@, etc.:

```
>>> traverseName(obj, u'@@index.html', request)
```

See also

```
traverse
```

B

ZCML Reference

Every component that is used within Zope 3 has to be registered, usually through ZCML. This reference gives an overview over most ZCML directives available in Zope 3.3. It explains their parameters in detail and gives examples for each one, usually ones from the book's example application. Some directives that are used very rarely are omitted in this references. For a complete and up-to-date version of the ZCML reference, please refer to Zope's built-in *APIDoc* tool.

Namespaces

Most Zope directives are part of a certain namespace. Only three special directives are available in all namespaces, `configure`, `include` and `includeOverrides`. Even though it is arbitrary from an XML point of view, it is a convention to use the namespace prefix as listed in Table B.1.

Table B.1. ZCML namespaces and their conventional namespace prefix

Namespace URL	Prefix
`http://namespaces.zope.org/zope`	`zope` (often also chosen as the main namespace)
`http://namespaces.zope.org/apidoc`	`apidoc`
`http://namespaces.zope.org/browser`	`browser`
`http://namespaces.zope.org/i18n`	`i18n`
`http://namespaces.zope.org/mail`	`mail`
`http://namespaces.zope.org/meta`	`meta`
`http://namespaces.zope.org/xmlrpc`	`xmlrpc`
`http://namespaces.zope.org/zcml`	`zcml`

These standard prefixes are also used in this reference. For example, if you are looking for the `adapter` directive from the `http://namespaces.zope.org/zope` namespace, search for `zope:adapter`.

Conventions

Several ZCML directives work in similar ways. That is because a lot of components in Zope 3 are managed in similar ways. The following list mentions a few common conventions shared among many directives:

- Some parameters allow more than one value being passed. Good examples for this are the *for* parameter of `zope:adapter` or the *interface* parameter of `zope:class`'s `implements` subdirective. Both take one or more interfaces, separated by at least one whitespace character. Any whitespace in between and around the items will be stripped.
- A few components that are registered by an identifier (e.g. named utilities like permissions and roles) require that their identifier is a dotted name. A dotted name is composed of several name elements dots as delimiters. A typical example for a dotted name is the way Python refers to modules and subpackages in packages (`worldcookery.recipe`). Dotted names are not only used to refer to Python objects, they are also used to uniquely identify registered components. By convention, the name of the Python package the component originates from is used as a first element of such a dotted name . For example, the *visitor* role in the WorldCookery application has the identifier `worldcookery.Visitor`.
- Menu items (whether configured stand-alone or within the view configuration) as well as permissions, principals and roles are configured with a title and description. The title of a menu item will usually be shown as a label within the menu, the description is often optionally available as a tooltip. With permissions, principals and the like, the title is used as a presentable name (as opposed to the ID which is used as an internal identifier), the description is shown when more information is requested by the user, for example through a mouse tooltip.

apidoc:bookchapter

Defines a chapter for the APIDoc Book section.

Parameters

id Identifier of the topic. This will also appear in the URL. This parameter is required.

title The chapter's title as it will appear in the menu. This parameter is required.

doc_path Relative path to a text file

parent Identifier of the parent chapter if this is a subchapter.

resources A list of additional files that are used by the chapter's text.

Examples

With the following directive, an APIDoc Book chapter for the *World Cookery* application is created, though without content:

```
<apidoc:bookchapter
    id="worldcookery"
    title="World Cookery"
    />
```

Directives like the following ones add the worldcookery package's doctests subchapters:

```
<apidoc:bookchapter
    id="filerepresentation"
    title="File representation"
    doc_path="filerepresentation.txt"
    parent="worldcookery"
    />
```

```
<apidoc:bookchapter
    id="folder"
    title="Recipe folder"
    doc_path="folder.txt"
    parent="worldcookery"
    />
```

See also

Chapter 23

apidoc:rootModule

Makes a module browseable n the APIDoc Code Browser

Parameters

module Dotted import name of the module. This parameter is required.

Examples

The following directive registers the `worldcookery` package with the API-Doc Code Browser:

```
<apidoc:rootModule module="worldcookery" />
```

See also

Chapter 23

browser:addMenuItem

Defines an entry in the *Add* menu of containers.

Parameters

title The text to be displayed for the menu item. This parameter is required.

description An optional description of the menu entry that is displayed together with the item or when the user requests more assistance.

icon Name of a browser resource that is associated with this menu item (e.g. as an icon).

for The interface that the menu item is registered for. This parameter is optional and defaults to `IAdding`.

menu Menu item that this entry is added to as a sub menu item.

class A class to be used as a factory for creating new objects. You need to specify either this parameter or a *factory*.

factory The ID of a factory that should be used to create new objects. You need to specify either this parameter or a *class*.

view The name of a custom add view that is to be displayed when the entry from the menu is selected. This parameter is optional.

order Number that indicates the relative position of the menu item.

filter An optional TALES condition that will be evaluated upon display of the menu. If the expression evaluates to a false value, the item is not displayed. The expression has access to the variables:

- context, the object the menu is being displayed for,
- request, the browser request,
- nothing

layer The layer that the menu item appears in. This parameter is optional and defaults to IDefaultBrowserLayer.

permission The permission that is required in order to display the menu entry. This parameter is optional because it can usually be inferred by the system; the underlying components are all protected by permissions. However, doing so may be expensive performance-wise.

Examples

The following is a typical specimen of the browser:addMenuItem directive: a simple title, a class, a permission and the name of the add form (which is usually generated by browser:addform):

```
<browser:addMenuItem
    title="[label-recipe] Recipe"
    factory="worldcookery.Recipe"
    view="worldcookery.Recipe"
    permission="worldcookery.EditRecipes"
    />
```

See also

browser:menu, browser:menuItem, browser:menuItems, browser:subMenuItem

browser:containerViews

Define several standard container views for a container implementation.

Parameters

for The interface for which the container views are to be registered. This parameter is required.

add The permission by which the adding view (+) will be protected. If not specified, no adding view will be registered.

contents The permission by which the contents page (contents.html) will be protected. If not specified, the contents page will not be registered.

index The permission by which the index page (index.html) will be protected. If not specified, the index view will not be registered.

layer The layer that the browser pages will be registered for. This parameter is optional and defaults to IDefaultBrowserLayer.

Examples

```
<browser:containerViews
    for="worldcookery.interfaces.IRecipeContainer"
    contents="worldcookery.EditRecipeFolders"
    index="worldcookery.ViewRecipeFolders"
    add="worldcookery.EditRecipeFolders"
    />
```

See also

browser:page

browser:defaultSkin

Sets the default browser skin.

Parameters

name Name of the default skin.

Examples

This directive is usually used in an overriding ZCML file because the `zope.app` package already defines a default skin. In the example application, we used the following line to change the default skin:

```
<browser:defaultSkin name="WorldCookery" />
```

See also

`browser:skin`

browser:defaultView

Defines the name of a browser view that should be used when no explicit view name is supplied.

Parameters

for Specifies the interface for which the default view name should be set. This parameter is required.

name Name that refers to a view that should be presented by default (if no view name is supplied explicitly). This parameter is required.

layer The layer that the default view name applies to. This parameter is optional and defaults to `IDefaultBrowserLayer`.

Examples

The `zope.app` package defines the default view for all objects as `index.html`. You can always make more specific definitions, for example the default view of all recipes could be changed to always the PDF view:

```
<browser:defaultView
    for="worldcookery.interfaces.IRecipe"
    name="pdf"
    />
```

See also

`zope:defaultView, zapi.getDefaultViewName`

browser:icon

Defines an icon for an interface.

Parameters

for The interface that the icon applies to. This parameter is required.

name Name of the icon. This name shows up in URLs, for example. This parameter is required.

resource The name of a browser resource containing the icon. You need to specify a value for either this parameter or the *file* parameter.

file A file containing the icon. You need to specify a value for either this parameter or the *resource* parameter.

title A descriptive title of the resource. This can, for example, be used in the image's *alt* tag. This parameter is optional.

layer The layer that the icon is registered for. This parameter is optional and defaults to IDefaultBrowserLayer.

Examples

From the example application:

```
<browser:icon
    name="zmi_icon"
    for="worldcookery.interfaces.IRecipe"
    file="recipe_icon.png"
    layer="worldcookery"
    />
```

See also

browser:resource

browser:menu

Defines a browser menu.

Parameters

id Identifier of the browser menu. This parameter is required and must be a dotted name.

title A descriptive title for documentation purposes. This parameter is required.

description An optional description of the menu.

interface Marker interface that identifies the menu.

class Class that is used to instantiate the menu object.

Examples

From the example application:

```
<browser:menu
    id="alternate_views"
    title="Menu containing a list of alternative views for an object"
    />
```

See also

`browser:addMenuItem`, `browser:menuItem`, `browser:menuItems`

browser:menuItem, browser:subMenuItem

Define a (sub)menu item.

Parameters

menu The identifier of the menu that the entry is to be defined for. This parameter is required.

submenu (`browser:subMenuItem` only) The identifier of the submenu that the entry is added to. This parameter is required.

for The interface the menu item is to be defined for. The entry will only be shown in the context of objects providing this interface. This parameter is required.

action Part of a URL relative to the object the menu is being displayed for. This parameter is required.

title The text to be displayed for the menu item. This parameter is required.

description An optional description of the menu entry that is displayed together with the item or when the user requests more assistance.

icon Name of a browser resource that is associated with this menu item (e.g. as an icon).

order Number that indicates the relative position of the menu item.

filter An optional TALES condition that will be evaluated upon display of the menu. If the expression evaluates to a false value, the item is not displayed. The expression has access to the variables:

- context, the object the menu is being displayed for,
- request, the browser request,
- nothing

layer The layer that the menu item appears in. This parameter is optional and defaults to IDefaultBrowserLayer.

permission The permission that is required in order to display the menu entry. This parameter is optional because it can usually be inferred by the system; the underlying components are all protected by permissions. However, doing so may be expensive performance-wise.

Examples

The following directive registers a menu item for the PDF-generating browser page:

```
<browser:menuItem
    for="worldcookery.interfaces.IRecipe"
    menu="alternate_views"
    title="PDF"
    action="@@pdf"
    permission="worldcookery.ViewPDF"
    />
```

See also

browser:addMenuItem, browser:menu, browser:menuItems

browser:menuItems

Define a number of browser menu items for the same menu and interface.

Parameters

menu The name of the menu that the entries are to be defined for. This parameter is required.

for The interface the menu items are defined for. The entries will only be shown in the context of objects providing this interface. This parameter is required.

layer The layer that the menu items appears in. This parameter is optional and defaults to IDefaultBrowserLayer.

Subdirectives

menuItem

Define a menu item within a group of menu items.

Parameters

action Part of a URL relative to the object the menu is being displayed for. This parameter is required.

title The text to be displayed for the menu item. This parameter is required.

description An optional description of the menu entry that is displayed together with the item or when the user requests more assistance.

icon Name of a browser resource that is associated with this menu item (e.g. as an icon).

order Number that indicates the relative position of the menu item.

filter An optional TALES condition that will be evaluated upon display of the menu. If the expression evaluates to a false value, the item is not displayed. The expression has access to the variables:

- context, the object the menu is being displayed for,
- request, the browser request,
- nothing

permission The permission that is required in order to display the menu entry. This parameter is optional because it can usually be inferred by the system; the underlying components are all protected by permissions. However, doing so may be expensive performance-wise.

subMenuItem

Define a menu item within a group of menu items.

Parameters

submenu Identifier of this menu item as a sub menu. This parameter is required and must be a dotted name.

other parameters same as menuItem

Examples

The browser:menuItems directive is very convenient when several menu items have to be registered for the same menu and possibly the same object interface:

```
<browser:menuItems
    menu="alternate_views"
    for="worldcookery.interfaces.IRecipe
    >
  <menuItem
      action="@@pdf"
      title="PDF"
      />
  <menuItem
      action="@@subscribe.html"
      title="Mail subscriptions"
      />
</browser:menuItems>
```

See also

browser:addMenuItem, browser:menu, browser:menuItem, browser:subMenuItem

browser:page

Registers a browser page (view for browsers).

Parameters

for The interface the page is registered for. This parameter is required.

name The name under which the browser page will be available. This value usually ends in .html. This parameter is required.

class A class that implements the browser page or that provides additional methods used by a Page Template (when used in combination with *template*). If used without a template, the class must either provide a __call__ method or you must specify a different method/callable attribute with the *attribute* parameter. This parameter is optional when used with the *template* parameter.

template Name of a Page Template file that is used to render the page. Page Template files typically end in .pt or .html. If you do not specify this parameter you need to specify at least a *class* that is responsible for the view generation.

attribute A callable attribute (e.g. method) of a view class (*class* parameter) that is to be called when the view is published. This parameter is cannot be used at the same time as the *template* parameter. It is optional and defaults to __call__.

layer The layer the browser page is registered for. This parameter is optional and defaults to IDefaultBrowserLayer.

permission The permission needed to use the browser page. This parameter is required.

menu Many browser pages are included in menus. It is convenient to name the menu in directive defining the page directive, rather than having to use a separate menuItem directive. This parameter is optional.

title The label of the entry in the browser menu that was specified in the *menu* parameter. This parameter is optional.

allowed_attributes A list of attributes that the *permission* should also apply to. By default, *permission* only applies to the methods necessary for publishing views, not accessing additional attributes of the view component. This parameter is optional.

allowed_interface An interface that specifies a list of attributes that *permission* should also apply to. This parameter has the same effect of *allowed_attributes*. This parameter is optional.

Examples

A regular browser page defined in Python is registered like so:

```
<browser:page
    for="worldcookery.interfaces.IRecipe"
    name="index.html"
    class=".recipe.ViewRecipe"
    permission="worldcookery.ViewRecipes"
    />
```

For convenience, browser pages can also be registered directly from Page Templates:

```
<browser:page
    for="worldcookery.interfaces.IRecipe"
    name="index.html"
    template="viewrecipe.pt"
    permission="worldcookery.ViewRecipes"
    />
```

See also

`browser:pages, browser:view, zope:view`

browser:pages

Define a number of browser pages that share common configuration parameters.

Parameters

for The interface the pages are registered for. This parameter is required.

class A class that implements the browser pages. This parameter is optional. If no class is specified, the directive handler will create one on-the-fly.

layer The layer the browser pages are registered for. This parameter is optional and defaults to `IDefaultBrowserLayer`.

permission The permission needed to use the browser pages. This parameter is required.

allowed_attributes A list of attributes that the *permission* should also apply to. By default, *permission* only applies to the methods necessary for publishing views, not accessing additional attributes of the view component. This parameter is optional.

allowed_interface An interface that specifies a list of attributes that *permission* should also apply to. This parameter has the same effect of *allowed_attributes*. This parameter is optional.

Subdirectives

page

Register a single page within the group of pages to be registered.

Parameters

name The name under which the browser page will be available. This value usually ends in .html. This parameter is required.

template Name of a Page Template file that is used to render the page. Page Template files typically end in .pt or .html. If you do not specify this parameter you need to specify at least a *class* that is responsible for the view generation.

attribute A callable attribute (e.g. method) of a view class (*class* parameter of the superdirective) that is to be called when the view is published. This parameter is cannot be used at the same time as the *template* parameter.

menu Many browser pages are included in menus. It is convenient to name the menu in directive defining the page directive, rather than having to use a separate menuItem directive. This parameter is optional.

title The label of the entry in the browser menu that was specified in the *menu* parameter. This parameter is optional.

Examples

This directive from the example application configures three browser pages for the same interface (`IRecipe`), using the same view class (`MailSubscriptionView`) and the same permission:

```
<browser:pages
    for="worldcookery.interfaces.IRecipe"
    class=".browser.MailSubscriptionView"
    permission="worldcookery.Subscribe"
    >
  <browser:page
     name="subscribe"
     attribute="subscribe"
     />
  <browser:page
     name="unsubscribe"
     attribute="unsubscribe"
     />
  <browser:page
     name="subscribe.html"
     template="subscribe.pt"
     menu="alternate_views" title="Mail subscriptions"
     />
</browser:pages>
```

See also

`browser:page`, `browser:view`, `zope:view`

browser:resource

Defines a browser resource.

Parameters

name The name under which the resource will be available. Resource URLs are of the form *site*/@@/*name* where *site* is the URL of the nearest site and *name* the value of this parameter. Sites are used for base URLs of resources so that their URLs do not change depending on the context and caches can do their work effectively. This parameter is required.

factory The resource factory that is called when a resource object is instantiated. This parameter is optional. The directive handler will automatically choose a factory implementation when none is given, depending on whether the *file*, *image* or *template* parameter was given.

file The name of a file containing the resource data. This parameter, *image* and *template* are exclusive of each other. When this parameter is given, a regular file resource is created.

image The name of an image file containing the resource data. If this parameter is used, an image resource rather than a regular file resource is created.

template The name of a Page Template file. If this parameter is given instead of *file* or *image*, a Page Template resource will be created. Page Template resources work like regular view Page Templates except that they do not have access to a context.

layer The layer the browser resource is registered for. This parameter is optional and defaults to IDefaultBrowserLayer.

permission The permission needed to use the browser resource. This parameter is not required and defaults to zope.Public.

Examples

From the example application:

```
<browser:resource name="sequence.js" file="sequence.js" />
```

See also

browser:resourceDirectory, zope:resource

browser:resourceDirectory

Registers a directory as a browser resource

Parameters

name The name under which the resource directory will be available. Resource URLs are of the form *site*/@@/*name* where *site* is the URL of the nearest site and *name* the value of this parameter. Sites are used for base URLs of resources so that their URLs do not change depending on the context and caches can do their work effectively. This parameter is required.

directory The name of the directory that is registered as a resource. Files within this directory will be accessible through URLs like *site*/@@/*name*/*filename*. The resource directory determins which kind of resource to create for a contained file based on the file extension.

layer The layer the resource directory is registered for. This parameter is optional and defaults to `IDefaultBrowserLayer`.

permission The permission needed to use the resource directory. This parameter is not required and defaults to `zope.Public`.

Examples

From the example application:

```
<browser:resourceDirectory
    name="wc"
    directory="wc"
    layer=".interfaces.IWorldCookerySkin"
    />
```

See also

`browser:resource`, `zope:resource`

browser:view

Defines a browser view, possibly with subpages.

Parameters

for The interface the view is registered for. This can also be a list of interfaces in which case a multi-view is registered. This parameter is required.

name The name under which the browser view will be available. It will be the base URL for the individual pages, e.g. `object`/@@*name*/*page* where `object` is the object that view is acquired for, *name* is the value of this parameter and `page` is the name of a subpage registered with the `page` subdirective.

class A class that implements the browser view. This parameter is optional. If no class is specified, the directive handler will create one on-the-fly.

layer The layer the browser view is registered for. This parameter is optional and defaults to `IDefaultBrowserLayer`.

provides The interface the view provides. This can be used if the view implements certain functionality, e.g. `IAbsoluteURL` or `IAdding`. This parameter is optional and defaults to `Interface`.

permission The permission needed to use the browser pages. This parameter is required.

menu Many browser pages are included in menus. It is convenient to name the menu in directive defining the page directive, rather than having to use a separate `menuItem` directive. This parameter is optional.

title The label of the entry in the browser menu that was specified in the *menu* parameter. This parameter is optional.

allowed_attributes A list of attributes that the *permission* should also apply to. By default, *permission* only applies to the methods necessary for publishing views, not accessing additional attributes of the view component. This parameter is optional.

allowed_interface An interface that specifies a list of attributes that *permission* should also apply to. This parameter has the same effect of *allowed_attributes*. This parameter is optional.

Subdirectives

`browser:view` has a `page` subdirective that is equivalent to the one of `browser:pages`. It is used to define subpages.

defaultPage

Define which subpage should be displayed by default if no subpage is specified explicitly in the URL.

Parameters

name The name of the subpage that should be displayed by default if no subpage is specified explicitly in the URL. If this directive is not specified, the first subpage defined will be the default one. This parameter is required.

Examples

Since subpages are quite uncommon, the browser:view directive is rarely used with subdirectives. A more common usage is to register a Python-based view component that is *not* a publishable browser page, for example the standard_macros view:

```
<browser:view
    for="*"
    name="standard_macros"
    class=".standardmacros.StandardMacros"
    permission="zope.View"
    allowed_interface="zope.interface.common.mapping.IItemMapping"
    layer=".interfaces.IWorldCookerySkin"
    />
```

See also

browser:page, browser:pages

browser:viewlet

Registers a browser viewlet.

Parameters

name The name of the viewlet. While the name does not necessarily have to be used for anything, it is needed to uniquely identify different viewlets for the same object, request, view and viewlet manager. This parameter is therefore required.

for The interface the viewlet is registered for. This parameter is optional and defaults to Interface (all objects).

view The view that the viewlet applies to. This parameter is optional and defaults to IBrowserView (all browser views).

manager The viewlet manager that the viewlet applies to. This parameter is optional and defaults to IViewletManager (all viewlet managers).

class A class that implements the browser viewlet or that provides additional methods used by a Page Template (when used in combination with *template*). This parameter is optional. If not provided, the directive handler will generate a class on-the-fly.

template Name of a Page Template file that is used to render the viewlet. Page Template files typically end in .pt or .html. If you do not specify this parameter you need to specify at least a *class* that implements the viewlet.

layer The layer the browser viewlet is registered for. This parameter is optional and defaults to IDefaultBrowserLayer.

permission The permission needed to use the browser viewlet. This parameter is required.

allowed_attributes A list of attributes that the *permission* should also apply to. By default, *permission* only applies to the methods necessary for publishing views, not accessing additional attributes of the view component. This parameter is optional.

allowed_interface An interface that specifies a list of attributes that *permission* should also apply to. This parameter has the same effect of *allowed_attributes*. This parameter is optional.

Examples

A simple, Page Template-based viewlet is registered with a directive like the following one:

```
<browser:viewlet
    name="10login"
    for="*"
    manager=".interfaces.IToolbar"
    template="login.pt"
    layer=".interfaces.IWorldCookerySkin"
    permission="zope.View"
    />
```

More complex viewlets are better implemented in Python, hence the *class* parameter is used to refer to the viewlet implementation:

```
<browser:viewlet
    name="remember"
    for="worldcookery.interfaces.IRecipe"
    manager=".interfaces.ISidebar"
    class=".remember.RememberViewlet"
    layer=".interfaces.IWorldCookerySkin"
    permission="zope.View"
    />
```

See also

browser:viewletManager

browser:viewletManager

Registers a browser viewlet manager.

Parameters

name The name of the viewlet manager as a content provider. This parameter is required.

for The interface the viewlet manager is registered for. This parameter is optional and defaults to Interface (all objects).

view The view that the viewlet manager applies to. This parameter is optional and defaults to IBrowserView (all browser views).

provides Interface that the viewlet manager provides. This is usually a marker interface based on IViewletManager and used to identify a particular viewlet manager in the browser:viewlet directive (*manager* parameter). This parameter is optional and defaults to IViewletManager.

class A class that implements the viewlet manager. This parameter is optional. If not provided, the directive handler will use the default implementation.

template Name of a Page Template file that is used to render the viewlet manager. The template has access to the manager's viewlets using the options/viewlet path expression. This parameter is optional. If omitted, the standard viewlet implementation will simply concatenate the output of all viewlets.

layer The layer the viewlet manager is registered for. This parameter is optional and defaults to IDefaultBrowserLayer.

permission The permission needed to use the browser viewlet. This parameter is required.

allowed_attributes A list of attributes that the *permission* should also apply to. By default, *permission* only applies to the methods necessary for publishing views, not accessing additional attributes of the view component. This parameter is optional.

allowed_interface An interface that specifies a list of attributes that *permission* should also apply to. This parameter has the same effect of *allowed_attributes*. This parameter is optional.

Examples

The following directive registers a viewlet manager for cases where the default implementation suffices:

```
<browser:viewletManager
    name="worldcookery.Headers"
    provides=".interfaces.IHeaders"
    layer=".interfaces.IWorldCookerySkin"
    permission="zope.View"
    />
```

A custom viewlet manager implementation with additional behaviour, such as sorting viewlets by name, can be chosen by using the *class* parameter:

```
<browser:viewletManager
    name="worldcookery.Toolbar"
    provides=".interfaces.IToolbar"
    class=".manager.SortingViewletManager"
    layer=".interfaces.IWorldCookerySkin"
    permission="zope.View"
    />
```

See also

browser:viewlet

configure

Grouping directive that starts a new configuration context, usually used as document element for ZCML files.

Parameters

i18n_domain Sets the i18n domain on the configuration context. This information is used for contained directives when strings are turned into translation messages. These will be attributed with the i18n domain that is acquired from the configuration context. An i18n domain should be a short identifier, usually chosen on a per-project or per-package basis. This parameter is optional and can be acquired from configuration contexts higher in hierarchy.

package Dotted name of a Python package which the contained directives are in context of. All contained directives that expect relative file paths for their parameters will evaluate these relative to the package's context. This parameter is optional and is usually set when a ZCML file is included by package.

Examples

By wrapping certain directives in a `configure` directive with a different package context, one can reuse files (e.g. Page Templates) from other packages in custom configuration. A typical use case is the *Preview* page for content types where the `preview.pt` template is located in the `zope.app.preview` package:

```
<configure package="zope.app.preview" i18n_domain="zope">
  <browser:page
      for="worldcookery.interfaces.IRecipe"
      name="preview.html"
      template="preview.pt"
      permission="worldcookery.ViewRecipes"
      menu="zmi_views" title="Preview"
      />
</configure>
```

See also

`include`, `includeOverrides`

i18n:registerTranslations

Register i18n message catalogs.

Parameters

directory Directory containing gettext translation files. The conventions is to use `locales` for this value. The i18n machinery expects a standard gettext directory layout inside this directory, i.e. `locales/`*lang*`/LC_MESSAGES/`*domain*`.mo` where *lang* is the language of the individual translation file and *domain* its domain. This parameter is required.

Examples

You will see this directive being used like this most of the time:

```
<i18n:registerTranslations directory="locales" />
```

See also

Chapter 9

include, includeOverrides

Includes another ZCML file, either regularly or in override mode.

Parameters

file The name of a configuration file to be included, relative to the directive containing the file the directive is being used in. This parameter is optional when the *package* parameter is given; in this case it defaults to `configure.zcml`. It cannot be used at the same time as the *files* parameter.

files The names of multiple configuration files to be included, expressed as a file-name pattern, relative to the directive containing the file the directive is being used in. The pattern can include the following elements:

- * matches zero or more characters
- ? matches a single character
- [*sequence*] matches any character in *sequence*.
- [!*sequence*] matches any character that is not in *sequence*.

The file names are included in alphanumerically sorted order, where sorting is without regard to case. This parameter is optional and cannot be used at the same time as the *file* parameter.

package Dotted name of a package from which files are included. If no *file* parameter is given, the `configure.zcml` file from that package will be included. This parameter will also set the package in the included file's configuration context. This parameter is optional when either the *file* or *files* parameter is given.

Examples

Include a package's `configure.zcml`:

```
<include package="worldcookery" />
```

Include a specific file from a package:

```
<include package="worldcookery" file="meta.zcml" />
```

Include a bunch of files using a file pattern. The following directives are used in an instance's `etc/site.zcml` to include ZCML snippets in `etc/package-includes`:

```
<include files="package-includes/*-meta.zcml" />
<include files="package-includes/*-configure.zcml" />
<includeOverrides files="wpackage-includes/*-overrides.zcml" />
```

See also

`configure`

mail:directDelivery

Registers a global utility for direct mail delivery (as opposed to queued delivery).

Parameters

name Specifies the name of the delivery utility. This parameter is optional and defaults to `Mail`.

mailer Specifies the name of the mail sending utility that is to be used for the actual delivery. This parameter is required.

permission Defines the permission needed to use this utility. This parameter is required.

Examples

Typically, a delivery utility is configured together with a mailer utility, e.g. an SMTP mailer:

```
<mail:smtpMailer
    name="worldcookery"
    hostname="localhost"
    port="25"
    />

<mail:directDelivery
    name="worldcookery"
    permission="zope.SendMail"
    mailer="worldcookery"
    />
```

See also

`mail:queuedDelivery`, `mail:smtpMailer`

mail:queuedDelivery

Registers a global utility for queued mail delivery.

Parameters

name Specifies the name of the delivery utility. This parameter is optional and defaults to `Mail`.

mailer Specifies the name of the mail sending utility that is to be used for the actual delivery. This parameter is required.

permission Defines the permission needed to use this utility. This parameter is required.

queuePath Specifies a path relative to the configuration file where the delivery utility can store its mail queue. Mails are stored in the *Maildir* format. This parameter is required.

Examples

Typically, a delivery utility is configured together with a mailer utility. The following example is taken from the example application:

```
<mail:smtpMailer
    name="worldcookery"
    hostname="localhost"
    port="25"
    />

<mail:queuedDelivery
    name="worldcookery"
    permission="zope.SendMail"
    queuePath="mail-queue"
    mailer="worldcookery"
    />
```

See also

`mail:directDelivery`, `mail:smtpMailer`

mail:smtpMailer

Registers a mailer utility that sends mail by connecting to an SMTP server.

Parameters

name Name by which the mailer utility is registered. This parameter is required.

hostname Host name of the SMTP server that mails are supposed to be sent to. This parameter is optional and defaults to `localhost`.

port Port of the SMTP server. This parameter is optional and defaults to `25`.

username A user name with which the utility will try to authenticate itself with the SMTP server. This parameter is optional.

password The password for the user that was specified with the *username* parameter for SMTP authentication. This parameter is optional.

Examples

See examples of `mail:directDelivery` and `mail:queuedDelivery`.

See also

`mail:directDelivery`, `mail:queuedDelivery`

meta:provides

Enables a ZCML feature that can be used in `zcml:condition`

Parameters

feature Name of the feature that is to be enabled. This parameter is required.

Examples

When enabled, the APIDoc tool registers a ZCML feature like so:

```
<meta:provides feature="apidoc" />
```

Other packages can then enable or disable APIDoc-related directives by using `zcml:condition`:

```
<apidoc:rootModule module="worldcookery"
    xmlns:apidoc="http://namespaces.zope.org/apidoc"
    xmlns:zcml="http://namespaces.zope.org/zcml"
    zcml:condition="have apidoc"
    />
```

See also

`zcml:condition`

meta:redefinePermission

Maps a permission to another one.

Parameters

from Original permission that is to be remapped.

to Name of the permission that the original one will be mapped to.

Examples

After defining fine-grained permissions, it is possible to map them back to more general ones if the flexibility is not needed by default:

```
<meta:redefinePermission
    from="worldcookery.ViewRecipes"
    to="zope.View"
    />
```

See also

Chapter 21

xmlrpc:view

Registers one or more XML-RPC views.

Parameters

for The interface the XML-RPC views are registered for. This parameter is required.

class A view class that provides the methods that can be called via RPC. This parameter is required.

methods A list of methods (or attributes) of the view class (*class* parameter) that are to be published via XML-RPC. This parameter is required unless the *interface* parameter is given instead.

interface An interface that specifies a list of methods (or attributes) of the view class that are to be published. Otherwise works like *methods*. This parameter is required if *methods* is not given.

name Optional name of the XML-RPC view. Normally, the names of the methods and attributes specified via *methods* or *interface* are registered directly as XML-RPC views on the object. In other words, they would be accessible via object/*methodname*. If this parameter is given, however, they will be available as subviews of this view, i.e. through object/*name*/*methodname*. In this case the view class (*class* parameter) should implement IPublishTraverse from the zope.publisher package.

permission The permission needed to use the views. This applies to both the case of methods being registered as individual views as well as the case of one view with subviews (*name* parameter). This parameter is optional; if it is not given, security protection should be ensured otherwise, e.g. through security declarations for the view class (*class* parameter).

Examples

The following directive taken from the example application registers two XML-RPC view methods for IRecipe objects as direct XML-RPC views (no *name* parameter given). This is the common way of registering XML-RPC views:

```
<xmlrpc:view
    for="worldcookery.interfaces.IRecipe"
    class=".recipe.RecipeView"
```

```
methods="info dublincore_info"
permission="worldcookery.ViewRecipes"
/>
```

See also

`zope:view`

zcml:condition

Executes a ZCML based on a condition

Parameters

`zcml:condition` is an attribute that can be applied to any ZCML directive. When present, the ZCML processor will execute the directive only when the condition evalutes to true. Conditions consist of two parts, a verb and an argument. There are currently four supported verbs:

have, not-have take one argument, a feature name, and check whether this feature is available or not available, respectively. Features can be defined with the `meta:provides` directive. By enabling or disabling features, one can easily enable or disable one or more ZCML directives and thus enable or disable certain application functionality.

installed, not-installed take one argument, a Python package name, and check whether this package is available or not available, respectively. If the package cannot be imported, the condition evaluates to false.

Examples

The following ZCML directive taken from the example application will only be executed if the `reportlab` package is found on the Python interpreter's module search path:

```
<include package=".pdf"
         xmlns:zcml="http://namespaces.zope.org/zcml"
         zcml:condition="installed reportlab"
         />
```

The following ZCML directive will only be executed if the `apidoc` feature is enabled.

```
<apidoc:rootModule module="worldcookery"
    xmlns:apidoc="http://namespaces.zope.org/apidoc"
    xmlns:zcml="http://namespaces.zope.org/zcml"
    zcml:condition="have apidoc"
    />
```

See also

meta:provides

zope:adapter

Registers an adapter.

Parameters

factory One or more callables that act as adapter factories. Usually only one factory is allowed for this value (most of the time the class that provides the adapter implementation). In case only one value is specified for *for*, you can specify several factories. When the adapter is to be instantiated for an object obj, the factories will be called in the following order: factory1(factory2(factory3(obj))). This parameter is required.

for One or more interfaces that the adapter is registered for. If more than one interface is specified, a multi-adapter is registered. This parameter is optional if *factory* has an adapts/adapter declaration.

provides The interface that the adapter provides, in other words, the interface that the adapter adapts to. This parameter is optional if *factory* implements exactly one interface.

name Name of the adapter. If specified, the adapter will be registered as a *named* adapter. This parameter is optional and defaults to an empty string (unnamed adapter).

permission An optional permission that is required to use the adapter. If not given, the adapter will always be available.

trusted Make the adapter a trusted adapter. Regular (untrusted) adapters are given a security-proxied object. in return, the adapter itself does not have any security protection (since the original object is already protected). With trusted adapters it is the other way around. They work with bare objects that have no security protection, while the adapters themselves are security-proxied and thus need security declarations. This parameter is optional and defaults to `False`.

locate Make the adapter a locatable adapter, in other words, ensure the adapter has an _parent_ attribute. This is necessary whenever a non-public permission is applied to the adapter so that security declarations can be inherited properly. This parameter is optional and defaults to `True`.

Examples

A simple adapter whose factory implements exactly one interface and already has an `adapts` declaration can be registered with the simplest `zope:adapter` directive:

```
<adapter factory=".size.RecipeSize" />
```

One application of named adapters are file factories in the context of file representation. The name is the extension of the object that is to be created:

```
<adapter
    factory=".filerepresentation.RecipeFactory"
    for="zope.app.folder.interfaces.IFolder"
    name=".recipe"
    permission="zope.ManageContent"
    />
```

When using annotations to store metadata, custom adapters usually provide a nice interface to data stored in annotations. When annotation data is retrieved from the object (e.g. through attribute annotations), the data will be security-proxied and most likely to be inaccessible to the adapter. That is why these adapters are registered as trusted ones. To ensure protection towards the data, security declarations are given for the adapter class itself. Consider an example from the example application:

```
<adapter
    factory=".rating.Rating"
    trusted="true"
    />

<class class=".rating.Rating">
  <require
      permission="worldcookery.Rate"
      interface=".interfaces.IRating"
      />
</class>
```

See also

getAdapter, getMultiAdapter, Chapter 11 (regular and named adapters), Chapter 14 (trusted adapters)

zope:class

Configures a class.

Parameters

class The class that is to be configured. This parameter is required.

Subdirectives

allow

Declares an attribute of the class to be publicly available.

Parameters

attributes The attributes that are to be allowed. You need to specify either this parameter or *interface*.

interface An interface that specifies the names of attributes which are to be allowed. You need to specify either this parameter or *attributes*.

factory

Configure a factory from class.

Parameters

id Identifier of the factory. This needs to be a dotted name, usually starting with the name of the current package. This parameter is optional and defaults to the dotted name of the class.

title Short title that characterizes the factory. The value provided here can be used as a title for a menu entry or in some other part of a user interface. This parameter is optional.

description Longer narrative description of what this factory does. This parameter is optional.

implements

Declares that the class given implements additional interfaces.

Parameters

interface One or more interfaces that the class should implement in addition to what it already implements through declarations in Python code. These usually are marker interfaces that tell Zope how the class should be used in certain circumstances. This parameter is required.

require

Protect methods and attributes of the class with a permission.

Parameters

attributes A list of attributes (this includes methods) that are to be protected with the permission (*permission* parameter). This parameter is optional, but you need to specify at least one of the *attributes*, *interface*, *set_attributes*, *set_schema* and *like_class* parameters.

interface An interface that defines a methods and attributes that are to be protected with *permission*. It otherwise works like the *attributes* parameter. This parameter is optional.

set_attributes A list of attributes whose modification shall be protected by *permission*. This parameter is optional.

set_schema A schema that specifies through fields a number of attributes whose modification shall be protected by *permission*. It otherwise works like the *set_attributes* parameter. This parameter is optional.

like_class Dotted name of a class whose security declarations should apply to the current class as well. This parameter is optional.

permission The permission that the specified attributes are to be protected with. This parameter is required.

Examples

The following ZCML snippet is a typical example of a content class being configured. It marks the class as attribute annotatable (by letting it implement an additional marker interface), and protects its attributes for read and write access:

```
<class class=".recipe.Recipe">
  <implements
      interface="zope.annotation.interfaces.IAttributeAnnotatable"
      />
  <require
      permission="worldcookery.ViewRecipes"
      interface=".interfaces.IRecipe"
      />
  <require
      permission="worldcookery.EditRecipes"
      set_schema=".interfaces.IRecipe"
      />
</class>
```

Allowing an attribute with the `allow` subdirective,

```
<class class="someclass">
  <allow attributes="someattribute" />
</class>
```

is equivalent to protecting it with `zope.Public`:

```
<class class="someclass">
  <require
      permission="zope.Public"
      attributes="someattribute"
      />
</class>
```

See also

Chapter 5

zope:grant

Grants permissions to roles and principals, and roles to principals.

Parameters

permission Specifies the permission to be granted to either a role (*role* parameter) or principal (*principal* parameter). This parameter is not allowed when *role* and *principal* are used.

role Specifies the role that is to be granted to a principal or that the permission is to be granted to. This parameter is not allowed when *permission* and *principal* are used.

principal Specifies a principal that a role or a permission is to be granted to. This parameter is not allowed when *permission* and *role* are used.

Examples

Grant a permission to a role:

```
<grant
    permission="worldcookery.ViewRecipes"
    role="worldcookery.Visitor"
    />
```

Grant a role to a principal:

```
<grant
    role="worldcookery.Visitor"
    principal="zope.anybody"
    />
```

See also

`zope:grantAll`, `zope:permission`, `zope:role`, Chapter 21

zope:grantAll

Grants *all* permissions to a role and/or principal.

Parameters

principal Specifies a principal that is to be granted all access. You need to give either this parameter or the *role* parameter.

role Specifies a role that is to be granted all access. You need to give either this parameter or the *role* parameter.

Examples

`grantAll` means that literally all permissions are granted to the given role or principal. In other words, these principals or roles will have unlimited access to everything. By default, the `zope.app.securitypolicy` package grants this kind of access to the `zope.Manager` role with the following directive:

```
<grantAll role="zope.Manager" />
```

See also

zope:grant, zope:permission, zope:role, Chapter 21

zope:interface

Registers an interface as a utility and optionally makes it a type.

Parameters

interface The interface that is to be registered. This parameter is required.

type An interface type that the interface should be marked with. This parameter is optional and defaults to IInterface.

name Name that the interface should be registered under. This parameter is optional and defaults to the dotted name of the interface.

Examples

Typically this directive is used to turn an interface into a type, for example a content type:

```
<interface
    interface=".interfaces.IRecipe"
    type="zope.app.content.interfaces.IContentType"
    />
```

It is also used to register interfaces under a certain name, for example skins:

```
<interface
    interface=".interfaces.IWorldCookerySkin"
    type="zope.publisher.interfaces.browser.IBrowserSkinType"
    name="WorldCookery"
    />
```

See also

Chapter 5, Chapter 10

zope:permission

Defines a new permission.

Parameters

id Identifier of the permission. This should a dotted name, usually starting with the name of the current package. This parameter is required.

title A short descriptive title that maybe used to describe the permission in user interfaces (rather than the identifier). This parameter is required.

description Longer narrative description for the permission. This parameter is optional.

Examples

Defining a permission is quite straight forward:

```
<permission
    id="worldcookery.ViewRecipes"
    title="View recipes"
    />
```

See also

zope:grant

zope:principal

Defines a global principal.

Parameters

id Identifier of the principal. This needs to be a dotted name. They usually start with the name of the current package. Note that principal IDs need to be unique throughout a whole Zope instance. This parameter is required.

login Specifies the principal's user name for login. This parameter is required.

password Specifies the principal's password for login. This parameter is required.

password_manager Name of the password manager utility that will be used to encrypt the password. This parameter is optional and defaults to `Plain Text`.

title Descriptive title for the principal. It usually describes the purpose of the principal (e.g. `Sample Manager`) or the full name of the person represented by the principal. This parameter is required.

description Longer prose description of the principal. This parameter is optional.

Examples

This directive is usually only used during development and for emergencies. A typical example of a usage of this directive is the initial administrative user account that is created when the `mkzopeinstance` script is run:

```
<principal
    id="zope.manager"
    title="Manager"
    login="manager"
    password_manager="Plain Text"
    password="secret"
    />
```

See also

`zope:grant`

zope:resource

Register a resource

Parameters

name The name under which the resource will be available. This parameter is required.

provides The interface the resource provides. This will cause the resource to be registered as one that provides this interface which will allow it to be looked up this way, too. This parameter is optional and defaults to `Interface`.

type Interface that specifies the request type this resource applies to. This parameter is required.

factory A factory (e.g. a class) that creates a new resource component. This is usually the class of the resource implementation, or some other callable that returns the resource object. You have to specify either this parameter or *component*.

component Component that is to be registered as a resource. You have to specify either this parameter or *factory*.

permission The permission needed to use the resource. This parameter is required.

allowed_attributes A list of attributes that the *permission* should also apply to. By default, *permission* only applies to viewing resources, not accessing additional attributes of the resource component. This parameter is optional.

allowed_interface An interface that specifies a list of attributes that *permission* should also apply to. This parameter has the same effect of *allowed_attributes*. This parameter is optional.

Examples

Browser resources are generally much easier to register because the browser:resource accepts various parameters to directly create resource factories from either files, images or Page Templates. With the zope: resource directive, you have to pass a *factory* manually, which means that for each resource you register you would have to write a little piece of Python code. This is why this directive is seldom used. In cases where you want Python components be represented as resources, it is very useful, though:

```
<resource
    name="worldcookery.css"
    factory=".resource.WorldcookeryCSS"
    type="zope.publisher.interfaces.browser.IBrowserRequest"
    layer="worldcookery"
    permission="zope.Public"
    />
```

See also

`browser:resource`

zope:role

Defines a global role.

Parameters

id Identifier of the role. This should be a dotted name, usually starting with the name of the current package. This parameter is required.

title Descriptive title of the role. This should be the full name of the role as it may appear in a user interface. This parameter is required.

description Longer prose description of the role. This parameter is optional.

Examples

From the example application:

```
<role
    id="worldcookery.Visitor"
    title="Visitor of the WorldCookery website"
    />
```

See also

`zope:grant`, `zope:principal`, Chapter 21

zope:securityPolicy

Sets the security policy of a Zope instance.

Parameters

component The security policy component. This should be a callable object that provides `ISecurityPolicy` itself. When called it should return objects providing `IInteraction`. Usually, this is the class implementing interactions. This parameter is required.

Examples

The security policy for a Zope instance is normally set in the `etc/securitypolicy.zcml` file. The default security policy implementation that comes with Zope resides in the `zope.app.securitypolicy` package which is why by default this file includes the following directive:

```
<securityPolicy component=".zopepolicy.ZopeSecurityPolicy" />
```

See also

Chapter 21

zope:subscriber

Registers a handler or a subscription adapter.

Parameters

handler A callable object that handles events. This is often just a function that returns nothing (None). You have to specify either this parameter or *factory*.

factory Subscription adapter factory. You have to specify either this parameter or *handler*.

for One or more interfaces that the subscription adapter is registered for, or that the handler subscribes to. This parameter is not required if *handler* or *factory* have adapts/adapter declarations.

provides The interface the subscription adapter provides. This parameter is required when using *factory*. It is not allowed when using *handler*.

permission The permission that is required to use the subscriber. This parameter is optional. If not specified, the subscriber will be available to everyone.

trusted Make the subscription adapter a trusted adapter. Regular (untrusted) adapters are given a security-proxied object. in return, the adapter itself does not have any security protection (since the original object is already protected). With trusted adapters it is the other way around. They work with bare objects that have no security protection, while the adapters themselves are security-proxied and thus need security declarations. This parameter only applies when using *factory*. It is optional and defaults to False.

locate Make the subscription adapter a locatable adapter. In other words, ensure the adapter has an __parent__ attribute. This is necessary whenever a non-public permission is applied to the adapter so that security declarations can be inherited properly. This parameter only applies when using *factory*. It is optional and defaults to False.

Examples

When a handler already has an adapter declaration that specifies the event type it is interested in, its registration is a simple call to zope:subscriber:

```
<subscriber handler=".dublincore.updateRecipeDCTitle" />
```

See also

zope:adapter, subscribers, Chapter 16

zope:utility

Registers a global utility

Parameters

component The component that is to be registered as a utility. You have to specify either this parameter or *factory*.

factory A callable that creates the utility object. This is often just a class with the utility implementation. You need to specify either this parameter or *component*. Note that unlike with views and other factory-dependent component types, utility factories are called *once* upon registration, not with every look-up.

provides The interface that the utility provides. This parameter is optional if *component* provides exactly one interface or if *factory* implements exactly one interface.

name The name of the utility. If given, the utility is registered as a *named* utility. This parameter is optional and defaults to an empty string (unnamed utility).

permission The permission needed to use the utility. This parameter is optional. If not specified, the component will be available to anyone.

Examples

From the example application:

```
<utility
    component=".recipe.recipeFactory"
    name="worldcookery.Recipe"
    permission="zope.Public"
    />
```

See also

`getUtility`, `getUtilitiesFor`

zope:view

Registers a view.

Parameters

for The interface the view is registered for. This can also be a list of interfaces when registering a "multi-view". This parameter is required.

type Interface that specifies the request type which the view applies to. This parameter is required.

name The name under which the view will be available. This parameter is required.

provides The interface the view provides. This parameter is optional and defaults to `Interface`.

factory A factory that creates the view component upon look-up. This is usually the class providing the view implementation itself. This parameter is required.

permission The permission needed to use the view. This parameter is optional.

allowed_attributes A list of attributes that the *permission* should also apply to. By default, *permission* only applies to the methods necessary for publishing views, not accessing additional attributes of the view component. This parameter is optional.

allowed_interface An interface that specifies a list of attributes that *permission* should also apply to. This parameter has the same effect of *allowed_attributes*. This parameter is optional.

Examples

Since zope:view simply registers an adapter, it is just a different spelling of zope:adapter. Using zope:adapter is preferred.

See also

zope:adapter, browser:view, xmlrpc:view

References

1. (2001) Apache Software License 2.0. Apache Software Foundation website <http://apache.org/licenses/LICENSE-2.0.txt>
2. Zope 3 Coding standards. Zope development home <http://dev.zope.org/Zope3/CodingStyle>
3. Ward G, Baxter A, (2006) Distributing Python Modules. Python website <http://docs.python.org/dist/dist.html>
4. Pilgrim M (2004) Dive Into Python. Dive Into Python website <http://diveintopython.org>
5. (2003) Dublin Core Metadata Element Set, Version 1.1: Reference Description. Dublin Core Metadata Initiative website <http://dublincore.org/documents/2003/06/02/dces/>
6. GNU gettext manual. GNU website <http://www.gnu.org/software/gettext/manual/gettext.html>
7. Abdelnur A, Hepper S, (2003) Java Portlet Specification. Java Community Process website <http://jcp.org/aboutJava/communityprocess/review/jsr168/>
8. METAL Specification Version 1.1. Zope community website <http://www.zope.org/Wikis/DevSite/Projects/ZPT/MetalSpecification11>
9. Bernstein D (1998) Maildir – directory for incoming mail messages. QMail website <http://www.qmail.org/man/man5/maildir.html>
10. Perence B (2004) The Open Source Definition. Open Source Initiative website <http://opensource.org/docs/definition.php>
11. van Rossum G (2001) Style Guide for Python Code. Python website <http://www.python.org/dev/peps/pep-0008/>
12. Eby P (2004) Python Web Server Gateway Interface. Python website <http://www.python.org/dev/peps/pep-0333/>
13. van Rossum G, Drake F L, (2006) Python Tutorial. Python website <http://docs.python.org/tut/tut.html>
14. Eby P J, Python Eggs. PEAK website <http://peak.telecommunity.com/DevCenter/PythonEggs>
15. Freed N, Borenstein N, (1996) Multipurpose Internet Mail Extensions (MIME) Part One. Internet Engineering Task Force (IETF) <http://www.ietf.org/rfc/rfc2045.txt>

16. Weibel S, Kunze J, Lagoze C, Wolf M, (1998) Dublin Core Metadata for Resource Discovery. Internet Engineering Task Force (IETF) <http://www.ietf.org/rfc/rfc2413.txt>

17. Goland Y, Whitehead E, Faizi A, Carter S R, Jensen D, (1999) HTTP Extensions for Distributed Authoring. Internet Engineering Task Force (IETF) <http://www.ietf.org/rfc/rfc2518.txt>

18. Resnick P (2001) Internet Message Format. Internet Engineering Task Force (IETF) <http://www.ietf.org/rfc/rfc2822.txt>

19. Crocker D (1982) Standard for the Format of ARPA Internet Text Messages. Internet Engineering Task Force (IETF) <http://www.ietf.org/rfc/rfc822.txt>

20. ReportLab API Reference. ReportLab website <http://www.reportlab.com/docs/reference.pdf>

21. ReportLab User Guide. ReportLab website <http://www.reportlab.org/rsrc/userguide.pdf>

22. Everitt P An Introduction to StructuredText. Zope community website <http://www.zope.org/Documentation/Articles/STX>

23. Eby P J, Building and Distributing Packages with setuptools. PEAK website <http://peak.telecommunity.com/DevCenter/setuptools>

24. TAL Specification Version 1.4. Zope community website <http://www.zope.org/Wikis/DevSite/Projects/ZPT/TALSpecification1.4>

25. TALES Specification Version 1.3. Zope community website <http://www.zope.org/Wikis/DevSite/Projects/ZPT/TALESSpecification1.3>

26. Test-driven Development. Wikipedia <http://en.wikipedia.org/wiki/Test-driven_development>

27. Kuchling A M What's New in Python 2.2. Python website <http://www.python.org/doc/2.2.3/whatsnew/whatsnew22.html>

28. Winter D (1998-2004) XML-RPC specification. XML-RPC website <http://xmlrpc.com/spec>

29. (2004) Zope Public License 2.1. Zope community website <http://zope.org/Resources/License/ZPL-2.1>

30. A reStructuredText Primer. Docutils website <http://docutils.sourceforge.net/docs/user/rst/quickstart.html>

Epilogue

Nearly two years have gone by and here I am again, finishing up my book. Looking back, I find that producing this second edition has been about as much as work as producing the first one. This is due to a number of factors. First of all, those of you who also bought the first edition will notice that the book has grown considerably. Five whole chapters were added, many others amended substantially. Furthermore, the book has been overhauled completely as my superb review team left no stone unturned regarding language and technical details. Without them this book would not be what it is.

Much has happened in the past two years since Zope X3 3.0 was released and the first edition of this book was published. The "X" was finally dropped and Zope 3 has had three stable releases since then. Zope 3 has been put into production by a growing number of Zope integrators who are developing and releasing reusable third-party extensions. This makes it clear: the Component Architecture works! It is even more important, however, to see Zope 2 and Zope 3 converging. Thanks to the Five project, Zope 2 developers now have access to the same great features as Zope 3 developers, and as a result, many Zope 2-based projects such as Plone are incorporating Zope 3 features and infrastructure. Years of experience with building web applications meet new and innovative technologies. What could be more exciting?

Zope 3 has also changed the Zope community in a lot of ways. Being a complete community effort, it set the cornerstone for the Zope Foundation that was incorporated earlier this year. The foundation spans an impressive collection of technology, such as the ZODB, the CMF, and Zope itself. Having these finally under community governance is a prerequisite for the long-term viability of the Zope project. Also thanks to Zope 3, the Zope community is looking outward again to other efforts in the greater Python world. The adoption of WSGI and eggs is hopefully only the beginning.

As much as things have changed over the past two years, one thing remains the same: the friendship I share with many of the members of the Zope community. It's not only the technology that makes me go to the annual conferences in Europe and the U.S. (four this year, a personal record!)—it's also these people. In fact, if it weren't for them, I don't know if I'd still be working on Zope. So, thank you, my Zope friends for making this worthwhile. Here's to another great and exciting two years to come!

Acknowledgements

After many months of work on this book, it is also time to thank those who helped me during that time. First I would like to thank everyone who bought, recommended and critiqued the first edition of this book. It showed me that the documentation effort for Zope 3 is a worthwhile engagement.

Special thanks go to

- Hermann Engesser and Dorothea Glaunsinger of Springer-Verlag for making this second edition possible.
- Jan Smith for the endless amounts of time she has spent in reviewing my writings, again! It wouldn't have been possible without her.
- Gary Poster for sharing his deep insight into Zope 3 many, many times. He is the technical reviewer whom every computer book author wants to have.
- Róman Joost for the new design of the *World Cookery* skin.
- Martin Aspeli and Paul Everitt for lots of invaluable review work.
- Michael R. Bernstein for reading the whole book front to back in record time and improving the text with many language refinements.
- Rocky Burt, Martijn Faassen, Sidnei da Silva, Martijn Pieters, David Whitfield Morriss for a lot of general technical advice.
- Phillip J. Eby for an inspiring foreword.
- Amos Latteier for suggesting improvements of the security chapter.
- Ian Bicking and Daniel Nouri for suggestions and help regarding workingenv.py.
- Andy McKay and Wichert Akkerman for some deployment insights.
- Robrecht van Valkenburg of Pareto for some great help with LaTeX.
- Dr. Helmut Hayd and Frank Burkhard of the Leipzig Max Planck Institute for Human Cognitive and Brain Sciences for their valuable feedback.
- Gabriele Brysch and Klaus Barthelmann of Haufe Electronic Publishing for stimulating discussions concerning Zope and Python.
- My Shanghai roommate Jendrik and all my other Shanghai friends for constantly distracting me the whole six months. That was an unforgettable time, guys!

Also thanks also to Fleetwood Mac, Deep Purple, the Dave Brubeck Quartet, and the Klazz Brothers for their enjoyable tunes. Special thanks to Jim Davis for Garfield who kept me in a good mood the whole year round.

Like the previous edition, this book was written using mostly Open Source software. Not much on the technical side has changed since then, with two exceptions. Firstly, my review team and I have tremendously benefited from a new issue tracker system called Trac, which also happens to be written in Python. Secondly, I switched from the bare subversion client to the subversion-based decentralized revision control system svk as I was on the road a lot and not always within reach of Internet access (major parts of this second edition were written on trains, planes and even city trams). Both Trac and svk boosted productivity enormously, so a lot of thanks go to those two projects as well!

Philipp von Weitershausen, Freiburg, September 2006

Epilogue to the First Edition

I came to Zope in the early 2.x days when I needed a software tool that would allow me to collaborate on a school website project. It was the time of DTML Documents and Python Methods and neither the CMF nor Plone and Silva existed. What was even worse was that documentation was scarce. Fortunately, the first Zope book to be published in English was being written by two Digital Creations employees, Amos Latteier and Michel Pelletier.

Then, over a year later, everything had changed. Now there were many books about Zope, some even in French, German, and other languages. Though that was not surprising because Zope seemed gain a lot of momentum in Europe. Zope also hit the big market at that point. NATO probably was the most advertised Zope customer at the time and maybe still is. However, most importantly, DTML stopped being cool and Page Templates began their long path to victory.

What always has been great about Zope is its community. Maybe this is why I stuck with Zope after all and did not go back to PHP or moved on to Java. I still enjoy hanging out on IRC (#zope at irc.freenode.net) because that is where you can feel the heart beat of the Zope community. It is also where I met all of the people that I ended up working with for some years now—before actually having met them in person. Now that Zope and its offspring Plone are even more successful, we can afford to hold our own conferences and actually see each other in person. Only sometimes I wish the old times back when he had those barbecues in Berlin with no more than 40 people.

Before the second barbecue in 2002, I participated in a Zope 3 sprint.[1] That was the time when I first got involved into Zope 3 development. It was exciting to help redesigning the framework I had been using for some time personally. During many "geddons,"[2] I did not only have the pleasure

---

[1] A sprint is a meeting of developers at which the software product in question is developed intensely for a couple of days.

[2] Merciless refactorings, derived from the word arma*geddon*.

of getting to know the Zope 3 source code inside out, I also was able to watch Zope 3 grow up and gain more momentum with every new feature, new geddon, or new event.

In late 2003 I was invited to Düsseldorf to give a tutorial on Zope 3 for the local Zope user group. At that event I realized that the new version of Zope needed good documentation from the start, otherwise it would have to overcome from the same initial hurdles of Zope 2 back then. Therefore, my goal was to provide an easy, but not too simple, a gradual, but not too horizontal introduction to Zope 3. I hope I have achieved that goal in this book. However, it would not have been possible without the community and their contributions to Zope and this book.

Special thanks goes to

- Hermann Engesser of Springer-Verlag for believing in Zope and this book.
- Jan Smith and Sidnei da Silva for their exceptional effort of reviewing the book. Thanks for everything, guys, that was incredible! I could not have done this without you.
- Róman Joost for his design of the World Cookery application skin as well as important feedback.
- Fred L. Drake for his advice during the initial phase of the book and for providing technical guidance.
- Jim Fulton for being a great mentor during the initial development phase of Zope 3.
- Stephan Richter for encouraging me to write a book in competition to his and some last-minute LATEXhelp.
- Aroldo Souza-Leite for inviting me to Düsseldorf where it all started.
- Kit Blake, Martijn Faassen and the Infrae crew for their invaluable support.
- Paul Everitt for his support and the foreword to the book. Keep up the good work, Paul!
- Marius Gedminas and Joe Geldart for technical advice.
- Philipp Latzel for being a good friend at my side and carrying me through difficult school assignments more than once.
- My roommates Max and Gregor for their patience with me during the hot phase of the writing period.

Thanks for the music of Frank Sinatra, James Darren, and Natalie Cole which kept me in a good mood throughout the whole writing and editing period. *It don't mean a thing if it ain't got that swing!*

This book was written 100% with the help of Open Source software! Originally written in DocBook XML using GNU Emacs and James Clark's nxml-mode, it was converted to LATEXusing an extended version of Ramon Casellas's and James Devenish's db2latex stylesheet package. The DocBook files and the source code to the example application were revision controlled in a subversion repository. Roundup, an issue tracking software written in

Python, was heavily used during the review process. The browser shown in most screenshots is Mozilla Firefox 1.0 (preview) for Mac OS X.

Philipp von Weitershausen, Dresden, October 2004

Index